Brownfields Redevelopment

ALSO OF INTEREST AND FROM MCFARLAND

Syringe Exchange Programs and the Opioid Epidemic: Government and Nonprofit Practices and Policies, edited by Joaquin Jay Gonzalez III and Mickey P. McGee (2021) • *Keeping Schools Safe: Case Studies and Insights*, edited by Joaquin Jay Gonzalez III and Roger L. Kemp (2021) • *Climate Change and Disaster Resilience: Challenges, Actions and Innovations in Urban Planning*, edited by Joaquin Jay Gonzalez III, Roger L. Kemp and Alan R. Roper (2021) • *Cities and Homelessness: Essays and Case Studies on Practices, Innovations and Challenges*, edited by Joaquin Jay Gonzalez III and Mickey P. McGee (2021) • *Senior Care and Services: Essays and Case Studies on Practices, Innovations and Challenges*, edited by Joaquin Jay Gonzalez III, Roger L. Kemp and Willie Lee Brit (2020) • *Veteran Care and Services: Essays and Case Studies on Practices, Innovations and Challenges*, edited by Joaquin Jay Gonzalez III, Mickey P. McGee and Roger L. Kemp (2020) • *Legal Marijuana: Perspectives on Public Benefits, Risks and Policy Approaches*, edited by Joaquin Jay Gonzalez III and Mickey P. McGee (2019) • *Cybersecurity: Current Writings on Threats and Protection*, edited by Joaquin Jay Gonzalez III and Roger L. Kemp (2019) • *Eminent Domain and Economic Growth: Perspectives on Benefits, Harms and New Trends*, edited by Joaquin Jay Gonzalez III, Roger L. Kemp and Jonathan Rosenthal (2018) • *Small Town Economic Development: Reports on Growth Strategies in Practice*, edited by Joaquin Jay Gonzalez III, Roger L. Kemp and Jonathan Rosenthal (2017) • *Privatization in Practice: Reports on Trends, Cases and Debates in Public Service by Business and Nonprofits*, edited by Joaquin Jay Gonzalez III and Roger L. Kemp (2016) • *Immigration and America's Cities: A Handbook on Evolving Services*, edited by Joaquin Jay Gonzalez III and Roger L. Kemp (2016) • *Corruption and American Cities: Essays and Case Studies in Ethical Accountability*, edited by Joaquin Jay Gonzalez III and Roger L. Kemp (2016)

Brownfields Redevelopment

*Case Studies and Concepts
in Community Revitalization*

Edited by JOAQUIN JAY GONZALEZ III,
TAD MCGALLIARD *and* IGNACIO DAYRIT

McFarland & Company, Inc., Publishers
Jefferson, North Carolina

Library of Congress Cataloguing-in-Publication Data

Names: Gonzalez, Joaquin Jay, III, editor. | McGalliard, Tad, editor. | Dayrit, Ignacio, editor.
Title: Brownfields redevelopment : case studies and concepts in community revitalization / edited by Joaquin Jay Gonzalez III, Tad McGalliard, and Ignacio Dayrit.
Description: Jefferson, North Carolina : McFarland & Company, Inc., Publishers, 2021 | Includes bibliographical references and index.
Identifiers: LCCN 2021032502 | ISBN 9781476683607 (paperback : acid free paper) ∞
ISBN 9781476643021 (ebook)
Subjects: LCSH: Urban renewal—Case studies. | Brownfields—Case studies. | City planning—Case studies. | Land use, Urban—Case studies. | Environmental policy—Case studies. | BISAC: BUSINESS & ECONOMICS / Development / Economic Development | POLITICAL SCIENCE / Public Policy / Environmental Policy
Classification: LCC HT170 .B77 2021 | DDC 307.3/416—dc23
LC record available at https://lccn.loc.gov/2021032502

British Library cataloguing data are available
ISBN (print) 978-1-4766-8360-7
ISBN (ebook) 978-1-4766-4302-1

© 2021 Joaquin Jay Gonzalez III, Tad McGalliard and Ignacio Dayrit. All rights reserved

No part of this book may be reproduced or transmitted in any form or by any means, electronic or mechanical, including photocopying or recording, or by any information storage and retrieval system, without permission in writing from the publisher.

Front cover: Demolition of an old hospital site in Belleville, Illinois on November 29, 2018 (Philip Rozenski/Shutterstock)

Printed in the United States of America

*McFarland & Company, Inc., Publishers
Box 611, Jefferson, North Carolina 28640
www.mcfarlandpub.com*

Jay dedicates this book to Jojo, brother and best friend.
Tad dedicates this book to Sharon and Thomas.
Ignacio dedicates this book to Eleanor, Camilla and Teresa.
And in remembrance of Charles Bartsch (1951–2018),
the father of brownfields.

Acknowledgments

We are grateful for the support of the Mayor George Christopher Professorship at Golden Gate University as well as GGU's Pi Alpha Alpha Chapter and the ICMA Student Chapter. We appreciate the encouragement from our wonderful colleagues and students at the Edward S. Ageno School of Business, the Department of Public Administration, and the Executive MPA Program, the International City/County Management Association (ICMA), and the Center for Creative Land Recycling.

Our heartfelt "THANK YOU!" goes to the contributors listed in the back section and the individuals, organizations, and publishers below for granting permission to reprint the material in this volume and the research assistance. They all expressed support for practical research and information sharing that benefits our citizens, communities, and cities.

Alaska Department of Environmental Conservation
Cheryl Ann Bishop
CIII Associates
Clark Henry
Coral H. Gonzalez
David J. Robinson
David S. Greensfelder
Ed Morales
Environmental Law Institute
Florida Department of Environmental Protection
Golden Gate University Library
Governing
Jay H. Dick
Kaiser Health News
Kaitlyn Krull
Karen Garrett
Kate O'Brien
Kerry Hansen
Kevin C. Desouza
Kim Briesemeister
Louisiana Department of Environmental Quality
Lyn Hikida
Marcus Humberg
Martha Faust
Mary Hashem
Michael Hunter
Michelle Hong-Gonzalez
The Montrose Group, Ohio
New York State Department of Environmental Conservation
North Dakota Department of Environmental Quality
Ohio Environmental Protection Agency
Oregon Business Development Department
Oregon Department of Environmental Quality
PA Times
Paul Harney
Paula Middlebrooks
Pennsylvania Department of Environmental Protection
PM Magazine
Rachel Jean-Baptiste
Roger L. Kemp
San Francisco State University Library
Severo C. Madrona, Jr.
Stuart Miner
theconversation.com
Todd S. Davis
Tom Carroll
U.S. Environmental Protection Agency
University of San Francisco Library
Washington State Department of Ecology
Willis Towers Watson

Table of Contents

Acknowledgments   vii

Preface   1

Part I. Introduction

1. City Governments and Brownfields Development
   ROGER L. KEMP   5

2. Overview of EPA's Brownfields Program
   U.S. ENVIRONMENTAL PROTECTION AGENCY   9

3. Redeveloping Brownfields Good for Environment and Economy
   DAVID J. ROBINSON   15

4. Brownfields as a Mainstream Investment
   TAD MCGALLIARD   18

5. Innovations in Environmental Remediation
   TAD MCGALLIARD   23

6. How Donald Trump Became Counties' Best Friend and Biggest Ally
   ALAN GREENBLATT   30

Part II. Challenges, Risks, and Opportunities
• *A. Challenges and Risks* •

7. Groundbreaking Environmentalism
   STEPHEN GOLDSMITH   37

8. Cleaning Up Toxic Sites Shouldn't Clear Out the Neighbors
   LINDSEY DILLON   40

9. Don't Give Up on Ambitious Green Architecture
   IAN MELL   43

10. Pittsburgh Steps Up
    RON LITTLEFIELD   45

11. Toxic Lead Can Stay in the Body for Years After Exposure
    STUART SHALAT ... 48

12. What Lies Beneath
    JAMES R. ELLIOTT and SCOTT FRICKEL ... 51

13. Lead Poisoning's Lifelong Toll Includes Lowering Social Mobility
    SHEFALI LUTHRA ... 54

• B. Opportunities •

14. Financial and Nonfinancial Incentives
    TAD MCGALLIARD ... 57

15. Societal Disruptions Are Opportunities for Economic Development
    KIM BRIESEMEISTER ... 67

16. Suburb City Managers Are Our First Responders
    TOM CARROLL and BRANDI BLESSETT ... 72

17. Improving Water Quality Doesn't Have to Wash Away Budgets
    RON LITTLEFIELD ... 77

18. Fighting Neighborhood Displacement, One Sewer Plant at a Time
    JAYANT KAIRAM ... 80

19. Setting the Stage for Leveraging Resources for Brownfields Revitalization
    U.S. ENVIRONMENTAL PROTECTION AGENCY ... 82

20. Key Steps in Successful Leveraging Strategies for Brownfields Projects
    U.S. ENVIRONMENTAL PROTECTION AGENCY ... 89

Part III. Practices and Innovations

• A. Federal •

21. Smart Growth
    U.S. ENVIRONMENTAL PROTECTION AGENCY ... 105

22. Brownfields Federal Programs and Cases
    U.S. ENVIRONMENTAL PROTECTION AGENCY ... 108

23. Brownfields Federal Tax Incentives and Credits
    U.S. ENVIRONMENTAL PROTECTION AGENCY ... 120

24. Leveraging: Harbor Point in Stamford, Connecticut
    U.S. ENVIRONMENTAL PROTECTION AGENCY ... 127

25. Leveraging: North Port Revitalization in Dubuque, Iowa
    U.S. ENVIRONMENTAL PROTECTION AGENCY ... 131

26. Leveraging: Commerce Corridor in Ranson and Charles Town, West Virginia
    U.S. ENVIRONMENTAL PROTECTION AGENCY ... 136

• B. State •

27. Florida Waste Cleanup Program
    FLORIDA DEPARTMENT OF ENVIRONMENTAL PROTECTION 140

28. State of Ohio's Brownfields Team
    OHIO ENVIRONMENTAL PROTECTION AGENCY 143

29. Brownfield Redevelopment Guide
    PENNSYLVANIA DEPARTMENT OF ENVIRONMENTAL PROTECTION 148

30. Oregon Brownfields Initiative
    OREGON DEPARTMENT OF ENVIRONMENTAL QUALITY
    and OREGON BUSINESS DEVELOPMENT DEPARTMENT 154

31. Brownfields in Alaska
    ALASKA DEPARTMENT OF ENVIRONMENTAL CONSERVATION 159

32. Brownfields: Transform the Past, Build for the Future
    NEW YORK STATE DEPARTMENT OF ENVIRONMENTAL CONSERVATION 165

33. Louisiana Brownfields
    LOUISIANA DEPARTMENT OF ENVIRONMENTAL QUALITY 171

34. Brownfields in Washington
    WASHINGTON STATE DEPARTMENT OF ECOLOGY 176

35. North Dakota's Brownfields Program
    NORTH DAKOTA DEPARTMENT OF ENVIRONMENTAL QUALITY 179

36. Tribal Brownfields and Response Programs
    U.S. ENVIRONMENTAL PROTECTION AGENCY 182

• C. City •

37. The Factories of the Past Are Turning into the Data Centers of the Future
    GRAHAM PICKREN 187

38. Cleaning Up House
    MARCUS HUMBERG, MARTHA FAUST, CHERYL ANN BISHOP
    and LYN HIKIDA 190

39. The Music City Miracle
    PAULA MIDDLEBROOKS 197

40. ICMA and CCLR's Case Experiences
    CLARK HENRY, TAD MCGALLIARD *and* IGNACIO DAYRIT 201

• D. International •

41. The Reuse of U.S. Military Bases in the Philippines
    SEVERO C. MADRONA, JR. 214

42.	Under the Hood KEVIN C. DESOUZA, MICHAEL HUNTER *and* TAN YIGITCANLAR	220
43.	Brownfield Sites Are Opportunities in the Heart of Towns and Cities PAUL NATHANAIL	226
44.	France Has a Unique Approach to Regenerating Inner Cities SEBASTIEN DARCHEN *and* GWENDAL SIMON	229
45.	An Old German Steel Region Gets a Mindful Modern Makeover CHRISTA REICHER	232
46.	Gasbrook Gasworks, Hamburg, Germany TAD MCGALLIARD	235

Part IV. Private and Nonprofit Environmental Professionals

47.	How Do Brownfields Companies Innovate? MARY HASHEM *and* STUART MINER	241
48.	What Developers Really Want TODD S. DAVIS	246
49.	Retail Revolution and Retrofit DAVID S. GREENSFELDER	249
50.	Brownfield Redevelopment and Environmental Insurance ED MORALES	254
51.	Land Recycling, Brownfields and the Center for Creative Land Recycling IGNACIO DAYRIT	259
52.	Municipal and Community Collaboration for Effective Brownfields Redevelopment ENVIRONMENTAL LAW INSTITUTE	265
53.	Working with the Private Sector to Redevelop Brownfields ENVIRONMENTAL LAW INSTITUTE	270
54.	Environmental Site Assessments TAD MCGALLIARD	275
55.	Remediation Planning, Reuse Planning and Site Design TAD MCGALLIARD	280
56.	Remediation Technologies and Remedies TAD MCGALLIARD	283

Part V. The Future

57.	The Importance of the Arts JAY H. DICK	295

58. How Civic Tech Can Address Urban Inequality
   STEPHEN GOLDSMITH — 299

59. Are Car-Free Bridges the Future?
   ALEX MARSHALL — 301

60. Reuses of Brownfields
   TAD MCGALLIARD — 303

61. Identifying Future Uses for Brownfields
   ENVIRONMENTAL LAW INSTITUTE — 306

62. As Cities Look at Options for Financing Infrastructure, They Keep an Eye Out for Low-Income Residents
   PAUL W. TAYLOR — 312

Appendices

A. Glossary and Acronyms of Brownfields and Economic Development Practices
   JOAQUIN JAY GONZALEZ III *and* IGNACIO DAYRIT — 323

B. Brownfields Revitalization Act (2002) — 330

C. Brownfields Utilization, Investment and Local Development (BUILD) Act (2018) — 332

D. Model Brownfields Legislation for States
   ENVIRONMENTAL LAW INSTITUTE — 335

About the Contributors — 354

Index — 357

Preface

In the early 1990s several rust belt cities sought President Bill Clinton's help in resurrecting their dying inner cores—suffocated by sprawling onto greenfields. And the shadow of Superfund liability.

Brownfields were born.

This was at a time when prominent incidences, like Love Canal, Three Mile Island, and the burning of the Ohio River tainted every attempt at land reuse. The problem these cities faced was the fear of environmental liability drove away economic development.

The mayors of these cities knew that their downtowns were not comprised of sites that belonged in the National Priorities List. In reality, there were many sites—the brownfields—which were far less contaminated and easier to assess and remediate. The primary objective of the brownfield movement was to remove the liability and facilitate the redevelopment of these sites, through funding assistance from the U.S. Environmental Protection Agency (EPA) for the purpose of economic development. Over time, the EPA gained other federal and state partners toward the redevelopment of brownfields into economically, environmentally and equitable uses.

So, what is a brownfield?

- Is it a site that is known to be contaminated? Maybe.
- Is it a site that is on a local, state or national registry of regulated sites? Not exactly.
- Is it a site which may pose potential financial, legal and regulatory risks for entities involved in such a site, such as past, current and future owners, occupants, developers and public agencies? Almost.

The practical definition of a brownfield is any site—with some notable exceptions to be discussed later—where state or federal resources can be used to remove uncertainties to, and facilitate its assessment, planning, cleanup and reuse.

That's a lot of sites, and there's probably one in your neighborhood.

In the articles that follow, we will take you around the neighborhoods of cities and states to acquaint you with the intricacies of brownfield projects past and present. Writing in Part I are contributors who will introduce you to the "basics," beginning with long-time city manager Roger L. Kemp's thoughts, the EPA's official definitions, the environmental and investment perspectives, on to President Trump's outreach to the many small and large counties all around our country.

The neighborhood-level drama begins in Part II with our authors delving deep into the multi-layered challenges, risks, and opportunities to our communities and our ecosystems. In Part III, our experts go into how we overcome challenges, mitigate risks, and grab opportunities using creative practices and simple innovations. Part IV's contributors describe the energy and spirit driving the leading-edge brownfield projects and partnerships of hardworking private and nonprofit environmental professionals. Part V's authors lead us to some areas for future exploration and experimentation. Finally, our Appendices provide essential resources such as a comprehensive glossary of brownfields and economic development terms and acronyms, the landmark 2002 and the new 2018 federal Brownfields laws, and a model legislation for those who wish to nudge their states into action.

The COVID-19 pandemic and the racial unrest that emerged during the writing and compiling of this volume reminds us of the critical importance of weaving in health, inclusiveness, diversity, equity, accessibility, and other justice considerations into whatever brownfield and economic development initiatives we do in our neighborhoods and cities moving forward.

Have a brilliant read!

Part I
Introduction

1. City Governments and Brownfields Development*

Roger L. Kemp

Many local governments have an Economic Development specialist who focuses on the development of vacant parcels of land that are ready for development, as well as long-standing vacant contaminated sites that are assumed to be brownfield sites. These economic development personnel are usually located in the Planning Department, and report to the Planning Director, or they are in the Office of the City Manager, and report to the City Manager. Very large communities might even have an Economic Development Department, where the Director would even have an economic development staff that would work together to promote and facilitate economic development in their community.

A typical developer looks to develop a piece of vacant land or rebuild on a site where the existing facilities can be rehabilitated or demolished and reconstructed. This is the norm, since a developer does not want to spend money to clean up a piece of property, since it is very costly to de-contaminate a polluted site. Most developers to not want to encounter this type of expense, since they do not have to if they purchase and develop a clean, non-contaminated, parcel of land, even if it was previously developed.

Therefore, a local government has economic development specialists work for them to facilitate the cleanup and development of such brownfield sites.

Brownfield Revenues

Over the years, there have frequently been many federal and state grant programs that have been approved that have authorized funds to promote the cleanup and development of brownfield sites in cities throughout our nation. Sometimes the federal government has adopted grants, which are typically allocated to our nation's state governments to give to their respective cities. Many state governments too have approved brownfield grants to give to their cities to cleanup and redevelop brownfield sites. The reasons for such brownfield cleanup grants from higher levels of government to our nation's cities are obvious. All levels of government—federal, state, and local—receive significant funds when brownfield sites in cities have been cleaned-up and redeveloped.

The reasons such grants become available from our federal and state governments

---

*Published with permission of the author.

is due to the additional revenues that all levels of government receive when such brownfield sites are cleaned-up and redeveloped. The revenues that each level of government receives once such polluted sites are redeveloped are as follows:

Federal Government. When a contaminated site is cleanup and redeveloped many jobs are usually created, and the federal government receives the federal income taxes paid on the salaries received by all of the employees that work for the new company that was built on the developed,

previously contaminated, site. Since there were no funds previously generated from such sites for many years, these are new funds generated for our federal government. Our federal government appreciates receiving these additional funds, especially when they are created from many of our cities, that are in numerous states throughout our nation. Federal government brownfield grants, due to the revenues that they ultimately generate, provide significant revenues to our federal government. Our federal government, in the long-term, receives much more revenues from these taxes then it previously paid for the cost of these brownfield cleanup grants.

State Governments. Just like with our federal government, when a contaminated site is cleaned-up and redeveloped, many jobs are created, and the state governments receives the state income taxes paid on the salaries by all of the employees that work for the new company that was built on the redeveloped, previously contaminated, site. Since there were no funds previously generated from this site for many years, these are new revenues generated for our state governments. Our state governments appreciate receiving these additional funds, especially since they were created by many of the cities located within their state. For this reason, state government brownfield grants, provide significant revenues to many state governments throughout the nation. Our state governments, also, in the long-term, receive more revenues from these taxes than they paid for the cost of these brownfield cleanup grants. State governments also receive sales taxes from the employees that work for the new company that was created on the cleaned-up redeveloped site.

City Governments. While city governments do not receive any of the income taxes generated from the employees that work for the new company that was redeveloped on the brownfield site, it does receive 100 percent of the property taxes that are created when this vacant site was fully redeveloped. Local governments receive all the property taxes, the largest local government revenue source, that will be generated from such a developed site. Cities also receive the property taxes on the company's personal property, like work-related equipment and technology. These taxes vary from state-to-state. Cities also receive property taxes from new employees that work for this company that move to their community because of the new jobs that they acquire. This is also an additional revenue source that cities may receive, primarily in property taxes from the homes that were purchased by the new employees that work for these companies.

Brownfield Sites

A brownfield site is one that was previously developed, currently not in use, and is thought to possibly be contaminated based on the use of the site by its previous owners. Such pieces of land were typically used previously for commercial or industrial purposes and are suspected to be polluted by soil contamination that was created by placing hazardous waste on the site. These sites exist in cities throughout our nation. In many states, sites previously used for gasoline stations or dry-cleaning stores automatically fall into this category, since chemicals from these land uses were left in the soil underneath and surrounding the buildings on such properties.

The U.S. Environmental Protection Agency (EPA) came up with the word "brownfield" in the early 1990s. This term applies to land sites that were previously contaminated, and that someone wants to redevelop for a new commercial or industrial use. According to the EPA, such parcels of land must be upgraded to be re-developed.

In 2002 President Bush signed into law the Small Business Liability Relief and Brownfields Revitalization Act (commonly called the "Brownfields Law"). This legislation provided grants and requirements for local governments for the assessment, cleanup, and revitalization of brownfield property sites. The law resulted in many acres of sites in cities throughout our nation being redeveloped for new commercial and industrial purposes.

If a piece of property in a city is declared a "brownfield site" a legal designation is imposed on it that would place restrictions, re-development conditions, and offer some financial incentives for the redevelopment of such designated brownfield sites.

Problems for Redevelopment

Generally, most brownfield sites are usually located in local government industrial property zones, and fewer of them are in commercial property zones. Industrial properties that are located on these sites created products, and commercial zones have companies that locate on these properties that sell such products to the public. Hence, most brownfield sites are in industrial property zones, and only a few of them are in commercial property zones. Some brownfield sites are even located in residential areas, since sometimes dry-cleaning establishments and gas stations are allowed in these property zones, even though, over time, they produced a high level of subsurface soil contaminants.

Many contaminated brownfield sites have remained vacant for many years in cities throughout America, due to the costs associated with the redevelopment of such properties. Frequently, the cost of the redevelopment of such sites would exceed the market value of the property. Over the years, however, due to other residential and commercial development, and as property values increased, such brownfield sites have received increased development attention, primarily due to the grants that are available from our state and federal governments to properly assess, cleanup, and redevelop such contaminated properties.

The Future

Due to federal government regulations that have been adopted over the years, our nation's state and local governments have implement brownfield regulations with the cooperation of the Environmental Protection Agency (EPA), one of the major departments of our federal government. This cooperative effort has resulted in the development of thousands of brownfield property sites in cities located in states throughout our nation.

Since our states and cities have been working together with our federal government's EPA department, over the years thousands of grants have been approved and issued to private companies to develop brownfield sites in many cities, in all of the states, throughout our nation. Also, as a private sector incentive for the development of brownfield sites, the costs of the improvement of such sites are tax deductible to the private companies that participate in such redevelopment efforts.

Over the years, I have worked in several cities throughout our nation. They include the largest city manager governments in California, New Jersey, and Connecticut. These cities include Oakland, California; Clifton, New Jersey; and Meriden, Connecticut. During my city management career in these communities, I have used all the state and federal brownfield site programs and grants available to local governments, and I am proud of my efforts over the years to develop contaminated sites in the cities that I have worked in.

2. Overview of EPA's Brownfields Program[*]

U.S. Environmental Protection Agency

What Is a Brownfield?

A brownfield is a property, the expansion, redevelopment, or reuse of which may be complicated by the presence or potential presence of a hazardous substance, pollutant, or contaminant. It is estimated that there are more than 450,000 brownfields[1] in the U.S. Cleaning up and reinvesting in these properties increases local tax bases, facilitates job growth, utilizes existing infrastructure, takes development pressures off of undeveloped, open land, and both improves and protects the environment.

Brownfields Program Environmental and Economic Benefits

EPA's Brownfields program empowers states, communities, and other stakeholders to work together to prevent, assess, safely clean up, and sustainably reuse brownfields. Revitalizing brownfield sites creates benefits throughout the community.

Through fiscal year 2019, on average, $17.45 was leveraged for each EPA Brownfields dollar and 9 jobs leveraged per $100,000 of EPA brownfields funds expended on assessment, cleanup, and revolving loan fund cooperative agreements.

Brownfield sites tend to have greater location efficiency than alternative development scenarios. Results of five pilot studies show a 32 to 57 percent reduction in vehicle miles traveled when development occurred at a brownfield site rather than a greenfield. Fewer vehicle miles traveled means a reduction in pollution emissions including greenhouse gases. These same site comparisons show an estimated 47 to 62 percent reduction of stormwater runoff for brownfield site development.

A 2017 study concluded that cleaning up brownfield properties led to residential property value increases of 5–15.2 percent within 1.29 miles of the sites.[2] Analyzing data near 48 of those brownfields, another study found an estimated $29 to $97 million in additional tax revenue for local governments in a single year after cleanup—2 to 7 times more than the $12.4 million EPA contributed to the cleanup of those brownfields.[3] Initial

---

[*]Public document originally published as U.S. Environmental Protection Agency, "Overview of EPA's Brownfields Program," https://www.epa.gov/brownfields/understanding-brownfields (September 2019).

anecdotal surveys indicate a reduction in crime in recently revitalized brownfields areas.

Opportunity to expand the assessment program and leverage funds and jobs has increased. Policy clarification allows the use of site assessment dollars for environmental assessments in conjunction with efforts to promote area-wide planning around brownfield sites. The use of funds for these purposes is particularly important in economically distressed areas. In certain instances, where assessments reveal immediate threats to the environment or human health, EPA could implement a more programmatic use of removal funds.

Environmental Contaminants Often Found at Brownfield Sites

Brownfield properties are often overlooked for reuse or redevelopment due to fear of environmental contamination. Understanding the types of contaminants present (or potentially present) and how people may be exposed to those contaminants will help a community plan cleanup and site reuse options that limit exposure risk.

U.S. EPA, states and tribes have programs that can help communities identify properties that are brownfields, determine whether the property is environmentally-contaminated, address contamination when needed and plan for site reuse that will bring new benefits to the community.

Below are the contaminants most reported from brownfields cleaned up using U.S. EPA grant funds:

1. **Lead** (Pb) (Metals) from Mining, fuel, paint, inks, piping, batteries, ammunition. Potential Health Effects: Damage to brain, nerves, organs, and bone; cancer

2. **Petroleum** (Oil) hydrocarbon compounds Drill and refining, fuel, chemical and plastic production. Potential Health Effects: Headache; nervous system, immune, liver, kidney, and respiratory damage; cancer

3. **Asbestos** (Fiber in rock) Mining and processing, piping, insulation, fire proofing, brakes. Potential Health Effects: Lung scarring, mesothelioma and lung cancer

4. **Polycyclic aromatic hydrocarbons** (PAHs) (Hydrocarbon compounds, combustion byproduct) Coal tar, creosote, soot, fire, industry/ manufacturing byproduct. Potential Health Effects: Liver disorders; cancer

5. **Other metals** (Metals) Metal fabrication, plating, mining, industry/ manufacturing. Potential Health Effects: Immune, cardiovascular, developmental, gastrointestinal, neurological, reproductive, respiratory and kidney damage; cancer

6. **Volatile organic compounds** (VOCs) (Manmade chemicals) Industry and commercial product solvents, degreasers, paint strippers, dry cleaning. Potential Health Effects: Eye irritation; nausea; liver, kidney and nervous system damage; birth defects; cancer

7. **Polychlorinated Biphenyls** (PCBs) (Manmade chemicals) Heat and electrical transfer fluids, lubricants, paint and caulk, manufacturing, power plant. Potential Health Effects: Disruption or damage to the immune, hormone and neurological system; liver and skin disease

8. **Arsenic** (As) (Metals) Pesticides, agriculture, manufacturing, wood preservative. Potential Health Effects: Nausea, vomiting and stomach pain; blood disorders; nerve damage; skin disease; lung and skin cancer

Contaminants can cause a range of health effects when a person is exposed, and the contaminant is absorbed into the body. Exposure pathways refer to the ways people come into contact or are exposed to a contaminant. The extent of exposure and absorption depends on how much contaminant is present, how a person is exposed, how often and how long they are exposed. Sensitive populations may be at a greater risk from exposures, such as children, the elderly and those with chronic conditions.

The three basic exposure pathways are (1) breathing, (2) eating or drinking, and (3) direct contact with the skin. Of the three, breathing and eating or drinking are the most common but all three can occur.

Reuse Possibilities for Brownfield Sites

Nearby residents and other local community members benefit when a brownfield site is transformed from an eyesore and safety concern into a new job center, recreational facility, housing, or other community amenity. Safely reusing a brownfield site is possible when a redevelopment plan helps guide site assessment and cleanup decisions.

Often, the process of assessing and cleaning up a single brownfield site sparks community interest to identify other sites for redevelopment! Successful brownfield site redevelopment across the country can be described through five main categories. Various public, private and community organizations redevelop brownfields to meet the many different needs that exist within a community.

- Reuse supported by a public or community organization may focus on a site with limited commercial potential or is a priority for the neighborhood.
- A private investor is likely more interested in a site and reuse that will provide a strong return on investment.
- Often, the goals of each party can be met through creativity and flexibility.
- For example, a brownfield site can be reused as commercial office spaces to serve as both a corporate headquarters and low-cost meeting space for community groups.

What Will Brownfields Redevelopment Look Like in Your Community?

- Green Space: Agriculture, community parks, trails, sports fields and facilities, open space and other recreational activities. These spaces also provide wildlife habitat and nature conservation opportunities.
- Residential: Multi-family homes, like apartments and condos, single-family homes and other residential purposes, such as university and senior housing.
- Industrial: Manufacturing buildings, warehouse, storage and distribution facilities, renewable energy production, research, and development parks.

- Mixed Use: Combination of two or more reuses (for example, an apartment building with retail and office spaces on the ground floor next to a public park).
- Commercial: Offices, retail, restaurants, and other businesses; municipal buildings and nonprofit centers.

Cleaning Up Brownfield Sites

Unsafe levels of environmental contamination on a brownfield may result from past or current industrial, commercial, residential, agricultural, or recreational uses and practices. Contaminants may be found in soil, water, or air. Cleaning up contaminants on a brownfield reduces or eliminates potential health risks to residents, workers, pets, and the surrounding environment.

How much cleanup is needed depends on the specific contaminants found at the brownfield, the extent of contamination, and how the property will be reused.

Risk levels. States and tribes use a risk-based cleanup approach to determine the required level of cleanup necessary at brownfield properties. These levels are set to pose minimal risk to human health and the environment, in accordance with federal standards. States and tribes require cleanup to meet risk-based standards based on contaminants present and the planned reuse for the brownfield.

Planned reuse for the brownfield. The amount of cleanup required at a brownfield depends on how the site will be reused. The risk of future exposure to contaminants may be greater for residents and workers who will spend much of their time living or working there. Children, elderly, pregnant women, and occupants who are ill can be especially sensitive to contaminants.

The risk-based cleanup will consider sensitivities of the specific populations and their time spent on the property. An effective brownfield cleanup protects the population from potentially harmful exposures by removing or containing site contaminants. For example:

- A residential site, where children may play or elderly live, requires a cleanup that removes contaminants above residential risk levels, so the property poses minimal risk from contaminant exposure.
- A factory with legacy contaminants associated with past uses may require cleanup in specific areas of the site to remove contaminants where workers could be exposed to levels above industrial standards. In low-access areas, such as power generation or vehicle storage, residual contaminants may be contained.

How Can My Community Clean Up a Brownfield Site?

Identify the planned reuse for the site and seek out experts who can help you navigate the cleanup process.

- Through experience, U.S. EPA, state, and tribal cleanup programs have learned a great deal about cleanup and contaminated site reuse. State and tribal programs oversee cleanups to ensure safe reuse standards are met.
- Cleaning up a brownfield requires assistance from an environmental professional

to create a site cleanup plan based on assessment findings and to conduct the cleanup according to state, tribal and local requirements.

The specific approach used to clean up a site depends on the way the site will be reused. Site reuse will dictate the need for clean soil; geotextile or cover/cap; land use controls; and whether lead or asbestos abatement is required. Various technologies are available to clean up contaminated properties. The technology selected will largely depend on cost and contamination characteristics of the site. The following are some of the commonly used methods for cleaning up brownfields and other contaminated sites:

- **Excavation**. Contaminants and contaminated soil on the surface or subsurface are dug up from the site and transported offsite for treatment or disposal in a landfill. Clean soil or other material can be used to fill the excavated area and create a level surface for reuse.
- **Tank removal**. Soil contaminated with gasoline or other fuels is dug up from the site to expose and remove the underground storage tanks and piping system. Then the soils under the tank can be examined for contamination and removed as needed.
- **Capping**. Creating or adding a barrier between the surface and contaminants by using a geotextile, a layer of clean soil or both. Capping protects areas of cleanup, reduces exposures, and prevents the spread of contamination.
- **On site or "In-situ" treatment**. Chemicals are injected into the soil to break down contaminants or convert them into less harmful or toxic substances. Solidification or stabilization adds binding or chemical agents to prevent contaminant movement.
- **Bioremediation**. Naturally occurring or adapted microbes consume organic contaminants. Active management at bioremediation sites includes adding nutrients, oxygen or chemicals that release oxygen to increase microbial growth, allowing them to degrade the contaminants over time to water, gas or less harmful or toxic substances.
- **Phytoremediation**. Plant root systems release substances which help plants neutralize, stabilize or increase microbial degradation of contaminants in contaminated soil or water near roots. Select plants can also take up contaminants through their roots, reducing soil and water contamination over time.
- **Lead and asbestos abatement**. Lead and asbestos are inspected and removed by specially trained licensed contractors. The training, inspection and abatement may be regulated by environmental or public agencies separate from brownfield programs. Lead and asbestos removal involve removal of contaminated material in contained areas using specialized equipment.

Types of Brownfields Grant Funding

EPA's Brownfields Program provides direct funding for brownfields assessment, cleanup, revolving loans, environmental job training, technical assistance, training, and research. To facilitate the leveraging of public resources, EPA's Brownfields Program collaborates with other EPA programs, other federal partners, and state agencies to identify and make available resources that can be used for brownfield activities. In 2020, the EPA funding programs consisted of the following:

- **Assessment Grants** provide funding for brownfield inventories, planning, environmental assessments, and community outreach.
- **Revolving Loan Fund (RLF) Grants** provide funding to capitalize loans that are used to clean up brownfield sites.
- **Cleanup Grants** provide funding to carry out cleanup activities at brownfield sites owned by the applicant.
- **Multipurpose (MP) Grants** provide funding to conduct a range of eligible planning, assessment and cleanup activities at one or more brownfield sites in a target area.
- **Environmental Workforce Development and Job Training (EWDJT) Grants** provide environmental training for residents impacted by brownfield sites in their communities.
- **Technical Assistance, Training, and Research Grants** provide funding to organizations to conduct research and to provide training and technical assistance to communities to help address their brownfields challenges.
- **State and Tribal Response Program Grants** provide non-competitive funding to establish or enhance State and Tribal Brownfields response programs.

Notes

1. The estimated 450,000 brownfields mentioned here and elsewhere in the text represents an estimate of the EPA for the number of sites that may be considered a brownfield. In actuality any property that is perceived to have environmental and related issues that may complicate cleanup is considered a brownfield, and nationwide numbers may far exceed this estimate.

2. Haninger, K., L. Ma, and C. Timmins. 2017. "The Value of Brownfield Remediation." *Journal of the Association of Environmental and Resource Economists 4(1): 197–241.*

3. Sullivan, K. 2017. "Brownfields Remediation: Impact of Local Residential Property Tax Revenue," *Journal of Environmental Assessment Policy and Management* 19(3).

3. Redeveloping Brownfields Good for Environment and Economy*

David J. Robinson

Up to 450,000 environmentally contaminated Brownfield sites exist in the United States according to the U.S. Environmental Protection Agency (EPA). These Brownfield sites are waiting for redevelopment as potential customers and workers in proximity often surround them. The redevelopment of Brownfields also promotes investment within the urban footprint rather than moving to adjacent, primarily rural counties whose cheap land and connections through the interstate highway system enabled cheap development since the 1950s.

A prime challenge for public administrators is continuing the growth and development of a region while managing the sprawl that stretches infrastructure, harms the environment and increases taxes. Many tools exist to address the sprawl in traditional development patterns, but tax and fee based Smart Growth Models may not fit slower developing regions that are still plagued by sprawl.

While not all regions have the mountains, ocean and 70 degree year-round weather of California or the dense population and wealth of the East Coast to keep growing even while applying Smart Growth fees on that growth, all regions and states have Brownfields within their existing urban footprint. Brownfield are environmentally contaminated real property, but do not include property listed on the EPA's Superfund List, facilities subject to unilateral administrative orders and facilities subject to the jurisdiction, custody or control of the United States government.

Addressing environmental contamination is often the major issue associated with the redevelopment of an urban site. First, the federal laws created to protect the environment must be addressed. Federal environmental laws designed to protect public health create liability for contamination at sites that unfortunately freeze development. Federal law creates liability for the environmental contamination of a site even if the current owner did not create the pollution. To protect themselves under federal law, the new property owners can establish a "bona fide prospective purchaser defense" before purchasing the property.

The new property owner can establish this defense if they can prove the pollution was caused by the act or omission of a contractually unrelated third party. Of course, the

---

*Originally published as David J. Robinson, "Redeveloping Brownfields Good for Environment and Economy," *PA Times*, https://patimes.org/redeveloping-brownfields-good-environment-economy/ (June 27, 2014). Reprinted with permission of the publisher.

new property owner cannot be contractually related to prior owners or be aware of the hazardous substances. To obtain protection, the new owner must undertake all appropriate inquiry into the previous ownership and uses of the property consistent with good commercial and customary practice. New property owners will need to hire an environmental consultant to perform Phase I and Phase II reviews of the site to determine the level of contamination and create an approved cleanup plan from state or federal regulators.

States who administer their own and federal environmental laws through a state environmental protection agency may have their own process to protect the new, prospective owner from punishment for owning contaminated land. Many states have reached Memorandums' of Understanding with the EPA to create a state-based process to protect new landowners.

Liability protection is not the only public policy needed to redeveloped Brownfield sites. It also takes money. Remediation of Brownfield sites is expensive. Remedies vary from simply capping the contamination to removing, not just the buildings, but also all the dirt at the site. Brownfield remediation can add a million dollar plus expense that can make even an attractive location simply unaffordable for most development.

The federal government is a source for funding Brownfield remediation. The EPA offers funding for Brownfield assessment, cleanup, development, and job training at contaminated sites. Assessment grants fund the Phase I and Phase II review of environmental consultants who can inventory, characterize, assess and conduct planning and community involvement related to Brownfield sites. The EPA grants range from $200,000 up to $700,000 to assess a site contaminated by hazardous substances, pollutants, contaminants or petroleum. Federal cleanup grants provide funding to remediate polluted site, but each applicant is constrained by funding and scope and they must have a 20 percent cost share. The main challenge with the federal Brownfield cleanup funding programs is they simply lack the overall funding to address the scale and scope of the challenge and its $200,000 per site cap on a per site cleanup funding does not come close to addressing most environmental contamination.

The federal government also provides Brownfield job training grants to encourage employment at formerly contaminated sites. Federal grants go to nonprofit organizations, colleges and universities, and regional, state and local government agencies in annual amounts up to $300,000 for up to five years (totaling $1,500,000). These grants may be used to address sites contaminated by petroleum, hazardous substances, pollutants or contaminants.

The federal Brownfield Revolving Loan Fund provides up to $1,000,000 in loans over five years for not for profit or governmental entities. This nonprofit restriction is a major challenge for the use of federal funding for widespread Brownfield redevelopment.

The challenges for the federal Brownfield program have not stopped the EPA from claiming success. According to the agency, $17.39 is leveraged for every EPA dollar expended. This program created 71,833 jobs nationwide. Storm water runoff from Brownfields redevelopment is 43 percent to 60 percent lower than alternative Greenfields scenarios. Furthermore, redeveloping Brownfields increases surrounding residential property values two percent to three percent.

Many state policy makers implement programs as well to address Brownfields and struggling urban sites. Again, according to the EPA, 12,864 Brownfields were remediated in 2010 by states, municipalities and tribal agencies, constituting a 10 percent increase over the previous year. Brownfields program leveraged more than $14,000,000,000 in Brownfields cleanup and redevelopment funding from the private and public sectors and created over 60,000 jobs.

Ohio points to many successful projects developed through its Brownfield redevelopment program known as the Clean Ohio Fund. The Akron Airdock is a 22-story long facility and was home to the famous Goodyear Blimp. In 2003, Lockheed Martin purchased it with the goal of using it for a new space age version of the blimp. Through the environmental protection provided by the Ohio Environmental Protection Agency's Voluntary Action Program, backed up by an EPA Memorandum of Understanding, a $3,000,000 grant of Clean Ohio Funds along with matching funds from Lockheed Martin and local government, this urban site is being redeveloped and is retaining over 500 jobs and creating nearly 100 more.

Public administrators at the local, state and federal government level, through effective public-private-partnerships, can clean polluted property and spur important job growth in urban markets. Successful strategies address both liability protection as well as funding for remediation to address development at these complex sites. However, the payoff in job creation and prevention of costly urban sprawl is substantial.

4. Brownfields as a Mainstream Investment*

Tad McGalliard

It can be argued that one of the most innovative and successful outcomes to emerge from the past 30 years of sustainability are the policies, programs, public private partnerships, and more that have been created to help clean up and reuse brownfields.

During this time, local governments have increased their knowledge about brownfields and have begun to mainstream their cleanup and redevelopment as part of their core responsibilities. Local governments lead or support brownfields redevelopment in several ways, as described next.

Planning for Better Places

Local governments are incorporating brownfield redevelopment goals and objectives into their commonly used plans and strategies, including those that are focused on sustainability and livability, economic development, regional transportation, disaster and hazard mitigation, small-area designations, parks, and recreation and open space.

The community of Russellville, Kentucky, for instance, met several goals in various plans through redevelopment of a former car dealership to create a new fire station and sports and recreation fields as well as green infrastructure.[1]

The award-winning Mecklenburg Livable Communities Plan (Mecklenburg County, North Carolina, http://livablemeck.com/plan/mlcp.pdf) includes key strategies, actions, and measures focused on brownfields and vacant land. Mecklenburg County, North Carolina, has been concerned about brownfield redevelopment goals and objectives for some time and developed a specific plan (http://livablemeck.com/plan/mlcp.pdf) to address them. Here's an excerpt from that plan:

- Promote the redevelopment, reuse, and rehabilitation of declining and vacant properties.
- Adjust and adopt local government policies and zoning regulations to provide flexible redevelopment of declining and vacant properties.

---

*Originally published as Tad McGalliard, "Brownfields as a Mainstream Investment," *PM Magazine*, https://icma.org/articles/article/brownfields-mainstream-investment, Nov. 27, 2017. Reprinted with permission of the publisher.

- Develop a temporary infill strategy, including audit of locations and countywide map to encourage infill and redevelopment.
- Preserve history through the repurposing of older structures and analyze architecture in communities to identify well-designed and culturally significant structures.
- Support developers' integration of local plans and use of other local government tools.
- Promote well-designed, artistic, and iconic structures in developed areas.
- Infill and redevelopment activity: Number of residential and commercial building permits in targeted reinvestment areas in Mecklenburg County, North Carolina.

Facilitating Engagement

Tools to connect community stakeholders—residents and businesses alike—in robust engagement approaches are more widely used now for brownfields projects than ever before. While such traditional approaches as public meetings are still available, it is far easier to reach constituents through online, social media, and specialized digital approaches.

The city of Pleasant Prairie, Wisconsin, for instance, used an online platform to solicit comments for a planning process involving the redevelopment of a former drive-in theater property. The city's platform received more than 335 comments on the various plan alternatives that were proposed for the project.[2]

Using and Adapting Local Financing Tools

Local governments continue to suggest that some of the biggest challenges for cleaning up and reusing brownfield properties are those associated with financing. Because of their location, contamination, and other factors, many brownfield properties remain upside down—that is, the site's value is less than the cost of cleaning it up for productive reuse.

Creativity in leveraging and layering financing is often required to make the economics of a redevelopment project work. Local governments have long used financial tools for economic development and have adapted many to support local brownfields priorities.

By far the tool local governments use most widely to mitigate financial challenges is tax increment financing (TIF). The Pittsburgh Technology Center, a $104 million development project that had struggled to get off the ground, is now one of the showcase redevelopment projects in the city of Pittsburgh, Pennsylvania. In addition to various sources of local and state government funding, a $7.4 million TIF program was used to finance the remainder of the project.[3]

In many places, communities have established other financial approaches to foster redevelopment, including property and income tax credits or adjustments, special tax districts, loan guarantees and revolving loan funds, direct grants, and municipal bond programs.

Many local governments have worked with development financing institutions to secure New Markets Tax Credit to help propel brownfields projects forward. While not widespread, some communities have begun to look toward foundation and philanthropic organizations as possible financial partners for redevelopment projects.

A project to redevelop a municipal dump into a library in Shepherdstown, West Virginia, received several hundred thousand dollars in foundation grants to support the initiative.[4]

Some communities have also created public-private partnerships (P3) to meet the goals of a local project. In Owensboro, Kentucky, the city's need for a new convention center led local developers to become partners on a local riverfront brownfields project that has stimulated redevelopment across the city's core, creating a robust pace of new public and private investments.[5]

Exercising Nonfinancial Tools

A variety of nonfinancial tools have been adapted or developed to support brownfields development. In many places, for example, local governments offer some level of support to conduct environmental site assessments of properties.

Tampa, Florida's brownfields program offers targeted environmental site assessments.[6] Other commonly used tools include infrastructure improvements to improve the value of areas, neighborhoods, and communities ripe for redevelopment; assistance with land aggregation and land banking; expedited permitting; planning, design, and engineering assistance; and density allowances.

The Value of Investing in Brownfields Redevelopment

According to recent ICMA survey data (*Brownfields and Local Governments 2018 Survey Report*), local government practitioners have these reasons to believe that their jurisdictions should invest human and financial resources in local brownfields actions:

- Protecting the environment as well as the public health of local and regional residents.
- Eliminating blight and increasing local tax bases.
- Creating jobs and economic opportunity.
- Prepping land for new commercial activities to develop.
- Creating more livable communities.

Across the U.S., thousands of brownfield properties have been redeveloped; however, there are likely hundreds of thousands more to go in large and small communities. Although precise numbers are hard to come by, most communities have some level of brownfields or redevelopment challenges.

The continued maturation of local expertise in dealing with these kinds of community issues is likely to be necessary for the foreseeable future. Local governments—in tandem with residents, elected leaders, and community organizations—have a lot at stake, and even more to gain.

The creativity, resourcefulness, and all-around management and leadership skills of the typical professional local government practitioner are just what the situation calls for and reason to be hopeful about the future.

Brownfields Conference 21 Years in the Making

For more than two decades, ICMA has partnered with the United States Environmental Protection Agency (EPA) on the National Brownfields Conference. Roughly equal in size to ICMA's own annual conference, the brownfields conference attracts several thousand registrants, more than 100 exhibitors, and offers more than 125 educational sessions, special events, and networking opportunities.

In 1996, a cross-section of stakeholders came together in Pittsburgh for the very first brownfields conference. The conference's return to Pittsburgh in December 2017 (*www.brownfields2017.org*) offers an opportunity to reflect on the maturation of the brownfields sector, as well as the continuing importance of local government policies, programs, and partnerships that support the cleanup and production of formerly used manufacturing and commercial properties.

Brownfields Roots

The period from 1965 to 2008 brought a series of national laws into existence that have basically established the framework for today's national, state, regional, and local environmental management system. During the 1960s, the Solid Waste Disposal Act and the National Environmental Policy Act were signed into legislation. In 1970, President Richard Nixon's administration founded EPA. The Clean Air Act of 1970 established regulatory requirements for air emissions from stationary and mobile sources of pollutants.

The Clean Water Act (1972), as the name suggests, set guidelines for the discharge of contaminants into U.S. waters. Other key legislation included the Endangered Species Act (1973), the Safe Drinking Water Act (1974), the Resource Conservation and Recovery Act (RCRA) (1976), the Pollution Prevention Act (1990), and the Comprehensive Environmental Response, Compensation, and Liability Act (CERCLA) (1980).

CERCLA, or Superfund as it's often called, provides mechanisms to clean up uncontrolled or abandoned hazardous sites and to protect environmental and public health from toxic exposures.

As of 2017, more than 1,000 sites remain on the National Priorities List (NPL), an EPA-maintained database of the dirtiest former commercial and government (e.g., former military bases) properties across the country.

The Conundrum

A key element of Superfund established that a polluter pays principle, which opened the door for regulatory agencies to define potentially responsible parties, or PRP, that could be on the hook for cleanup costs associated with sites listed on the Superfund NPL.

In the years after Superfund authorization, local governments across the U.S. took note that lenders for real estate deals, particularly in urban areas, were increasingly risk averse to investment on formerly used properties, citing a fear of becoming a PRP.

Interpretations of the regulatory framework associated with the Superfund law suggested that all past, present, and future property owners of formerly used sites could be liable for contamination. With this mindset, many owners of various kinds of properties—even such small parcels as gas stations—abandoned their sites and declared bankruptcy rather than face the prospect of expensive lawsuits. And, because future property owners were held liable, the sites remained undesirable to developers and investors.

In the early 1990s, EPA created the national brownfields program to develop research, programming, and grant funding to help local communities overcome the challenges of potentially contaminated properties. In a significant move, the Small Business Liability Relief and Brownfields Revitalization Act (2002) amended Superfund by clarifying CERCLA liability protections and providing funds to support various state, tribal, and local partners.

Notes

1. http://dca.ky.gov/Case%20Studies%20Library/CaseStudy2012RussellvilleFireStation.pdf.
2. http://www.pleasantprairieonline.com/openvillagehall/index.asp?pd_url=http%3A%2F%2Fwww.peakdemocracy.com%2Fp%2F173#peak_democracy.
3. https://www.cmu.edu/steinbrenner/brownfields/Case%20Studies/pdf/pittsburgh%20technology%20center%20-%20LTV.pdf.
4. https://www.epa.gov/sites/production/files/2015-11/documents/shepherdstown_success_story.pdf.
5. http://www.lanereport.com/22530/2013/07/owensboro-new-downtown-riverfront.
6. https://www.tampagov.net/economic-and-urban-development/programs/brownfields-assessment-grant-program.

5. Innovations in Environmental Remediation

Tad McGalliard

Brownfields are defined by the United States Environmental Protection Agency (EPA) as "real property, the expansion, redevelopment, or reuse of which may be complicated by the presence or potential presence of a hazardous substance, pollutant, or contaminant."[1] In practice, brownfields could be anything from a former corner gas station, a failing retail center, an obsolete industrial space, to an abandoned mill. They are found in every community and often present challenges to public and private efforts at revitalization. This paper will explore some of the reasons for the challenges and present solutions that have worked for communities across the United States and internationally.

Industrial sites are perhaps the most recognizable type of brownfield. As a result of increasing globalization, the industrial sector of the American economy began to decline in the 1950s and 1960s. Offshoring became more prevalent, a trend that only accelerated deindustrialization in the following two decades. Consequently, the inventory of vacant (and often contaminated) surplus industrial sites increased. The lack of demand for industrial space in most parts of the country, combined with liability concerns influenced by federal policy, served to exacerbate the problem of reuse or redevelopment of industrial brownfield sites.

While the most contaminated land tends to be at the site of former industrial operations, brownfields are not limited to any particular land use. Leaking underground storage tanks are found at almost every older gas station. Other auto service uses, and dry cleaners are frequently hot spots for contamination. Unlike former industrial sites, these neighborhood-serving uses are often embedded in or adjacent to residential areas, which can add another dimension of complexity to redevelopment, but also lend urgency to the characterization and cleanup of contamination.

As consumer preferences shift toward online shopping and mixed-use retail options, traditional shopping malls and retail centers across the country are shutting down, creating another source of brownfield sites. As tenants move to newer developments, dwindling rents and market dynamics make redevelopment or improvements cost-prohibitive to property owners. The resulting vacancies and deferred maintenance make obsolete malls and strip centers a source of retail brownfields, often complicated by former dry cleaners or automotive uses.

Regardless of initial use, it is often easier and more profitable to develop on greenfields than to redevelop a site with known or suspected contamination, particularly in suburban or rural areas where land is cheaper and more plentiful outside of the developed urban or commercial core.

Challenges to Brownfield Remediation and Reuse

The EPA estimates that there are over 450,000 brownfield sites in the United States, with varying levels of contamination.[2] Despite the relative ease with which some of these sites could be remediated and put to productive use, federal policies originating in the 1980s have discouraged investment in contaminated property. Although these policies were intended to enforce cleanups at the country's most contaminated sites, in some cases innocent purchasers, lenders, landlords, and current owners were held liable for contamination they did not create. This disincentivized investment into properties with known or suspected contamination, as buyers and developers were reluctant to assume the responsibility for costly cleanup efforts. Combined with the effects of rapidly changing economic and development patterns, the 1980s were a crucial turning point in the legal and regulatory treatment of contaminated properties in America. For the past 40 years, the fear of environmental liability has been one of the strongest disincentives to redevelopment for both developers and their sources of funding.

While environmental liability insurance has been available since 1978, the process of establishing a policy with sufficient coverage may be prohibitive to greenfield developers.[3] Projects that are incorrectly or underinsured may end up costing thousands or millions of dollars if something goes wrong. And even if no unforeseen circumstances arise, the cost of cleaning up a brownfield can be challenging, especially for smaller developers. A 2007 study by the Northeast Midwest Institute (NEMWI) estimates that the average cost to remediate a brownfield is just over $600,000—approximately $774,000 in 2021 dollars—which does not include the traditional costs of redeveloping the site.[4] For larger and more complex sites, remediation alone can cost up to $700 million.[5]

High cleanup costs and uncertain environmental liability create an additional challenge in acquiring funding. Traditional sources of real estate funding—both debt and equity—are often reluctant or refuse to fund brownfield properties before the remediation is complete. Thus, typical acquisition, construction, and development loans are not readily available for brownfield sites. Once a brownfield project has been insured and funded, the approval and implementation of a remediation and redevelopment plan presents the next challenge. Many brownfield properties have been vacant or underused for many years; back taxes and deferred maintenance create a reuse challenge. Site infrastructure may be crumbling, adjacency to other blighted properties may make potential investors warier, and unanticipated costs, setbacks, and project delays can extend the remediation process. Market values may change significantly during the cleanup portion of the project, leaving little incentive to redevelop once remediation is complete. Local and state agencies may delay approvals for projects; many smaller cities and towns that are inexperienced with brownfield development may have to be educated on how to handle environmental issues and the cleanup process. Limitations on future uses may be governed by the severity of the original contamination; finding an appropriate end user may take more time than it would for a comparable greenfield development. These factors may further deter developers and local governments from taking on brownfield projects.

Despite the high cost and challenges, brownfield redevelopment projects can be extremely rewarding. Taking into account both direct and indirect financial benefits, such as increased adjacent property values, the average value of brownfield remediation is 6.5 times greater than the cleanup cost.[6] Brownfield redevelopment can also revitalize neighborhoods by removing blight and increasing the "eyes on the street" phenomenon, inspire a sense of community, celebrate historic character, and resolve long-standing environmental concerns. While beginning a redevelopment project may initially seem daunting, there are many tools that local governments can use to facilitate the redevelopment process and attract developer interest in their brownfield properties.

Big Idea Themes

The presence or perceived presence of contamination often has repercussions that extend beyond the physical limits of the site, from disinvestment in the neighborhood caused by perceived blight to public health issues caused by contamination. In addition to the more obvious environmental benefits of remediation and redevelopment, land recycling produces various financial and nonfinancial benefits.

While the prospect of brownfield redevelopment may be daunting, the resultant economic, environmental, and community revitalization make it a key component of smart growth strategies.

Nonfinancial Benefits

Among the least recognized benefits of brownfield redevelopment are the indirect improvements to the surrounding neighborhood, leading to what the NEMWI refers to as the "linchpin effect."[7] While this effect can be difficult to quantify, there is substantial evidence to support the claim that the redevelopment of a brownfield can be a catalyst for the redevelopment of a neighborhood. NEMWI refers to the Tide Point project in Baltimore, Maryland, which involved the redevelopment of a historic Proctor and Gamble waterfront soap factory into 400,000 square feet of office space, which has been the international headquarters of Under Armor since 2011.[8] In the seven years after the project's completion in 2000, property tax valuations in the area rose from $3.8 million to $50.1 million. Within the neighborhood, residential and commercial property values rose fivefold from 1995 to 2007.[9] Similar success stories have been observed across the country.

San Antonio's Pearl Brewery redevelopment features an 850,000-square-foot mixed-use development, including a 146-key hotel, 432 residential units, and a mix of office, retail, and educational uses, including the third location of the Culinary Institute of America.[10] Originally the site of a brewery that operated for 118 years (including clandestine operations during Prohibition), the property was contaminated by the time of its closure in 2001, and the historically industrial neighborhood had suffered from disinvestment and blight since the 1970s. After a three-year master planning process that included remediation and removal of blighted structures, the Pearl redevelopment has been a resounding success. It attracts thousands of visitors on a weekly basis and continues to spur economic development in the surrounding area. The Pearl District continues to grow; an additional 344,000 square feet of commercial development and 223 additional residential units are scheduled to be completed in 2019. Infrastructure investments made by the city of San Antonio have further incentivized redevelopment in the neighborhood.[11]

Like Tide Point and the Pearl District, which are located in downtown ports and inner-ring industrial areas, many brownfields benefit from their close proximity to urban centers. Once revitalized, these brownfields have the potential to restore the urban fabric and contribute to downtown and community vibrancy, whether through increased economic activity, the creation of public space, or the restoration of natural habitats.[12]

Additionally, the investment in brownfield sites can encourage community activism and a sense of ownership in the redevelopment area. While many redevelopment plans focus on public participation during the planning process, maintaining meaningful community engagement after the plans are complete is equally important. Community engagement can maximize positive outcomes and minimize the impacts of gentrification for communities that have endured despite unfavorable economic and living conditions. By creating places designed with the community in mind, the long-term success of the project is more likely. Other negative externalities of untreated brownfields, such as crime rates and environmental justice concerns, can be improved when increased activity contributes to the "eyes on the street" phenomenon and inspires a sense of pride in local community members.

Brownfield redevelopment also presents an opportunity for historic preservation. Historic manufacturing buildings have been redeveloped into multifamily dwellings and mixed-use, commercial, and light industrial uses across the United States. The Ponce City Market in Atlanta used state brownfield tax credits to help fund the adaptive reuse of the 1926 Sears, Roebuck & Company building. Before its redevelopment as a 350,000-square-foot food hall with over 500,000 square feet of office and 259 residential units, extensive remediation had to occur to remove contamination from site soil, groundwater, asbestos, and lead paint from the building's interior.[13] In Milwaukee, Wisconsin, a 1939 gas station that operated for over 50 years and experienced leaking fuel storage tanks was converted into a neighborhood coffee shop.

For projects that involve historic preservation, federal grants and tax credits are available from the National Parks Service; many states also have grants or tax incentives available. For many cities, specialized industrial or manufacturing operations defined the character of a neighborhood; the residences nearby were owned by working-class families who invested generations of labor into making consumer goods, cars, airplanes, or chemicals.[14] Preservation of these locally significant landmarks connects future growth with historic legacy. When feasible, adaptive reuse is also the most environmentally friendly approach to redevelopment—even new "green" buildings constructed with up to 40 percent recycled materials still take 65 years for the energy savings to surpass the savings caused by preserving an existing building.[15] However, the environmental benefits of brownfield redevelopment extend far beyond historic preservation.

Environmental Benefits

The most obvious and immediate effects of environmental remediation are visible on the project site itself, but the "ripple effect" caused by remediation can extend much further. In addition to the restoration of natural habitat and ecological integrity, brownfield redevelopment also has long-term positive regional implications for sustainability.

First, redevelopment of brownfields preserves existing greenfields. The NEMWI estimates that 1 acre of redeveloped brownfield preserves as much as 4.5 acres of previously undeveloped land.[16] This is partially attributable to the tendency of brownfield sites to be located in close proximity to existing city or town centers, as well as the frequent necessity of maximizing usable space to make redevelopment financially feasible.[17]

The reduction of sprawl and the construction of mixed-use buildings—frequent characteristics of brownfield redevelopment—also lowers vehicle miles traveled (VMT), as uses are located closer to their users.[18] Higher density development, especially near urban centers, encourages use of alternative modes of transportation, further reducing vehicle miles traveled. The Urban Land Institute (ULI) estimates that compact development on former brownfields can reduce VMT between 20 percent and 40 percent, which would result in a 7 percent to 12 percent decrease in driving-related greenhouse gas emissions (GHG) by 2050.[19] In 2016, light-duty vehicles and medium- and heavy-duty trucks generated over 23 percent of total GHG emissions in the United States,[20] meaning that prioritizing brownfield redevelopment would result in an approximately 1 percent to 3 percent reduction in total GHGs for the United States by 2050, just by building on brownfields instead of greenfields.[21]

In several studies focused on larger cities conducted by the United States Conference of Mayors, the reduction in vehicle miles traveled also translated to improved air quality, resulting in a 36 percent to 73 percent reduction in volatile organic compounds (VOCs), and a 40 percent to 87 percent decrease in nitrogen oxides (NOx) compared to similar greenfield developments.[22] The reduction in VMT and corresponding air quality improvement has additional positive impacts on public health, including encouraging more active, healthy lifestyles.

Compact development also improves stormwater runoff quality, particularly after any soil contamination is addressed. At densities of 8 units per acre or greater, runoff rates per home are reduced by 74 percent when compared to development at densities of 1 unit per acre.[23] Provided that the higher density trend in brownfield redevelopment continues, there is significant potential for improvement. In addition to the energy conserved through adaptive reuse (when feasible), there is the potential to capitalize on the inherent environmental benefits of brownfield redevelopment by constructing certified green buildings.

Financial Benefits

The NEMWI estimates that the average site cleanup costs approximately $600,000 ($774,000 in 2021 dollars), exclusive of sites with petroleum contamination.[24] However daunting the cost of cleanup may be, brownfields can become financially profitable uses, and can stimulate further reinvestment in the project area. Local governments can spur interest in and remove barriers to redevelopment by funding initial site assessments and producing rough estimates of the scope of the cleanup. Once the first public investment in the site has been made, it may be used to leverage funding from private developers. Although some communities may balk at contributing public funds to a private cleanup and development project, the benefits to doing so can be significant. Often an outreach effort is necessary to educate elected officials, constituents, and other stakeholders on the positive returns on such public investment.

Redevelopment projects vary significantly in the ratio of public to nonpublic funding—with $1 in public funding leveraging from $2.41 to $63 in other funding sources.[25] For EPA projects, nearly $17 were leveraged for every federal dollar spent.[26] The average investment ratio for public to nonpublic investment is 1:7—thus, every public dollar invested generates a significant amount of outside funding. And public money for brownfield programs need not come exclusively from the local government—the NEMWI estimates that 45 percent of public money comes from state governments, 30–35 percent from local governments, and 20–25 percent from the federal government. These ratios vary from project to project but serve as an approximation of each level of government's typical level of contribution.[27]

The long-term financial impacts of redevelopment for local governments are significant. After the initial investment and any tax-revenue sharing periods are over, tax revenues can increase substantially from pre-development levels. Additionally, the cost of providing infrastructure is significantly lower than comparable greenfield developments. Studies that have compared brownfield and greenfield developments—even compact ones—find that redeveloping brownfields results in infrastructure savings between 10 percent and 65 percent, with the savings averaging between 20 percent and 30 percent.[28] A Carnegie Mellon University study analyzing residential brownfield projects compared to greenfield residential projects in Baltimore, Chicago, Minneapolis, and Pittsburgh found that, on average, brownfield developments are 6 times closer to the city center, have 5 more households per acre, and a walkability index twice as high as greenfield developments.[29]

Additional benefits are seen in job creation. As of October 2019, the EPA Brownfields Program has leveraged more than 144,800 jobs. Through the end of FY 2016, 8.9 jobs were leveraged per $100,000 in EPA funding.[30] As opposed to greenfield development, brownfields are often located in economically distressed areas and tend to bring jobs to areas with greater need. A study referenced in a paper published by the National Center for Environmental Economics found that positive public benefit is maximized when jobs are reallocated to areas that have historically higher levels of unemployment and poverty.[31] With the addition of new jobs and the removal of the threat of contamination, further community revitalization is poised to occur. In fact, the EPA estimates that property values rise 5 percent—15.2 percent near brownfields sites when cleanup is complete.[32] Although redevelopment is often an environmental, economic, and community benefit, many local governments remain uncertain about how to approach these projects.

Notes

1. U.S. EPA, OLEM. "Overview of the Brownfields Program." Overviews and Factsheets. U.S. EPA, January 8, 2014. https://www.epa.gov/brownfields/overview-brownfields-program.
2. Ibid.
3. Hannah, John. "Brownfield Redevelopment: A Risk versus Reward Proposition." International Risk Management Institute, Inc., December 2000. https://www.irmi.com/articles/expertcommentary/brownfield-redevelopment-a-risk-versus-rewardproposition.
4. Paull, Evans. "The Environmental and Economic Impacts of Brownfields Redevelopment." Northeast Midwest Institute, July 2008.
5. Cone, Marla. "When Superfund Expenses Go `Mega.'" latimes.com, January 26, 2007. http://articles.latimes.com/2007/jan/26/nation/na-mega26.
6. Haninger, Kevin, Lala Ma, and Christopher Timmins. "The Value of Brownfield Remediation." *Journal of the Association of Environmental and Resource Economists 4*, no. 1 (March 2017): 197–241. https://doi.org/10.1086/689743.

7. Paull, Evans. "The Environmental and Economic Impacts of Brownfields Redevelopment." Northeast Midwest Institute, July 2008.
8. Sernovitz, Daniel J. "Under Armour to Buy Tide Point for $60.5M." *Baltimore Business Journal*, January 27, 2011, sec. Commercial Real Estate. https://www.bizjournals.com/ baltimore/news/2011/01/27/under-armour-to-buy-tide-pointfor.html.
9. Paull, Evans. "The Environmental and Economic Impacts of Brownfields Redevelopment." Northeast Midwest Institute, July 2008.
10. Yona, Batel. "Pearl, 2017–2018 Global Awards for Excellence Winner." ULI Americas, November 13, 2017. https://americas.uli.org/awards/pearl-2017-global-awards-excellence-finalist/.
11. *Ibid.*
12. Brandt, Jessica. "Guide to Leveraging Brownfield Redevelopment for Community Revitalization: Building Capacity in Washington State." State of Washington Department of Ecology, September 2010. https://fortress.wa.gov/ecy/publications/documents/1009054.pdf.
13. Arnall Golden Gregory LLP. 2014. "A Case Study in Brownfield Development—Ponce City Market." Georgia Environmental Conference.
14. Olin, Bob. "Sherman Perk Building History." shermanperkcoffeeshop. Accessed January 2, 2019. http://shermanperkcoffeeshop.com/Building_History.html.
15. U.S. EPA, OA. "Smart Growth and Preservation of Existing and Historic Buildings." Overviews and Factsheets. U.S. EPA, February 26, 2014. https://www.epa.gov/smartgrowth/smartgrowth-and-preservation-existing-and-historic-buildings.
16. Paull, Evans. "The Environmental and Economic Impacts of Brownfields Redevelopment." Northeast Midwest Institute, July 2008.
17. Stanislaus, Martha. "Building Vibrant Communities: Community Benefits of Land Revitalization." U.S. EPA, August 24, 2009. https://www.epa.gov/sites/production/files/2015-09/documents/comben.pdf.
18. *Ibid.*
19. Brandes, Uwe, Rachel MacCleery, Sarah Jo Peterson, and Matthew Johnston. "Land Use and Driving: The Role Compact Development Can Play in Reducing Greenhouse Gas Emissions: Evidence from Three Recent Studies." Urban Land Institute, 2010.
20. U.S. EPA, OAR. "Fast Facts on Transportation Greenhouse Gas Emissions." Overviews and Factsheets. U.S. EPA, August 25, 2015. https://www.epa.gov/greenvehicles/fast-factstransportation-greenhouse-gas-emissions.
21. Paull, Evans. "The Environmental and Economic Impacts of Brownfields Redevelopment." Northeast Midwest Institute, July 2008.
22. *Ibid.*
23. *Ibid.*
24. *Ibid.*
25. *Ibid.*
26. U.S. EPA, OLEM. "Overview of the Brownfields Program." Overviews and Factsheets. U.S. EPA, January 8, 2014. https:// www.epa.gov/brownfields/overview-brownfields-program.
27. *Ibid.*
28. Paull, Evans. "Analysis of the Economic, Fiscal, and Environmental Impacts of the Massachusetts Brownfields Tax Credit Program." Redevelopment Economics, October 2012. http://www.redevelopmenteconomics.com/yahoo_site_admin/ assets/docs/Infrastructure_Costs_-_brownfields-greenfields_final2.208110246.pdf.
29. Hendrickson, Chris, Deborah Lange, Yeganeh Mashayekh, Amy Nagengast, and Shegnan Zhang. "Estimation of Comparative Life Cycle Costs and Greenhouse Gas Emissions of Residential Brownfield and Greenfield Developments." Carnegie Mellon University, Department of Civil and Environmental Engineering, November 12, 2013. https://www.cmu.edu/steinbrenner/ brownfields/Current%20Projects/files/bf_gf-life-cyclecomparison-paper-final-submittal.pdf.
30. U.S. EPA, OSWER. "Brownfields Program Accomplishments and Benefits." Overviews and Factsheets. U.S. EPA, January 8, 2014. https://www.epa.gov/brownfields/brownfields-programaccomplishments-and-benefits.
31. Howland, Marie. "Employment Effects of Brownfield Redevelopment: What Do We Know from the Literature?" *Journal of Planning Literature* 22, no. 2 (November 2007): 91–107. https://doi.org/10.1177/0885412207306616.
32. U.S. EPA, OLEM. "Overview of the Brownfields Program." Overviews and Factsheets. U.S. EPA, January 8, 2014. https:// www.epa.gov/brownfields/overview-brownfields-program.

6. How Donald Trump Became Counties' Best Friend and Biggest Ally[*]

ALAN GREENBLATT

Editor's note: Republican and Democratic administrations and legislatures since 1993 have supported the EPA's brownfields program. Established under President Clinton (D), the program has received steady support and was reauthorized twice under Republican administrations in 2002 and 2018, and continues to receive support under President Biden.

Couy Griffin came riding into town on a horse. Back in February, Griffin led a dozen "Cowboys for Trump" on a 170-mile ride from a farm in Cumberland, Md., to the White House, intending to show support for the president and present him with a hat. They didn't make it past the gate, but President Trump got wind of the event—they were featured on *Fox & Friends*—and called up Griffin, who was already at the airport on his way home to New Mexico, to thank him.

Griffin, who serves on the Otero County, N.M., commission, had the presence of mind not just to flatter Trump, but to bring up policy concerns. Griffin told the president that his county is home to Lincoln National Forest, which he said was mismanaged and presented a severe fire hazard that one day could wipe out the entire neighboring village of Cloudcroft. Trump promised to investigate the matter. It wasn't lip service. Griffin soon found himself on a conference call with USDA and Forest Service officials. "Commissioner Griffin, I want to start out by saying you definitely have the ear of the president of the United States on this," said Jim Hubbard, the agriculture undersecretary who oversees the Forest Service.

Not many county officials can bank on being able to draw the president's attention to a parochial matter, but counties in general are finding greater success communicating their concerns to the White House than they have had for a long time, if ever. Top administration officials have consulted with counties about opioids and opportunity zones, disaster response and environmental management. "They're not just talking to us—we've seen real action on things we've been pushing for years," says Christian Leinbach, who chairs the county commission in Berks County, Pa. "We couldn't even get our concerns heard through channels in the Obama administration."

---

[*]Originally published as Alan Greenblatt, "How Donald Trump Became Counties' Best Friend and Biggest Ally," *Governing*, https://www.governing.com/topics/politics/gov-trump-counties.html (June 25, 2019). Reprinted with permission of the publisher.

The White House has invited every county commissioner in the country to attend a series of 35 summits held at the Old Executive Office Building. All told, more than 2,000 have come. Each of the summits featured at least one cabinet secretary; half included Vice President Mike Pence. Trump himself spoke at the last one.

These weren't grip-and-grin occasions where county commissioners took selfies or grabbed napkins embossed with the White House seal. At each event, the White House Office of Intergovernmental Affairs promised to guide them through the federal government as a whole, handing out names and contact information of individual officials who could help them out with problems or concerns, whether at EPA, HUD, the Army Corps of Engineers, or elsewhere. To many of these visiting politicians, it felt like concierge service. Handing out business cards may be no big deal, but county officials around the country say they consistently get quick responses—and quite often results—whenever they reach out to the administration. "It's refreshing for us at a county level to see this level of responsiveness," says Chris Villines, executive director of the Association of Arkansas Counties.

The Trump White House is doing more than acting as a liaison between counties and federal departments. It has created a new competitive grant program that will provide $225 million for rural counties to repair and replace bridges. It's proposed $340 million to clean up sewage that runs from Mexico into 25 border counties from San Diego to Brownsville, Texas. The administration has invited county commissioners to participate formally in the rulemaking process for rewriting regulations, including federal oversight of waterways that some county officials complain burdens them with excessive red tape. "We've always had an open door at the White House with recent presidents," says Matt Chase, executive director of the National Association of Counties (NACo). "What is different about the Trump White House is they're sustaining the outreach. They're inviting any and all county commissioners to tap into the administration."

It amounts to something of a winning streak for counties, traditionally described by academics as "the forgotten governments" of America. Last year, the Interior Department sent out a record $552.8 million to counties through the payments in lieu of taxes (PILTs) program. The 2018 law reauthorizing the Federal Aviation Administration included several grant programs that flow directly to counties, which are involved in a third of public airports. Thanks in large part to lobbying from counties, that law also contains a provision limiting the Federal Emergency Management Agency to a three-year window for conducting audits on disaster funds, ending the practice under which FEMA sometimes would "claw back" money from counties a decade after paying out grants. EPA's brownfields program offers new liability protections to state and local governments. In December 2018, Trump signed a five-year farm bill that includes increased assistance for rural counties and schools, allows counties to exclude prisoners from population caps on eligibility for rural development programs and gives them greater flexibility in using federal broadband funds.

Policies such as brownfield liability or PILTs aren't going to make a lot of headlines. Day-to-day issues on which counties and the federal government interact can fly so low under the radar that they don't command much attention even from policymakers in Washington, let alone the press.

But most key state and federal programs have to be executed by counties when they get to the local level—transportation, Medicaid, public health, mental health and services for children, youth and seniors among them. Counties own nearly half the roads in the country and are largely responsible for stormwater and sewage. Yet presidents and governors routinely have given them short shrift, treating them as places to dump their problems, rather than partners in devising solutions. No matter how often county officials parrot the line that they provide more services than cities do, even to city residents, they rarely have commanded the attention that cities and states are able to claim. Counties have traditionally been treated like red-headed stepchildren by federal officials. It's always easier to deal with 50 states than 3,069 counties.

Counties still aren't getting everything they might want from this administration. Trump has made it a crusade to cut back on Medicaid and Affordable Care Act spending; many of those dollars flow through counties. The president also sought deep cuts to the Supplemental Nutrition Assistance Program (SNAP), still better known as food stamps. Counties administer SNAP in just 10 states, but those states are home to nearly a third of the people who receive the benefit. Trump's budgets have called for eliminating Community Development Block Grants, a rare source of flexible federal funding for localities.

But to the extent counties are looking for relief from federal regulations and unfunded mandates, their desires align with the larger goals of an administration looking to slice through the federal rulebook. "We've listened to state and local leaders where they think there's not smart regulation that's hampering opportunity and growth," says Doug Hoelscher, who directs the White House Office of Intergovernmental Affairs. "We don't always give 'yes' answers, but I think we give answers on a lot more things than prior administrations."

Every administration takes a different approach to federalism. Although George W. Bush had been governor of Texas and selected several governors as cabinet secretaries, his Office of Intergovernmental Affairs functioned as a command center, giving states and localities their marching orders. Barack Obama, the first president elected from a big city in nearly a century, quickly scored points among state and local officials with a more open approach. Under Obama, HUD, EPA and Transportation at least talked publicly about knitting together programs on the local level in a more collaborative way.

But the primary conduit for Obama policies was the nation's cohort of big-city mayors. While past presidents tended to do business with states, to the extent they cared about other levels of government at all, Obama worked directly with mayors on a variety of programs he couldn't get through Congress, including minimum wage increases, paid sick leave requirements, early childhood education and community policing.

It made sense for Obama to find common cause with mayors. For half a century and more, big cities have been dominated politically by liberal Democrats. Counties have been different. Hillary Clinton ran extremely well in 2016 in the biggest ones, carrying 88 of the 100 most populous counties, but that largely was the extent of her success. All told, she carried fewer than 500 counties, while Trump won more than 2,500. He took two-thirds of the vote in rural counties and small towns. Paying close, ongoing attention to friendly counties may be rare for a president, but it makes perfect political sense for Trump. "We typically think of the president as the leader of the whole nation, but presidents also act like members of Congress do," says Michael Sances, a political scientist at the University of Memphis. "They try to do things for their own base to shore up their reelection prospects."

The mere act of talking to county officials is a way of keeping Trump's bond with supporters from rural and small-town areas who complain about being ignored by Washington. "Having that reputation is something that's noticed back home, outside the beltway," says Hoelscher, the White House intergovernmental affairs director. "It's not the biggest news above the fold, but usually with these initiatives it's local news that these local leaders are coming to the White House."

The administration isn't devoting its downward attention exclusively to counties. During his first two years in office, the president met with governors in person 65 percent more often than Ronald Reagan had at the same point in his term. His office is also launching a series of summits for state legislators, similar to those organized for county commissioners.

For county officials, however, after long neglect in Washington, a White House invitation is so unusual and unexpected that they sometimes think it must be a prank. Amy Galey, a commissioner from Alamance County, N.C., reported her email to her county's IT department, convinced it was an attempt at hacking.

But the communications keep coming. When Hurricane Michael was bearing down on the Atlantic Coast last October, the Office of Intergovernmental Affairs called county officials even before the storm landed, making sure they had access to the federal contacts and resources they'd need. They keep following up after disaster strikes. "Our lead here from FEMA is in constant contact with us, almost on a daily basis, sending us fact sheets about what needs to be done, what eligible moneys are available, the process you should use," says Mary Ann Borgeson, a commissioner in Douglas County, Neb.

There have been complaints that when counties in red states such as Nebraska get in trouble, they are given A-plus treatment, but when solidly Democratic California counties suffer historic wildfires, the president criticizes them for bad forest management. Trump's 2017 tax-cut package eliminated deductions for personal losses from wildfires and earthquakes—twin calamities in California—but maintained the tax break for victims of hurricanes in the predominantly Republican Southeast. In June 2018, Congress approved a $19 billion disaster relief package intended to provide help primarily to victims of hurricanes and flooding.

The county customer service ethic promoted by the White House has started permeating down to various federal agencies. Judd Freed is the director of emergency management for Ramsey County, Minn., which includes St. Paul. He notes that there are plenty of apps on his phone that are great at telling him the weather where his brother lives, but his department relies on moment-to-moment information from the National Weather Service regarding local conditions practically on a block-by-block basis. "Under the Obama administration, we did have pretty good access to them," Freed says. "Under the Trump administration, they have made an outstanding effort to remain accessible to us."

It's less than likely the average voter will ever know that the administration went to bat for her county on sharing weather data or ending FEMA clawbacks. But voters will hear about bridges being built, or possibly that their public works department is saving money thanks to environmental deregulation. "The focus of the national media is on the acrimony and the disruptions going on in Washington, D.C.," says San Diego County Supervisor Greg Cox. "The White House certainly understands that counties have a lot of responsibilities. So far, we've seen some pretty substantive things being addressed."

The county courthouse gang may not be the machine bosses they once were, but having local officials talk up the president can't hurt in the places Trump relies on most for votes. Even during the 2016 campaign, Trump's people were unusually alert to the value of doing outreach with NACo and counties. "The goal here might be to sway Republicans who weren't totally sold on Trump in 2016, showing he can be pragmatic," says Sances, the Memphis professor. "If they hear from county officials that, despite the tweets, he's doing real things to help us here, that explicit messaging will convince some people on the fence."

Trump has won over some reluctant county officials individually. A few Republican commissioners who've attended the White House summits have admitted to reporters that they backed other candidates in the primaries in 2016, but have since come to believe that Trump has their interests at heart. "I don't agree with everything the Trump administration has to say—especially President Trump," says Leinbach, the commissioner in Berks County, Pa., "but I've got to tell you his actions speak very loud."

Griffin, the "cowboy commissioner" from New Mexico, goes a lot further. Initially, he dismissed Trump as "a New York Yankee real estate tycoon who we know is not one of us." Now he believes Trump will "go down as the greatest president that we've ever had."

Despite the access he's gotten to decision makers in the Forest Service and USDA, though, Griffin still hasn't gotten what he wants from them in terms of cleaning up the national forest. He's confident that Trump will make it right. The president, after all, has already invited him to return to the White House, telling Griffin there are 20 acres on the South Lawn where he can ride his horses when he comes back to deliver his hat.

PART II
Challenges, Risks, and Opportunities

• A. Challenges and Risks •

7. Groundbreaking Environmentalism*

Stephen Goldsmith

Most urban parcels in the middle of Northeast or Midwest cities have some form of environmental contamination caused by a previous use. Would-be developers of these parcels typically face a long and unpredictable regulatory cleanup process that leaves many properties languishing for years in a state of neglect.

So it was big news last month when New York City Mayor Michael Bloomberg gathered with a group of city and state officials in the Williamsburg neighborhood of Brooklyn for a development groundbreaking. The big news wasn't the development, but the fact it was being built on a contaminated site. Home to a former gas station, it had been vacant for four years—the type of site most developers avoid because of the fear of environmental red tape.

Instead, the contaminated dirt will now be removed. The new development, which includes a diner, 50 new apartments and several small retail shops, will not only energize the neighborhood, but also add to the city's tax rolls. It was the first municipally run "brownfield" development in the nation. Hopefully, it won't be the last.

The project's success was possible because environmental regulators came to see their role as, "How can we enable environmentally beneficial development?" In this case, city and state regulators worked together with the developer to create a clear path to cleanup and rebuilding.

This is an important shift. Historically, environmental officials have imposed unrealistic demands on developers. Overlapping environmental agencies can grind a developer down with their inconsistent rules and goals. Most states assign remediation of contaminated "brownfields" to environmental enforcement agencies, which are philosophically removed from economic development concerns.

Ironically, the primary reason these contaminated areas remain barren, ugly, and often dangerous is not because the cleanup costs are too great, but because regulatory uncertainty jeopardizes the developer's business models and financing arrangements.

Over the past 20 years, I can think of no other area that better illustrates where the perfect has been the enemy of the good. To me, excessive mandates on would-be developers creates a situation where public officials earn reputations for being environmentally friendly at the expense of economically downtrodden and environmentally compromised communities.

---

*Originally published as Stephen Goldsmith, "Groundbreaking Environmentalism," *Governing*, https://www.governing.com/blogs/bfc/economic-development-environmentalism.html, May 18, 2011. Reprinted with permission of the publisher.

Finding a way to redevelop a contaminated site is often the best solution, both environmentally and economically. To make redevelopment possible requires dropping vendettas against long-gone former polluters, and insulating newcomers from some of the risks of decontaminating and rebuilding on these sites.

Risk on brownfields comes in three flavors:

- Environmental risk: These arise because the actual field conditions and ultimate cleanup requirements may be unknown prior to investigation and cleanup.
- Liability risk: These include both the threat of government enforcement under environmental law, and third-party personal injury or property damage claims brought by individuals.
- Regulatory risk: These arise through burdensome processes established by states to approve a cleanup plan, and the possibility that future regulators will further change the standards.

The first two of these risks are manageable. Environmental risk is usually small and typically does not impede brownfield development. After three decades, the cleanup industry understands well the science and processes necessary to produce reasonable levels of safety. Although significant, liability risk is also manageable. Risks from third-party claims can be managed through the purchase of pollution liability insurance; while risks from government enforcement can be addressed through state cleanup programs that provide a liability release in exchange for enrollment.

It is regulatory risk, however, that creates the greatest barrier to cleanup and redevelopment of contaminated sites. Regulatory risk stems from the uncertainty about the future and the unpredictability of the time and cost of navigating the environmental regulatory process. This risk poisons development and cripples land transactions.

Regulatory risks include confusing, conflicting, and often overwhelming amounts of guidance on regulatory processes—guidance that is often poorly calibrated and promulgated in a way that does not match environmental severity. This problem is complicated by inefficient or non-existent processes for negotiation, conflict resolution and approval of documents, coupled with a typical lack of urgency on the part of the regulators to keep projects on schedule.

Unfortunately, regulators lack development experience and awareness of the impact of regulatory risks on the development project and on its economic and societal value. Staff are often poorly schooled in efficiency and the use of time-saving methods that would benefit developers.

New York City's new Brownfield Cleanup Program is an attempt to minimize a developer's risk, especially the regulatory risk. In NYC, the director of Environmental Remediation, Dr. Daniel Walsh, has decoupled cleanup regulation from state oversight by establishing a municipally run brownfield cleanup program that adopts state standards but not the state regulatory process. Instead, he has introduced innovative approaches to efficient project management that shorten reviews, speed the cleanup and give developers confidence in the regulatory process.

This joint program is possible because the New York State Department of Environmental Conservation, now led by Commissioner Joe Martens, took the unusual and commendable step of allowing the city to negotiate liability protection on behalf of both jurisdictions. Now, developers can get the liability protection they need and can count on a regulatory program that delivers the predictability and support that fosters their development plan.

The rebirth of a neighborhood in Brooklyn was made possible because enlightened state and local officials envisioned a new way of looking at an old problem.

Without any government regulation, contaminated areas undoubtedly would be improperly developed. Absent private investment contaminated lots stay contaminated and dangerous. Creating the conditions to enable environmentally sound development should be the goal. In Brooklyn, we have seen how environmental improvement and economic development can work hand in hand.

8. Cleaning Up Toxic Sites Shouldn't Clear Out the Neighbors*

Lindsey Dillon

San Francisco has embarked on a project to transform its industrial southeast waterfront into a bike-friendly destination called the Blue Greenway. When completed, the Blue Greenway will be a 13-mile network of parks, bike lanes and trails along the southeastern edge of the city.

Among its many benefits, the project creates green space and waterfront access in the low-income Bayview Hunters Point neighborhood. The Blue Greenway is part of a larger transformation of Bayview Hunters Point. This older, neglected neighborhood is still full of vacant lots and a large, abandoned naval base, but it is becoming a landscape of hip townhomes and new coffee shops. Its transformation includes the complicated cleanup of many toxic waste sites—most notoriously, a military radiation lab on the former Hunters Point Naval Shipyard.

The Blue Greenway project cleans up toxic land along its route with funding from the Environmental Protection Agency's Brownfields Program, which supports the cleanup and reuse of contaminated sites. Brownfield redevelopment projects like the Blue Greenway are intended to bring environmental and economic benefits to run-down urban areas. And yet, as I have found in my own research, they can also contribute to gentrification and economic displacement.

Recycling Land

Brownfields are contaminated sites such as old gas stations, dry cleaning facilities, former factories and power plants. In the case of the Blue Greenway, they are small, vacant lots in old industrial areas and median strips along the road.

Brownfields are less heavily contaminated than sites on the EPA's Superfund list, which can take decades to clean up. The brownfields program is designed to move more quickly and make contaminated sites available for reuse. Ideally, returning these sites to use stimulates the economy and revitalizes neighborhoods. The program is widely popular with people who live near brownfield sites, as well as with city

---

*Originally published as Lindsey Dillon, "Cleaning Up Toxic Sites Shouldn't Clear Out the Neighbors," *The Conversation*, https://theconversation.com/cleaning-up-toxic-sites-shouldnt-clear-out-the-neighbors-74741 (July 10, 2017). Reprinted with permission of the publisher.

politicians and the private sector, which profits from the business of cleanup and redevelopment.

Even EPA Administrator Scott Pruitt, a forceful advocate of cutting back federal environmental protection, has voiced support of the brownfields program, calling it "absolutely essential." When the agency released US$56 million in brownfield grants in May, Pruitt lauded the program for "improving local economies and creating an environment where jobs can grow."

EPA's brownfield program was developed in the mid–1990s to provide incentives for states and companies to voluntarily clean up toxic spills and vacant industrial sites. At that point, Superfund was the only federal program that managed toxic cleanups. Superfund cleanups are federally mandated, top-down projects in which EPA has significant enforcement authority—notably, to make polluters pay for the cleanup.

In contrast, the brownfields program is more market friendly. It decentralizes authority to states and offers incentives for voluntary cleanups, such as grants, tax breaks and other subsidies.

The brownfields program emerged at a moment when many U.S. cities sought to redevelop their postindustrial areas. In contrast to Superfund, which at that time had little to say about land reuse, brownfields projects aimed not just to clean up industrial sites but to redevelop and reuse them. The word "brownfield" itself is a real estate term: Brownfields are the opposite of "greenfields," or undeveloped land.

In this way, brownfields redevelopment projects are often framed as environmental solutions to urban deindustrialization. As the U.S. Conference of Mayors stated in a 1999 report, the brownfields program helps "recycle America's land."

Preventing "Green Gentrification"

However, these projects also raise questions about environmental justice. Many brownfield sites are concentrated in low-income communities of color. This spatial concentration of toxic sites is, in part, an effect of redlining—the practice of denying loans to racial minorities based on color-coded neighborhood maps of financial risk. It is also an effect of 20th-century patterns of inner-city disinvestment and discriminatory zoning policies, which allowed for the siting of hazardous industries in low-income neighborhoods. Together, these and other factors have produced well-documented geographical entanglements of race and toxic waste.

At its best, brownfield redevelopment can transform vacant lots into parks and bring other amenities to neglected neighborhoods. It is most successful when local communities are meaningfully involved in the planning process, and when it is combined with other policies aimed to reduce social and economic inequalities.

One successful example is Fruitvale Transit Village in East Oakland, California, where a nonprofit called The Unity Council led the transformation of an old rail parking lot into a mixed-use development. The complex includes a senior center, a library, a health clinic and a mix of market-rate and affordable housing.

But these projects can also contribute to green gentrification by increasing land values and rents and displacing low-income residents. One example is New York City's High Line, an old elevated rail line that was "recycled" into a destination by converting it into a walkable pathway, lined by native plants. Today the High Line is an enormously popular attraction. It also has spurred development that has priced many small businesses and less wealthy households out of the neighborhood.

Fewer Cleanups

Ideally, EPA's Office of Environmental Justice could help to address some of the inequalities produced by brownfields cleanups. However, President Trump's proposed 2018 budget for the EPA eliminates this office. It also cuts funding for the brownfield program, by 30 percent, from $48 million to $33 million, along with large cuts to Superfund cleanups and emergency response capabilities and other hazardous waste management programs.

These cutbacks threaten the lives and livelihoods of all U.S. residents, and are unpopular among both Democrats and Republicans. Yet because of the legacies of race and industrial zoning patterns, their effects will fall hardest on already marginalized communities.

What Can Be Done?

One way to protect communities from both toxic waste and green gentrification would be to increase funding for EPA's Brownfield Environmental Workforce Development and Job Training Program (EWDJT), if it survives the Trump administration. Many brownfield communities struggle with unemployment, and residents are easily priced out of neighborhoods as they become more expensive to live in. The Brownfield EWDJT creates jobs for low-income residents, which can help them reap some of the benefits of brownfield redevelopment.

State support for affordable housing and community land trusts also can complement brownfield cleanups. Successful community land trusts are managed by nonprofits that buy land and build affordable homes. The homes are sold to local residents, while the nonprofit retains ownership of the land. This strategy can protect low-income neighborhoods from commercial developers.

More broadly, our notions of "sustainability" and "urban greening" ought to include values of justice and equity. Otherwise, important projects like the Blue Greenway will build sustainable waterfronts for the urban elite, rather than spreading the environmental benefits of toxic cleanup to the many.

9. Don't Give Up on Ambitious Green Architecture*

Ian Mell

London's proposed "Garden Bridge" is no more. After years of controversy, the city's mayor has finally sunk the idea into the Thames.

The notion of a bridge covered in plants and trees spanning the river did have some merit. But it needed to be in the right place, with the right design, and the project needed to generate support from local Londoners. Thomas Heatherwick's proposal appeared to lack awareness of this.

Nonetheless, the Garden Bridge's failure should not be an excuse to rein in our ambitions. To deliver more innovative urban greening in London and beyond, there remains value in thinking bigger, bolder, and greener.

To deliver visions of such urban oases we should continue to dream. But we must also be realistic. Long before such a project even makes it onto the drawing board, architects, politicians, and the public need to agree on certain vital questions. Who will eventually own it? How it will be funded? And who will be able to access it?

Don't Do This: The Garden Bridge Trust

The Garden Bridge was an example of what not to do. A lack of transparency lead to approximately £37m of taxpayer funding being lost in the project; the level of private funding lost remains unknown. Likewise, the pseudo-public nature of the bridge would have restricted access for groups, cyclists, and buskers, instead providing a corporate space underwritten by ongoing public investment.

But this sort of thing can work, and there are many examples where derelict or brownfield land in urban centers has been transformed into multi-functional public spaces. Millennium Park, in the heart of Chicago, was built on a former rail yard and car park. The High Line in New York turned a disused elevated train line into a park, and there are similar projects in Atlanta and Seoul. Each brought disused transport infrastructure back into public use.

There is now a clamor among cities across the world to develop the "next" High

---

*Originally published as Ian Mell, "Don't Give Up on Ambitious Green Architecture—Despite London's Garden Bridge Folly," *The Conversation*, https://theconversation.com/dont-give-up-on-ambitious-green-architecture-despite-londons-garden-bridge-folly-82602 (August 16, 2017). Reprinted with permission of the publisher.

Line—the latest proposal being a "Camden Highline" in north London. Such enthusiasm to follow the success of New York illustrates how cities want their brands to be associated with projects that are innovative yet also green and sustainable.

Get Locals on Board

One of the big ideas behind the Garden Bridge was to create such an oasis in one of the world's busiest and most polluted cities. Where successful interventions have occurred, they have been achieved with community (public and business) backing. The redevelopment of the Historic 4th Ward Park in Atlanta or the Cheonggyecheon River restoration project in Seoul would be very different projects without public support. Likewise, the Olympic Park site in London is largely publicly accessible 24/7, making it a multi-functional and valuable public space.

Even in Milan where the Bosco Verticale—a pair of tree-covered skyscrapers—shows the architectural merit of innovation on private property, it is complemented by a new public park, allotments, and communal spaces. What each of these projects does is to find a balance between funding, ownership, and access, which helps to limit conflicts over use.

Future projects should therefore take notice of what these investments got right, and the Garden Bridge got wrong. Developing truly valuable parks and open spaces is a delicate process. It requires a mixture of funding from public and private sources but should not be held hostage to the demands of private investors.

Publicly-funded projects need to meet the needs of the public and should reflect both local community and wider city-level aspirations. This may mean negotiating a prize-winning design for a more intuitive space that is functional for older people, families, or children. The Maggie Daley Park in Chicago is an excellent example of this.

There is also a need to ensure that ownership is transparent and that everyone knows their rights of use. This should be publicly and not privately focused, as there is a wealth of evidence to highlight the social, health, and economic value of accessible parks and gardens.

Finally, the Garden Bridge should be a cautionary note for future investments. There are many projects in London, across the UK and globally that have worked with various partners to design, develop, and manage parks and open spaces successfully. They have managed to grasp the needs of local communities, work with complex design and funding issues, and negotiate ownership and access rights. These projects are the ones we should be promoting as best-practice examples of what make a good public park. As they (nearly) say, one bad apple does not spoil the whole bunch.

10. Pittsburgh Steps Up*

Ron Littlefield

Pittsburgh is home to more than 700 sets of steps to help people traverse the hilly city. As they aged, it became an open question about whether they are a public asset or liability. It hints at a problem common to cities as infrastructure ages and needs change.

Over the years, when seeking to compare my own city with others, Pittsburgh often served as my default community. For example, when legendary newsman Walter Cronkite announced in October 1969 that my city, Chattanooga, had the dirtiest air in America, my immediate reaction was, "What about Pittsburgh?"

Truthfully, both cities were gritty and grimy industrial relics back then and air quality was just part of the problem. Pittsburgh was famous for its furnaces, but for a brief not-so-shining moment, little Chattanooga and its aging iron foundries was able to nudge Pittsburgh and other Rust Belt cities out of the running for the dubious title of "dirtiest."

Beyond pollution, we have a few more characteristics in common. Both Chattanooga and Pittsburgh are "physiographically challenged"—that means hilly—cities with historic incline railways serving as unique features of the public transportation system. Both are also traversed by major rivers that have largely been used to serve commercial interests over recreation or quality of life—which translates to more pollution. But most notably, like many other aging industrial cities, we have dealt with diminished economic opportunities and declining populations.

A major cultural shift was needed. As Pittsburgh began to clean up and change, other cities (including mine) struggling with similar issues began to take notice.

I still remember when Willard Scott, another broadcast legend, exclaimed early one morning on the *Today Show*, "Pittsburgh looks like fun!" He then went on to describe how the city was turning things around. It was reclaiming the rivers, building waterfront parks and amenities, promoting festivals and celebrating all that made it what it had been and what it had become. Pittsburgh had become a model for turning adversity into advantage.

The "hill and valley" terrain of cities like Pittsburgh and Chattanooga present unique challenges and opportunities. So, when I visited Pittsburgh, I tried to take note of how the city was managing to address this demanding natural feature. I also followed the city's redevelopment efforts in city planning circles and local government trade publications—looking for ideas to steal. Just as Pittsburgh's industry had been world class, so was

---

*Originally published as Ron Littlefield, "Pittsburgh Steps Up," *Governing*, https://www.governing.com/cityaccelerator/blog/pittsburgh-steps-up.html (May 2, 2017). Reprinted with permission of the publisher.

its remediation of industrial brownfields. As those of us who follow the fortunes of cities in transition were drawn to admire Pittsburgh's expensive new condominiums perched on slag heaps, somehow it was easy to completely overlook the city's sidewalks. Let me explain.

Pittsburgh has something that is almost totally unique: Its sidewalks include a large number of public stairways—23 miles of pedestrian facilities made up of steps. It's another product of the city's industrial heritage and topography. When the mills were built in the valley near the rivers and the residential areas developed up on the hillsides, it was necessary to provide some means for the workers to get from home to job.

One solution was the inclines. At one time, Pittsburgh had more than a dozen inclines, but now has only two. (By comparison, Chattanooga once had three but now has only one.) The steps were a necessary response to a public transportation challenge addressing both the steep topography and the public's limited ability to pay. A book by Dr. Bob Regan quotes Ernie Pyle from a 1937 column about Pittsburgh, "The well-to-do people drive to work. The medium people go on street cars and inclines … and the poor people walk up the steps."

Dr. Regan, a geophysicist affiliated with the University of Pittsburgh, has spent a good part of his professional life walking and studying the steps of his city. He has produced two books on the subject: The Steps of Pittsburgh, published in 2004, and Pittsburgh Steps, published in 2015. Intrigued by the subject, I bought a copy of the more recent edition and devoured the text, which is richly supported by maps, charts, and photographs. I then telephoned Dr. Regan for an interview. He was kind enough to oblige.

Dr. Regan explained why Pittsburgh's steps are unique. He said that while historically hilly cities like Cincinnati and San Francisco once had numerous public steps, most communities have attempted to phase them out over the years. By his latest count, however, Pittsburgh still has 739 sets of steps—with 344 of those sets counted as legal city streets. Although the city isn't building more, it is still finding them as some are almost completely camouflaged by overgrowth.

Dr. Regan declined to try and place a value on the city's collection of steps as a significant piece of public infrastructure. He said the steps were first built in the early 1900s and mostly of wood. As they were heavily used and became worn over time, many were replaced with concrete and steel. "They tried to replace railings using aluminum a few years ago," he said. "Unfortunately, those didn't last very long." The value of the metal combined with the sometimes remote locations of the steps made them an easy target for scavengers.

He described how even today some "orphan" structures are reachable only by steps and stressed how difficult repair and replacement will be due to the need to carry materials up or down steep terrain. How will those responsible for public works determine priorities? "Look for the most used steps," he said. "One way is to look for those that have been shoveled when it has snowed."

When I asked Dr. Regan for some fun facts about Pittsburgh's steps, he mentioned the special events that were created around these unique assets. The numerous climbs, runs and walks utilizing the steps were briefly discussed in our phone conversation but are more thoroughly covered in his book. Dr. Regan was particularly proud of an event known as "Step Trek," which has been described as "a vertical party."

Those unique steps are just one more reason for city lovers like me to envy Pittsburgh. Yes, Willard Scott, Pittsburgh does look like fun, and in dealing with adversity and making use of what makes the city special, Pittsburgh presented a new challenge for the rest of us.

City Accelerator is helping Pittsburgh identify public/private alternatives to conventional arrangements for financing infrastructure, and the preservation of the city's steps is a major focus. More than a century ago, Pittsburgh's steps were a creative and innovative solution to the pressing problems of urban development. Today, the steps might be unique but the need to find new ways to finance infrastructure is almost universal. We can't wait to see what creative and innovative solutions will emerge.

11. Toxic Lead Can Stay in the Body for Years After Exposure*

Stuart Shalat

Editor's note: Lead contamination is a national epidemic. The sources are not just from lead pipes mentioned in the article, but from legacy manufacturing products and applications. Issues like lead pipes often overlay with lead contamination in brownfields situations, and are part of the big picture issues tackled by brownfields professionals. This article offers additional insights on lead poisoning.

The ongoing water crisis in Flint, Michigan, has highlighted just how harmful lead contamination is. What you may not realize, however, is that lead exposure is a problem throughout the U.S.

The Centers for Disease Control and Prevention estimate that over four million households with children in the U.S. are exposed to elevated levels of lead. At least half a million children have blood lead levels above five micrograms per deciliter, the threshold that prompts a public health response.

Lead used to be commonly used in gasoline, household paints and even coloring pigments in artificial turf through the end of the last century. And although today lead is no longer used in these products, there is still plenty of it out there. Lead does not break down in the home or the environment, and the result is that we still have to be concerned about lead poisoning today.

As a university-based researcher who focuses on children's health, I have spent the past 30 years trying to understand how exposure to environmental toxins happens, and how to prevent it.

So where and how do people come into contact with lead, and what does it do to their bodies?

Lead in Water Is Easily Absorbed by the Body

Lead is one of the oldest materials utilized for the construction of plumbing systems. In fact, the word "plumbing" even has its origins in the Latin word for lead, "Plumbium."

---

*Originally published as Stuart Shalat, "Toxic Lead Can Stay in the Body for Years After Exposure," *The Conversation*, https://theconversation.com/toxic-lead-can-stay-in-the-body-for-years-after-exposure-53607 (February 4, 2016). Reprinted with permission of the publisher.

While Congress banned the use of lead pipes in 1986, with the passage of the Safe Drinking Water Act, the crisis in Flint illustrates that lead pipes are still out there.

While lead in soil and in-house dust represents significant sources of exposure, drinking contaminated water may represent the greatest risk. Water is readily absorbed through the intestines, quickly resulting in elevated levels of lead in the bloodstream. A child's gastrointestinal tract absorbs lead more completely than an adult's.

The U.S. Environmental Protection Agency (EPA) sets a level for drinking water sources of 15 parts per billion (ppb) as requiring immediate notification of consumers.

If you have ever seen a large gasoline tanker truck on the highway, 15 ppb would correspond to 15 drops of a chemical, diluted in that entire truck. That is how little an exposure of 15 ppb is. Even these small amounts of lead in the water, over time, can affect people's behavior and impair intellectual development.

Once lead is in the body, it can also be stored in bone for years. Even after exposure stops, the lead can come back into the bloodstream and continue to damage the brain and other organs for years to come.

Lead Is a Toxin

Lead is known to cause problems with blood formation, kidney function, heart, reproduction, gastrointestinal symptoms, peripheral nerve damage (tingling in hands and feet) and even death. The effects on many of these organs can be permanent, and like all toxins the dose is critical. The higher the exposure and the longer it continues, the greater the damage.

Numerous research studies, some in the early 1940s, have shown that lead affects the development of a child's intelligence. Even minuscule levels can decrease a child's measured IQ.

In the brain, lead can disrupt the function of mitochondria in neurons, preventing the cells from functioning properly. It can also affect the release of neurotransmitters, which is how neurons communicate with each other, and alter the structure of blood vessels in the brain. Taken together this damage can lead to reduced IQ, learning disabilities, decreased growth, hyperactivity and poor impulse controls, and even hearing impairment. This is why lead exposure in children is especially concerning.

It is recognized that poor nutrition can increase the uptake of lead into the body. For instance, calcium, which is an essential mineral for bone growth in children and for cellular function, can decrease lead absorption. If an individual has inadequate calcium in their diet, their body will absorb more lead. Additionally, since lead can replace iron in the formation of red blood cells, iron deficiency also leads to more lead being absorbed into the blood.

A diet rich in beneficial minerals, particularly iron and calcium, can lower, but not eliminate, the uptake of lead from environmental sources.

However, people with low incomes might have trouble buying enough food or getting a balanced diet, robbing them of the protection that good nutrition provides. Flint is an economically disadvantaged community, making the lead exposure there of even greater concern.

Treating Lead Poisoning

The damage lead causes cannot be reversed, but there are medical treatments to reduce the amount of lead in the body. The most common is a process called chelation—a patient ingests a chemical that binds to lead, allowing it to be excreted from the body.

Chelation, though, is not without its risks. The chemical doesn't just increase the removal of lead, but also of essential minerals such as calcium. In children, the use of chelation therapy must be carefully monitored to avoid serious complications that can include permanent kidney damage or even death. The treatment is often reserved for only those children with very high lead levels.

Regulations Curbed New Lead Additions to the Environment

Because lead causes irreversible damage, making sure that people aren't exposed to lead is especially important.

Lead exposure in the U.S. has been minimized by two government actions. In 1973, the Environmental Protection Agency decided to begin phasing out lead as a gasoline additive. The phase-out was complete in 1996.

Interestingly, this was not done for health reasons, but to allow the catalytic converters that cars required to meet new air pollution standards to function. However, the phase-out dramatically reduced the amount of lead deposited on the ground, where children could be exposed and ingest it while playing.

Then in 1977, the Consumer Product Safety Commission banned the use of lead paint from residential properties and homes. This action was solely based on health concerns.

Together, these actions greatly reduced lead in the environment, with an added benefit of reducing blood lead levels in children.

But Plenty of Lead Is Still Out There

But there is still plenty of lead out there. And those who are poor or live in the shadow of abandoned industrial sites are often at greatest risk.

Much of the housing stock in the U.S, especially in eastern cities, dates to before lead paint was banned. Many homes, particularly in poor communities, still contain lead, and if the paint surfaces are not well maintained, the paint may flake off and form dust that can be inhaled and ingested. Another problem is that untrained individuals may attempt to remove the paint, which can make the problem even worse by generating large quantities of dust in the process.

Elevated lead levels can be found in many communities, often associated with metal smelting operations. Plants that manufacture or recycle car batteries can also be a problem. After the companies close, these sites (called Brownfields because they are often not cleaned up) create long-term persistent hazards for children in these communities.

It is no coincidence that these unremediated sites are often located in economically disadvantaged communities of color. Only by concerted community and government action can the sites by identified and cleaned up. This will take many decades, but it will prevent future health hazards for generations to come.

12. What Lies Beneath*

JAMES R. ELLIOTT *and* SCOTT FRICKEL

Editor's note: This article describes Sites Unseen, *which includes sites that were under the EPA's Superfund program. While many practical approaches to reuse and redevelopment are the same, the statutes that apply to assessment, cleanup and legal liability are distinct from brownfields sites.*

Philadelphia's hip Northern Liberties community is an old working-class neighborhood that has become a model of trendy urban-chic redevelopment. Crowded with renovated row houses, bistros and boutique shops, the area is knit together by a pedestrian mall and a 2-acre community garden, park and playground space called Liberty Lands.

First-time visitors are unlikely to realize they're standing atop a reclaimed Superfund site once occupied by Burk Brothers Tannery, a large plant that employed hundreds of workers between 1855 and 1962. And even longtime residents may not know that the 1.5 square miles of densely settled land around the park contains the highest density of former manufacturing sites in Philadelphia.

Over the past 60 years, more than 220 factories operated in this same small area. Nearly all did business before the mid–1980s, when the U.S. Environmental Protection Agency started requiring businesses to report releases of toxic materials

In our book, "Sites Unseen," we set out to discover how many such former sites exist and why, over time, they simultaneously seem to proliferate and disappear from view. The data we collected from state manufacturing directories dating back to the 1950s don't tell us whether specific addresses we found are presently contaminated. But they do provide richly textured maps of where and for how long hazardous industrial activities operated in four very different cities—New Orleans, Minneapolis, Portland and Philadelphia. Our findings strongly suggest that these and many other American cities now face a legacy hazardous waste problem they don't even know they have.

Hazardous Waste Legacies

According to data recently released by the EPA, in 2017 industrial facilities (excluding mining operations) released 1.1 billion pounds of hazardous waste at the point of

---

*Originally published as James R. Elliott and Scott Frickel, "What Lies Beneath: To Manage Toxic Contamination in Cities, Study Their Industrial Histories," *The Conversation*, https://theconversation.com/what-lies-beneath-to-manage-toxic-contamination-in-cities-study-their-industrial-histories-104897 (December 20, 2018). Reprinted with permission of the publisher.

production or "on site." That number is an understatement, because government records rely on voluntary reporting and exclude smaller manufacturing facilities that also pollute. And there is virtually no public documentation of similar releases before the 1980s.

To investigate the scope and scale of this problem, we identified relic and active sites from state manufacturing directories, which can be found in public libraries nationwide. These guides are largely untapped sources of information about where manufacturing activities occurred, for how long, and what each facility produced. In each city we analyzed, we were surprised to learn that government databases ostensibly designed to identify hazardous sites actually captured less than 10 percent of historically existing manufacturing sites.

Through follow-up surveys, we learned that 95 percent of relic manufacturing sites are used today for activities other than hazardous industry. We found coffee shops, apartments, restaurants, parks, childcare centers and much more at these locations. These patterns corroborate processes which we now suspect drive both the spread of contaminated urban lands and the concealment of their past uses.

Erasing Sites' History

Like other businesses, most hazardous industrial facilities operate for a time, then go out of business or move their operations elsewhere. This constant turnover is an ongoing, fundamental feature of urban economic development. And because urban land is limited and valuable, those lots typically are redeveloped for non-industrial uses when they become available.

Our data show that hazardous industrial sites turn over every eight years, on average. This means that an individual lot can be redeveloped multiple times, sometimes over the span of just a few decades. For example, one Portland, Oregon address that we investigated housed a neon sign and sheet metal fabricator during the 1950s, then the office of a dry bulk trucking company, and is now a doggy day care center.

These interlocking processes of land use and reuse have far-reaching environmental impacts that social scientists are only beginning to recognize. Lot by lot, small but ongoing changes in urban land uses spread toxins across urban areas. At the same time, pressures for redevelopment often cover up the evidence.

In these ways, large, long-lived industrial sites, like the former Burk Brothers Tannery in Philadelphia, represent the tip of the iceberg of urban industrial activities and resulting contamination. Government agencies typically identify and clean up these large, visible sites that are known or widely suspected to be contaminated. And often they offer developers incentives to build on them, including liability waivers.

All the while, thousands of smaller, less prominent but potentially polluted sites go unnoticed, contributing to a much more systemic environmental risk.

Look Back to Move Forward

Based on the research we did for our book, we believe the problem of relic industrial waste is far greater and more vexing than many scholars, regulators and developers appreciate. And this complexity has important implications for environmental justice and the question of who lives, works and plays in neighborhoods burdened by relic industrial contaminants. Communities can't set priorities for cleaning up contaminated land until they identify relevant sites.

Environmental justice studies that use more limited government data on hazardous sites provide consistent evidence that polluting industries and environmental hazards are more frequently imposed on poor and minority communities. But our findings suggest that, over time, risks also accumulate over broader areas—including white working-class neighborhoods of yesteryear, lower-income and minority neighborhoods that superseded them, gentrifying areas such as Philadelphia's Northern Liberties that are now selectively following, and whatever comes after that.

It is a basic social fact of urban life that industrial hazards accumulate and spread relentlessly. The sooner this problem is recognized, the sooner Americans can reclaim their cities and the environmental regulatory systems that are designed to ensure our collective well-being.

One way forward is for regulatory agencies to undertake historical investigations of relic industrial sites, using the same publicly available sources that we have used. Concerned citizens and neighborhood groups can do so as well, and the DIY User's Guide at the end of our book describes how to do it.

13. Lead Poisoning's Lifelong Toll Includes Lowering Social Mobility*

Shefali Luthra

Cynthia Brownfield was lucky. When her daughter, then 2 years old, tested for high levels of lead in her blood, she could do something.

Brownfield, a pediatrician in St. Joseph, Mo., got her home inspected and found lead in the windows. She got them replaced and had her pipes fixed, too. Her daughter, now 12, was probably affected, says Brownfield. But quick action minimized the exposure. Her daughter is now a healthy, fully-functioning preteen.

"We were in the financial position where we could hire a plumber and change the windows," she said. But others—even her own patients—may not be so fortunate. This reality may have implications even more far-reaching than generally accepted.

Findings published Tuesday in JAMA break new ground by suggesting the effects of childhood lead exposure continue to play out until adulthood, not only harming an individual's lifelong cognitive development, but also potentially limiting socioeconomic advancement. Specifically, Duke University researchers tracked a generation of kids based on data collected through a nearly 30-year, New Zealand–based investigation known as the Dunedin Multidisciplinary Health and Development Study.

They studied the development of more than 1,000 New Zealanders born between April 1972 and March 1973. Because at that time gasoline still contained lead, exposure was common, creating a sizeable sample that included people across class and gender. More than half in that data set had been tested for lead-exposure at age 11, and the study tracked brain development and socio-economic status over the years—making for "a natural time" to use them to study lead's health effects, said Aaron Reuben, a PhD candidate in neuropsychology at Duke University, and the study's first author.

By the time study participants reached age 38, a pattern emerged: Children who were exposed to lead early in life had worse cognitive abilities, based on their exposure level. The difference was statistically significant. They were also more likely to be worse off, socioeconomically, than those who had not been exposed to lead. The study found that no matter what the child's IQ, the mother's IQ, or the family's social status, lead

---

*Originally published as Shefali Luthra, "Lead Poisoning's Lifelong Toll Includes Lowering Social Mobility, Researchers Find," *Kaiser Health News*, https://khn.org/news/lead-poisonings-lifelong-toll-includes-lowering-social-mobility-researchers-find/ (March 28, 2017). Kaiser Health News is a nonprofit news service covering health issues. It is an editorially independent program of the Kaiser Family Foundation that is not affiliated with Kaiser Permanente. Reprinted with permission of the publisher.

poisoning resulted in downward social mobility. That was largely thanks to cognitive decline, according to the research.

"Regardless of where you start out in life, exposure to lead in childhood exerts a downward pull to your trajectory," Reuben said.

Though this research was set in New Zealand, it offers insight into a problem experts said is fairly ubiquitous in the United States and across the globe. The CDC estimates that as many as half a million children between ages 1 and 5 had blood lead levels high enough to cause concern: 5 micrograms per deciliter and up. At least 4 million households across the country have children experiencing significant lead exposure.

Last year's water crisis in Flint, Mich., brought lead exposure front and center as a public health concern. Meanwhile, a Reuters investigation published this winter found elevated lead levels in almost 3,000 communities around the country. The Centers for Disease Control and Prevention recently changed its guidelines to suggest that any childhood exposure to the chemical is harmful, and is pushing to get rid of lead poisoning in kids by 2020.

In the U.S., children at risk are typically poorer and racial minorities—in part because they more often live in older houses with lead paint. This is a stark difference from the research population, which tended to be white. However, because the study spanned a period of time in which lead was still used in gasoline, the lead exposure measured in the study spanned a wider class spectrum.

That adds greater consequence to these findings, many said.

"Kids who are poor, or who have some of these other social determinants of health that are negative—they end up with a double whammy. Whatever health consequences they have from being poor, those are added to the additional consequences of being exposed to lead," said Jerome Paulson, an emeritus professor and pediatrician at George Washington University. Paulson has researched lead's effects on children, although he wasn't involved with this study.

"If you want to talk about 'breaking out of poverty,' kids who have lead exposure are probably going to have more difficulties," he added.

That said, these conclusions aren't perfect. For instance, the research doesn't account any variation in how the children who were tested may have been previously exposed to lead, or how their continued lead exposure through adulthood may have differed. Those who worked in jobs like construction, for instance, may have had greater lead exposure than those in white-collar jobs, Paulson noted. But on the whole, he said, it makes a strong case for the long-term impact of childhood lead exposure.

Pennsylvania, Maryland and Massachusetts, which all have cities with concentrated areas of older housing, have identified lead poisoning as a major child health hazard. The CDC has also embraced "primary prevention"—testing homes for lead and removing it before people move in and risk exposure. But securing resources for lead testing, screening and abatement poses its own set of challenges.

The JAMA study illustrates, in part, one such difficulty. Lead poisoning happens over years, not overnight. So illustrating the impact, even if it's ultimately significant, is hard to do.

"Prevention doesn't have a lot of pizzazz. If you prevent something from happening, it's a wonderful thing, but it's hard to measure and take credit for," said David Bellinger, a neurology professor at Harvard Medical School and a professor in the environmental health department of the university's public health school, who wrote a commentary that ran alongside the JAMA paper.

And funding for such programs is often unreliable, said Donna Cooper, the executive director of Public Citizens for Children and Youth, a Pennsylvania-based nonprofit that advocates on behalf of young people. For instance, the White House's initial budget plans would boost some lead abatement funds but slash other grants used for similar purposes. And for many states, she said, even what's long been available isn't enough to meet the scope of the concern.

"We have very clear CDC guidance on what should be done, and no money to back it up," Cooper said. "It ebbs and flows with the headlines."

• B. Opportunities •

14. Financial and Nonfinancial Incentives
Tad McGalliard

The financial uncertainties associated with redeveloping a brownfield can be prohibitive to generating developer interest. The imposition of environmental liability on innocent parties under CERCLA has been lessened with the Brownfields Law and BUILD Act but acquiring sufficient funding and managing other forms of risk, including financial, market, third-party lawsuits, etc., can still prove difficult. The heavy upfront costs of developing brownfields and longer, more complex development period makes brownfields particularly susceptible to changes in financial markets and economic downturns. Fortunately, public financing tools can help close funding gaps and reduce development risks.

Financial Uncertainty: Liability and Cleanup Costs

CERCLA was passed in 1980 to allow the federal government to address environmental risks at abandoned sites that presented a significant detrimental impact to human health and the environment. While the intent of the legislation was to hold the parties responsible for contamination accountable for the cost of cleanup, the imposition of liability affected all potentially responsible parties, which included any past or current owners, regardless of responsibility for contamination. This legal construct of retroactive, strict, joint and several liability significantly chilled private investments in the cleanup and redevelopment of contaminated property.

The definition of liability under the original CERCLA legislation understandably made potential developers wary of any contaminated site, regardless of its designation as a Superfund site by the EPA. A potentially contaminated site could present millions of dollars' worth of cleanup costs and associated liability—the extent of which is difficult to determine without investigation, which can also be expensive. Additionally, the original CERCLA legislation offered few options for PRPs to defend themselves from responsibility for contamination. Defendants had to prove that the contamination was a result of (1) an act of God; (2) an act of war; or (3) actions by a third party contractually unrelated to the party held responsible. However, winning a claim was unlikely, especially until the Superfund Amendments and Reauthorization Act (SARA) of 1986, which clarified what constituted a "contractually unrelated" party. Even as amended, private developers generally remained wary of brownfields until the passage of the Small Business Liability Relief and Brownfields Revitalization Act (Brownfields Law) in 2002.

The Brownfields Law expanded funding for the Superfund Act, provided funding for state-level response programs, provided liability relief for contiguous property owners and "bona fide" prospective purchasers, and clarified cleanup responsibility requirements for innocent landowners. The act also provided exemptions for parties who could prove that they did not contribute or contributed minimally to onsite contamination and exempted certain small municipal solid waste generators. As a result, the Brownfields Law had a significant effect on the feasibility of brownfield redevelopment. It provided states with power to fund brownfield programs and limited EPA oversight of cleanups conducted under state jurisdiction. The liability exemption for bona fide prospective purchasers (BFPPs) ensured that developers could purchase a potentially contaminated property without the risk of being treated as a PRP. Decreased liability for bona fide purchasers led to somewhat increased investment interest from lending institutions and other parties, which helped make brownfield redevelopment a more financially feasible scenario. The increase of public funding also provided a basis for many of the public financing tools used today, which will be discussed later in this section.[1]

The BUILD Act was passed by Congress in spring 2018 as part of the Omnibus Spending Bill, and included several further changes to CERCLA and the EPA's Brownfields Program. First, it extended protection of local governments, which were previously only exempted from liability if they obtained control of the site involuntarily. Second, it allowed lessees to be exempted from liability in the same manner as bona fide prospective purchasers, although lessees have to go through the same validation process as purchasers. Third, the BUILD Act expanded grant eligibility to certain nonprofit organizations. Fourth, it established a new multipurpose brownfield grant, increased funding for remediation grants from $200,000 to up to $650,000, although total program funding was not increased. Finally, it made other changes to CERCLA, including allowing grant money to be applied to certain petroleum contaminated sites (which were previously excluded from CERCLA funding), allowing grant funds to be used for certain administrative costs, and expanding grant funding eligibility to certain publicly owned sites acquired before the Brownfields Law was passed.[2]

Need for Financial Incentives

Despite reduced liability for new bona fide or noncontributing property owners, remediation costs alone can be prohibitively expensive. The NEMWI estimates that the average cost of cleanup is around $600,000 ($740,000 in 2019 dollars), but cleanup costs can reach nearly $1 billion for "mega-Superfund" sites. Historically, the maximum EPA grant funding for cleanup of non–Superfund sites under the Brownfields Law was only $200,000. Under the BUILD Act, the maximum grant amount for cleanup has increased to $500,000, and with the introduction of multipurpose grants, funding up to $1 million is available from the EPA for heavily contaminated sites.[3] Although these numbers are encouraging, the total pool of EPA brownfield funding has not increased to match the higher allowable grants. Thus, more money is available, but to fewer sites. The grants are highly competitive and there is no guarantee of being awarded. In order to make redevelopment a reality, financial and nonfinancial incentives offered by local governments are often critical to help bridge a project's financing gap.

Importance of Public Financing Incentives

In addition to assessment and remediation costs, redevelopment also includes typical development costs, such as infrastructure improvements, soft costs (such as engineering and architecture), and vertical construction if the existing buildings cannot be salvaged for adaptive reuse.

Public-private partnerships, land value finance mechanisms, and government loans and grants are all proven methods of closing the financing gap on brownfield projects and providing long-term public benefit. Public-private partnerships (P3s, alternatively abbreviated as PPPs) are cooperative agreements between governmental and nongovernmental entities and have financial and nonfinancial benefits to both parties. P3s are beneficial in creating stronger relationships between public and private parties; they combine the expertise of private entities with the stability of public entities. P3s can also expand funding options—grant funding available only to the public sector can be used on projects with private sector involvement and private financing. P3s can be particularly useful for sites where contamination makes it difficult to secure traditional funding.

Nonfinancial benefits of P3s may include improved community relationships and support, streamlined approvals processes, and partnership on larger-scale redevelopment plans. P3s also can be established between property owners and municipalities to expedite the determination of remedial responsibility and financing. One of the benefits of P3s is that they are entirely customizable to best serve the needs of both parties.

Many P3s are established between private developers and local redevelopment agencies (RDAs), which also are known as community redevelopment agencies, urban renewal authorities, urban renewal agencies, or other similar names. While RDAs have historically played a controversial role in redevelopment, modern RDAs, where they exist, have a useful role in redeveloping brownfields. RDAs are typically formed by the municipalities they serve, although many receive state funding. Except for California, all states have some form of urban renewal law, which often includes options for Tax Increment Financing (TIF) and other financing structures.[4]

When creating a P3, the most important part is to clearly define the roles and responsibilities of all parties and to establish a clear vision for the end result.[5] Appointing a designated brownfields coordinator may help direct the redevelopment process, especially for marginally viable sites, by identifying and focusing available resources.

Land Value Finance Mechanisms

Land Value Finance Mechanisms (LVFM) are typically public financing incentives that reduce lender's risk, minimize loan carrying costs for the borrower, improve project cash flow, and in some situations, provide loans or grants to pay for remediation and redevelopment costs.[6] Among the most popular LVFMs is Tax Increment Financing (TIF), also known as Revenue Allocation Districts (RADs) in New Jersey, Tax Allocation Districts (TADs) in Georgia, and Tax Increment Reinvestment Zones (TIRZs) in Texas.

The earliest use of TIF dates to the mid–20th century, where it was enacted in response to decreasing tax bases in city centers caused by post–World War II suburban flight. Since the 1970s, its use has become increasingly common, with 49 states offering some form of TIF structure by 2004,[7] although popularity and regulations vary from state to state. Although the enabling legislation is enacted at a state level, it is the local municipality's choice to use it or to establish an RDA. TIF is a tax-sharing revenue structure, where a local government freezes the taxable value of a property or area at its predevelopment rate, generally for a period of 10 to 25 years. After development is complete, any increase in property value above the predevelopment rate is then used to finance the debt issued for the cost of installing infrastructure. The use of TIF is usually subject to a set of conditions; documenting a condition of blight (as defined by state statute) is often required in order for a TIF district to be established. An applicant for TIF often must also provide evidence that the development would not be able to occur "but-for" the availability of TIF funds.

While TIF has been the dominant funding tool for the past few decades, it does have some limitations when applied to brownfield redevelopment. Although the standards vary state by state, TIF funds are sometimes limited to infrastructure improvements, which may exclude the cost of cleanup. As the most unpredictable cost of developing a brownfield site is excluded, the assurance of funding for infrastructure improvements can have limited value, especially if the site is already well-connected to existing infrastructure.

Under TIF, vertical development must also be assured. When project timelines and costs increase due to unforeseen environmental costs, markets are more likely to change and halt the redevelopment process before vertical development can be completed, or even begin. However, TIF can be instrumental in closing the funding gap in projects with narrower profit margins.

When TIF is unavailable or impractical, there are alternative LVFMs that allow tax revenues to be directed toward redevelopment. In 2011, the state of California dissolved its RDAs, which were the entities responsible for creating and administering TIF districts. This action was in response to the program's consumption of property tax revenues—in 2009–2010, 12 percent of California's property taxes were being diverted to RDAs.[8] As an alternative, California approved Enhanced Infrastructure Financing Districts (EIFD) in 2015, which allow cities, counties, and special districts to issue TIF-like EIFD bonds under certain circumstances.[9] Unlike most state TIF statutes, California EIFDs allow funding to be applied to brownfield remediation and mitigation, as well as to other public works projects, particularly those focused on increasing sustainability. Cooperating entities within the EIFD form a joint power authority and create financing plans to which all members must agree. While sales and hotel tax, community facilities bonds, and other various sources of funding may be used, school district and community college funds are not available to be used in the financing plan, which resolves local governments' primary concern about traditional TIF districts.

Special Assessment Taxes (SAT) involve levying an additional tax on properties within a defined special district, typically corresponding to the area that will benefit from the improvements funded by the tax.[10] Like urban renewal entities, SAT districts go by various names depending on location and type of service provided. Community Facilities Districts (California), Metropolitan Districts (Colorado), and Community Development Districts (Florida) are all types of SATs used to fund infrastructure improvements. SATs can also be used for more specific needs, such as Business Improvement Districts or Transportation Improvement Districts. These special taxing districts typically require a majority of the affected property owners to agree to the special assessment. SATs are most easily implemented when most of the property in the district is held by a few owners. SATs are also a more stable source of funding than TIFs, as the assessment is made on existing value, rather than projected value. Like TIF, these funds can be used to finance infrastructure improvements that will serve the site and provide public benefit to the surrounding area.

Land Value Tax (LVT) involves separating the taxable value of the land from the taxable value of the structures built on top of it. Unlike SAT, LVT is typically assessed on all the properties within a jurisdiction. Proponents of LVT argue that it discourages speculative land holding, as the land is usually taxed at a higher rate than the structure, and encourages high-density development that maximizes profit.[11] In Harrisburg, Pennsylvania, LVT was an effective means to reduce the number of unoccupied buildings in the downtown from over 4,200 in the early 1980s to less than 500 by the mid–1990s.[12] The combination of the revitalization generated by brownfield redevelopment and the high-density development encouraged by LVT together can create significant public benefit.

Federal Funding Options

The EPA offers a wide variety of grants and loans that are available exclusively for brownfield projects.[13] The following grants and programs are available on a federal level, with applications generally opening every one to two years.

Three types of assessment grants:

- Community-Wide Assessment Grants are available for up to $300,000 and are used when a specific site has not been identified; funds usually are applied to assess several sites. The Community-Wide Assessment Grants partially replace Area-Wide Planning Grants, which were discontinued after FY 2017.
- Site-Specific Assessment Grants are available for a single site. Grant funds are usually limited to $200,000 but may be increased to $350,000 based on the size and level of contamination onsite.
- Assessment Coalition Grants are awarded to a coalition of three or more entities working together; each entity receives a portion of the award. Funds are available up to $600,000 and must be applied toward at least 5 different brownfield sites. Entities are typically adjacent municipalities or a coalition of municipal and nonprofit members.
- EPA Cleanup Grants provide funding for cleanup activities on one or more sites, although the applicant for the grant must be the owner of the site(s). With certain hardship exceptions available for local governments with populations of 50,000 or less, tribes, and nonprofits, qualifying recipients must provide a 20 percent match to the amount of the EPA grant, although this may be provided as money, labor, materials, or in-kind services. As of 2019, Cleanup Grants are available up to $500,000, but eligible entities may qualify for up to $650,000.
- Multipurpose Grants may be applied to planning, assessment, and remediation costs on multiple sites, although they cannot be used in "distinctly different" geographic areas. Grants are usually capped at $800,000, but the 2018 Better Utilizing Investments to Leverage Development (BUILD) Act made grants up to $1,000,000 available. As with the cleanup grant, the applicant must own the

site(s) included in the multipurpose grant proposal and contribute $40,000 worth of money, labor, materials, or in-kind services; there is no option to request a waiver for this cost share.
- The Environmental Workforce Development and Job Training (EWDJT) Program provides grants of up to $200,000 that allow governments, nonprofits, and other organizations to invest in the training and job placement of community members who are under- or unemployed in areas that are affected by the presence of brownfields. Job training is geared toward sectors that are related to brownfield cleanup and ongoing maintenance and monitoring, as well as other jobs within the environmental field. EWDJT Grants are not offered every year, but applications are usually due in winter of the years they are offered.
- Revolving Loan Fund (RLF) Grants may be granted to a single entity or a coalition of two or more entities. Grants are available up to $1,000,000 per applicant; these funds may be distributed as low-interest or forgivable loans to subrecipients, including private, for-profit entities. RLF loans are paid back over time, making funds available for other borrowers. Project periods may be up to 5 years, and as with cleanup grants, recipients must provide a 20 percent match, which may also be waived under certain circumstances.[14] Solicitations for proposals are not planned for FY 2019, although additional funds may be available for existing recipients.
- Numerous technical assistance, research, and training resources are available from the EPA's partners through the Technical Assistance to Brownfields Communities (TAB) program, the Technical Assistance Services for Communities (TASC) program for communities affected by Superfund sites, the Targeted Brownfields Assessment program, the Council of Development Finance Agencies (CDFA), Groundwork USA, the Hazardous Materials Training and Research Institute at Eastern Iowa Community College, and the University of Louisville. Each partner provides various resources and programs for different aspects of the redevelopment process.
- State and tribal grants are awarded annually to help fund state and tribal brownfield programs, as well as certain assessment and cleanup activities. The program receives $50 million annually in federal funding, which is split among state and tribal environmental response programs.
- Federal.

Opportunity Zones are part of a tax incentive established by the 2017 Tax Cuts and Jobs Act, through which individuals and corporations can invest capital gains into a Qualified Opportunity Fund (QOF). Depending on the length of time an investment in a QOF is held, the investor can reduce the tax that would be levied on the original investment, and in some circumstances completely avoid capital gains tax on the increase in value of the Opportunity Zone investment. Opportunity Zone areas were nominated by states in early 2018 and certified by the Secretary of the U.S. Treasury in mid–2018; eligible tracts had a median income of 80 percent or less of area median income, or had a poverty rate over 20 percent. There are 8,762 Opportunity Zones in all 50 states, Washington, D.C., and 5 U.S. territories. Remediation of and business investments on brownfield sites are attractive investments for a QOF and QOFs are already stimulating investment in areas that historically have been less able to attract developer interest.[15]

The New Markets Tax Credit (NMTC) Program is another program designed to help economically distressed communities attract private capital by providing investors with a Federal tax credit. Established in 2000, investments made through the NMTC Program are used to finance businesses in neglected, underserved low-income communities.

With the right combination of private equity, state and local partnerships, creative financing mechanisms, and government grants and loans, redevelopment can become financially feasible, even on challenging properties. In addition to the nonfinancial resources that generally can be found on the state and local level, the environmental benefits and vast number of financial resources available for brownfield projects should strongly encourage infill development.

Nonfinancial Incentives and Support

On top of financial uncertainties, developers may be overwhelmed by the environmental problems and lengthier timelines associated with cleanup plan approvals that delay redevelopment. Using the tools and programs discussed here, local governments can provide nonfinancial resources to educate staff and promote redevelopment opportunities to the private sector.

Marketing

The first step toward establishing a successful brownfields program is marketing. Creating and maintaining a database of sites available for redevelopment can be used to stimulate developer interest and connect potential partners. Sites like brownfieldslistings.com provide an online marketplace of properties across the country available for redevelopment, a forum for local governments and developers to post Request for Proposals (RFPs) or Request for Qualifications (RFQs), and project boards where community members can go for project information and updates. Similar online listing sites can be found on the state or local level; the EPA also has a map of brownfield sites that have received EPA funding—from run-of-the-mill dry cleaners to Superfund sites—available online as the "Cleanups in My Community" map.[16] Some of these sites have received small grants to fund site assessments and are not yet remediated; others have been recipients of substantial EPA grants to fund cleanup. GIS data for various local, state, and federal programs can also be found at data.gov. On a local level, the relevant local information can be synthesized and distributed to developers to raise awareness of available brownfield properties.

Collecting data in a concise, centralized place takes some of the guesswork out of initial redevelopment plans. EPA TAB partner Kansas State University (KSU) has created a Brownfields Inventory Tool (BiT), which allows the user to organize information on general site data, cleanup details, contaminants found onsite, institutional and engineering controls, sampling data, previous and current sources of funding, and redevelopment plans, among other things.[17] Brownfield program coordinators can create pages for each site targeted for redevelopment, then compile individual site pages into an easily navigable database of local brownfield sites.

The BiT is intended to be used internally and maintained as a reference resource, but individual entries can be shared with interested parties. Using the information saved within the BiT, brownfields program staff have an opportunity to assemble a regularly released brownfield opportunities newsletter, featuring basic information on multiple sites with links to grants and other funding opportunities and more in-depth site information. Mailing lists could include all local developers, regardless of experience with brownfield redevelopment projects. Combined with a redevelopment roadmap, a list of brownfield opportunities may be enough incentive to attract new developers to the community's challenged sites.

Redevelopment roadmaps are step-by-step guides to the actions necessary to prepare a site for redevelopment, from initial site assessments to the completion of vertical development. A roadmap should show not only the steps for redevelopment, but an overview of the permits and approvals necessary to proceed, as well as the agencies and organizations typically consulted in redevelopment projects. The roadmap may also include grant funding opportunities available at the state and federal level, or other sources of project financing. Redevelopment roadmaps may be prepared by brownfields staff for their jurisdiction in general, or on a project-by-project basis. The CDFA Brownfields Technical Assistance Program uses EPA funding to help communities prepare redevelopment roadmaps; CDFA's expert staff provide specific and actionable advice to help kickstart the redevelopment process.[18] As these roadmaps generally contain a section on community engagement, publishing a redevelopment roadmap can also help ensure the community is involved as key development decisions are made and project milestones are reached.

City Regulations and Incentives

The challenges of brownfield development offer an opportunity to find innovative approaches to some municipal regulatory and entitlement requirements. Local governments often can provide low- or no-cost solutions that allow a flexible approach to redevelopment projects. Prioritizing brownfield redevelopment and infill projects over greenfield development provides numerous economic, environmental, and quality-of-life benefits.

For instance, providing flexibility to zoning and site design regulations can be the difference between a feasible and infeasible redevelopment project. The median cost for one structured parking space is $19,700 (2017 US$) therefore, for brownfields in urban areas, consider a reduction or elimination of parking requirements.[19] For larger or more suburban projects, a 10 to 20 percent reduction in parking would significantly reduce project construction costs. For new construction buildings, reducing setbacks and increasing permissible floor-area ratio (FAR) can also help developers meet minimum required profits for particularly complex sites. While the regulations should always be in line with the community's vision for the area, maximizing available space makes the project more feasible from a financial perspective, and also compounds the environmental benefits of redevelopment—dense development takes better advantage of adjacency to transit, further reduces demand for greenfield development, and promotes walkable neighborhoods.

At times, infill projects provide the opportunity for historic preservation. While some buildings are beyond repair, too contaminated for reuse, or of no historic significance, rehabilitating and adapting existing structures where feasible is the most sustainable option. However, the lengthy approval process and stricter regulations of historic preservation may deter some developers from investing the requisite time and money necessary to restore a historic building. When possible, local governments should provide flexibility to brownfield projects located in historic districts. Allowing flexibility in certain restoration requirements helps make historic preservation on a brownfield more financially feasible, while allowing for the use of historic preservation tax credits and grants. Providing guidance on which historic preservation resources are available for brownfield projects increases the likelihood of a successful adaptive reuse.

One of the best ways to ensure a comprehensive, efficient, and effective review process is to provide staff who are dedicated to brownfields. While this may not be feasible for many municipalities—nearly 70 percent of respondents from the ICMA survey did not already have a dedicated brownfield professional employed by the local government—partnerships with federal- or state-level programs may be an option. In 2011, New Jersey instituted the Camden Collaborative Initiative, which placed an environmental professional from the New Jersey Department of Environmental Protection (NJDEP) with the city of Camden to manage their redevelopment program. While the brownfield expert worked closely with the city, they were still employed by NJDEP, and worked to facilitate partnerships with various governmental, quasi-governmental, nonprofit, and private partners. The program was so successful that it was expanded to Trenton and Perth Amboy in 2015, and to Bayonne in 2018. The program has resulted in the successful remediation and redevelopment of multiple sites thus far, and has generated significant community buy-in, ensuring long-term follow through.[20] If providing dedicated staff is infeasible, municipalities can still work closely with regulatory agencies and developers to effectively and efficiently address brownfield challenges.

Liability Solutions

Since the passage of CERCLA, fear of liability has been the most significant deterrent to potential brownfield developers. The strict and retroactive liability enacted by CERCLA made developers hesitant to take on a site with even the possibility of contamination. While subsequent legislation has made CERCLA less onerous for innocent purchasers, state level statutes can provide further indemnification to encourage redevelopment. In the late 1990s and early 2000s, the state of Michigan enacted several innovative policies that strongly incentivized brownfield redevelopment, including limiting owner liability, increasing reliance on private and voluntary action, increasing public funding and increasing flexibility in cleanup standards.[21] Innocent purchasers of potentially contaminated sites are required to perform a baseline environmental analysis (BEA) to determine that there is actually contamination onsite. One benefit of the mandatory BEA has been the discovery that many sites were not actually contaminated or were significantly less contaminated than was originally suspected.

To the extent possible, local governments should work with state regulatory agencies to implement risk-based cleanup standards. For sites with higher levels of contamination, cleanup to residential standards may not be environmentally or financially feasible. To prevent this from prohibiting redevelopment, alternate, risk-based cleanup standards allow for the remediation plan to reflect the end use of the property—commercial/ industrial standards are still protective of human health and the environment, but allow for the assumption that occupants will spend less time there than they would for residential uses. To prevent residential or more sensitive uses from being built on site in the future, institutional controls can be enacted that run with the deed of title. For larger sites, a phased development and occupancy approach, which allows the property to begin generating income while the rest of the site is still under construction, should be considered.

Even with limited financial resources, local governments can still incentivize brownfield redevelopment within existing departments and programs. Often, a local government plays a key role between developers and state agencies. Building strong relationships between all parties can keep the redevelopment process running as smoothly and efficiently as possible, without expending an unrealistic amount of resources.

Notes

1. U.S. EPA, OLEM. "Summary of the Small Business Liability Relief and Brownfields Revitalization Act." U.S. EPA, July 24, 2014. https://www.epa.gov/brownfields/summary-small-businessliability-relief-and-brownfields-revitalization-act.

2. Mroz, Eric S. "The 2018 B.U.I.L.D Act: Redevelopment of Contaminated Properties." Drewry Simmons Vornehm, LLP, July 30, 2018. https://dsvlaw.com/the-2018-b-u-i-l-d-act-privateredevelopment-of-contaminated-properties/.

3. "Brownfields Utilization, Investment, and Local Development Act (BUILD Act) Bill Summary." Environmental Protection Agency, June 2018. https://www.transportation.gov/BUILD grants.

4. "FAQs: Denver Urban Renewal Authority." Denver Urban Renewal Authority. Accessed August 9, 2018. http://renewdenver.org/redevelopment/faqs/.

5. Bartsch, Charles. "Promoting Brownfield Redevelopment: Role of Public-Private Partnerships." Northeast Midwest Institute, April 2006. http://www.nemw.org/wp-content/ uploads/2015/06/2006-Promoting-BrownfieldRedevelopment_Public-Private.pdf.

6. ICF International. "Financing Brownfields: State Program Highlights." Environmental Protection Agency, September 2007. https://nepis.epa.gov/Exe/ZyPDF.cgi/P1002PSZ.PDF?Dockey=P1002PSZ.PDF.

7. Farris, Sherri, and John Horbas. "Creation vs. Capture: Evaluating the True Costs of Tax Increment Financing." *Journal of Property Tax Assessment and Administration* 6, no. 4 (October 2009): 5–28.

8. Svorny, Shirley. "Why California Dissolved Its RDAs." *Regulation*, no. Summer 2014 (2014).

9. Day, Linda. "A New Financing Tool for California: Enhanced Infrastructure Finance Districts." *Planetizen*, August 31, 2016. https://www.planetizen.com/node/88347/new-financing-toolcalifornia-enhanced-infrastructure-finance-districts.

10. "Special Assessment Districts." Urban Regeneration, The World Bank. Accessed November 7, 2018. https://urban-regeneration.worldbank.org/node/19.

11. Foldvary, Fred E. "Geo-Rent: A Plea to Public Economists." *Econ Journal Watch* 2, no. 1 (2005): 106–32.

12. Hartzok, Alanna. "Pennsylvania's Success with Local Property Tax Reform—The Split Rate Tax." *American Journal of Economics and Sociology*, no. April 1997 (April 1997). http:// www.earthrightsinstitute.org/news-4/publications/land-valuerights/226-pa-tax-reform.

13. U.S. EPA, OSWER. "Types of Brownfields Grant Funding." Overviews and Factsheets. U.S. EPA, July 15, 2014. https://www.epa.gov/brownfields/types-brownfields-grant-funding.

14. U.S. EPA. "Revolving Loan Fund Overview." U.S. EPA, 2017. https://www.epa.gov/sites/production/files/2017–09/documents/17–08.pdf.

15. Internal Revenue Service. "Opportunity Zones Frequently Asked Questions." IRS, 2018. https://www.irs.gov/newsroom/opportunity-zones-frequently-asked-questions.

16. "Cleanups in My Community." Environmental Protection Agency, March 19, 2019. https://ofmpub.epa.gov/apex/cimc/f?p=cimc:map:0:::71:P71_WELSEARCH:NULL|Cleanup||||true|fa lse|false|false|false|false|||sites|Y.

17. "TAB Program." Technical Assistance to Brownfields. Accessed January 4, 2019. https://www.ksutab.org/.

18. "Kalispell Core Area and Glacier Rail Park Roadmap to Redevelopment." Accessed October 18, 2018. https://www.kalispell.com/DocumentCenter/View/216/CDFA-KalispellCore-Area-and-Glacier-Rail-Park-Roadmap-to-RedevelopmentPDF?bidId=.

19. Cudney, Gary. "Parking Structure Cost Outlook for 2017." Carl Walker, 2017.

20. "Community Collaborative Initiative." State of New Jersey Department of Environmental Protection, July 17, 2018. https:// www.nj.gov/dep/cci/index.html.

21. Hula, Richard C., and Rebecca Bromley-Trujillo. "Cleaning Up the Mess: Redevelopment of Urban Brownfields." *Economic Development Quarterly* 24, no. 3 (2010): 276–87. https://doi.org/10.1177/0891242410365711.

15. Societal Disruptions Are Opportunities for Economic Development*

KIM BRIESEMEISTER

Editor's note: Societal disruptions stemming from the impacts of COVID-19 and the protests against racism are symptoms of economic inequities from health, economic and environmental inequities. As the author suggests, these are also opportunities to study and have discussions on responses and recovery, including economic development.

Societal disruptions have always created tremendous opportunities for economic development, but what sets today's disruption apart is the accelerated pace at which change is occurring. To remain competitive, city leaders must rewrite their economic development plans to account for the disruption, and perhaps even more importantly, implement those plans expeditiously.

Cities that want to be in an optimal position for economic growth should focus on three key areas:

- Rezoning to attract new development opportunities,
- Strengthening city/county and/or regulatory relationships, and
- Marketing opportunity zones or targeted redevelopment sites.

Evaluating your city's status in these categories is essential so that once the analysis is complete, the planning phase can commence. I have always been a strong proponent of creating a step-by-step plan to tackle city issues, then working the plan aggressively.

The Retail Apocalypse?

While the term "retail apocalypse" is commonly cited, I don't believe the news is all bad for retail stores. Yes, there are issues, but there are opportunities as well, and cities who proactively update zoning codes to stay ahead of the changing retail trends will fare better than those who are complacent.

First, let's address what we are facing. According to data from Green Street Advisors,

---

*Originally published as Kim Briesemeister, "Societal Disruptions Are Opportunities for Economic Development," PM (December 2019, Vol. 101: 11) by ICMA, the International City/County Management Association; reprinted with permission.

roughly a third of shopping malls are at risk of dying off as they exist today. When a mall loses a major anchor store, the chance of the mall's survival is drastically reduced.

Other problem retailers can be found along major U.S. corridors as mom and pop shops and big box electronic/home stores close and remain vacant, leaving struggling strip centers and blighted empty buildings.

However, new concepts are beginning to emerge that are changing the way people shop. These innovations may reveal the next generation of how shopping will transform underutilized retail centers.

One concept to explore is called Neighborhood Goods, a new type of department store with retail "pop-up" areas where multiple vendors can rent space on a short-term basis to introduce or test merchandise.[1] Their first location, a 14,000 square foot space, opened in November 2018, in Plano, Texas.

Cameras are omnipresent, recording consumer shopping habits, and since most people assume they are being watched everywhere anyway, they are not bothered. This invaluable market research of monitoring how people buy things, combined with in-person interaction, is creating a new form of retail strategy.

While online shopping has radically altered our relationship with retail, it's also providing innovative options for the next phase of growth through the reinvention and re-use of existing space.

The Mall Reimagined

If your city has a dying mall, this real estate asset offers one of the largest potential prospects for new uses on the site. Although malls are privately owned, cities with aggressive economic development teams can proactively work with the owners on a revised plan for the real estate.

Begin by assessing what your community really wants and needs to grow economically—not just now, but also 20 years from now. Then ensure there is an authentic connection to the overall brand of your city. Consider cities such as Charleston, South Carolina; Austin, Texas; Kansas City, Missouri; and Boca Raton, Florida. Whether or not you like their brand is irrelevant, it's that they have one and have built upon it to their advantage. Austin, for example, is building a brand around the music industry, so if they have failing real estate assets, they could target musical uses, such as a school or even a performance venue, to the vacant or underutilized parcel.

For cities with a strong tourism industry, hotels or visitor attractions could be zoned into large sites encouraging and expanding the tourist brand. Another city could create codes that encourage a medical office expansion if the site is near a hospital, thus growing a medical brand for the city.

It helps tremendously if a city already has a brand to build upon when attracting new businesses or is considering how to repurpose a dying mall. If your city doesn't have a brand, begin to create one.

Back to retail and malls. I believe the innate desire for human interaction will continue to drive people to places where they can shop in a physical location and interact with other people.

In addition to the human connection, most Baby Boomers still like to touch stuff before they buy it. Even as online purchases increase, certain goods and services may transition more slowly and continue to be sold in traditional retail physical environments. Generation Z also likes to shop, but they want unique handmade items, preferring experiences over materialism. This is leading developers to devise entertainment, dining, and shopping centers that have a pop-up and personalized feel.

Finally, the aging population is also a key factor in new development as some malls are looking to transition into micro-housing units that are directly connected to medical and dental facilities along with restaurants, entertainment, and specialty grocers.

Cities that consider the changing retail environment and nuances of human interaction can create an economic strategy that proactively repurposes the reuse of malls and other large real estate, becoming a magnet for good economic growth.

Change Your Zoning Laws

One of the most powerful tools a city has is its ability to control, manage, and manipulate growth through its zoning laws. Bad zoning codes can stunt a city's growth faster than a poor crime rating, and good zoning codes can change the face of a city in a very short time. Cities that say they have strong economic development goals are only as strong as their zoning code, so begin by reviewing your zoning laws for obstacles and opportunities.

    1. **Conduct an analysis of underutilized surface parking areas or garages in your city, including mall parking lots, old big box centers, city owned parking, etc.** Look for both public- and private-owned parcels. The loss of retailers has led to many empty or underutilized parking areas leaving tremendous opportunities for new growth. Using the options previously discussed, plan for new uses, or a complete redevelopment of these sites, including new residential development inside the mall footprint, new public gathering spots, green spaces, and pedestrian connections. Consider changing access roads and create walkable connections to the surrounding neighborhoods.

    2. **For major high traffic corridors with strip center frontage, cities should check if parking requirements, or some other regulatory requirement, are limiting new businesses from filling those vacant spaces.** If you can find out why the retailers won't rent space, you're halfway there.

    3. **Change zoning in the middle of a city center on key sites, or on perimeter parcels near town, to allow small-scale distribution centers in commercial areas.** The tremendous growth of online orders is pushing Amazon, grocery chains, and other big retailers to find new distribution centers inside traditional neighborhoods or city centers. Economic growth will occur in your city when these retailers can create a distribution system near their client base making their delivery system more efficient. The assumption traffic; however, if zoned correctly, these buildings will likely create less traffic than retail or commercial use.

    4. **Review strip center zoning to determine if it can be changed from consumer-oriented retail uses to a new flex category, thus modifying the parking requirements, as ingress/egress of the site.** By altering the traffic and parking flow, there may be opportunities for new green space or plazas for gathering.

    5. **Conduct a feasibility analysis to determine if shallow retail strip centers abutting residential neighborhoods can be rezoned for live/work, creating a**

transition. Taking a live/work zoning category a block deeper into a single-family neighborhood may not be popular or appropriate in a strong and healthy single-family neighborhood, so a thorough examination of the surrounding area will be critical.

      6. **Consider a form-based code**. Very few cities have embraced the concept of a form-based code, which provides development guidelines but also flexibility within the building footprint, which is enticing to developers.

Zoning Case Study

One city wanted to revitalize their downtown, but they were struggling to define their brand. They didn't have any obvious assets to build upon, such as a beach or mountains, medical centers, educational uses, or courthouses. My company suggested a "culinary district" brand for them because they did have strong catering businesses, kitchen designers, specialty food stores, and culinary retail shops. Uniquely, they had a huge 180,000 square foot industrial building that used to be a Sears distribution center right on main street, but it was zoned retail. We suggested they rezone it industrial to accommodate a brewery, and within one month they landed Funky Buddha Brewery, which set the stage for a complete revitalization of their downtown.

The City-County Connection

There are often disconnects between the cities and counties, but for this new phase of growth to be successful, those gaps should be tightened, and a uniform vision realized. The county must be as progressive as its most progressive city for overall economic development to be successful. Investors and developers analyze locations and a burdensome governmental process can be enough to send a potential investor to the next county where easier permitting and a business-friendly environment await.

Some of the biggest stumbling blocks that must be addressed immediately include:

- Outdated systems,
- Declining and failing infrastructure,
- Bureaucracy, and
- Lack of long-term progressive goals for moving people or goods around.
- City leaders can help move this relationship into a better place by focusing on three key areas:
- Defining an overall strategy for how the city wants to grow,
- Forming public/private relationships to attract good growth, and
- Creating a shared vision for growth that removes development obstacles at all governmental levels.

Opportunity Zones and Targeted Redevelopment Sites

Last, but not least on our checklist, we visit a "good" disruption created by the IRS. Opportunity zones were added to the tax code by the Tax Cuts and Jobs Act in 2017, with the first set of opportunity zones being announced on April 9, 2018. As defined by the IRS, an opportunity zone is "an economically distressed community where new investments, under certain conditions, may be eligible for preferential tax treatment."[2] Cities who obtained this status are now determining the best ways to fulfill the promised potential. Other cities, without these zones, who are looking to emulate elements of the model, can create their own targeted redevelopment sites including a thoughtful set of incentives to attract private investment.

The IRS code has reams of details about Opportunity Zones, but essentially, it's a substantial tax break on capital gains that's re-invested in disadvantaged communities. The federal government's goal is purportedly to attract much needed funding in areas that are struggling economically. What city leaders need to concern themselves with is how to they make their city stand out to attract some of that investment!

Leaders must ensure that their city is ready to do business whether they have an official opportunity zone or not. These are the best steps:

- Begin with a thorough analysis of zoning laws, land-use, utilities, infrastructure, roads, and right of ways.
- Create your vision and position your Opportunity Zone or redevelopment site as a place to do business.
- Develop marketing concepts and creative pieces that will attract investors utilizing the city brand.
- Establish a dedicated department and point person in the city. Ensure there's a real estate expert in house who can promote the advantages of investing in the city.

In conclusion, disruption creates opportunities. Embrace that concept. Great leaders view periods of rapid change as an exciting time leading to new innovations. As you move forward to create a successful city, be confident in your plan and work those steps!

Notes

1. https://neighborhoodgoods.com/about.
2. https://www.irs.gov/newsroom/opportunity-zones-frequently-asked-questions.

16. Suburb City Managers Are Our First Responders*

Tom Carroll *and* Brandi Blessett

The pattern of decline is familiar. Millions of Americans living in first suburbs[1] used to work factory assembly lines and shop floors. But as manufacturing employment has shrunk, residents within America's first suburbs face wage stagnation. In turn, they are forced to invest less in their homes, which increasingly show signs of age. As decline manifests, homeowners with wherewithal often leave. This sets in motion a downward economic cycle, which collectively make the first suburb poorer year over year. The gradualness of the decline often makes it very difficult for those living amidst it to perceive it.[2]

Despite a rich academic literature focusing on first suburban decline, scholars have offered few actionable policy solutions.[3] Most articulated policy options place the responsibility for fixing this problem at the state and federal levels, where little action has occurred. The reality is state governments have been cutting local aid for the last decade,[4] and the federal government is mired in worse political gridlock than normal.

As a result of shrinking state budgets and federal government gridlock, first suburban leaders have been left to contend with decline on their own. An example of the state of the decline in first suburbs can be seen near the city of Cincinnati, in which city leaders in modest first suburbs must act with urgency. Furthermore, first suburban decline has accelerated in the decade after the 2008 recession.

The city of Cincinnati (296,943) is the central city in Hamilton County (802,374). Hamilton County currently has a total of 49 separate units of local governments, including Cincinnati. In 2018–2019, ICMA funded a research fellowship that, among other things, analyzed the state of first suburbs in Hamilton County.

The results are not encouraging. Of the 33 first suburbs in the study, only eight have a total tax base that has equaled or exceeded the pre–2008 recession values in nominal dollars. When adjusted for inflation, only two Hamilton County first suburbs have exceeded their 2008 tax bases. Eight of the 33 communities have experienced double digit increases in the rates of poverty since 1999. Six first suburbs have poverty in excess of 20 percent, which is considered to be a tipping point.[5] Nineteen of the 33 first suburbs have had a loss in population since 1990. Hamilton County is thus like so many other parts of the Midwest, as some affluent first suburbs are stable, but too many others are in various states of

---

*Tom Carroll and Brandi Blessett, "Suburb City Managers Are Our First Responders," *PM* (December 2019, Vol. 101: 11) by ICMA, the International City/County Management Association; reprinted with permission.

decline. The suburbanization of poverty is clear and present in Hamilton County, and a financial recovery from the Great Recession has not occurred evenly.

What Can Be Done?

If state and federal help is not forthcoming and the warning lights are flashing for middle class first suburbs, what can city managers do to reverse decline, or at least manage it? Unfortunately, there is no silver bullet. We offer four strategies: (1) governance; (2) more than mere economic development; (3) housing; and (4) leadership, inclusion, and equity.

1. Governance

A local government's tax base ultimately reflects the economic resources of the community itself. As first suburbs decline, local governments are themselves unable to keep up. Norwood is a Cincinnati first suburb once-home to a General Motors plant that closed in 1987. Norwood spent $962 per capita on their police and fire departments in 2016. Nine miles away is Blue Ash, Ohio, a nearby first suburb with substantial income tax from employment centers. Blue Ash spent $974 per person on their police and fire departments in 2016, virtually identical to Norwood. Yet Blue Ash's public safety spending is a mere 31 percent of its income tax collections, whereas Norwood's $962 is 112 percent of its income tax collections.[6] As a result, Norwood is in fiscal emergency. Nearby, Springdale spends $808 per person per year, and Forest Park spends $519; both communities have much in common with Norwood.

The above comparison of public safety spending is simple, yet insightful. The research on first suburbs in Hamilton County shows that communities, even in the same urban county, spend widely differing amounts of money on public services. Norwood has had substantial revitalization and private investments over the last 10 to 15 years but is an example of a first suburb that is facing a fiscal emergency because it has not benchmarked against nearby peers to find less expensive service models. Benchmarking against peers is the key to helping communities like Norwood adapt.

2. More Than Mere Economic Development

Many ICMA members have expertise in economic development, brownfields remediation, zoning, and public finance. These same skills are the essential ingredients needed to help first suburbs. Traditionally, local government economic development reacts to the marketplace and closes project funding gaps.

What is different about economic development in declining first suburbs is that the free market is experiencing a market failure and the role of economic development is to correct it. This requires an interventionist government role beyond conventional economic development. Rather than simply closing funding gaps, local leaders must find a way to alter the market—assume risk and intervene in the real estate market—in a way that the private sector will not do.

One such example of market intervention is the City of Kettering, Ohio, which borders the city of Dayton. Kettering budgets $500,000 annually for revitalization.

If unspent, the balance accumulates, and Kettering uses the money to acquire strategic property and undertake catalytic redevelopment projects. This is in line with a 2002 Brookings Institution recommendation that first suburbs create a third budget priority, in addition to operating and capital budgets: "revitalization." Kettering has the budget discipline to do this, whereas first suburbs like Norwood spend too much on funding operations, thus shorting reinvestment. First suburbs need to treat revitalization as the third leg of the budget stool, along with capital and operations.

The case of Lockland, Ohio, is additionally illustrative. Lockland has owned a formerly polluted former mattress factory site of about nine acres along I-75 for many years. Had it been privately owned, the property would be developed today as a warehouse. But Lockland recognized that this site is the community's one chance to get advanced manufacturing to add jobs and income taxes. By controlling the land, Lockland defends itself from a lesser land use the free market would generate today and controls the eventual outcome of this site's redevelopment.

Similarly, the former city manager of Silverton, Ohio, negotiated a cashless land swap that gave an underutilized portion of a park to the local school system for a new school site. This resulted in Silverton receiving the 5.8-acre former school site once the new school was built. It took five years for the new school to be opened, and in that time, Silverton assembled adjacent properties into a ten-acre site. Private developers would likely not have undertaken this assemblage. By amassing 10 acres—zoned and shovel-ready—Silverton attracted private partners who are now building a mixed-use New Urbanist redevelopment. The project will grow Silverton's tax base 15–18 percent on a mere two percent of its land area.

The examples of several Southwest Ohio communities—Kettering, Lockland, and Silverton—show that first suburbs can intervene in and alter the real estate market. Assembling and controlling catalytic sites is the best way to correct the market failures that are occurring.

3. Housing

Aging housing is the most important driver of modest first suburban decline.[7] As new homes are constructed, higher-income families buy them and leave behind aging houses for families with lower incomes. This is known as "filtering."[8] Mass-produced homes built right after World War II, lacking architectural diversity, are particularly prone to filtering. Over time, a once middle-class community becomes relatively poorer, and the homes sell or are rented to people with increasingly modest backgrounds. Since the Great Recession and subsequent recovery (2008–2015 [estimate]), real estate investment trusts have been finding ways to corporatize being slumlords, buying large quantities of modest single-family homes in targeted first suburbs to achieve efficiencies with property management.[9]

City managers in first suburbs must recognize that their existing housing stock is not going to improve with age. The first line of defense is property maintenance. The city of Cleveland Heights has one of the most progressive property management teams in Ohio consisting of rental registration, rental inspections, point of sale inspections, and foreclosure prevention programs. Cleveland Heights stays on top of its housing because it has seen what has happened in other nearby communities.

Beyond the traditional housing program, first suburban managers need to create new and different housing options in the community.[10] And the opportunity here is to rebuild first suburban homes with greater density, greater environmental sustainability, resilience against severe weather, accessibility, and affordability. At the same time local governments must embrace teardowns, increase density, foster mixed-use redevelopments, and champion affordable housing while also bringing in more market rate housing options.

4. Leadership, Inclusion, and Equity

Most first suburbs are facing growing levels of poverty, and many new residents are either people of color or immigrants. Suburbanized poverty creates a geographic service gap between suburban poor residents and the social and charitable organizations that tend to be located in the central city. As a result, poor suburban residents struggle to access the support they need. The City of Springdale is working to connect their expanding low-income areas to downtown Cincinnati through better bus services.[11] The City of Kettering has a senior services coordinator whose job is to connect seniors to service providers in the Dayton area, so seniors can remain in their homes. While most first suburbs are not geared to provide social services, the suburbanization of poverty means local government professionals need to improve our capacity to connect our residents to those who can help.

Of perhaps greatest importance is the need for city managers in first suburbs to spearhead community engagement to bring together increasingly diverse residents and forge community ties, especially during community decline. Cleveland first suburbs Shaker Heights and Cleveland Heights have been engaging with the local community for decades, welcoming diverse new residents. As leaders, we must create forums to foster greater dialogue, engagement, connections, and friendships across socioeconomic backgrounds. Your community's future may well depend on it. White flight is still very much a reality and is the fastest accelerator of first suburban decline.

Conclusion

The decline of first suburbs has been a gradually building crisis, and a decade after the Great Recession many first suburbs are far from recovered. Reversing decline, or at the very least achieving a new level of stability, will take decades. But year after year, we can start to achieve the desired stability needed to help lift these communities.

Most city managers have the foundational tools and training to address the challenges of today's first suburbs. What is needed is a new sense of urgency, good government guided by benchmarking, a focus on interventionist actions to correct market failures, a vision and plan to rebuild aging housing, and a commitment to inclusion. These are formidable tasks, yet we have no choice but to try to reverse this trend.

NOTES

1. First suburbs—defined as generally inner-ring communities just outside central cities that have older housing, aging infrastructure. and, at times, struggling neighborhoods and. commercial areas.
2. Hanlon, Bernadette. 2009. *Once the American Dream: Inner-Ring Suburbs in the Metropolitan United*

States. Temple University Press. Florida, Richard. 2017. *The New Urban Crisis: How Our Cities Are Increasing Inequality, Deepening Segregation, and Failing the Middle Class—And What We Can Do About It*. Basic Books.

3. Hexter, Kathryn W., Edward W. Hill, Benjamin Y. Clark, Brian A. Mikelbank, and Charles Post. 2015. "Revitalizing Distressed Older Suburbs: Case Studies in Alabama, Michigan, Ohio, and Pennsylvania." *The New American Suburb: Poverty, Race and Economic Crisis*.

4. Maciag, Mike, and JB Wogan. 2017. "With Less State Aid, Localities Look for Ways to Cope" *Governing*, February.

5. Kneebone, E. and Berube, A. 2013. *Confronting Suburban Poverty in America*. The Brookings Institution.

6. In Ohio, most cities rely predominantly on a local income tax. Cities can levy property taxes and other fees, but in most cases, a municipality's primary source of revenue is the local income tax collections. Income tax collections are thus a key performance indicator for Ohio municipalities.

7. Bier, Thomas. 2017. Housing Dynamics in Northeast Ohio: Setting the Stage for Resurgence. https://engagedscholarship.csuohio.edu/msl_ae_ebooks/4/.

8. Hanlon, Bernadette. 2009. "A typology of Inner-Ring Suburbs: Class, Race, and Ethnicity in the U.S. Suburbia." *City and Community*. 8: 3.

9. REITs are Real Estate Investment Trusts. *Wall Street Journal*, January 4, 2018.

10. Cleveland State professor emeritus Tom Bier believes that huge quantities of first suburban homes are going to have to be torn down and rebuilt in the next fifty years. The authors certainly hope he is not correct in terms of scope.

11. Swartsell, Nick. 2018. "As Some Suburban Hamilton County Enclaves Get Poorer, More Rely on Limited Transit Options." *City Beat*.

17. Improving Water Quality Doesn't Have to Wash Away Budgets*

Ron Littlefield

Editor's note: The brownfields industry focuses as much on the reuse and environmental quality as it does assessment and cleanup of contaminated sites. Infrastructure is a common issue in all these disciplines. Sewer and stormwater management directly and indirectly affect the capacity of cities to grow, and to maintain a clean and safe environment.

From where I sit, Saint Paul is 1,006 miles away, but there is much about that Northern metropolis that seems familiar and close to home.

Of all the efforts that have demanded my time and attention during 40 years of public service, nothing really compares with the intense effort and immense funding needed to address water quality. Like Saint Paul, my city, Chattanooga, is a river city. It is also an old industrial community with the predictably harsh legacy of contaminated sites and vacant brownfields. I feel their pain. And I also admire Saint Paul's aggressive and innovative response to the daunting challenges that cities like ours face as we try to restore our environmental health.

As I was conducting a little research for this piece, I was not particularly surprised to learn that Saint Paul and its "twin," Minneapolis, were built with combined sewer systems. Many old cities (Chattanooga included) share that early Industrial Age infrastructure, but the cost and difficulty of attempting sewer separation today often presents an almost insurmountable obstacle. In September 1999, the U.S. Environmental Protection Agency (EPA) published a Combined Sewer Overflow Management Fact Sheet on this relatively common urban problem and Saint Paul is prominently mentioned.

Among the approximately 1,000 communities served by combined storm and sanitary sewers, Saint Paul, South Saint Paul and Minneapolis are listed among the cities that had achieved complete or partial separation by 1999. In fact, the Minneapolis/Saint Paul area is credited with one of the largest sewer separation projects, involving more than 21,000 acres of drainage area. The fact sheet states, "By December 1996, 189 miles of storm sewers and 11.9 miles of sanitary sewers had been installed."

The project not only reduced flooding and improved water quality, but the city also took the opportunity during construction to pave streets, install streetlights, add handicap ramps to sidewalks, install new gas and water mains and replace lead water service

---

*Originally published as Ron Littlefield, "Improving Water Quality Doesn't Have to Wash Away Budgets," *Governing*, https://www.governing.com/cityaccelerator/blog/improving-water-quality-doesnt-have-to-wash-away-budgets.html (April 25, 2017). Reprinted with permission of the publisher.

connections. (If only Flint, Mich., had taken similar action on its lead pipes in advance of its recent and devastating problems.) In 1984 dollars, the construction costs for Saint Paul averaged $15,400 per acre, but clearly the city was determined to take advantage of the situation and make the infrastructure investment count for much more than its original purpose. Perhaps this early effort set the stage for its present day "shared and stacked" approach to making water quality projects do double or even triple duty.

A topical piece by Camille LeFevre in the MinnPost explains the policy in greater detail. The article notes: "This new method of managing stormwater ... means the system does more than one thing on a site (say, irrigation plants and/or trees) to provide additional community services or amenities beyond just managing rain runoff." One example is a tree trench system that stretches for five miles along both sides of a transit line, which includes 1,000 new trees, nine rain gardens and stormwater planters that filter rainwater and prevent oils from the street from reaching the river. Additional benefits include cleaner air and new pockets of habitat for wildlife.

Wes Saunders-Pearce, water resource coordinator for Saint Paul, said participating in the City Accelerator is something that "galvanized our ability to frame innovative green stormwater management as a benefit to the development community and local cities." The partnership enabled the development of a five-year plan to extend benefits to three additional brownfield sites in the city: West Side Flats, Snelling-Midway and the site of a former Ford plant. According to Saunders-Pearce, by focusing on these three "opportunity sites" and utilizing the financial assistance provided by the City Accelerator—along with the "peer to peer knowledge exchange" from other communities in the program—Saint Paul will be able to expand its study of barriers in the community to capital outlay and the cost of long-term operations and maintenance.

The development of the now vacant Ford site was the subject of a separate MinnPost article written by Peter Callaghan. The 135-acre property on the Mississippi River sounds very much like a 100+ acre site proximate to the Tennessee River in Chattanooga that formerly was the location for two significant foundries. We have been planning and wrestling with the future of that large and well-situated property for years—not unlike other cities with similar sites left over from the age of heavy industry. But Saint Paul is taking a progressive step with its "shared and stacked" philosophy.

Another site in the list, West Side Flats, was the subject of a master plan published in 2001. The document is richly illustrated and almost classical "Olmstead/Central Park like" in its presentation of what the area might become. Architects, urban planners and other such "planning junkies" (like me) will find it interesting and inspiring. More recent articles on the subject indicate that after 16 years, Saint Paul continues to follow the plan and progressively chip away at accomplishing the proposed list of features.

The third "opportunity" site, Snelling-Midway, is the selected location for a large soccer stadium that has become somewhat controversial, but the plan still follows the community's philosophy to achieve more than a single purpose. The stadium is intended to serve as a catalyst to redevelop the surrounding neighborhood into a more livable and walkable urban village.

The great and lasting value of the City Accelerator is that it explores territory that many other communities will find familiar. Saint Paul is not alone in its long-term plans to build a better community while attempting to address the environmental sins of the past—and all within the constraints of a limited budget. We are all in this together. Cities across America are facing hundreds of millions of dollars in financial responsibility to effectively address water quality issues resulting from problems as diverse as our aging sewer systems to industrial brownfields to surface water contamination related to pavement, landscaping and other common elements of urban development.

Wes Saunders-Pearce is quoted in the December 2016 article by Camille LeFevre as confirming that, while Saint Paul is not alone in its efforts or even necessarily first in terms of projects with layers of multiple benefits, the city remains uniquely and totally invested in the greater cause at hand. "And we're leading nationally with what we're trying to accomplish. We're way out front in terms of trying to understand how to make these systems replicable through financial mechanisms that can be institutionalized, instead of finding grants here and there."

Cities everywhere faced with similar challenges (and that means most of us) should watch closely and prepare to steal ideas from Saint Paul.

18. Fighting Neighborhood Displacement, One Sewer Plant at a Time*

JAYANT KAIRAM

Editor's note: Assessment and cleanup of brownfields sites are often overlain by environmental, economic and land use issues. Part of the solution involves proactive interaction among stakeholders to anticipate outcomes from redevelopment.

Bayview-Hunters Point, a low-lying, four-square-mile pitch of southeast San Francisco, has seen its fair share of transition, and even drama. Occupied by the Ohlone people before the arrival of the Spanish, it once hosted slaughterhouses that fed the city's growing population. To support the wars of the 20th century, the Navy made dramatic investments in the shipbuilding industry there. And in 1982, long before Candlestick Park was turned into dust, Dwight Clark made a miraculous endzone catch to bring home a championship to a city that badly needed some good news.

During the Great Migration, blacks came to the region on the promise of good blue-collar jobs at the shipyards, and "the Bayview," as the community is known to locals, became a bastion of black home ownership. Even today, as the community continues to reckon with crime and poverty, the area's majority of black and Asian-American residents forge strong and diverse social networks bound by churches, neighborhood groups, youth organizations and community gardens.

Now the Bayview is undergoing yet another transition. Massive real estate projects on the sites of the decommissioned Navy shipyard and Candlestick Park are bringing thousands of new homes and associated commercial activity, signaled by the appearance of craft breweries, coffeehouses and rising real-estate prices that are displacing long-time residents. This is happening even as the realities of environmental injustice continue to burden the community. Only recently were its gas-fired power plants shut off, and questions around remediation of a former Navy radiation lab remind everyone of the public-health risks the community has long grappled with.

And yet there are things poised to happen in the Bayview that could provide an opportunity for San Francisco—and for other cities whose own disadvantaged neighborhoods face similar issues—to tackle the intertwined problems of racial and environmental injustice, residential displacement, and the need for the kinds of jobs that support strong communities.

---

*Originally published as Jayant Kairam, "Fighting Neighborhood Displacement, One Sewer Plant at a Time," *Governing*, https://www.governing.com/gov-institute/voices/col-neighborhood-displacement-utilities-job-creation-long-term-careers.html (June 4, 2018). Reprinted with permission of the publisher.

The Bayview is not just vacant industrial lots and brownfields. It's also the location of San Francisco's Southeast Treatment Plant, which handles 80 percent of the city's sewage flows. The plant was built in the 1950s and, like many of the country's aging water facilities, is in desperate need of modernization. A $7 billion upgrade plan is on deck for the city's entire 100-year-old sewer system, including transforming the antiquated Southeast plant into a cutting-edge facility incorporating state-of-the art operational efficiencies, seismic retrofits and technologies to reduce odor and other environmental nuisances.

The San Francisco Public Utilities Commission (SFPUC), the agency that owns and operates the plant, is taking a deliberate approach to ensure that those upgrade dollars are maximized for community benefit. Practices like project labor agreements and local contract-assistance programs are complemented by a robust suite of apprenticeships and internships coordinated with the school district and community-based organizations.

The SFPUC's focus is not simply about being a good neighbor. It is essential that it compliment shorter-term construction and contractor jobs with permanent, long-term careers. This is in due in part to the fact that the agency is staring at 50 percent retirement eligibility for its nearly 3,000-person workforce over the next decade. It's a challenge faced by other large infrastructure and utility entities across the country: It's estimated that one in three water-utility workers will retire in the next 10 years. These well-paying jobs—including mechanics, machinists, electricians and facility operators—cover all aspects of the work and provide a path toward management and executive opportunities.

The SFPUC is partnering with other regional water agencies in a consortium called Baywork to identify and develop career pipeline programs for these positions. This type of assessment is a necessary step to ensure that the agencies are planning strategically and bringing in the relevant educational and training partners—be they high schools, community colleges or for-profit entities—as they identify a new generation of "green collar" jobs that can offer at-risk youth and other residents career professions in the neighborhoods where they grew up.

Much of the opportunity that water infrastructure presents for stemming residential displacement and supporting surrounding communities results from the simple reality that it cannot move. Water infrastructure is anchored firmly, typically in places that are racially diverse, historically marginalized, burdened with environmental harm and hit by loss of industry, but now also on the precipice of gentrification. Yet they are neighborhoods where minority home ownership and social networks hold on in the face of speculative development agendas. With a growing interest in anti-displacement policy, focused on housing preservation via land trusts, inclusionary zoning and other means, it's also essential to elevate the place-based job creation ladders and retention strategies that can ensure that these communities will be able to leverage the economic opportunities before them.

19. Setting the Stage for Leveraging Resources for Brownfields Revitalization*

U.S. ENVIRONMENTAL PROTECTION AGENCY

Brownfields, abandoned properties, and blight affect communities across America. Grants from the U.S. Environmental Protection Agency (EPA) provide essential funding to communities for brownfields assessment, cleanup, area-wide planning activities, and revolving loan funds. However, after using the funding available from EPA's Brownfields program, local communities often struggle to secure adequate resources to complete brownfields revitalization projects. Cleanup costs can be substantial, expensive infrastructure upgrades may be needed to support revitalization efforts, design and engineering costs can be daunting, and redevelopment costs may be prohibitive, especially in distressed or small communities with weak markets and at sites with limited reuse potential.

Many communities struggle to find and attract sufficient funding for brownfields redevelopment projects. It often is difficult for communities to identify how best to invest limited local resources. Sound initial investments of local funds in brownfields revitalization can attract the interest and support of outside investors and lead to additional funding. In addition, finding, understanding, and meeting the qualifications for federal, state, and philanthropic grant and loan programs can be confusing, time-consuming, and difficult. EPA developed this guide to assist communities in overcoming these challenges.

What Does "Leveraging" Mean?

Essentially, leveraging is the use of existing resources or funding to attract additional resources or funding. Wise use of existing investments may lead to other investments (funding or other types of resources) from other parties.

It is a good idea for communities to begin their brownfields redevelopment projects by establishing strong leadership, assembling a team of committed partners, engaging with the citizens, and carefully assessing how to make the best use of limited local dollars so that initial local investments will leverage additional funding.

This guide will help you get started.

---

*Public document originally published as U.S. Environmental Protection Agency, *Setting the Stage for Leveraging Resources for Brownfields Revitalization*, https://www.epa.gov/brownfields/setting-stage-leveraging-resources-brownfields-revitalization (September 2019).

How Does Leveraging Work?

Initial investments, when made strategically, can result in attracting additional investments because they establish commitment to a project, instill confidence in the potential success of a project, and address the sustainability of the project. Initial local investments can include:

- using available local funds for planning, site assessments, or property purchases, and focusing personnel on identifying and securing sources of seed money for a project (e.g., government or foundation grants) and those that will leverage additional investment (i.e., community planning grants or brownfields assessment/cleanup grants).

Examples of leveraged funding include:

- When a local government uses its own local resources to purchase property and conduct an environmental assessment of the property, or when a local government obtains a brownfields assessment grant and uses those funds to assess the environmental conditions at the property, the community can use the results of that investment to attract private investment.
- The initial investment in the property purchase or the environmental assessment demonstrates commitment on the part of the local government to the reuse or redevelopment of the property.
- The same initial investment in the environmental assessment of a property provides information to potential investors or developers that can delineate the level of risk associated with further investments in the property or project.
- Many non-profit funders require that grant applicants demonstrate local commitment to a project by committing matching funds or in-kind resources, such as staff time and the use of locally-owned equipment.
- Private investors and developers often judge a project's potential for success by the degree of local investment or commitment to a project.
- Redevelopment projects established within local government master plans as priority projects may have a better chance of attracting private investment than projects merely listed in an RFP or real estate posting.
- Projects or properties where local governments invested in infrastructure improvement, transit upgrades, or beautification projects may have a greater advantage in attracting additional funding due to the demonstration of local commitment.
- Federal and state agencies may give preference to grant applicants who can demonstrate commitments of resources from other funding sources, particularly when the locality uses those resources in effective ways to make genuine progress toward meeting project goals.

Examples of other types of resources that can be leveraged include:

- Strong local leadership: Projects where local leadership shows a willingness to collaborate with other partners and investors demonstrate a potential for sustainability. Potential investors are attracted to projects where local leaders are committed to working with them over the long-term for the mutual benefit of all investors.

- Strong public participation and the ability to demonstrate community commitment to a project also can be leveraged to attract the collaboration and investment of private partners. Investors need a sense of commitment and a level of confidence that their investments will lead to success and an acceptable rate of return.
- Technical assistance and in-kind contributions from project partners demonstrate local commitment to the project, which often is essential when applying for state and federal grants and in attracting outside developers.

Setting the Stage for Leveraging Resources for Brownfields Revitalization

This guide is intended to help local communities successfully leverage resources for brownfields and community revitalization. It focuses primarily on what communities can do before they solicit funding to organize themselves and make the preparations necessary for mounting a successful leveraging effort.

The following sections of this guide provide:

- A background on brownfields and the challenge of funding revitalization.
- A step-by-step guide to help localities organize efforts to pursue and secure funding from a variety of sources for brownfields and community revitalization.
- Success-story case studies showing how three communities (Dubuque, Iowa; Charles Town/Ranson, West Virginia; and Stamford, Connecticut) successfully leveraged numerous sources of funding for brownfields and community revitalization.
- An overview of assistance available from U.S. EPA for enhancing community capability to leverage available resources for brownfields projects.

Brownfields and the Funding Challenge

Brownfields impact communities across America. It is estimated that there are more than 450,000 brownfields in the U.S. Brownfields and vacant properties can present risks to human health and the environment, contribute to blight, and hinder community revitalization. These sites can be as large as abandoned factories or whole areas of a community or as small as abandoned gas stations and dry-cleaning establishments. Addressing brownfields can be particularly challenging in economically distressed communities or in areas where the real estate reuse market may be weak or stagnant.

The cleanup and revitalization of brownfields can bring tremendous benefits to communities. Benefits may include increasing environmental protection and reducing health risks, increasing local tax bases, creating new businesses and jobs, reducing or eliminating blight, making use of existing infrastructure, and reducing the sprawl caused by the development of lands on the outskirts of the community.

EPA's Office of Brownfields and Land Revitalization (OBLR)

OBLR provides grants and technical assistance resources to support brownfields assessment and cleanup activities in local communities. In addition to funding, available resources include information sharing on successful brownfield strategies and best practices, liability resolution tools, and access to technical assistance.

Since the Brownfields program was launched 20 years ago, EPA has provided nearly 3,300 grants to local governments and nonprofit organizations, leveraging $24.2 billion in cleanup and redevelopment funding from a variety of public and private sources, and leveraging about 1,700 jobs. These EPA brownfields resources include:

- **Brownfields Assessment Grants**—EPA provides grants annually of up to $200,000 to single localities or up to $600,000 for coalitions of communities, to support the investigation and assessment of brownfield properties and reuse planning at those sites. Applying for Brownfields Assessment grants often is the first step that a locality takes to launch a brownfields program.
- **Targeted Brownfields Assessment (TBA) Support**—TBA support generally is provided to communities that do not have an EPA assessment grant or do not have the capacity to manage a grant, but have a brownfield property where the assessment of the property could spur redevelopment. For TBAs, EPA does not provide funding directly to a community. Instead, EPA provides contractor resources to communities to assess and characterize brownfields on their behalf.
- **Brownfields Multipurpose Grants**—since 2018, EPA provides grants bi-annually of up to $800,000 to local governments and nonprofits to support a community-driven planning process for a specific area with one large or several brownfield sites, and the cleanup of one of these sites. Project areas typically include a neighborhood, downtown commercial district, community waterfront or old industrial corridor. These grants help communities create an area-wide plan and implementation strategies for cleaning up/reusing brownfields, upgrading infrastructure, creating new development opportunities, and leveraging resources for revitalization.
- **Brownfields Cleanup Grants**—EPA provides grants annually of up to $500,000 to local governments and nonprofits for cleanup of specific brownfield sites that are owned by the applicant.
- **Brownfields Revolving Loan Fund (RLF) Grants**—EPA provides grants bi-annually of up to $1,000,000 to state or local governments to capitalize a revolving loan fund, which can be used to provide subgrants to local government and nonprofit entities, and make loans to local, nonprofit or private-sector entities to support cleanup of brownfield sites.
- **Environmental Workforce Development and Job Training (EWDJT) Grants**—EPA provides grants of up to $200,000 to local and nonprofit organizations to recruit, train, and place predominantly low-income and minority, unemployed or under-employed residents of communities affected by hazardous waste sites. Job training participants receive training in the skills needed to secure full-time, sustainable employment in the environmental field and in the assessment and cleanup of brownfields taking place in their communities.

EPA brownfields grants can catalyze significant brownfields activities at the local level, help a community build a brownfields program, and clean up and revitalize specific sites. Any community that seeks to address brown-fields is encouraged to explore these EPA funding opportunities.

At the same time, EPA brownfields grants often do not provide sufficient funding to enable a community to address all of the challenges that must be tackled at brownfields properties. Brownfields redevelopment projects often involve several stages or phases, and each phase may require significant resources and effort. Further, many of the activities necessary for redevelopment of contaminated sites at various phases of the brownfields redevelopment process may not be eligible for funding with EPA brownfields grants, so other funding sources often must be tapped or leveraged to complete brownfields redevelopment projects.

Brownfields revitalization project costs can be daunting to many local communities. Identifying and leveraging resources to support necessary tasks at each phase of the redevelopment process is critically important to success. This is particularly true in small or economically distressed communities or in weak market areas that do not have vibrant commercial or economic reuse potential. These costs also can be challenging in situations where the brownfield reuse does not create direct economic returns or revenues, as is the case when a site is reused for green space or a public park facility.

EPA's Office of Brownfields and Land Revitalization will continue to help communities create effective strategies for leveraging resources for brownfields cleanup and revitalization projects. As part of EPA's Next Generation Brownfields initiative, OBLR plans to offer the following resources and assistance in 2016 and beyond:

- Brownfields Federal Programs Guide—EPA issued the 2015 Brownfields Federal Programs Guide in September 2015. The Brownfields Federal Programs Guide provides in-depth information on resources available from more than 20 federal agencies and offices and highlights federal tax incentives that can support brownfields revitalization. (See: www.epa.gov/sites/production/files/2015-09/documents/brown-fields-federal-programs-guide-2013.pdf).
- Resource Roadmaps—EPA will conduct a webinar focusing on how to create a resource roadmap as a useful tool to guide efforts for leveraging resources for brownfields and community revitalization. The interactive webinar will be recorded and made available to EPA Brownfields grantees and communities. EPA also plans to issue a memorandum to grantees and EPA regional offices clarifying that brownfields assessment grants and Area-wide Planning Grants may be used for reuse planning activities, including the creation of Resource Roadmaps for revitalization at eligible brownfield properties.
- Meet the Funders Webinars—EPA will collaborate with other federal agencies, philanthropic foundations, and nonprofit organizations to conduct a series of in-depth webinars that engage funders and their staff to explore ways that they can leverage their programs for local brownfields revitalization efforts. This Meet the Funders series will educate funding organizations about the needs and challenges of local communities on brownfields revitalization issues and provide in-depth information and tips on how to leverage resources with their support. These webinars will be recorded and made widely available.
- Building the Federal Family of Brownfields Agencies—EPA is dedicated to continuing its long collaborations with the federal family of agencies that provide funding, technical assistance, and other resources to support local brownfields and community revitalization. This will include efforts to promote intra-agency collaboration within other EPA program offices as well as inter-agency collaboration with other federal agencies and organizations. EPA will

work on community and economic development issues with HUD, the Economic Development Administration, and the U.S. Department of Agriculture's Rural Development program. EPA will foster infrastructure investments for brownfields revitalization with the U.S. Department of Transportation, the U.S. Army Corps of Engineers, and other agencies. EPA will promote green strategies and climate smart brownfields with the U.S. Department of Interior, the National Oceanographic and

- Atmospheric Administration, and the U.S. Department of Energy. EPA supports the approach of giving funding preference and prioritization for additional federal funding to localities that have developed strong brownfields revitalization plans, solid public and stakeholder support, and proactive strategies for leveraging resources.
- Promoting Economic Development and Community Revitalization, Particularly in Communities with Weak Markets—Distressed, small, disadvantaged communities often lack the capacity to catalyze economic development and revitalize brownfields. EPA will continue its commitment to supporting brownfields revitalization in small, rural, underserved and struggling communities with brownfields grants, a focus on ensuring environmental justice, area-wide planning support, and robust technical assistance.
- Technical Assistance—The EPA's Office of Brownfields and Land Revitalization will continue to work with its 10 regional offices, the Technical Assistance to Brownfields Communities (TAB) centers, and a variety of other nonprofit and educational partners to provide technical assistance to communities on brownfields, including on leveraging strategies. (See: www.epa.gov/brownfields/brownfields-technical-assistance).

Leveraging Resources Beyond EPA Brownfields Grants

Success in leveraging resources for Brownfields revitalization is not limited to the very complex and large-scale revitalization projects undertaken by Dubuque, Iowa; Stamford, Connecticut; and Charles Town/Ranson, West Virginia, which are profiled in the case study examples in the next section of this guide. Here are a few examples of no-less-successful leveraging efforts undertaken by communities for smaller-scale projects:

The Town of Coventry, Rhode Island used EPA Brownfields state program funds, and Brownfields Assessment and Cleanup grants that were awarded to the Rhode Island Department of Environmental Management (RIDEM) to help assess and remediate a former unauthorized dump, the vacant Sandy Bottom property. The property was transformed into the Sandy Acres Recreational Area, which includes two acres of restored wetlands.

Leveraging: Coventry leveraged funds from the U.S. Fish and Wildlife Service to support flood plain expansion and improve the environment in Coventry; RIDEM funds for wetland restoration and park construction; and remediation funds from the Town's sewer commission to install new sewer pumping station on property. The local public works and department of parks and recreation cleared trees and removed contaminated soils and solid waste from the property.

The Earth Conservancy used 12 EPA Brownfields Cleanup grants (totaling $2.4 million) to leverage the resources necessary to reclaim nearly 2,000 acres of former mine-scarred coal lands in Luzerne County, Pennsylvania. These lands are being reused in a variety of ways, including open space, recreational trails, the site of a community college dormitory, for roadways, and for residential, commercial, and industrial development.

Leveraging: The Earth Conservancy leveraged a range of resources including state funds from the Pennsylvania Department of Environmental Protection's Growing Greener Program and from the Pennsylvania Department of Community and Economic Development. The Earth Conservancy also leveraged resources from the U.S. Department of Interior's Office of Surface Mining Reclamation and Enforcement, and from local partnerships.

The City of Fairborn, Ohio, used a Brownfields Cleanup grant to help remediate an old cement manufacturing plant and redevelop the property for use as the National Center for Medical Readiness at Calamityville, a realistic tactical training center for emergency disaster response medicine associated with Wright State University.

Leveraging: The former site owner donated the property to the City of Fairborn, which leveraged additional resources from Wright State University and the Clean Ohio Fund.

The Ironbound Community Corporation in Newark, New Jersey used its Brownfields Area-Wide Planning grant to develop a community-supported reuse plan that transforms a former vacant lot in the East Ferry Street neighborhood into a community garden and open-air market.

Leveraging: The Ironbound Community Corporation leveraged a range of resources for the project, including private funds to help with personnel costs at the site; a USDA Farmer's Market Promotion Program grant; HUD Community Development Block Grant funds (provided via the City of Newark); an EPA Environmental Justice small grant; and an EPA Targeted Brownfields Site Assessment.

The Northwest Regional Workforce Investment Board (WIB) Inc., in Waterbury, Connecticut used EPA Environmental Workforce Development and Job Training grant funds to recruit, train, and place unemployed and underemployed Waterbury residents, including veterans and ex-offenders, in environmental jobs. Funds were used to train participants in several environmental skills areas.

Leveraging: The Northwest Regional WIB leveraged many additional resources through local, state, and federal sources including the Northwest Construction Careers Initiative, the Connecticut Green Jobs Funnel Initiative, and the Workforce Investment Act.

20. Key Steps in Successful Leveraging Strategies for Brownfields Projects*

U.S. Environmental Protection Agency

The importance of being strategic and purposeful when leveraging funding for brownfields and community revitalization efforts cannot be overstated. Communities cannot depend on "pennies from heaven" to fund revitalization projects. Nor can they wait until a grant solicitation is issued to devise a plan and then rush to apply to the funding agency within the usual 30 to 60-day application period. Well-crafted plans are key: The most successful communities tend to be thoughtful, purposeful, and strategic when identifying, pursuing, leveraging, and using resources for brownfields revitalization.

The steps outlined here are based on the experiences of many communities that developed and implemented successful strategies to leverage funding for brownfields revitalization.

1. Organize a Project Team with Local Leadership from the Top, and Designate a Manager

Brownfield success is about people. The most successful localities establish brownfields project teams, led by strong leaders from local government. Project teams should include prominent local leaders, brownfields "champions," and a cross-sector team representing key organizations and stakeholders (e.g., local chamber of commerce, local community development corporations, prominent business leaders, local civic organizations, philanthropy, and religious organizations).

A task force or working group might include participants from within local government as well as other involved and interested stakeholders (for example, landowners, developers, or neighborhood representatives). The team also might include technical experts or consultants involved in the project. This project team can play many roles, including guiding the overall project, making key decisions, allocating resources and staff to the project, promoting inter-governmental and public-private collaboration, acting as

---

*Public document originally published as U.S. Environmental Protection Agency, "Key Steps in Successful Leveraging Strategies for Brownfields Projects." *Setting the Stage for Leveraging Resources for Brownfields Revitalization*, https://www.epa.gov/brownfields/setting-stage-leveraging-resources-brownfields-revitalization (September 2019).

liaison with the public and key stake-holders, and pursuing funding necessary to complete the revitalization project.

Local leadership is important. Addressing brownfields challenges and working towards community redevelopment requires leadership from top elected officials and an effective team of staff, stakeholders, and volunteers. Maintaining the commitment to a long-term project—even when local administrations change—is essential. The mayor, county executive, township supervisor, or other top elected official should be a visible and determined leader who facilitates community engagement by working in partnership with the council, business community, and local citizens.

It often is advantageous for the mayor or chief executive to dedicate a lead staff person or volunteer to focus the community's efforts on revitalization. A manager should be designated to: keep the project team cohesive, working well and on task; coordinate communications through various mechanisms (such as email distribution groups, web-sharing project sites); and schedule and coordinate meetings, track progress, and recommend next steps for the group. The team manager could be the locality's brownfields manager, the revitalization project manager, somebody designated by the group itself, or even a senior community leader.

It is essential to regularly brief local government leaders (e.g., the mayor, county executive, city manager, or other senior elected and appointed leadership) about planned and ongoing community revitalization projects. They should be ready to represent the project to external stakeholders, the public, and funding organizations. It also is a good idea to hold a briefing session and seek input from the municipal council, planning commission, or other officials whose support will be needed, particularly when it comes to planning and funding efforts. It is important to engage these officials early and often in the process, not just when it is time to seek funding for the redevelopment project. An essential key to community revitalization is the involvement of as many facets of the community as possible.

2. Articulate a Clear Community Vision and Identify Brownfields Revitalization Priorities

Planning for community revitalization requires leadership, patience, and determination. It also requires community engagement and involvement. Community revitalization is an incremental process that addresses a series of challenges along the way. Leadership must step up. A strong team must be formed. The community must be engaged. A vision must be established, and priorities must be set. Community members must understand how the cleanup and revitalization of brownfields can help fulfill their broader community goals. Success will come when the project team connects brownfields opportunities to revitalization priorities and a broader community vision. When communities "begin with the end in mind," they can generate momentum to overcome difficult brownfields challenges.

A community vision for any brownfields revitalization project offers the opportunity for residents to establish what they value about their community and what they want their community to look like in the future. The process of developing a vision helps community leaders and residents to take a realistic look at their community, establish an honest appraisal of community assets and needs, and set collaborative goals for the future. This information is critical for developing a strategy for change and revitalization. The process of developing a community vision is essential to establishing momentum, creating collaborative goals, and ensuring community-wide participation. The process starts with developing a clear community vision for revitalization developed with significant community and stakeholder engagement. The project team needs to answer:

- What do citizens want their community to look like in the future?
- What are the possibilities or opportunities for revitalization?
- What are the most important goals for revitalization (such as, increasing the supply of affordable housing, boosting tourism, revitalizing a waterfront, attracting more commercial development or advanced manufacturing businesses, or expanding green space)? Which revitalization goals are most important to the community?
- How can brownfields revitalization promote the overall community vision?

The project team must engage with residents and stakeholders, assess community needs, establish initial priorities, and develop a plan for continued public participation. Because the level (and cost) of brownfields cleanup often depends on the type of future use intended for a site, it is essential to establish a clear community vision for the future. Community leaders need to confirm reuse plans early so that a remedial plan can be developed with the end use in mind.

Questions that may guide the team in establishing priorities for brownfields redevelopment include:

- Which neighborhood or areas in the community are most in need of revitalization?
- Where are prime real estate parcels located? Which properties or areas are the most promising for redevelopment? Are these properties currently hindered by potential contamination?
- Which properties have sufficient community, stakeholder, and political support for moving forward toward reuse and revitalization?
- Which properties have a reuse vision or concept that is viable and exciting and is consistent with the overall community vision?
- Which project, if accomplished, will produce the most benefits and have the greatest catalytic effects on community revitalization?

Successful brownfields revitalization is possible when communities see brownfields not as liabilities, but as opportunities for economic development, blight reduction, and community revitalization. Despite environmental contamination, many brownfields are in prime locations that may be easily accessible via public transportation or served by existing infrastructure. A successful community vision and brownfields revitalization plan will identify the assets and opportunities presented by brownfields properties and build a redevelopment plan around them.

Most communities cannot tackle all their brownfield sites at once or devote the resources necessary to redevelop every vacant, contaminated, or abandoned property simultaneously. It is unlikely that sufficient resources will be available. In addition, the capacity of the local team will be overwhelmed if priorities are not established and resources identified incrementally.

Communities should focus efforts and resources on priority sites and connect these efforts to the overall community priorities that are most important to local citizens.

Success builds upon itself when projects are approached incrementally and guided by clear, established priorities consistent with an overall community vision.

3. Build and Maintain Local Stakeholder and Citizen Support

Obtaining significant public support for brownfields revitalization projects is critical to leveraging success. Community leaders and the project team must effectively market brownfields redevelopment projects to citizens. This requires clearly communicating what the completed project will look like, the benefits that are likely to result, and how the project will help the community realize its overall vision for the area. The goal is to continually build public support for and commitment to a shared revitalization vision.

Early and frequent stakeholder involvement and citizen engagement in the brownfields revitalization process is critical. Projects with widespread and enthusiastic public support have a greater chance of success. Community engagement leads to community investment. Projects that are well planned and supported by a community tend to be more competitive when applying for funding opportunities.

It is important to think beyond traditional public hearings or forums where local officials announce what will happen and hear limited public comments. Using a variety of methods to engage community members usually is the most effective approach. This can include providing information through the traditional media, on websites, or through public information sessions; using newsletters and social media; holding planning charrettes and workshops; and conducting to conduct outreach and promote information sharing.

One very effective method for engaging key stakeholders is to create an advisory board or an informal council that might include organizational and grassroots representatives, elected leadership from every level of government, and funders supportive of the project. A community can recruit a robust cross-section of stakeholders to participate in such an advisory board, keep them informed, and convene the body periodically to provide updates. An advisory board can be invaluable when funding officials visit the community, stakeholder support letters are needed for grant applications, and for demonstrating broad public support for projects in grant or loan funding applications.

Moreover, when brownfields are revitalized by the private sector, it is important for localities to engage with private landowners, developers, and potential users to ensure that cleanup and redevelopment are conducted in a fashion that supports the property's expected reuse, and in a way that can effectively leverage public and private resources. Actions by localities that reduce the risk and uncertainty from environmental contaminants, upgrade infrastructure to the site, improve the overall neighborhood context for the project, and reduce time delays for development will lead to more successful projects. Public-private collaboration also will lead to more successful leveraging and private-sector investment than brownfield projects that are left to fend for themselves without public-private partnership.

It also may be beneficial to coordinate with the congressional delegation and their staff in local district offices and in Washington, D.C. Provide information to these officials and their staff early and throughout the revitalization process, share briefing sheets and updates with them, visit them in their offices, and invite them to tour the local project and meet with key stakeholders. Local officials can lead these interactions, which also should include the key members of the project team who are managing implementation of the project. The better-informed federal representatives are, the better they can act as champions for local efforts.

4. Delineate Brownfield Project Components and Project Phases

Brownfield projects are not monolithic endeavors. A brownfield project usually includes several components, each with multiple stages or phases. A successful funding strategy starts with clearly delineating each project component and phase.

Components of a brownfields redevelopment effort might include demolition, site preparation, and projects related to economic development, housing, green space, waterfront restoration, stormwater management, trail restoration and development, community gardens, forestry, municipal and transportation facilities, and other project components not listed. Mixed-use development projects often combine many of these components.

Individual phases of a project (e.g., planning, property acquisition, site characterization and assessment, cleanup, construction, infrastructure improvements) should be identified at the beginning of the brownfields revitalization process. Funding needs and sources of available funding may be different for different phases of a project. When seeking project funding, it can be helpful to consider funding opportunities for individual project phases. For example, rather than trying to assemble funding for the entire project at once, it often makes sense to determine costs for next phases of each project and seek funding and support for that phase.

5. Create Estimates of Project Costs

Once priority projects are identified and their key components and phases are delineated, it is useful to estimate project costs for each key project and its core components. With well-estimated project costs, a community can better identify the best potential funding sources, understand, and estimate the levels of matching-share funds that will be needed, and tailor efforts to gain support for funding requests. Cost estimates can become more precise as the project moves forward from planning-level cost estimates toward final cost estimates. Some communities use their own staff while others hire professionals such as planners, engineers, or construction experts to develop accurate cost estimates. Funders such as a government agency or private foundation sometimes will finance the use of expert consultants as part of the planning process. However, sometimes it is necessary for a locality to make an investment for expert project cost estimating.

6. Identify the Best Funding Sources for Project Components and Phases

Once a community confirms its priority projects, delineates project components and phases, and develops solid cost estimates, it is ready to seek sources of funding for brownfields revitalization. Consider the following potential sources of funds or investment for brownfield projects:

- Site redevelopers or private sector investors.
- Banks and other traditional lenders.
- Regional agencies (such as metropolitan planning organizations, industrial development authorities, or economic development districts).
- Federal or state tax incentives.
- Community foundations and regional, corporate, and national philanthropies.
- State and federal funding agencies.
- Local funds and incentive tools (also see #8 below).

Information about potential sources of funding for brownfields revitalization projects is available in a variety of sources. EPA's 2015 Brownfields Federal Programs Guide is a comprehensive resource with detailed information on more than 100 federal sources of funding and technical assistance for brownfields projects available from more than 20 federal agencies. This publication is a great first stop when searching for federal brownfields resources.

One way to keep informed about federal funding opportunities is to create customized subscription feeds from the Federal Register, which provides timely copies of nearly every federal funding solicitation issued. Another excellent way to stay abreast of federal-agency funding opportunities is to subscribe to the email listservs maintained by EPA and many other federal agencies, through which they often convey updates on sources of available funding.

The information available in individual states on resources for brownfields and community revitalization varies widely.

Check the state government's website and individual state agencies for program and funding information. It also may be possible to subscribe to state email listservs for information on funding, starting with the state's Brownfields program. Private, charitable, and corporate philanthropic foundations also can be sources of funding for local redevelopment projects.

Many foundations are ramping up their giving towards "impact investing," which is an approach that seeks to create a positive economic return from contributions to the awardee, while also fostering positive social, environmental, or community improvements—the types of results often associated with brownfields revitalization. There are more than 85,000 philanthropic foundations in the U.S. However, there are only a few centralized clearinghouses or tracking systems for these funders. Given that foundations provide more than $50 billion annually in charitable giving, localities certainly should include philanthropies in their targeted efforts to secure resources for brownfields and community revitalization.

One approach for staying well informed about funding opportunities from any source is to contact the program and funding managers at each organization directly. Often, it is a good idea to call or meet with representatives from a foundation to introduce and discuss a community project. Most officials are eager to provide information about their programs and are interested in supporting solid local projects. It always is a good idea to read the organization's funding solicitations (or the past year's solicitation, if no current funding program is open) and other background information online before contacting a funding official. Prepare for each meeting by researching the organization's primary goals, funding objectives and past funding decisions.

Also, be prepared to outline your community's project. Demonstrate knowledge of the foundation's programs and funding opportunities and demonstrate strong enthusiasm for your project. Identifying potential funding sources for brownfields and community revitalization is a significant task. Localities should consider assigning this task to the brownfields project team, project team leader, or to the locality's grants manager who can conduct necessary research and match available resources to specific brownfields priorities and needs. Keep in mind that each funding source includes different priorities and different restrictions regarding the use of funds.

For example, EPA's Brownfields Cleanup Grants can be used only for cleanup activities at brownfields owned by the grant applicant. Such funding cannot be used for construction and redevelopment activities. It is essential that the project team segregate brownfields redevelopment efforts into distinct phases and identify funding opportunities for each phase. Limited local funding should be used as essential seed money or for complying with matching-share requirements for funds sought from outside sources. Costs should be tracked meticulously and documented for future reference.

Grants, loans, and other forms of direct funding from federal, state, or philanthropic sources are not the only sources of financing for brownfields projects. Tax credits and other tax-related incentives often are critical components of the financing strategy for brownfields projects. Use of tax-related incentives can spur public and private investment in a project by reducing the tax burden, and thus the overall cost of a project, for investors when they make certain types of investments. For this reason, it is important to identify and assess the feasibility of using available federal tax incentives and credits for various components of a brownfields revitalization project. Examples include New Markets Tax Credits (NMTC), Low Income Housing Tax Credits (HTC), Historic Rehabilitation Tax Credits, and Energy Efficiency and Renewable Energy tax credits and incentives and the Brownfields Expensing Tax Incentive, when available. EPA's 2015 Brownfields Federal Programs Guide discusses many of the tax-related provisions that often are factored into brownfields financing strategies. Many of these tax credits and incentives are available subject to authorization by Congress. Please consult EPA's Brownfields website (www.epa.gov/brownfields) for the latest information on rules or interpretation regarding their use. Additional tax-related incentives may be available at the state level. Localities also may create local tax-related incentives, which are discussed in sections 8 and 9.

7. Create a "Resource Roadmap" for Priority Projects

Creating a Resource Roadmap can be very useful for developing a strategy for leveraging funding for brownfields and community revitalization. A Resource Roadmap is a document, sometimes in matrix form, that identifies revitalization priorities, their key components and phases, and the estimated cost for each project component and phase (or at least the most important next phases). The Resource Roadmap can be a handy guide for project teams pursing grant and loan funding. It also can be a great information tool to provide to local leadership (such as a city council) and funding champions (such as state and local legislators). The Resource Roadmap can help map out potential sources of funding and how to meet matching-share requirements for individual funding sources, as discussed below.

8. Develop a Strategy for Matching-Share Contributions and Leveraging Local Funding Sources

Confirming matching-share funds and leveraging local resources often are critical steps in securing external grants or investments. Most grants require recipients to provide a significant matching share, which demonstrates the community's commitment to the project and may instill the confidence of potential funders and investors in the feasibility of the project.

Beyond any required match, funding organizations also will want to see that the applicant community can leverage additional resources. Leveraging typically refers to additional contributions toward the project, but not necessarily direct financial matching. For example, if a private investor is willing to build a $10 million commercial center on a brownfield that needs an expensive cleanup, the value of the developer's capital project is considered leverage, even though it is not direct funding for the cleanup effort.

Identifying committed matching funds and available leverage often requires significant planning well in advance of the time that the actual funding application is prepared. This involves significant municipal financial planning and capital budgeting and making requests to key funding stakeholders (such as municipal department heads, city council, and/or state officials) well before grant applications are due.

Early in the revitalization process, localities should create a matching/leveraging strategy for each project and associated funding request. (This information should be reflected in the Resource Roadmap described in Step 7 above.) It usually is necessary to identify potential sources of matching funds and to secure matching-share commitments from partners (including partners in various departments of the local government or from within the applicant's own organization). Pitches should be made to potential match contributors by highlighting the benefits and potential outcomes of the project. Securing these resources early helps build momentum and commitment for the project. It usually is fine for a contributor to agree to make its matching-share contribution or leveraged resources contingent upon receipt of the grant or loan for which the applicant is applying. This information should be added to the Resource Roadmap as commitments are secured.

It also can be valuable to determine what non-financial or in-kind resources the applicant locality can contribute to a project. Some funding programs will accept in-kind contributions, such as the value of staff time or the labor of public work crews, as part or all the required matching share for a grant. For in-kind contributions to meet matching-share requirements, an applicant determines the specific value of the in-kind contribution, documents show that value was derived, and obtains a letter of commitment from the contributor that conveys the value of the contribution. However, even when in-kind contributions can contribute to a funding match, funders often will also seek some level of "cash" match, which demonstrates that the applicant has "skin in the game." Also keep in mind that some funding sources may restrict the types of funding or in-kind contributions that can be used as matching funds (e.g., some federal grants prohibit the use of other federal resources as matching funds).

9. Assess the Feasibility of Debt Financing

Early in the process, a locality also should assess whether it has the capacity (and desire) to use debt or other financing strategies to cover major capital costs and to build upon the external grants or other resources that will be part of the overall funding package. For example, a major infrastructure upgrade at a brownfield site, such as the construction of a new complete-street roadway or a new building, could entail millions of dollars and is unlikely to be financed completely by federal, state, or philanthropic funding sources. The locality may need to consider using bonds, debt (e.g., bank loans, or other financing tools) to cover major capital costs.

The locality must understand its ability to service debt from future project revenues, prospective redeveloper payments, user fees, general municipal revenues, increased tax revenues associated with the revitalization, or other repayment streams.

A locality should consider the range of available debt financing tools by creating a pro-forma analysis of the potential costs of servicing debt or municipal financing tools and its ability to cover those costs. It is a good idea to consult early with counsel and experienced financial consultants. It also is a good idea to explore the potential for using government-backed or subsidized financing tools to lower capital costs, such as the U.S. Department of Housing and Urban Development's (HUD) Section 108 Guaranteed Loans, the Federal Home Loan Banks' Community Investment Program lending tools, the U.S. Department of Agriculture's (USDA) lending tools, EPA's Brownfields Revolving Loan Funds, or state government lending support programs.

Many communities use bonding or tax-abatement tools to for site clearance activities (including cleanup), infrastructure upgrades or other improvements to support brownfields revitalization, often in combination with grants or other resources leveraged into the project. Commonly used bonding tools include general obligation bonds, assessment districts that service the bond debt through assessments on the commercial development or housing that is built in the previously under-utilized area, tax abatement tools, or tax increment financing.

General Obligation Bonds: Virtually all communities can issue general obligation or "G.O." bonds for any proper public purpose that pertains to its local government and affairs. Economic development practitioners can make a strong case that bond pool or bond proceeds to support brownfield cleanup and reuse projects will create jobs and enhance the local tax base, which are appropriate public purposes. Communities traditionally issue G.O. bonds for acquiring land, preparing sites, and making infrastructure improvements—key elements in a brownfield redevelopment strategy. Moreover, the community's ability to repay this bond debt is enhanced by the growth in property tax revenues as more brownfields are brought back to productive uses.

Tax Increment Financing: TIF traditionally is used for a variety of economic revitalization efforts, usually in economically distressed, abandoned, or under-utilized areas—which describes a typical brownfield. TIF is the most common form of local support for brownfield reuse, and a key part of any strategy to address financing gaps.

All but a few states have passed legislation enabling municipalities to use TIFs. The TIF process uses the anticipated growth in property taxes generated by a future development project to finance public sector investment. Some states also allow localities to use projected sales tax revenue growth in a project area as TIF. TIFs are built on the concept that new value will be created and that this future value can be used to support the financing of the activities needed now (such as cleanup or infrastructure improvements) to create that new value. The key to TIF is the local commitment of incremental tax resources for the payment of redevelopment costs.

TIF is used for specific purposes of the redevelopment, such as acquiring and preparing the site, cleanup of contamination, upgrading utilities, streets, or parking facilities, and carrying out other necessary site preparation and improvements. This makes TIF an ideal tool for brownfield projects. In addition, TIF programs are easily used with other types of funding, such as grants or loans.

Tax Abatements: Tax abatements are reductions or forgiveness from tax liabilities. Usually, tax abatements involve either reduce rates for a specific period, typically five or ten years; or they freeze values at some point in time, usually at a pre-improvement stage. Tax abatements are commonly used to stimulate investments in building improvements or new construction in areas where property taxes or other conditions discourage private investment.

Special Service Areas or Taxing Districts: Localities can use taxing districts or "special service area" designations as a way to raise cash to finance extra services, improvements, or facilities that will benefit the targeted area. Current property owners in a special service area agree, or a redeveloper can commit future property owners or users, to accept and pay a special real estate levy or fee. These proceeds are used to pay for the defined services or activities. The jurisdiction uses this additional revenue to finance the improvements, either earmarking it directly for the area, or using it to issue bonds to fund the projects.

Many communities use this approach for main street or central business district improvement initiatives. Projects commonly include security, maintenance, storefront rehabilitation, and business attraction or retention efforts. Some communities use this tool to finance infrastructure upgrades in commercial districts or at industrial parks. Property owners in a defined brownfields area could use this approach to raise funds to cover cleanup costs at blighted sites, especially at small orphan sites that hinder the whole area.

10. Create a Briefing Sheet for Each Priority Project

Many communities have found it valuable to prepare a compelling briefing sheet that can be used to succinctly convey to the public, key stakeholders, and funders the scope, objectives, benefits, status, progress, supporters, funding secured, challenges, and outstanding needs of the overall brownfields redevelopment project or for each major component of a large project. For example, one briefing sheet could focus on transportation infrastructure elements of a project, while another might address parks and recreational plans for a brownfield area. Briefing sheets can be professionally designed if there is in-house design capacity or resources to spare, but even home-grown designs will be sufficient.

Tips from communities for creating an effective briefing sheet include:

- Keep it short: no more than two pages (one sheet, front and back).
- Liven up the sheet with graphics or pictures, such as "before" pictures, site groundbreaking photos, and the organization/sponsor logo. Remember the adage that "a picture is worth a thousand words" … and maybe a million dollars. Consider creating an artist's rendering of the reuse vision for priority brownfield sites.
- Include specific funding requests or opportunities currently being sought.
- Include the lead point of contact for inquiries about the project.

- Continuously update the briefing sheet as goals are achieved, funding secured, new partnerships are formed, or as project objectives change.

Distribute and email these briefing sheets widely and often. The briefing sheets can help create a buzz about the project and build support for funding efforts. It is surprising how the briefing sheets can circulate and give a boost to a project.

11. Seek State Backing

Often, the best sources of funding and technical assistance resources are available through state agencies that support economic development, environmental, and infrastructure priorities. State funding is important for leveraging federal funding and can offer a critical source of funding to meet matching-share requirements. Many states provide targeted economic development assistance funds, brownfields financing assistance, tax incentives, infrastructure grants, subsidized loans, or other incentives to support brownfields and community revitalization.

Moreover, many federal funds are funneled through state agencies or require that localities partner or work with the state government to be eligible or competitive for funding. Regardless of whether a locality is seeking funding from state agencies, it usually is valuable to coordinate closely with state officials. Involving state elected officials in the revitalization process can be helpful in several ways. They can help connect localities with other communities across the state that are addressing similar situations. They also can become effective champions for local brownfields revitalization initiatives.

12. Collaborate with Federal Agency Officials

It is critical to engage early with relevant federal agency and program officials so that they are familiar with the community's brownfield project and its key components. Officials at EPA, the Department of Commerce, the Department of Transportation, HUD, the U.S. Army Corps of Engineers, the U.S. Department of Agriculture, and other agencies can support and help guide local projects.

Federal program managers routinely host webinars and workshops to explain their funding programs and how they can be used. These sessions can provide excellent opportunities to interact with funding officials on a community's specific projects. Also consider making regular visits to the regional offices of federal agencies and to their headquarters offices in Washington, D.C. Keep in touch by phone and email and invite federal officials to your community for site and project tours. Communities should consider planning collaborative forums, workshops, or roundtable events that include federal officials and a variety of other stakeholders to build understanding and ongoing support for revitalization initiatives.

13. Prepare for Grant Writing

Prepare ahead of time to write effective applications for grants or other kinds of resources. Do not wait until the funding notice is issued or the application submission deadline is at hand. Most agencies with grant opportunities have information posted on their websites on previous funding opportunities or suggestions for getting started early. Communities can use this information to help identify the information they need to gather, which will help them get a jump start on preparing their applications. Well-prepared communities typically have the most competitive funding applications.

Strategies for preparing effectively for the grant-writing process include:

- Determine if your community or organization is eligible for the grant or funding resources.
- Determine whether the activities for which you are seeking funding are eligible under the funding opportunity. If not, move on and consider other grants and resources.
- Identify and refine your project. Make sure the project you plan to apply for is a good "fit" for the grant type and that your project is far enough along in the planning stage to discuss in a firm, concrete manner in the application.
- Determine the most appropriate organization to be the applicant for the grant or funding resource. Are they eligible? Do they have the necessary grant management experience, capabilities, and capacity?
- Identify and confirm key partners, stakeholders and supporting organizations.
- Follow the application instructions. Provide requested information and address all criteria. Again, your project should be well-defined at this stage in your planning process so that you can provide specific information about the project, project goals, partners, support, costs, leverage funding, and community engagement or any other items requested in the funding solicitation. Remember, details matter! Be sure to provide detailed information about how your project relates to the criterion, make necessary linkages, and explain connections. Don't leave the reviewers guessing.
- Estimate project costs, solidify matching funds, and confirm leveraged dollar commitments.

Remember: Follow the instructions and answer every question thoroughly. This may seem obvious, but many applicants skip questions, omit required information, violate rules for the application, or fail to answer the questions that are asked. These problems can be avoided with careful preparation and by paying meticulous attention to instructions and evaluation criteria included in the solicitation.

It is always a good idea to prepare an outline based on the requirements in the Request for Proposal (RFP). This helps ensure that you do not forget to address an evaluation criterion, and that you include key information and address all other factors listed in the grant solicitation. Be sure to use suggested or required application formatting. Because some funding solicitations can be unclear, it is easy to miss important details that should be addressed in your application. Following an outline will help ensure that you don't leave out key information. Preparing an outline also allows you to allocate and devote space to address all evaluation criteria without exceeding page limitations. Be sure to ask questions if the solicitation is unclear.

If your application is unsuccessful, always request a debriefing from the funding agency to learn what the strengths and weaknesses were in your proposal. Use this feedback to improve subsequent applications.

14. Celebrate Success

It has been said that "nothing succeeds like success," and this certainly is true when it comes to obtaining funding. Success can come by accomplishing significant project milestones and by obtaining the next grant. Effective communities always are looking for opportunities to celebrate success, thank funding agencies and key supporters, hold groundbreaking celebrations and ribbon-cutting events, cultivate media coverage, send newsletters, and spread the word in other ways.

Part III
Practices and Innovations

• A. Federal •

21. Smart Growth[*]

U.S. Environmental Protection Agency

Editor's note: Unless a contaminated site is demonstrably causing direct health and environmental impacts, the other reasons to do so are to improve economic conditions, provide social benefits and to improve the environment. These are the tenets of Smart Growth, and why brownfields are inextricably linked.

"Smart growth" covers a range of development and conservation strategies that help protect our health and natural environment and make our communities more attractive, economically stronger, and more socially diverse.

Development decisions affect many of the things that touch people's everyday lives—their homes, their health, the schools their children attend, the taxes they pay, their daily commute, the natural environment around them, economic growth in their community, and opportunities to achieve their dreams and goals. What, where, and how communities build will affect their residents' lives for generations to come.

Communities of all sizes across the country are using creative strategies to develop in ways that preserve natural lands and critical environmental areas, protect water and air quality, and reuse already-developed land.

- They conserve resources by reinvesting in existing infrastructure and rehabilitating historic buildings.
- By designing neighborhoods that have homes near shops, offices, schools, houses of worship, parks, and other amenities, communities give residents and visitors the option of walking, bicycling, taking public transportation, or driving as they go about their business.
- A range of different housing types makes it possible for senior citizens to stay in their neighborhoods as they age, young people to afford their first home, and families at all stages in between to find a safe, attractive home they can afford.
- Through smart growth approaches that enhance neighborhoods and involve residents in development decisions, these communities are creating vibrant places to live, work, and play.
- The high quality of life makes these communities economically competitive, creates business opportunities, and strengthens the local tax base.

---

[*]Public document originally published as U.S. Environmental Protection Agency, "Smart Growth," https://www.epa.gov/smartgrowth (January 2020).

Based on the experience of communities around the nation that have used smart growth approaches to create and maintain great neighborhoods, the Smart Growth Network developed a set of 10 basic principles to guide smart growth strategies:

The Smart Growth Network's *Getting to Smart Growth* series provides 200 policies that communities can consider implementing to make sure that development happens how and where they want it.

- Mix land uses.
- Take advantage of compact building design.
- Create a range of housing opportunities and choices.
- Create walkable neighborhoods.
- Foster distinctive, attractive communities with a strong sense of place.
- Preserve open space, farmland, natural beauty, and critical environmental areas.
- Strengthen and direct development towards existing communities.
- Provide a variety of transportation choices.
- Make development decisions predictable, fair, and cost effective.
- Encourage community and stakeholder collaboration in development decisions.

How Does EPA Work on Smart Growth Issues?

EPA helps communities improve their development practices and get the type of development they want. We work with local, state, and national experts to discover and encourage development strategies that protect human health and the environment, create economic opportunities, and provide attractive and affordable neighborhoods for people of all income levels.

EPA's Office of Community Revitalization works on smart growth issues by:

- Conducting research.
- Producing reports and other publications.
- Providing examples of outstanding smart growth communities and projects.
- Working with tribes, states, regions, and communities through grants and technical assistance.
- Through partnerships, bringing together diverse interests to encourage better growth and development.
- Supporting education and outreach by contributing to Smart Growth Online and the New Partners for Smart Growth conference.

Why Does EPA Work on Smart Growth Issues?

EPA's mission is to protect human health and the environment. How and where communities develop affects human health and the environment. Therefore, EPA works on smart growth issues to help communities develop in ways that are better for health and the environment.

Policies and regulations vary by community and by state. Many federal policies, particularly those related to the environment, transportation, and housing, affect how communities develop, but the federal government generally does not directly regulate development. The federal government can help states and municipalities better understand the impacts of development patterns, but development decisions are predominantly under state and local jurisdiction.

Besides the Office of Community Revitalization, other EPA programs that work on issues related to smart growth include:

- Brownfields and Land Revitalization
- Protecting Children's Environmental Health
- Office of Environmental Justice
- Office of Water
- Transportation and Air Quality

What Are Some Environmental Benefits of Smart Growth Strategies?

Development guided by smart growth principles can minimize air and water pollution, reduce greenhouse gas emissions, encourage cleanup and reuse of contaminated properties, and preserve natural lands. Where and how we develop directly affects natural areas and wildlife habitat and replaces natural cover with impervious surfaces such as concrete or asphalt. Development patterns and practices also indirectly affect environmental quality since they influence how easily people can get around.

Smart growth practices can lessen the environmental impacts of development with techniques that include encouraging compact development, reducing impervious surfaces, safeguarding environmentally sensitive areas, mixing land uses (e.g., homes, offices, and shops), promoting public transit, and improving pedestrian and bicycle amenities.

Air Quality. Compact communities with a mix of uses and transportation options make it easy for people to choose to walk, bicycle, or take public transit instead of driving. People who choose to drive generally can drive shorter distances. Less travel by motor vehicles can reduce air pollution by smog-forming emissions and other pollutants. For instance, the Tempe, Arizona Transportation Center is a hub for light rail and buses and includes storage and repair facilities for bicycles.

Climate Change. Transportation options and land use patterns that reduce air pollution also cut the emissions of greenhouse gases that contribute to climate change. Using energy-efficient, green building techniques can reduce greenhouse gas emissions from energy use. Smart growth strategies can also help communities prepare for the impacts of climate change. Like Tupelo Alley, a mixed-use, LEED Gold building near public transit in Portland, Oregon.

Water Quality. Compact development and open space preservation can help protect water quality by reducing the amount of paved surfaces and by allowing natural lands to filter rainwater and runoff before it reaches drinking-water supplies. Green infrastructure techniques, which mimic natural processes to capture, hold, absorb, and filter stormwater, can be incorporated into streets, sidewalks, parking lots, and buildings. Like rain gardens in Washington, D.C., which captures and reuses stormwater.

Open Space Conservation. Preserving natural lands and encouraging growth in existing communities protects farmland, wildlife habitat, outdoor recreation, and natural water filtration that ensures clean drinking water. For example, a wildlife refuge path in Delaware is a recreational amenity in a place that also provides habitat for animals and valuable ecological services.

22. Brownfields Federal Programs and Cases*

U.S. Environmental Protection Agency

Editor's note: The process of and resources for redevelopment brownfields leverage many other federal and state programs. Some of the programs are geographic in nature, while others cover a sector of the economy. Used properly, communities can accelerate brownfield reuse planning and implementation.

This article outlines the key programs, cases, and incentives offered by the federal government that can be used to support brownfield projects. When considering potential sources of assistance for brownfield efforts, keep in mind that many federal programs may not specifically use the term "brownfields." Nevertheless, they still may offer resources applicable for brownfields cleanup and redevelopment.

Appalachian Regional Commission

The reclamation and reuse of brownfields and formerly mined lands align with Appalachian Regional Commission (ARC)'s asset-based development approach to community and economic development, and exemplify a way that communities can meet ARC's five investment goals—investing in entrepreneurial and business development strategies that strengthen Appalachia's economy. The communities of Central Appalachia are increasingly interested in the potential to create economic opportunity through the creative reuse and redevelopment of abandoned and formerly mined lands.

CASE: Poe Mill Park, Greenville, SC. Funding from ARC was critical for creation of a new park on the site of a former textile mill in Greenville, South Carolina. In FY 2018, ARC awarded a grant to the Greenville County Redevelopment Authority's Poe Mill Brownfield Remediation Completion project. The project area is the site of an old textile mill that closed in 1977. The abandoned structures subsequently burned down in 2003. Since 2009, various local entities have collaborated to remediate the site (mainly by removing asbestos- and heavy metals-laden materials) so that it can be turned into a neighborhood park and a regional attraction with an amphitheater. The new park will

---

*Public document originally published as U.S. Environmental Protection Agency (2019), "Overview of Brownfields Federal Programs," in *2019 Brownfields Federal Programs Guide* (Washington, D.C.: EPA).

provide a local gathering place and is expected to catalyze further economic growth in the area.

The Greenville County Redevelopment Authority used $800,000 in EPA brownfields grants to assess and clean up the Poe Mill Historical Plaza and Poe Mill parking lot after the fire. The Redevelopment Authority and its partners will complete a multiphase remediation process and prepare the site for redevelopment by demolishing structures on the property, distributing a one-foot deep layer of clean soil fill on the entire site (minus the existing paved area) to encapsulate the contaminated soils below, and seeding the non-paved areas.

Department of Agriculture—Rural Development

The U.S. Department of Agriculture (USDA) Rural Development (RD) is committed to helping improve the economy and quality of life in rural America by providing financial programs to support essential public and private facilities and services such as water and sewer systems, housing, health clinics, emergency service facilities, and electric and telecommunications infrastructure. USDA-RD provides grants, loans, and loan guarantee assistance for a variety of business, commercial, and industrial brownfield redevelopment projects in small towns and rural areas.

CASE Bedford Solar Farm, Bedford, VA. In 2017, Bedford Solar received a $3 million USDA Rural Development loan to build a three-megawatt solar plant to provide electricity to Bedford, a small rural town in Virginia. Built on a brownfield, Bedford Solar entered into an agreement with the Bedford Town Council, which was approved in November 2016. The developer agreed to lease the land from the town and pay to develop the solar farm. The farm was complete in December 2017 and is expected to stimulate local economic growth and development. It began providing electricity in January 2018, reducing energy costs, attracting new business with sustainable renewable energy, and creating local jobs.

Department of Agriculture—U.S. Forest Service

U.S. Forest Service Cooperative Forestry programs, delivered through state forestry agencies, provide information and assistance to communities involved in brownfields projects. These programs help communities manage natural resources to enhance forest health and ecosystem services and to promote community resilience and economic development.

CASE: Muskegon Lake Cleanup and Restoration, MI. With funding provided by the U.S. Forest Service through the Great Lakes Restoration Initiative, the nonprofit Delta Institute is working with the Western Michigan Shoreline Regional Development Commission to plant 5,500 hybrid poplar trees on eight brownfield sites to aid the $75 million cleanup and restoration of Michigan's Muskegon Lake. The trees are expected to help reduce pollution from five types of contaminants through the process of phytoremediation. Phytoremediation is the process of using trees and vegetation to take up harmful contaminants, such as petroleum hydrocarbons and heavy metals from soil and groundwater. Phytoremediation is being used as an interim land management strategy in to help remediate the soil and prepare the site for a more permanent redevelopment solution.

Department of Commerce—Economic Development Administration

The Economic Development Administration (EDA) provides grants to help communities and regions suffering from economic distress build capacity for economic development. EDA assistance is available to units of state and local government, nonprofits, Indian tribes, and institutions of higher education in rural and urban areas experiencing chronic high unemployment or underemployment, low per capita income, or a severe disruption to the economic base of the community or region.

CASE: New Belgium Brewing Co., Asheville, NC. In 2013, EDA awarded a $1.12 million grant to Asheville, North Carolina, to fund infrastructure improvements on a former brownfield site. These transportation improvements and waterline upgrades helped the New Belgium Brewing Co. establish a brewery, tasting facility, and distribution center for its craft beers. The project enhances the emerging beverage cluster in western North Carolina and is part of a project undertaken by Asheville to redevelop a former livestock market and salvage yard. New Belgium specifically sought a brownfield property for its East Coast expansion "to prevent taking agricultural land out of production or eliminating natural habitat, to lovingly bring what was once a source of jobs and industry back into productive use, and to find a location near other amenities, increasing density and walkability." The infrastructure improvements funded by EDA were completed in 2016. To date, the project has created 130 jobs and generated over $123 million in private investment.

Department of Commerce—National Oceanic and Atmospheric Administration

The Department of Commerce's National Oceanic and Atmospheric Administration's (NOAA) mission is science, service, and stewardship. NOAA works to understand and predict changes in climate, weather, oceans, and coasts; to share that knowledge and information with others; and to conserve and manage coastal and marine ecosystems and resources.

CASE: South Wilmington Wetland Park, Wilmington, DE. In 2009, the City of Wilmington, Delaware, was awarded $200,000 in EPA community-wide brownfields assessment grant funds to conduct Phase I and Phase II environmental site assessments, cleanup planning, and reuse planning at several vacant and contaminated parcels within the 27-acre South Wilmington Wetland Park. This project helped catalyze a decade of action toward the development of a wetlands park and stormwater management facility that will clean a contaminated brownfield area, reduce flooding in the Southbridge neighborhood, separate combined sewers, restore aquatic and wildlife habitat, create pedestrian trails and wetland boardwalks for community recreation and enjoyment, and create a new open space and environmental education center for the community. In 2018, Wilmington leveraged a nearly $3 million National Coastal Resilience Fund grant from NOAA and the National Fish and Wildlife Foundation (NFWF) to support this South Wilmington Wetland Project. The $23.9 million project is currently underway and is expected to help buffer the impacts of sea level rise, reduce urban stormwater runoff, and boost the ecological, economic, and social benefits of the wetlands

Department of Defense—U.S. Army Corps of Engineers

The U.S. Army Corps of Engineers (USACE) assists the development and management of the nation's water resources in an environmentally sustainable, economic, and technically sound manner. USACE provides comprehensive planning, design, construction, engineering management, and technical support to the Army and to the nation. In addition, USACE responds to engineering-related brownfields questions and project inquiries from any community within the U.S. and its territories for major water resource-related endeavors.

CASE: Hub Site, Meriden, CT. In a unique partnership with the U.S. Army Corps of Engineers, the U.S. Department of Transportation, and the U.S. Department of Housing and Urban Development, the City of Meriden, Connecticut, transformed an abandoned shopping mall complex, the HUB site, into a 14-acre urban greenspace with walking trails, an amphitheater, a daylighted stream, and a farmers market. The site was a brownfield due to prior industrial and commercial uses. The mall closed after severe flooding occurred in the 1990s and the city acquired the site through condemnation. Meriden used $480,000 in EPA brownfields assessment and cleanup grants for environmental remediation. The state provided $14.9 million for demolition, site design, and construction. The daylighting of Harbor Brook that runs through the property was an important aspect of the project, and a key part of the city's flood control efforts. The city partnered with the U.S. Army Corps of Engineers to achieve these flood control goals, using funding from the Corps and congressionally earmarked funds ($144,300) directly from the EPA Clean Water Fund.

Department of Energy

The U.S. Department of Energy (DOE) supports brownfields reuse by providing technical assistance in the fields of energy use and environmental remediation and in the Los Alamos National Laboratory (LANL) Sustainable Design Guide providing technical assistance in the field of environmental cleanup and stabilization.

CASE: Las Colonias Park, Grand Junction, CO. The 130-acre Las Colonias Park within the Greater Downtown Plan for the River District in Grand Junction, Colorado, is an example of beneficial reuse under DOE's LM program. Grand Junction's Downtown Plan identifies the River District as a critical community area connecting the riverfront to several underserved neighborhoods. The area was used for operation of a uranium mill from 1950 to 1970. The mill site has since been cleaned up by DOE and was turned over to the City of Grand Junction by the State of Colorado in 1997 for public use. A park was planned but the project was delayed several times due to lack of funding. Remarkably, despite several delays and the development of two new master plans (in 2008 and again in 2013) the original goal of the park remained the same: providing a space for the passive experience of nature through the creation of amenities that enhance the community without endangering the environment. The city's plan for the land includes revitalizing a neglected riverfront area with a native arboretum, trail connections, riparian restoration, shelters, wetlands, parking, a boat launch, and an outdoor amphitheater. The ambitious plan for the park will restore and enhance the banks of the Colorado River, celebrate the history of the area, and help revitalize the local economy.

Department of Health and Human Services—Agency for Toxic Substances and Disease Registry

The Agency for Toxic Substances and Disease Registry (ATSDR) is directed by congressional mandate to perform specific functions concerning the effect on public health of hazardous substances in the environment. Sites such as brownfield and land reuse sites may be the source of potentially harmful exposures because of contamination from previous property uses. Addressing public health concerns and issues related to the restoration of contaminated properties is essential. Community health considerations are important parts of ATSDR's land revitalization activities.

CASE: Joplin, MO. On May 22, 2011, a tornado altered the Joplin, Missouri, landscape along a nearly ¾ to one-mile wide and six-mile long path. The storm impacted about 8,000 structures including homes, businesses, schools, churches, and a hospital. Public infrastructure, such as utilities and storm sewers, and the natural environment also were affected. The tornado's path included a two-mile corridor, along East 20th Street between South Main Street and South Highview Avenue, with nearly all development, infrastructure, and environmental elements damaged or destroyed. ATSDR's Brownfields/Land Reuse Action Model was used to characterize existing conditions and highlight community revitalization efforts in the 20th Street Corridor, especially as they relate to human health. The City of Joplin, state and private initiatives, as well as federal agencies worked together to improve Joplin's infrastructure, environment, and its economy. They used the ATSDR Brownfields/Land Reuse Action Model to organize these efforts into one framework that incorporates health themes and enables planning, avoids duplication of effort, and provides dataset access. In addition, during community meetings in June 2013, 135 community members participated in a voluntary health engagement activity that linked design characteristics to health. Participants provided their three top choices from a list of healthy community design ideas. This project is an example of the opportunities available through ATSDR's Brownfields/Land Reuse Health Program to turn brownfield sites into economically sustainable, safe, and healthy places for everyone to enjoy.

Department of Health and Human Services—National Institute of Environmental Health Sciences

The mission of the National Institute of Environmental Health Sciences (NIEHS) is to discover how the environment affects people to promote healthier lives. NIEHS's The Environmental Career Worker Training Program (ECWTP), formerly the Minority Worker Training Program (MWTP), focuses on delivering comprehensive training to increase the number of disadvantaged and underrepresented workers in areas such as environmental restoration, construction, hazardous materials/waste handling, and emergency response. Since 1995, the ECWTP has provided pre-employment and health and safety training to approximately 12,000 people from underserved communities nationwide. ECWTP assists communities in developing a more comprehensive training program to foster economic and environmental restoration of brownfields.

CASE: Arizona State University. NIEHS's Worker Training Program (WTP) supports training and outreach to underserved and rural communities. Arizona State University (ASU), part of the Western Region Universities Consortium, offered courses to Native Americans in New Mexico and Arizona, as part of a program coordinated with the U.S. Department of the Interior Bureau of Indian Affairs (BIA), through the Navajo Region Division of Environmental and Safety Management. In 2017, ASU trained 467 Native American workers in 20 courses for the BIA. ASU is the only provider of Hazardous Waste Operations and Emergency Response training, as well as other key hazardous materials courses, for BIA in the region.

Department of Health and Human Services—Office of Community Services

The Office of Community Services (OCS) works in partnership with states, communities, and other agencies to address the economic and social services needs of the urban and rural poor at the local level by providing grant monies and technical assistance to these organizations. OCS provides grants to community development corporations and community action agencies to increase the capacity of individuals and families to become self-sufficient and to revitalize communities. Brownfield projects with a job creation focus may want to explore the following OCS funding opportunities.

CASE: Bartlett Station, Roxbury, MA. Bartlett Station is a major development project on a former brownfield site located in the heart of one of most impoverished neighborhoods in Roxbury, Massachusetts. One component of this project is the build-out of a new 86,000-square-foot building with 12,150 square feet of ground-floor retail space, funded through a $488,000 Office of Community Services Community Economic Development (CED) grant to Nuestra Comunidad Development Corporation, along with a variety of other federal, state, local, and private funding sources. The development project is revitalizing a low-income neighborhood by replacing a vacant, blighted property with new mixed-income rental housing and a quality grocery store, Good Food Market, which will provide needed goods and services. The commercial growth and expansion of this once-vacant site also is creating full-time jobs with living wages and benefits for members of the community.

Department of Housing and Urban Development

The overall mission of the U.S. Department of Housing and Urban Development (HUD) is to create strong, sustainable, inclusive communities and quality affordable homes for all. HUD has several brownfield applicable programs: Community Development Block Grant Program (includes the Entitlement Communities Program and several non-entitlement communities' programs); Indian Community Development Block Grant (ICDBG) Program; Section 108 Loan Guarantee Program; and Lead-Based Paint Hazard Reduction (LHR) Grant Program.

CASE: Sun Valley Homes, Denver, CO. The Housing Authority of the City and County of Denver, and the City and County of Denver were awarded a $30 million FY 2016 HUD Choice Neighborhoods Implementation Grant for the Sun

Valley neighborhood—Sun Valley EcoDistrict. Sun Valley was one of the neighborhoods addressed by the South Platte River corridor study under a 2010 EPA Brownfields Area Wide Planning Grant. To support the goal of implementing sustainable redevelopment solutions, Denver and the Denver Housing Authority also received land revitalization technical assistance from EPA to identify green stormwater management alternatives that were incorporated into the Sun Valley Homes master plan. A new light rail station was completed in 2013 and now connects the Sun Valley to downtown and the surrounding region. Local partners plan to build 750 new, mixed-income housing units; create new open space; and increase opportunities for local businesses, and access to quality jobs and education to residents. In the northern part of the neighborhood, the Denver Broncos plan to construct a $351 million Entertainment District with retail, commercial, and residential developments. The city also continues to invest in the neighborhood's light industrial area to attract new businesses.

Department of the Interior—National Park Service

The National Park Service (NPS) preserves natural and cultural resources, and manages the National Park System for the enjoyment, education, and inspiration of this generation and future generations. The NPS cooperates with partners to extend the benefits of natural and cultural resource conservation and outdoor recreation throughout this country and the world.

CASE: Comiskey Park, Dubuque, IA. In 2013, Dubuque was awarded an EPA brownfields assessment grant to begin cleanup efforts at polluted sites near Comiskey Park, named after a baseball great who played for the Dubuque Rabbits on a former baseball field at this location during the 1879–1882 seasons. Comiskey Park is the only accessible outdoor space for Dubuque's historic Washington and North End neighborhoods. These neighborhoods have older building stock, mixed-density commercial and residential development, and a diverse multi-ethnic population, most of whom have low and moderate incomes. Through its brownfields assessment work, the city was able to identify properties for remediation and reuse. In 2017, the city also secured a $508,000 grant from the National Park Service's Outdoor Recreation Legacy Partnership program to purchase, remediate, and develop an adjacent 1.95-acre brownfield parcel to expand Comiskey Park for recreational and green infrastructure uses. Improved recreational opportunities at Comiskey Park also will support mixed-use neighborhood redevelopment initiatives identified during Dubuque's brownfields assessment efforts.

Department of the Interior—Office of Surface Mining Reclamation and Enforcement

The mission of the Department of the Interior's Office of Surface Mining Reclamation and Enforcement (OSMRE) is to ensure that coal mines are operated in a manner that protects citizens and the environment during mining, the land is restored to beneficial use following mining, and the effects of past mining are mitigated by aggressively pursuing reclamation of abandoned coal mines. Supports local governments in the assessment, reclamation, and redevelopment of abandoned mine lands.

CASE: Pittsburgh Botanic Garden, Oakdale, PA. Funding from the OSMRE Abandoned Mine Land (AML) program has been used to reclaim historic coal AML sites located in Allegheny County, Pennsylvania, 10 miles west of Pittsburgh. With additional funding from other sources, the site has been developed as the Pittsburgh Botanic Garden, which opened to the public in 2014. Continued reclamation using OSMRE AML funds has addressed a dangerous highwall, mine subsidence, and acid mine drainage, and supported expansion of usable land in the garden to 465 acres. Current plans for the garden include a total of 18 distinct gardens, five diverse woodland experiences, an amphitheater for outdoor concerts and performances, an event center, and a botanic research facility when fully completed. The expansion is expected to create jobs, attract visitors, and generate millions of dollars in revenue.

Department of Labor

The U.S. Department of Labor (DOL) fosters, promotes, and develops the welfare of wage earners, job seekers, and retirees of the United States; improves working conditions; advances opportunities for profitable employment; and assures work-related benefits and rights. DOL administers a variety of federal labor laws, including those that guarantee workers' rights to safe and healthful working conditions, a minimum hourly wage and overtime pay, and freedom from employment discrimination. DOL's Employment and Training Administration (ETA) does not execute a specific brownfields initiative, its mission and discretionary grant investments often complement and support local redevelopment efforts that require workers who are trained and skilled to handle environmental cleanup and sustainable redevelopment of Brownfields.

CASE: City of Springfield, MO. The Missouri Job Center—Ozarks Region, in partnership with the City of Springfield, utilized funding from the Department of Labor in conjunction with EPA Environmental Workforce Development and Job Training funds to provide additional training to graduates of the city's "Green for Greene" job training program. By braiding these two resources, program graduates can obtain a Class A Commercial Driver's License, which is an employer valued certification, in combination with 13 other certifications offered through the program. The certifications included are: 40-Hour HAZWOPER, OSHA 10-Hour Construction, Asbestos Worker/Handler, Lead/Mold Abatement, Lead RRP, Confined Space, Trenching/ Excavation, Flagger, Silica, Forklift, Bloodborne Pathogens, and First Aid/CPR. With the co-enrollment, the Missouri Job Center is also able to provide supportive services to eliminate barriers and increase retention. Most recently, the Center leveraged DOL funds to provide wages to youth eligible program participants during the training. These wages allowed participants experiencing financial hardships the opportunity to participate, complete the program, and excel. To date, 64 graduates have successfully completed the program, earning an average hourly wage of $15.25.

Department of Transportation—Federal Highway Administration

The Federal Highway Administration (FHWA) works to ensure that America's roads and highways continue to be safe and technologically up to date. It provides financial and technical support to state, local, and tribal governments for constructing, improving, and preserving America's highway system. Encourages the appropriate consideration of brownfield in transportation planning, FHWA's National Environmental Policy Act (NEPA) process, and state-related project development process.

CASE: Grays Ferry Crescent, Philadelphia, PA. The U.S. Department of Transportation (DOT), along with the City of Philadelphia; the Pennsylvania Departments of Environmental Protection, Community and Economic Development, and Conservation and Natural Resources; the Delaware Valley Regional Planning Commission; and several other local organizations partnered on a $2 million project to clean up and redevelop a swath of brownfields along the Schuylkill River into an extension of the Schuylkill Banks Trail and Greenway. The cleanup of contamination, including metals associated with pigments and paint-making, began in August 2008. Construction on the trails began in March 2010. The project created a 3,700-foot-long bicycle and pedestrian trail, plus several walking trails that total an additional 1,600 feet. Funding from the DOT Federal Highway Administration's Congestion Mitigation and Air Quality Improvement Program was used to support several priority projects for the Pennsylvania Region identified by the Delaware Valley Regional Planning Commission (DVRPC). This funding included $400,000 for the creation of a separated two-way bike lane on the Grays Ferry Bridge and nearby streets, which connects the Grays Ferry Crescent section of the Schuylkill River Trail to the entrance of Bartram's Garden; and $250,000 for the Schuylkill River Development Corporation for an additional 1,200 feet of trail along the Schuylkill River as part of the effort to connect South Street and the Grays Ferry Crescent segment.

Department of Transportation—Federal Transit Administration

The Federal Transit Administration (FTA) supports the use of brownfields in transportation projects as part of efforts to improve communities through FTA transportation investments. Because many brownfields are in urban areas where transit is a viable transportation option, FTA programs can play a role in local efforts to find an economically productive use for a brownfield site. FTA funds are specifically designated for transit projects, but funds also may be used to assess or clean up any part of a brownfield site that is proposed for use as part of a transit project. FTA shares best practices and offers technical assistance to transit agencies working with other state and local government agencies on transit projects involving brownfield sites.

CASE: Conover Station, Conover, NC. Conover, North Carolina, transformed an abandoned manufacturing plant into a vibrant, mixed-use development and transit center. After the Broyhill Furniture plant closed, the town purchased the site in 2005. Despite the site's environmental challenges, Conover saw its potential and envisioned a redevelopment that also would preserve the Warlong Glove building as its centerpiece. The town used EPA brownfields grants to assess and clean up the site, along with an EPA loan through the Land of Sky Regional Council's brownfields revolving loan fund. Grants from the Federal Transit Administration and the Clean Water Management Trust also contributed to the $4.4 million project—the largest new construction in downtown Conover in several decades. Today, the 6.8-acre former brownfield is the site of Conover Station, a multi-modal transportation hub for trains, buses, and cabs that also houses a library, computer lab, and coffee shop. In 2012, the Manufacturing Solutions Center opened a state-of-the-art, 30,000-square-foot center adjacent to the Warlong Glove building, to promote job creation in the region. A 40,000-square-foot commercial building housing a large fitness center opened on the site in late 2015. Soon the Conover Station site also will include a public park with walking trails, a stormwater pond, and playground.

Federal Housing Finance Agency

The Federal Housing Finance Agency (FHFA)'s FHLBank community development programs include the Affordable Housing Program (AHP), the Community Investment Program (CIP), and the Community Investment Cash Advances (CICA) program. The AHP is a housing program, while the CIP can be used both for housing and for targeted community development. The CICA program is used only for targeted community development. Although these programs were not designed exclusively for brownfield development or tax credits, they can be used to help finance these types of projects. Each FHLBank offers the AHP, CIP, and CICA programs.

CASE: Station Center, Union City, CA. The Federal Home Loan Bank of San Francisco was one of the funding sources for development of Station Center, a 157-unit mixed-use, affordable apartment complex built on a former brownfield in the East Bay town of Union City outside of San Francisco. The complex, which was certified LEED Platinum, incorporates a variety of energy-efficient features, and includes 8,600 square feet of commercial space at street level, along with a playground, fitness center, community rooms, and garden plots for residents. Station Center is a central feature in Union City's vision to revitalize the city by creating Station District, a new city center with housing, parks, and retail near public transportation, and jobs for its residents. The centrally located site between two rail lines was an underused brownfield that formerly housed the Pacific State Steel Corporation and PG&E Pipeyard. Other funding sources for the project included the Redevelopment Agency of the City of Union City, Housing Authority of the County of Alameda, California Community Reinvestment Corporation, California Tax Credit Allocation Committee, and private banks.

General Services Administration

The General Services Administration (GSA) leverages the buying power of the federal government to acquire the best value for taxpayers and its federal customers. GSA works with federal landholding agencies to review and identify surplus federally owned brownfields. It seeks to redeploy these brownfields in close coordination with local community planning objectives. GSA serves as the "honest broker" in returning these properties to productive use.

CASE: Twin Cities Army Ammunition Plant, Arden Hills, MN. GSA used its brownfields expertise to redeploy 543 acres of the former Twin Cities Army Ammunition Plant (TCAAP). TCAAP was used for small arms ammunition production dating back to World War II. Due to extensive soil and groundwater contamination, the site was listed on the National Priorities List (NPL) in 1983. GSA worked with the U.S. Army to identify a portion of TCAAP as excess to the Army. Through close coordination with the

City of Arden Hills and Ramsey County, GSA developed a real estate strategy for reuse of two parcels in line with community redevelopment objectives and property remediation needs. The first transfer of 116 acres created a public park and wildlife corridor. GSA structured a negotiated sale to Ramsey County to expedite site remediation and redevelopment of the 427-acre second parcel. Fee transfer of the property to Ramsey County occurred after the soil remediation was completed in 2015. The redevelopment of the site will include a mix of commercial, residential, light industrial and other uses and is expected to be a catalyst for economic development in the region.

National Endowment for the Arts

Established by Congress in 1965, the National Endowment for the Arts (NEA) is the independent federal agency whose funding and support gives Americans the opportunity to participate in the arts, exercise their imaginations, and develop their creative capacities. NEA encourages livability by addressing community priorities such as public safety, health, blight and vacancy, environment, job creation, equity, local business development, civic participation, and community cohesion.

CASE: Ripple Project, Martin County, FL. In 2015, Martin County, Florida, received the second of two NEA Our Town grants to support the Ripple Eco-Art Project. The project combines interactive landscapes, green infrastructure, and art features to mitigate the water quality impacts of human use and stormwater runoff pollution along the St. Lucie River waterfront in the historic Old Palm City area. By holding water onsite in artistically designed green infrastructure features, the Ripple project reduces the amount of runoff generated during a rainstorm, alleviating erosion, and habitat damage. In addition, the project will filter out pollutants such as oil, bacteria, sediment, and nutrients as the collected water seeps through vegetation and soil. Martin County has prioritized Old Palm City's revitalization and wants to implement creative placemaking projects that will engage residents, showcase the historic community, and protect the polluted St. Lucie River. The Our Town project, which brings the arts and sciences together through community engagement and design, will serve as a model for future Martin County capital development efforts.

Small Business Administration

The U.S. Small Business Administration (SBA) recognizes that small business is critical to the nation's economic recovery and strength, to building America's future, and to helping the United States compete in today's global marketplace. The SBA encourages the redevelopment of brownfields. SBA loan guarantees are available to small businesses interested in locating on revitalized brownfield. Typically, this occurs through the use of one or more of the following factors: (1) indemnification; (2) completed remediation; (3) "No Further Action" letter obtained; (4) "minimal contamination" achieved; (5) cleanup funds approved; (6) escrow account available; (7) groundwater contamination originating from another site; (8) a pledge of additional or substitute collateral; or (9) other factors, such as the existence of adequate environmental insurance.

CASE: Avondale Textile Mills, Graniteville, SC. In 2005, a freight train derailment just outside the Avondale Mills rocked the small, unincorporated city of Graniteville, in Aiken County, South Carolina. About 40 tons of chlorine vapor and liquid were released. The accident caused a public health emergency that required evacuation of 5,400 residents, killed 10 people, and left hundreds in respiratory distress. Damage to buildings and machinery from the accident caused the struggling Avondale Mills plant to close its doors after 161 years in operation, and at least 1,200 jobs were lost. Since then, the city and Aiken County have been working to revitalize Graniteville. Cleanup and redevelopment of 15 shuttered textile mills and a steam plant, including the Avondale Mills, are at the heart of the effort, which is expected to take up to 20 years to complete. A $1.278 million SBA Section 504 loan is a critical element of the nearly $29 million package of funding from various public and private sources that already has been assembled by Aiken County and its redevelopment partners for this massive effort. This includes $800,000 in brownfields assessment grants to conduct environmental site assessments and prepare the sites for remediation; and a $200,000 EPA Environmental Workforce Development and Jobs Training grant to train up to 60 local workers in environmental remediation jobs to help restore the closed mills across Graniteville and the surrounding area.

23. Brownfields Federal Tax Incentives and Credits*

U.S. ENVIRONMENTAL PROTECTION AGENCY

EPA's brownfield grants serve as seed funding—other funds are necessary for planning, assessment, cleanup and redevelopment. Effective brownfields redevelopment approaches often incorporate and leverage federal and state incentive and assistance programs to help provide the funding and financing needed to overcome brownfields redevelopment challenges.

The information in this article reflects the most recent reforms and extensions authorized by the Tax Cuts and Jobs Act of 2017 (P.L. 115–97), which became effective on January 1, 2018. [P.L. 115–97] P.L. 115–97 substantially changed the federal tax system, introducing permanent corporate tax cuts, along with individual changes, which are set to expire.

Opportunity Zones

The Tax Cuts and Jobs Act of 2017 created a new investment option for capital gains, "Qualified Opportunity Funds." Qualified Opportunity Funds (QOFs) promote investment in the development of real estate and businesses in "Qualified Opportunity Zones." Qualified Opportunity Zones (OZs) are census tracts of low-income and distressed communities designated by state governors and certified by the Department of Treasury. Investors who invest their capital gains in QOFs can defer and reduce their capital gains tax burdens. Given that there may be as much as $6.1 trillion in unrealized capital gains assets in the U.S., the Opportunity Funds investment option may represent a significant chance for communities to attract new capital for the cleanup and redevelopment of brownfields located in the 8,762 designated Opportunity Zones.

The Opportunity Zone law offers deferred taxes, then significant tax breaks, to a broad array of investors who deploy and hold their capital gains in businesses and capital improvement projects located in Qualified Opportunity Zones (QOZs). To realize preferential tax treatment, investors must place their capital gains into a Qualified Opportunity Fund. QOFs may be either a corporation or partnership established solely for the purpose of investing in QOZs, in exchange for an equity interest in that QOZ

---

*Public document originally published as U.S. Environmental Protection Agency (2019), "Federal Tax Incentives and Credits," in *2019 Brownfields Federal Programs Guide* (Washington, D.C.: EPA).

project. The program will allow investors to establish QOFs for a targeted area, or even a single-purpose project in a QOZ. These QOFs must hold at least 90 percent of their assets in QOZ property, which includes qualifying stock, partnership interest, or business property located within a QOZ.

Each state nominated a limited number of population census tracts to be designated as QOZs. A population census tract was eligible for designation as a QOZ if it satisfied the definition of "low-income community" (LIC) (which is the same as the federal definition for New Markets Tax Credit) or is contiguous with an LIC that is designated as a QOZ, and the median family income of the non–LIC tract does not exceed 125 percent of the median family income of that contiguous LIC QOZ. Opportunity Zones have now been designated in all 50 states, the District of Columbia, and five U.S. territories. To qualify as a QOZ property, assets must either have their "original use" in a QOZ; or the QOZ property must be "substantially improved" (which generally requires making investments with a cost at least equal to the asset's purchase price) within 30 months of the property's acquisition. During "substantially all" of the QOZ's holding period, substantially all use of such property must be in a QOZ.

CASE: Confluence Corridor, Glenwood Springs, CO. The City of Glenwood Springs, Colorado, will leverage the federal designation of two downtown census tracts as Opportunity Zones to advance its EPA-funded Confluence Corridor Brownfields Area-Wide Plan (AWP). The AWP focuses on redeveloping vacant and contaminated properties into vibrant, mixed-use development at the confluence of the Roaring Fork River and Colorado River in the heart of downtown. Glenwood Springs used an EPA Region 8 Targeted Brownfields Assessment to understand the environmental conditions at its long-vacant, former wastewater treatment plant that occupies a prime site for redevelopment. The area-wide plan envisions a mix of more than 400,000 square feet of commercial, retail, and housing, along with a multi-modal transit center and riverfront recreational parks and nature areas within the Opportunity Zone boundary. The City of Glenwood Springs created a Glenwood Springs Opportunity Pitchbook highlighting shovel-ready and investment-ready projects in its Opportunity Zone brownfields; hosted forums with local investors, bankers, and developers to educate the community about the incentive; issued a request for proposals from developers of the Confluence Corridor that uses the Opportunity Zone designation as a key incentive; and is reaching out directly to Opportunity Fund managers about investing in the confluence Opportunity Zone brownfields.

New Markets Tax Credits

The New Markets Tax Credit (NMTC) program is designed to stimulate the economies of distressed urban and rural communities and create jobs in low-income communities by expanding the availability of credit, investment capital, and financial services. The NMTC program was created through the Community Renewal Act of 2000. The program is administered by the Community Development Financial Institutions (CDFI) Fund within the U.S. Department of the Treasury. Each year, tax credits are allocated through the CDFI Fund and distributed to qualified Community Development Entities (CDEs). CDEs include a range of for-profit and nonprofit organizations, such as banks, community development corporations, CDFIs, organizations that administer community development venture capital funds or community loan funds, small business development corporations, specialized small business investment companies, and others.

There are nearly 6,000 organizations certified as CDEs, including subsidiaries (CDE partners), and approximately 1,100 certified CDFIs. Since 2000, the CDFI Fund has completed 14 allocation rounds and made 1,105 awards totaling $54 billion in tax allocation authority. Each federal dollar put in the program has leveraged over $8 in private investments. Demand for the tax credits has remained high since the program's inception, particularly as CDFI allocations dropped from $7 billion in 2015 to just half of that in the 2017 round. In the 2017 round, 230 applicants requested a total of $16.2 billion in NMTC Allocation Authority, of which 73 CDEs received $3.5 billion in NMTC Allocation Authority (or 32 percent of the total applicant pool).

NMTCs can be a viable option for many brownfields redevelopment projects, given the typical priorities and target investments of NMTC allocation recipients. Given their focus on distressed areas, which often include blighted and abandoned buildings, NMTCs have significant potential to support brownfields projects. Brownfields developers can approach existing CDEs to help fund their projects or, in certain circumstances, brownfields developers can consider applying for CDE certification themselves.

CASE: Hazelwood Green, Pittsburgh, PA. In the Hazelwood neighborhood on the banks of the Monongahela River, Pittsburgh's last steel plant closed in 1998 after 130 years of operation as the Hazelwood Coke Works, and later as Jones & Laughlin Steel and then LTV Steel. The trio of Pittsburgh's philanthropic foundations—R.K. Mellon, the Heinz Endowment, and the Claude Worthington Benedum Foundation—purchased the 178-acre site in 2002 under the ownership group Almono LP and spent a generation remediating and preparing the site for redevelopment. They used a range of resources, including EPA Brownfields Grants. In 2017, Almono re-launched the "Hazelwood Green" project on the site, which is planned approximately 8 million square feet of mixed-use, transit-oriented development that is in the process of documentation for LEED Neighborhood Development. The project is designed to meet ambitious goals for livability, neighborhood wellness, and community empowerment.

Owned by Regional Industrial Development Corporation (RIDC), the property's historic Mill 19 building is slated to become a one-of-a-kind technology and advanced manufacturing hub launched by Carnegie Mellon University, with 218,000 square feet of net-zero energy, mixed development that will include the Advanced Robotics for Manufacturing (ARM) Institute, the Manufacturing Futures Initiative, and the Catalyst Connection nonprofit manufacturing assistance center. It also will employ innovative new technologies, including robotics, 3-D printing, and machine learning. Restoration and redevelopment of the Mill 19 building cost $46.6 million. The Urban Redevelopment Authority of Pittsburgh, a public agency that runs a New Markets Tax Credit entity named Pittsburgh Urban Initiatives, allocated $6 million in NMTC equity resources to Mill 19 to complete the capital stack for the project.

Low-Income Housing Tax Credits

Low-Income Housing Tax Credits (LIHTCs) were created under the Tax Reform Act of 1986 to provide incentives for the use of private equity in the development of affordable housing for low-income Americans. These credits are intended to ensure an attractive minimum rate of return on investments in low-income housing. LIHTCs may be used as part of a brownfields financing package if affordable rental housing is part of a project. The credits are used successfully in many states as part of mixed-income housing developments and as infill projects on brownfields sites. The program is administered at the state level by state housing finance authorities. Each state receives an allocation of federal tax credits determined by a formula based on its population.

Each state can issue LIHTC tax-exempt bonds up to its ceiling. These bonds are then used to attract investment capital for the development of low-income housing. Development capital is raised by a private housing developer, often working closely with a local government housing authority, to "syndicate" the credit to an investor or a group of investors. This is done by selling the rights to future tax credits in exchange for upfront cash. As these credits are syndicated, developers obtain the equity capital necessary to build or rehabilitate structures for low-income housing.

The tax credit is paid to LIHTC investors annually over a 10-year period. The funds generated through syndication vary from market to market and from year to year because they are set by market price. Typically, prices range from the mid-$0.80s to low-$0.90s per $1.00 tax credit under normal economic conditions.

State-Administered Program: State housing agencies administer the LIHTC program by reviewing tax credit applications submitted by developers and then allocating the credits. This process allows each state to set its own priorities and address its specific housing goals.

- Some states consider infill, vacant property reclamation, and mixed use as priorities in their allocation plans, which can make brownfield sites more attractive to housing developers as they compete for LIHTC allocations.
- Some states promote projects located in specific geographic areas or distressed rural or urban areas, which may encourage investment in brownfields.

The Housing and Economic Recovery Act of 2008 (HERA) required states to include energy-efficient construction as an allocation priority. As a result, to the extent that brownfields housing projects include "green" technologies and sustainable development provisions, they may become more attractive to developers seeking LIHTCs. As an IRS requirement, projects that serve the lowest-income tenants and guarantee low-rent affordability for the longest time-period are given priority. Owners must keep the rental units available to low-income tenants for at least 30 years after completion of the project. Both for-profit and nonprofit brownfields developers can use LIHTCs to help finance low-income housing projects. The tax credit program can be used either to construct new buildings or to rehabilitate existing buildings. All activities associated with the development of housing, including cleanup and demolition, can be claimed as expenses associated with the development of low-income housing for the purposes of claiming the low-income housing tax credit.

Over the past 20 years, states received significant levels of LIHTC allocations that supported the development of many housing units. The program continues to provide nearly $8 billion annually in budget authority to issue tax credits. Almost all new affordable multifamily construction undertaken since 2000 received a subsidy under this program. Some of the projects were conducted on brownfield sites, but the full potential for the development of low-income housing on brownfield sites is yet unrealized.

CASE: Soundview Landing, Norwalk, CT. As the oldest public housing complex in the state of Connecticut, Washington Village (located on Norwalk Harbor on the Long Island Sound) was in severe deterioration and distress even before Superstorm Sandy flooded the complex. Many low-income families were displaced, and the flood caused further damage to the troubled complex, including black mold and other problems. Located in a low-income neighborhood but poised for revitalization because of its waterfront location, proximity to the South Norwalk Multimodal Train Station, and the emerging renewal of the overall area, Washington Village is now transformed into "Soundview Landing." Soundview Landing is the result of years of community-based planning by the City of Norwalk Redevelopment Agency and its partners, who used HUD Choice Neighborhood Planning Grant resources to create a "Neighborhood Transformation Plan" for the housing complex and its surrounding area. This was followed by a $30 million HUD Choice Neighborhood implementation grant to help finance the redevelopment, along with resources leveraged from the HUD Disaster Resilience program, EPA's Brownfields Program, the State of Connecticut, and local and private sector sources.

A key to financing the project was the allocation of $3,763,750 to the project in two rounds of federal Low-Income Housing Tax Credits from the Connecticut Housing Finance Authority. This enabled leveraging of more than $40 million in private equity. The private developer for the property, which partnered with the Norwalk Housing Authority to conduct this project, was able to leverage those LIHTC funds with state bonds, $8.8 million in brownfields funds provided by the State of Connecticut and the Federal Home Loan Bank of Boston, federal grants, and private equity and debt. The development transformed the blighted housing into a $144 million, mixed-income project designed to ensure storm resiliency from future storms. Soundview Landing has 165 housing units, including 82 public housing units, 41 affordable LIHTC and workforce housing units, 42 market-rate units, and 273 apartment units, all served by a new public park, community gardens, and a specially designed public road to ensure dry egress for residents during storm events.

Historic Rehabilitation Tax Credits

Historic rehabilitation tax credits were adopted by Congress to discourage unnecessary demolition of sound older buildings and to slow the loss of businesses from older urban areas. These tax credits encourage private investment in the cleanup and rehabilitation of historical properties. The National Park Service administers the program in partnership with the Internal Revenue Service (IRS) and State Historic Preservation Offices (SHPOs). Nearly 1.6 million historic buildings are in or contribute to historic districts listed in the National Register of Historic Places, with many more added each year. The NPS estimates that 20 percent of these buildings qualify as income-producing. The historic rehabilitation tax credit is well-suited for packaging with other economic development grant and loan programs. Using the historic preservation tax credit generally does not preclude the use of other federal, state, tribal or local funding sources or other programs designed to encourage rehabilitation. Because historic rehabilitation tax credits focus on older buildings, they are an ideal brownfields financing tool. Their use at brownfields properties is rapidly accelerating across the country. The tax credits help attract redevelopment capital to many projects in blighted and ignored areas not ordinarily considered for investment. These projects encompass a wide range of properties and project types, including offices, hotels, retail stores, warehouses, factories, and rental housing.

CASE: Historic Millwork District, Dubuque, IA. Iowa's oldest city, Dubuque, traditionally prospered on logging, mill working, and manufacturing. Those industries declined and vanished over several decades, leaving more than one million square feet of vacant, former-factory space and many brownfields within Dubuque's Millwork District. The Millwork District and its 19 contributing industrial buildings were added to the National Register of Historic Places in 2008. Between 2002 and 2016, the Dubuque community leveraged $34 million in Federal Historic Tax Credits and $14 million in State of Iowa Historic Tax Credits to complete the rehabilitation and reuse of its historic assets. The effort, which cost more than $202 million, included the redevelopment of the Novelty Iron Works building; the Rouse, Dean & Company foundry; the Power Plant building; and the Dubuque Linseed Oil Paint Company. With revitalization completed in 2012, the historic Millwork District now employs 2,500 workers and includes one million square feet of mixed-use development and entertainment spaces heated by an innovative district energy system.

Energy Efficiency and Renewable Energy

As communities become more concerned about the economic and environmental impacts of the use of fossil fuels and energy waste, renewable energy technologies are expected to play a greater role in meeting future electricity demand. The U.S. Energy Information Administration estimates that renewable-generated electricity will account for 31 percent of total U.S. electricity generation in 2050. Technology innovation, reduced costs, federal tax credits, loan and grant programs, and state requirements will help facilitate this growth.

Identifying and using land in areas that are amenable to high-quality renewable energy alternatives will be an essential component to developing new renewable energy sources. EPA screened more than 80,000 potentially contaminated sites and solid waste landfill covering nearly 43 million acres across the United States for suitability to renewable energy generation facilities. Tracked sites include brownfields Superfund sites, Resource Conservation and Recovery Act (RCRA) sites, abandoned mine lands, and landfills. Maps depicting the locations of these EPA-tracked sites and their potential for supporting renewable energy generation can be found at: https://www.epa.gov/re-powering/re-powering-mapper. These maps enable users to view screening results for various renewable energy technologies at each site. Through coordination and partnerships among federal, state, tribal, and other government agencies, as well as utilities, communities, and the private sector, new renewable energy facilities may be developed on many potentially contaminated properties.

Combining energy incentives with contaminated land cleanup incentives can allow investors and communities to create economically viable, nonpolluting, renewable energy redevelopment projects on brownfields particularly sites where local economic conditions prohibit more conventional reuse of the site. Over the past decade, several statutes created, expanded, or extended incentive programs such as tax incentives, loans, grants, and loan guarantees to encourage renewable energy generation and energy efficiency projects. This section contains information about the federal tax incentives that are available to potential developers considering the siting of renewable energy generation and energy efficiency projects on brownfields.

CASE: Annapolis Energy Park, Annapolis, MD. The 16.8-megawatt Annapolis Renewable Energy Park broke ground in 2017. When complete, it will be the largest solar project installed on a closed landfill in the United States. This solar facility has the capacity to generate over 20,000 MWh of clean electricity per year on an 80-acre former city landfill resulting in more than $5 million in energy revenues for the power offtake users of the facility: the City of Annapolis, Anne Arundel County, and Anne Arundel County Public Schools. As a capped landfill with a significant elevation and no tree cover, the property was an ideal location for a solar field. State officials report that the solar field will help Maryland electric service providers meet the state requirement that they obtain 25 percent of power from renewable sources by the year 2020. The solar park was built by a private sector developer, BQ Energy, under a land-lease arrangement with the City of Annapolis. BQ Energy was able to take a federal Investment Tax Credit covering 30 percent of eligible capital project costs, allowing the company to pass a lower-cost energy supply to the public parties taking the energy output.

24. Leveraging

*Harbor Point in Stamford, Connecticut**

U.S. Environmental Protection Agency

Located along the Long Island Sound, Stamford (population 128,278) is the third largest city in Connecticut. The South End waterfront was Stamford's industrial area since the 1600s. In the 20th century, Stamford became a thriving neighbor of New York City and today the city boasts one of the mightiest concentrations of corporations in the nation.

Nevertheless, Stamford struggles with blight, pockets of severe poverty, and many long-vacant brownfields. The city's key transportation assets—Interstate 95 and its location along Amtrak's busy Northeast Corridor linking Boston, New York, and Washington, D.C.—also have posed a long-time challenge for the South End, isolating about 350 acres in the South End from downtown and the rest of the city. The waterfront area had limited accessibility from the interstate and was marked with contaminated and vacant properties, compounding its economic distress.

Under the leadership of former Mayor Dannel Malloy, a team of public and private entities set their sights on revitalization of Stamford's South End. They focused on cleaning up clusters of brownfields to transform the waterfront into a vibrant and attractive residential, commercial, and mixed-use development. Another critical goal was to reconfigure the connection between Interstate 95 and the South End to make the area more accessible to commuters and residents, allowing travelers to better utilize the Stamford Intermodal Transportation Center, a hub for regional train, bus, and vehicle traffic.

The revitalization of the South End got underway in 1997, when Stamford was designated an EPA Brownfields Showcase Community. This enabled the city to leverage resources from the 20 federal agencies participating in the Showcase Community initiative. Stamford subsequently won two EPA Brownfields Assessment grants, a Brownfields Revolving Loan Fund (RLF) grant, a Brownfields Cleanup grant, and a Brownfields Job Training grant—all of which focused on the revitalization of the South End waterfront. In fact, Stamford was the first community in the nation to put a Brownfields Revolving Loan Fund into action, transforming a former waterfront fueling depot into a charming waterfront residential village.

---

*Public document originally published as U.S. Environmental Protection Agency, "Leveraging Case Study: Harbor Point in Stamford, Connecticut." *Setting the Stage for Leveraging Resources for Brownfields Revitalization*, https://www.epa.gov/brownfields/setting-stage-leveraging-resources-brownfields-revitalization (September 2019).

Over the next several years, Stamford built upon the initial support from EPA's Brownfields program by leveraging more than $250 million in public funding for revitalization and infrastructure upgrades from the following sources:

- U.S. Department of Transportation: Stamford secured more than $215 million from federal and state transportation agencies to rebuild and improve the transportation network around its redeveloped brownfields neighborhoods. This includes $10.5 million from DOT in Transportation Investment Generating Economic Recovery (TIGER) grants and $19 million in Federal Transit Administration (FTA) Bus Livability Discretionary Grant funding to upgrade its Intermodal Transit Center.
- Revamping and modernizing outdated roadways and regional transit has been essential to revitalizing the South End. With additional federal and state support, the Connecticut Department of Transportation is working with Stamford to rebuild a constrained rail underpass that restricts downtown access to the South End's main corridor. Stamford also secured about $75 million through the FTA's New Starts and Bus and Bus Facilities grant programs, the Federal Highway Administration's (FHWA) Job Access and Reverse Commute and Intelligent Transportation Systems grant programs, and other funding sources for the Stamford Urban Transitway, a new complete-street corridor providing access to the brownfields area and the Intermodal Transportation Center. FHWA also provided $1.1 million to improve streetscapes in the Waterside neighborhood and reconstruct the West Main Street pedestrian bridge connecting distressed areas of the community to the Intermodal Transportation Center.
- U.S. Department of Housing and Urban Development: Stamford obtained $6.4 million from HUD's Block Grant Disaster Recovery program allocation to the State of Connecticut. This funding supported replacement of an elderly-housing property and was used to supplement an additional $8.1 million in public and private money for construction of a new elderly home and support services facility. Stamford also obtained $850,000 from HUD's Healthy Homes Program.
- U.S. Department of Commerce: In 2013, Stamford secured $800,000 from the Department of Commerce's Economic Development Administration (EDA) for reconstructing the Dyke Lane Pumping Station, which was damaged by flooding. EDA's disaster relief funding will improve flood control and help protect the South End from the impacts of climate change and natural disasters.

Stamford took the following key steps to increase its effectiveness leveraging funding for revitalization of the South End:

- Building a Project Team Through Local Leadership: At the outset of this project, Mayor Malloy convened a multi-agency task force and designated a point-person for brownfields revitalization, which helped make brownfields redevelopment a city priority. This level of commitment continued under Stamford's next mayor, as did the involvement of key community leaders.
- Establishing the South End as a Priority: As factories were closing in the South End, the city and private developers assessed opportunities along the waterfront. As a result, revitalization of the South End soon became a driving force and the city's top revitalization priority, a status that was maintained for two decades.

- Seeking External Support: Stamford realized that the city could not achieve the massive revitalization effort on its own. The city used its EPA Brownfields Showcase Community designation as an opening to approach other federal agencies that support revitalization and brownfields redevelopment. As a result, Stamford cultivated and has maintained strong relationships with state and federal agencies.
- Engaging the Community: Stamford identified additional community needs and engaged the community in waterfront revitalization plans through many community meetings. The city formed a "swat team" of business leaders, community groups, landowners, and other stakeholders to assess and promote redevelopment potential.
- Tackling the Redevelopment Piece by Piece: Over the course of two decades, Stamford built the transportation infrastructure necessary to open up brownfields areas and attract private investment to the South End. The city worked through projects one phase at a time, recognizing that it was impossible to acquire all the necessary funding at one time. Instead, Stamford tackled parts of each project one by one and sought funding for the along the way for critical next steps in the overall transportation and infrastructure project. This approach enabled the city to make steady progress toward achieving its ambitious goals. The strategy also helped spark major private-sector investment in the area.
- Committing Local Matching-Share Funding: Stamford learned early that it was critical to have "skin in the game" and to offer local matching funds to successfully leverage additional funding for its revitalization effort. The city's annual capital budgets included money designated to serve as its local match for various state and federal grants. The city also established a TIF district that provided $186 million in investment for public infrastructure upgrades, which complemented the local, state, and federal funding already being acquired.
- Creating Briefing Sheets and Other Compelling Project Communication Materials: Throughout the South End revitalization process, Stamford created and updated communications materials that helped the city make its case to potential funders and private investors, and to build support among elected representatives and other stakeholders whose support was critical. In addition to briefing sheets, these materials included project progress reports, project maps, and PowerPoint presentations. These compelling communications materials helped potential funders and investors understand Stamford's short- and long-term goals and enabled the city to build support for specific funding requests and other related initiatives.
- Celebrating Success: Stamford's leaders made sure to celebrate progress at each step of the long revitalization process. The city celebrated both large and small accomplishments along the way with groundbreakings, ribbon-cuttings, site tours for state and federal officials, and community celebrations. They also paid attention to media outreach and sent thank you notes to funders and supporters along the way.

The public funding that began with support from EPA's Brownfields program has leveraged $5 billion in private-sector investment. Investments include the Harbor Point and Metro Green projects, which are LEED gold-certified, mixed-use, transit-oriented development projects that incorporate luxury living space along with affordable and workforce housing, food and retail, nightlife, parks, schools, and water-front activities.

Stamford's success is an example of how EPA Brownfields funding was critical to revitalization of a contaminated former industrial area into one of the most significant mixed-use developments in the nation.

25. Leveraging

North Port Revitalization in Dubuque, Iowa*

U.S. Environmental Protection Agency

Located on the banks of the Mississippi River near the borders of Wisconsin and Illinois, Dubuque is Iowa's oldest city and home to a population of 58,436. Though Dubuque was originally established as a fur-trading post and lead mining community, it later flourished as a manufacturing and meatpacking hub—a major artery for the Midwest United States through its railroad and shipping connections for commercial and industrial use. Unfortunately, the 1980s brought significant challenges due to the collapse of the farm economy, resulting in high unemployment and a loss of more than 10 percent of Dubuque's population. The Dubuque Packing Company closed down and John Deere, the city's largest employer at the time, reduced its workforce by almost three-quarters. All told, Dubuque lost 10 percent of its population and had the highest unemployment (24 percent) in the nation.

In the 1990s, President Bill Clinton and the U.S. Department of Interior designated the Upper Mississippi River as an American Heritage River, which spurred Dubuque officials and residents to come together for a planning process to restore the city's connection with the Mississippi River. At that time, the 120-acre Port of Dubuque was plagued by environmental issues, undervalued property, a hodge-podge of heavy industrial uses, and many vacant brownfields. Residents and tourists alike were physically and psychologically disconnected from the river. In 2001, the City initiated a planning and design effort to craft a comprehensive, long-term vision for the Port. The City engaged local property owners, developers, and residents to gather input on the most appropriate plan and best strategies for advancing the area. Based upon feedback and collaboration across sectors, the Dubuque City Council adopted the 2002 Port of Dubuque Master Plan.

Dubuque's "North Port" revitalization was launched with EPA Brownfields Assessment and Cleanup grants awarded to the city in 2002 and 2003. Bordering the Mississippi River, the area has been the home to shipbuilding and repair facilities, railroads, bulk petroleum and coal storage operations, food processing plants, farm machinery manufacturers, and lead mining activities since the early 1800s. These brownfield resources were key to unlocking the North Port's revitalization potential and instrumental to

---

*Public document originally published as U.S. Environmental Protection Agency, "Leveraging Case Study: North Port Revitalization in Dubuque, Iowa." *Setting the Stage for Leveraging Resources for Brownfields Revitalization*, https://www.epa.gov/brownfields/setting-stage-leveraging-resources-brownfields-revitalization (September 2019).

helping the city pivot from a declining former industrial town into a Midwest tourist destination. The 2002 Brownfields Assessment grant was used to conduct 12 Phase I and six Phase II environmental site assessments within the North Port. EPA Assessment funding also was used to develop cleanup plans, reuse plans, and leveraging strategies. The 2003 Brownfields Cleanup grant was used to clean up a petroleum plume within the Port of Dubuque that had contaminated soil and groundwater across several acres of prime riverfront property along the Mississippi River.

Dubuque has since leveraged the EPA Brownfields Assessment and Cleanup grants to secure public and private resources to further the community's goals. These grants were crucial in leveraging more than $800 million in public grants and private investment, including substantial federal and state funding:

- **U.S. Department of Commerce**: Dubuque prepared land and upgraded infrastructure using grant funding from the U.S. Department of Commerce, Economic Development Administration's (EDA) Public Works grant program. In 2013, Dubuque was awarded a $1.2 million EDA Disaster Relief Grant to daylight the Bee Branch Creek and prevent flooding in the neighborhood adjacent to the Port.
- **U.S. Department of Transportation**: Dubuque leveraged over $16 million in U.S. Department of Transportation funding including a TIGER grant, Transportation Enhancement grant and Transportation, Community, and System Preservation (TCSP) grant from DOT's Federal Highway Administration(FHWA), and the Federal Transit Administration's State of Good Repair grant for a complete street, pedestrian, and riverfront boardwalk network to support the mixed-use development of the North Port revitalization, historic train depot and freight house restoration projects, and the construction of a new intermodal facility that will serve the Port redevelopment.
- **U.S. Department of Housing and Urban Development**: Dubuque secured $800,000 in grant funding from the U.S. Department of Housing and Urban Development for the Riverfront Discovery Center at the North Port redevelopment.
- **U.S. Department of Interior**: Dubuque secured over $1 million from the National Fish and Wildlife Service and the National Park Service to support the Riverfront Development Center and other activities at the Port area.
- **U.S. Department of Health and Human Services**: Dubuque leveraged $3 million in grant funds from HHS for the development of exhibits at the River Discovery Center in the North Port revitalization area.
- **National Endowment for the Humanities**: Dubuque secured more than $1 million in grants for the Port Discovery Center and other cultural activities in the North Port area.
- **Institute for Museum and Library Services**: IMLA provided Dubuque more than $100,000 to support planning for this riverfront restoration.
- **U.S. EPA**: EPA selected Dubuque to receive Building Blocks technical assistance in 2013 to create plans and strategies for using green infrastructure to manage stormwater and protect the water quality of the Mississippi and its tributaries.
- **State of Iowa**: Dubuque worked closely with the State of Iowa, and leveraged an impressive $48 million in grants from community tourism, "Vision Iowa," and

other state programs to support riverfront development, the Mississippi River Museum and Aquarium, and other key components of the North Port project.

To accomplish this leveraging for the Port revitalization, Dubuque organized and took several key steps to be effective:

- **Project Team with Local Leadership**: The City of Dubuque and Dubuque Area Chamber of Commerce partnered with the Dubuque County Historical Society, the local nonprofit organization, which led the nationally recognized $188 million America's River campaign. This team was closely supported by the Office of the Mayor, the Dubuque City Council, and "America's River Advisory Committee" composed of local, regional, and national river leaders, and a "4th Street Peninsula Working Group" formed for the project and including leaders from municipal departments and other stakeholders. Dubuque also designated a team to manage and coordinate this robust group of collaborators, including the assistant city manager, director of planning, city engineer, and others to assist in leading the effort.
- **North Port Established as a Priority**: Dubuque recognized that its overall strategy for resilience and revitalization depended upon reclaiming the historic asset that helped create the community but had been disconnected from the people—the Mississippi River. Dubuque used its national designation as an "American Heritage River" pilot community as an organizing force to establish priorities and, through that effort, the community identified the Port area as the place with the best geography and reuse potential. This led Dubuque to confirm the revitalization of North Port as a top community priority for focus, staff time, and funding.
- **Dubuque Engaged and Energized the Community**: The North Port brownfields revitalization was the culmination of the "Port of Dubuque Master Plan" process. The Master Plan grew from a ten-month, place-based community planning and design effort—launched with the support of federal resources—to craft a comprehensive, long-term vision and redevelopment concept for the 4th Street Peninsula and the South Ice Harbor. A variety of stakeholder and public participation opportunities were employed in the planning process that included monthly stakeholder luncheons, design workshops, site tours, regular committee meetings, city council work sessions and a public open house. Through this effort, the business community, citizens, key stakeholders, and elected leaders became champions for this initiative.
- **Tackling the Redevelopment Piece by Piece**: Dubuque's municipal and port staff identified the key components that would be necessary to trigger private-sector reinvestment at this deteriorated riverfront area. These included cleanup of a petroleum plume, demolition of obsolete buildings and structures, preparation of the land for redevelopment, stormwater management to protect the Mississippi River, design and construction of new transportation and pedestrian/bike networks, creation of public spaces and public art, reclaiming of the riverfront for public boardwalks, planning and construction of major tourism attractions, and other public improvements. Dubuque identified and secured resources, including local funding and external grants, to finance each phase of the various component projects involved in the overall development. Over time, success

built upon success, and the momentum of the redevelopment increased as the community and funders became more excited and certain about the prospects for redevelopment. This momentum culminated in major investments by the private sector, and the new North Port became a reality.
- **Committing Local Funding**: Dubuque enhanced its ability to leverage grants, private investment, and other external resources by committing its own local funding to the success of the project. Altogether, the City of Dubuque, the America's River campaign and private investors devoted more than $188 million to the project, including upfront investment in the visioning and planning of the Port Master Plan, funding for major infrastructure upgrades, and matches to state and federal grants. To date, nearly $800 million has been invested at the Port of Dubuque through the America's River campaign, private investment, and public infrastructure investment.
- **Establishing Compelling Materials**: Each year during the North Port revitalization and the seven-year America's River campaign, Dubuque created or updated its project materials for potential funders, elected representatives, and other targeted supporters. Project materials included briefing sheets, progress reports, and resource-roadmap matrices of grants that would be sought. These tools proved to be useful tools that allowed potential funders to understand Dubuque's short- and long-term funding strategies and helped them to respond to and support the initiative.
- **Dubuque Cultivated Strong Relationships with State and Federal Agency Officials**: Dubuque was committed to informing state and federal agency leadership and program managers about the needs, progress, and key next steps on the North Port revitalization. Local officials made repeated visits to the state capital, regional federal agency offices, and Washington, D.C., to brief officials on the North Port/ America's River project, worked very closely with the Iowa congressional delegation, and invited state and federal agency and elected officials to Dubuque to tour the site and better understand key needs.
- **Dubuque Celebrated Success!**: Dubuque made sure that its state and federal supporters, as well as the local community, were able to celebrate progress on the North Port/America's River revitalization. For example, when the Obama Administration launched the national Partnership for Sustainable Communities in Dubuque in 2009, they toured and were briefed on the Port revitalization activities, which helped Dubuque continue the resource-leveraging effort.

The initial EPA brownfields funding and the other resources that were leveraged from these early grants spurred additional public and private investment that made possible the development at North Port of the Grand River Conference and Education Center, River's Edge Plaza, Riverwalk, National Mississippi Museum and Aquarium, Alliant Amphitheater, Grand Harbor Resort and Waterpark, and Diamond Jo Casino.

Beyond the direct funding leveraged, these investments produced more than 700 jobs and created new recreational and entertainment attractions for community members and visitors, reinvigorating a depressed economy and community. Due to the innovative and exemplary use of its brownfields grants and resulting leverage and revitalization, the North Port project was awarded the Phoenix Award for EPA Region 7 in 2005.

Dubuque is poised to repeat the success at North Port by redeveloping the adjacent South Port. In 2013, Dubuque was awarded a $400,000 EPA Brownfields Assessment grant to conduct environmental investigations, assessments, and reuse planning at the 33-acre South Port area on the Mississippi River. Like North Port before its revitalization, South Port currently is an area of heavy industrial and port use that has experienced a steady decline over the past 40 years, leaving brownfields and vacant properties, some of which have been closed for decades. Dubuque's goal is to redevelop the South Port as a new downtown neighborhood where people can reconnect with the Mississippi River in a walkable, transit-oriented environment. The City also seeks to extend its Riverwalk from the North Port to the Mines of Spain Recreation Area.

Recently, the City partnered with the University of Iowa's "Iowa Initiative for Sustainable Communities" to engage residents and begin to identify reuse options for the South Port. In 2013, Reimagining the South Port of Dubuque study was released. This study recommended a variety of entertainment, recreational, commercial, retail, and other mixed-use development. Like with North Port, Dubuque has established a Steering Committee and brownfield project teams and has already begun to engage the community. Dubuque was very pleased when, in 2015, the EPA awarded Dubuque a Brownfields Area-Wide Planning grant to support the revitalization of South Port and is certain that this Area-Wide support will enable Dubuque to leverage even more public support and private investment in the future.

EPA Brownfields grants were the keys to unlocking the revitalization potential of Dubuque's Port area and were catalysts for the larger effort to transform Dubuque from a declining former industrial town into a Midwest tourist destination. EPA funding not only helped support development of major conference and event centers, plazas, museums, resorts, and casinos, but also led to the creation of the local jobs that are integral to the construction, operation, and servicing of the redevelopment and the expansion of the local economy.

26. Leveraging

Commerce Corridor in Ranson and Charles Town, West Virginia*

U.S. Environmental Protection Agency

Ranson and Charles Town (combined population, 10,000) are adjacent small cities in Jefferson County in the eastern panhandle of West Virginia, within a 90-minute drive of Washington, D.C. The Ranson/Charles Town area traditionally was the industrial epicenter of Jefferson County. The decline of America's manufacturing industry hit the community particularly hard-leaving many residents without jobs, diminishing the local tax base, and leaving significant brownfields behind that slowed economic growth and decreased residential and commercial property values. At least 15 brownfields impact the heart of the urban area along the 1.5-mile border between the two cities and the Evitts Run Creek, which traverses the community. In 1999, Ranson/ Charles Town launched an effort to turn this blighted and polluted corridor into a new "Commerce Corridor" with new downtown development and community park and recreation assets.

In 2001, EPA awarded the City of Ranson a Brownfields Assessment grant and kicked off the revitalization of the Commerce Corridor in a ceremony with EPA's Administrator. The cities obtained additional Brownfields Assessment grants in 2004 and 2006. These grants were used to conduct 20 environmental site assessments and to develop sophisticated brownfields reuse plans. In 2010, Ranson obtained an EPA Brownfields Area-Wide Planning grant that was used to engage key stakeholders in the process of creating a robust plan for revitalization, an infrastructure upgrade strategy, a highest-and-best-use analysis for key brownfield parcels, and a "Resource Roadmap" to identify sources of leveraged funding for the reuse and implementation of properties in the Commerce Corridor (See: www.ransonrenewed.com).

EPA awarded a Brownfields Cleanup grant to Ranson in 2011 to remediate a contaminated, closed brass foundry. Ranson and Charles Town also used a $900,000 EPA Brownfields Revolving Loan Fund (RLF) grant to address brownfields on Evitts Run Creek. RLF funding was used to clean up a particularly challenging manufactured gas facility that plagued the community for decades. RLF funds also were used to create the West Side Revitalization Master Plan that will guide the cleanup and reuse of

---

*Public document originally published as U.S. Environmental Protection Agency, "Leveraging Case Study: Commerce Corridor in Ranson and Charles Town, West Virginia." *Setting the Stage for Leveraging Resources for Brownfields Revitalization*, https://www.epa.gov/brownfields/setting-stage-leveraging-resources-brownfields-revitalization (September 2019).

blighted brownfields along the Evitts Run Creek. Reuse plans include creating a park, recreation areas, and an economic development zone in Charles Town's most distressed neighborhood. (See: www.charlestownwv.us/index.asp?Type=B_BASIC&SEC={3CB2F7DC-ADE5-4A41-868D-39BFC5BBA55D}.)

Ranson and Charles Town launched the Commerce Corridor effort by forming a multi-stakeholder Commerce Corridor Council that includes public, private, non-profit, neighborhood, state, and federal stakeholders. The council guided and supported the initiative, including the funding and leverage efforts involved. Under this framework, Ranson and Charles Town developed a comprehensive brownfields inventory, prioritized sites for assessment, engaged the community and key stakeholders, and established a strong vision and area-wide plan for revitalization. The cities also leveraged public and private resources, upgraded infrastructure, and attracted private sector investment to the revitalization effort.

In 2006, Ranson and Charles Town joined with the Urban Land Institute in a comprehensive economic reuse planning project that convened top experts in real estate, finance, brownfields, and sustainability to identify strategies for brownfields reuse. The overall brownfield effort was fueled by a robust commitment from Ranson and Charles Town staff and the support of environmental, planning, and funding consultants retained with EPA grant support.

In the 15 years since receiving the first Brownfields Assessment grant in 2001, Ranson and Charles Town have seen tremendous progress and benefits to the community:

Environmental Remediation: The cleanup of sites included the removal of numerous abandoned underground storage tanks, the remediation of contaminated soil, and the abatement of asbestos materials.

Ranson Civic Center: In 2008, the City of Ranson used local funding to purchase a former Maytag spray-painting facility that had sat idle since 1989. The facility was cleaned up and repurposed in 2010. Today, this former brownfield is Ranson's Civic Center, a 40,000 square-foot facility with an adjacent, quarter-acre pocket park situated next to the Boys & Girls Club of Jefferson County and the Evitts Run Park system. The Civic Center is home to the Ranson Parks and Recreation Commission, which uses the facility for public athletic events, social functions, trade shows, job fairs, and youth and family activities.

The Civic Center, which can hold 1,500 people, has two full basketball courts, bleachers, and batting cages; an office area; full-service concession and eating areas; multi-purpose flex flooring; new lighting, sound systems and wireless Internet; and a stage for performances. Outside the Civic Center, a community group established the Ranson Community Garden, which employs homeless members of the community who cultivate crops that provide healthy foods to support the Jefferson County Homeless Coalition and other community needs.

American Public University Headquarters and Campus: The American Public University System (APUS), one of the foremost online universities in the nation, made Ranson its headquarters and invested more than $100 million in the Commerce Corridor brownfield area. APUS continues to build a high-tech educational campus that already provides more than 650 jobs to local residents. The campus includes an academic center, finance center and solar array, and information technology center.

APUS Academic Center: The Academic Center is a $12 million, 45,000 square-foot, four-story, LEED gold-certified building situated on another former brownfield. The

Veiner Metal Salvage Yard operated for more than 100 years until it was closed in the 1960s. The property remained vacant until the Academic Center was built in 2010.

The Academic Center includes meeting and office space for more than 140 APUS faculty, academic staff and student advisors; and a library with one of the nation's major collections for research in military studies and military history. The building can house 330 employees and already produced 170 initial new high-skills jobs.

The architecture for the Academic Center and other APUS buildings preserves and complements the character and history of Charles Town and blends old and new design elements. Environmentally friendly materials and construction features were used to reduce greenhouse gas emissions and to contribute to a healthier work environment for employees and a cleaner environment for the community. Energy-efficient design features include advanced thermal insulation of windows and walls, variable lighting and cooling to manage energy use, and 99 roof solar panels that provide a portion of the center's energy requirements.

APUS Finance Center and Solar Array: APUS expects to obtain LEED-gold certification for the 105,000 square foot, four-story Finance Center that straddles the Ranson and Charles Town border. The $18 million, privately financed center boasts the largest solar array in West Virginia; its 170-space parking lot has1, 660 solar panels that generate enough electricity to supply 30 average-sized homes. The solar array/parking lot also has 14 electric car charging stations. The building's roof was designed to eliminate the heat island effect, and the building was constructed of materials derived from recycled content including structural steel, studs, drywall, hardware, and floorings. It is landscaped with native and adaptive plants. The facility currently houses 245 employees and has the capacity for 450 staff.

APUS Information Technology Center: APUS also will seek LEED certification for its Information Technology (IT) Center, which was completed in late 2015. The IT Center was built on the former Maytag appliance manufacturing facility in the Commerce Corridor. The large brick building includes a metal dome that houses a 240-pound, state-of-the-art telescope that will provide a new other-worldly view to the people of Ranson and Charles Town, and to APUS students across the globe who can remotely access the telescope. The IT Center also has an outdoor pavilion for musical and cultural events.

New Jobs Development: On the Charles Town side of the border, there are new jobs on the redeveloped brownfields where a former lumber facility was located for decades. The site provides professional office space for a land use planning and engineering firm, and a high-performance automotive supply company.

Creation of the Charles Town/Ranson Commerce Corridor enabled the two communities to leverage more than $15 million in additional grants and other resources to move forward the revitalization of the downtown area. Funding was obtained from the following sources:

U.S. Department of Transportation: Ranson and Charles Town secured two very competitive TIGER grants from the U.S. Department of Transportation. The first TIGER grant was used to plan the Green Corridor revitalization through the brownfield area, creating a complete street, and using green infrastructure elements to transform the central roadway. The second TIGER grant was used to construct the corridor with $10 million in federal, state, local and private-sector funding. TIGER funding also was used to plan and engineer a new transit center in downtown Charles Town, which provides regional bus and rail transit passengers with a hub for accessing public transit to the Washington, D.C., metropolitan area.

U.S. Department of Housing and Urban Development: HUD provided the City of Ranson with a range of resources for brownfields and community revitalization. HUD resources include a Sustainable Communities Challenge grant that enabled Ranson to hire top land use planners to create a new comprehensive land use plan and Ranson Smart Code to promote smart and sustainable development. Ranson also received a $1.5 million HUD Brownfields Economic Development Initiative grant and up to $3.5 million in HUD Section 108 Loan Guarantee funding to remove a dilapidated, vacant brass foundry; upgrade infrastructure; and prepare for development of a mixed-use downtown center.

U.S. Department of Agriculture: Building upon the TIGER funding for design of a new downtown transit hub, the City of Charles Town used $3.8 million in USDA Community Facilities loan resources to fully restore the historic Charles Washington Hall as a community center, indoor farmers market, café, performing arts space, and regional transit.

National Endowment for the Arts: Recognizing the community revitalization that began with Charles Town's EPA Brownfields grants, NEA awarded an "Our Town" grant to the city to establish the Washington Heritage Arts and Cultural District, an arts and cultural district in the area around the Commerce Corridor and Green Corridor. The NEA funding catalyzed diverse groups of arts, cultural, historic, civic, and private-sector leaders to promote vibrant activities in the downtown area for residents and tourists.

U.S. EPA: In addition to the Brownfields grants, the City of Ranson received technical assistance through EPA's Building Blocks for Sustainable Communities program to help the city identify strategies to spur growth in the urban core and thus, avoid sprawl. EPA also provided expert contractor technical assistance to Ranson to assist with development of a green infrastructure plan for handling stormwater runoff from brownfield redevelopment areas into the Chesapeake Bay watershed.

National Fish and Wildlife Foundation: Charles Town secured a $100,000 Chesapeake Bay Stewardship Fund grant from the National Fish and Wildlife

Foundation to design a community recreational pond on the old Public Works site and the city dump, both within the core of the brownfields revitalization area. The pond also will serve as a major stormwater management facility to protect the Shenandoah and Potomac Rivers and the Chesapeake Bay. Charles Town also seeks to use its EPA Brownfields RLF funding as matching share for other funding used for the construction of this green facility.

The joint and collaborative efforts of the two small cities are transforming Ranson and Charles Town from a failed manufacturing area with stagnant downtowns, into a mecca for technology, education, arts, culture, tourism, and sustainability. EPA Brownfields grants sparked this transformation in part because the cities worked together to leverage additional local, state, federal, philanthropic, and private-sector funding.

As a result, these communities are recognized nationally as models for small-town sustainability. The Charles Town/Ranson Commerce Corridor initiative was a key feature on the White House's anniversary celebration for the HUD/DOT/EPA Partnership for Sustainable Communities (See: www.whitehouse.gov/blog/2011/06/16/partnership-sustainable-communities-marks-two-trailblazing-years) and EPA's three-year celebration of that Partnership. Ranson/Charles Town won the 2013 Phoenix Award for brownfields revitalization and the National People's Choice Award for the best brownfields project, and in 2014, the communities won the national Brownfields Renewal Award for outstanding economic development of brownfields.

• B. State •

27. Florida Waste Cleanup Program[*]

FLORIDA DEPARTMENT OF ENVIRONMENTAL PROTECTION

Editor's note: With CERCLA as the guiding rule, each state has its own environmental laws which address their priorities and are tailored to their economic conditions, hydrogeology, geography and natural resources and social factors. State brownfields programs usually fall under the states' environment, conservation or natural resources departments. Like the Federal government, other state line departments complement the reuse aspects of site cleanup and assessment.

Waste Site Cleanup Section

The prevention and cleanup of contamination by hazardous waste is one of the nation's major concerns. But nowhere is it of greater importance than in Florida, where ground water is the source of almost 90 percent of the state's drinking water. The recreational benefits and fish and wildlife habitats provided by Florida's surface waters must also be protected. Florida's natural resources are vital to the quality of life its residents and visitors expect and enjoy. While Florida is not normally thought of as an industrialized state, sources of pollution do exist, and generated wastes need proper treatment and disposal. Florida's environmental laws can and do help to prevent contamination by today's activities, but actions in the past have left Florida a legacy of hazardous waste sites.

The Waste Site Cleanup Section is responsible for the remediation of hazardous waste sites where enforcement has been unsuccessful or only partially successful, and for coordination with the U.S. Environmental Protection Agency during EPA managed remediation of National Priority List Superfund sites in the state of Florida. The section is also responsible for the cleanup of contamination resulting from the operation of eligible dry-cleaning facilities.

Site Investigation Section

The Florida Department of Environmental Protection (DEP) Site Investigation Section (SIS) conducts environmental assessments throughout Florida. These assessments are vital to protecting the state's residents and visitors, as well as our fragile environment.

---

[*]Public document originally published as Florida Department of Environmental Protection, "Florida Waste Cleanup Program," https://floridadep.gov/waste/waste-cleanup (January 2020).

Assessments typically emphasize soil and groundwater impact determinations. Groundwater produced from aquifers provides almost 90 percent of Florida's population with fresh, clean drinking water. Sites requiring assessment are prioritized and referred to Site Investigation staff by the DEP district offices. Staff also provide technical support and assistance to various law enforcement agencies to assist in the investigation of environmental crimes.

Since its inception in 1982, Site Investigation staff have conducted or supervised environmental assessments at more than 750 sites. Examples of sites assessed include electronic manufacturing facilities, dry cleaning facilities, maintenance yards, printing facilities, chemical storage tanks, agricultural fields and golf courses. Staff also conduct large-scale investigations to determine the sources of groundwater contamination affecting public and private supply wells.

Site Investigation personnel consist of scientists, licensed monitor well drillers and technicians. To support various assessment needs, SIS maintains and operates a Geoprobe Model 6600 direct push unit with hydraulic profiling and electrical conductivity capabilities, as well as a Geoprobe Model 5410 direct push unit. Overflow assessments are conducted by licensed environmental firms and include all phases of study. Subcontracted services such as mobile laboratory, borehole geophysical and ground penetrating radar are common. Contracted work is directed by experienced DEP contract managers.

The State-Owned Lands Cleanup Program is included within the Site Investigation Section. The program is funded by the Florida Legislature to address potential health-related and environmental issues on state-owned properties. The program began in 2001 and is available to all state agencies. Site Investigation Section contract managers oversee all activities, which are generally conducted by private environmental firms. Almost 400 areas of concern on 85 state properties have been assessed.

Federal Programs Oversight

The Federal Programs Section works with the United States Environmental Protection Agency (USEPA), Air Force, Navy, Army Corps of Engineers (USACE), Defense Logistics Agency (DLA), and National Aeronautics and Space Administration (NASA) to oversee environmental restoration contaminated sites using applicable state and federal regulations, including Florida Statute and Florida Administrative Code, the Comprehensive Environmental Response Compensation and Liability Act (CERCLA) and the Resource Conservation and Recovery Act (RCRA). Environmental restoration under this section includes assessment and remediation of the following types of sites:

- Hazardous waste
- Petroleum
- Installation Restoration Program (IRP)
- Military Munitions Response Program (MMRP)
- Base Closure and Realignment Commission (BRAC)
- Formerly Used Defense Sites (FUDs)

FUDS Program

The USACE and the Florida Department of Environmental Protection are working together as a team to protect human health and the environment at FUDs. This program establishes a framework for the efficient and effective cleanup of past Department of Defense disposals, discharges or releases of hazardous substances, petroleum products and unexploded ordinance on or from FUDS. Environmental restoration shall be conducted in a manner that meets the requirements of the applicable statute and regulations, including CERCLA the National oil and Hazardous Substance Pollution Contingency Plan (NCP) and Florida law regulating the cleanup of sites contaminated with hazardous waste products.

The CERCLA Site Screening Group

The Comprehensive Environmental Response Compensation and Liability Act (CERCLA) Site Screening Group conducts CERCLA site assessments on sites with confirmed or suspected contamination to document whether a release of hazardous substances has occurred and to evaluate potential threats to nearby receptors, including but not limited to, drinking water wells and surface water bodies. Research and file review is conducted by DEP staff. Fieldwork, when required, is accomplished using a combination of DEP staff, EPA staff and private contractors. The information collected during the assessments is used to complete a Hazard Ranking System (HRS) evaluation. The HRS score and the supporting site information are then evaluated by EPA in determining whether the site should be included on the National Priorities List (NPL) and cleaned up under the Superfund program.

Brownfields Program

The primary goals of the Brownfield Redevelopment Act are to reduce public health and environmental hazards on existing commercial and industrial sites that are abandoned or underused due to these hazards; create financial and regulatory incentives to encourage voluntary cleanup and redevelopment of sites; derive cleanup target levels and a process for obtaining a "No Further Action" letter using Risk-Based Corrective Action principles; and provide the opportunity for Environmental Equity and Justice. Please view the Memorandum of Agreement between the Florida Department of Environmental Protection and the United States Environmental Protection Agency–Region 4 for complete information.

28. State of Ohio's Brownfields Team[*]

Ohio Environmental Protection Agency

The Ohio Environmental Protection Agency is a trusted leader and environmental steward using innovation, quality service and public involvement to ensure a safe and healthy environment for all Ohioans.

Ohio EPA's goal is to protect the environment and public health by ensuring compliance with environmental laws and demonstrating leadership in environmental stewardship. Everyone needs clean air to breathe and clean water to drink. We want to keep our environment clean, but we enjoy modern conveniences that create pollution, like air emissions from electric plants and automobiles and hazardous waste like leftover paint and cleaning chemicals.

The Ohio Environmental Protection Agency is a state agency whose goal is to protect the environment and public health by ensuring compliance with environmental laws. Those laws and related rules outline Ohio EPA's authority and what things we can consider when making decisions about regulated activities.

Ohio EPA was created on October 23, 1972. It combined environmental programs that previously had been scattered throughout several state departments. Ohio EPA's Central Office is located in Columbus, and five district offices manage the Agency's programs throughout the state. The director of Ohio EPA is appointed by the governor and serves as a cabinet member.

Ohio EPA establishes and enforces standards for air, water, waste management and cleanup of sites contaminated with hazardous substances. We also provide financial assistance to businesses and communities; environmental education programs for businesses and the public; and pollution prevention assistance to help businesses minimize their waste at the source.

Ohio EPA has several regulatory divisions that play different roles in environmental protection. Each division issues permits to regulate industries that pollute in a specific area, like air emissions or wastewater discharges to rivers and streams. The permits include requirements for operating, monitoring and reporting compliance. There are a few core responsibilities that each regulatory division of Ohio EPA fulfills:

---

[*]Public document originally published by the Ohio Environmental Protection Agency, "State of Ohio's Brownfields Team," https://epa.ohio.gov/About (January 2020).

- Review permit applications and issue permits to facilities.
- Investigate citizen complaints.
- Monitor to make sure all environmental standards are met (usually accomplished by collecting samples of air, water or soil and testing them for pollutants in a laboratory; and reviewing sampling and monitoring data submitted by a facility).
- Provide technical assistance to help regulated facilities understand and follow environmental laws and permit requirements.
- Take enforcement action against facilities that violate environmental laws and permit requirements.

Non-regulatory divisions provide financial assistance to businesses and communities; site cleanup and spill response; environmental education programs for businesses and the public; pollution prevention assistance to help businesses minimize their waste at the source; laboratory analysis; and criminal environmental investigations. Ohio EPA's Central Office is located in Columbus. *Five district offices* manage the Agency's programs at the local level. They are located in Bowling Green, Twinsburg, Dayton, Columbus and Logan.

The District offices review permit applications; investigate citizen complaints; investigate and oversee cleanups of spills and releases; monitor compliance with environmental standards; provide technical assistance to help regulated facilities understand and comply with environmental laws and permit requirements; initiate enforcement action against facilities that are not in compliance; provide environmental information and other assistance to the public; coordinate public records requests; and give public presentations.

The Division of Air Pollution Control ensures compliance with the federal Clean Air Act and the Emergency Planning and Community Right-to-Know Act as part of its mission to attain and maintain air quality at a level that will protect public health and the environment. The division reviews, issues and enforces permits for installation and operation of sources of air pollution and operates an extensive outdoor air monitoring network. The division also oversees an automobile emission testing program to minimize emissions from mobile sources.

The Director's Office is charged with upholding the Agency's mission to protect human health and the environment. The office directs all activities of the Agency including policy development and rulemaking, enforcement, strategic planning, coordinating state and federal initiatives, and providing outreach, education and assistance to the regulated community and citizens.

The Division of Drinking and Ground Waters ensures compliance with the federal Safe Drinking Water Act and evaluates potential threats to source waters that supply more than 5,000 public drinking water systems in Ohio. The division has a lead role for statewide ground water protection in cooperation with other state and federal agencies; implements a ground water quality monitoring program; and provides technical support to the Agency's waste management divisions.

The Office of Environmental Education administers the Ohio Environmental Education Fund, awarding up to $1 million annually in grants for projects targeting pre-school through university students and teachers, the general public and the regulated community. The office also administers the Ohio Clean Diesel School Bus grant program, Diesel Emission Reduction Grants, and a scholarship program for university students in environmental science and engineering.

The Office of Employee Services maintains current employment information, posts available positions with the state job bank and collects and screens employment applications submitted to the Agency. Staff provide assistance to Ohio EPA administrators and staff on matters regarding Civil Service laws and rules, discipline, employment, benefits, recruitment, position descriptions and personnel policies. The Office of Equal Employment Opportunity pursues fair and equal treatment for all individuals employed by or seeking employment with Ohio EPA and also monitors the Agency's compliance with all laws, rules and regulations governing nondiscrimination.

The Division of Environmental and Financial Assistance houses several of the Agency's core programs that focus on compliance assistance and community development. It includes three offices: the Office of Compliance Assistance and Pollution Prevention (OCAPP); the Office of Financial Assistance (OFA); and the Office of Outreach and Customer Support (OCS).

OFA staff members provide technical assistance to help small community wastewater plants improve operations and efficiency and administer two low-interest state revolving loan fund programs that finance municipal wastewater treatment, water quality improvement and drinking water projects. Eligible projects include building or renovating drinking water plants or wastewater plants and sewers, restoring aquatic habitat, improving home sewage disposal systems and best management practices for agriculture or forestry to reduce and prevent water pollution. Funding is also provided for recycling, litter cleanup and scrap tire management activities.

OCAPP helps thousands of small businesses annually comply with environmental regulations through on-site assistance, help completing forms, training events, plain-English publications and other services and helps entities identify and implement pollution prevention (P2) measures that save money, improve performance and benefit the environment. The division recognizes outstanding efforts of businesses, communities and other entities making a commitment to environmental stewardship through Ohio EPA's Encouraging Environmental Excellence (E3) program.

OCS staff members connect Ohio businesses and communities with the division's services through in-person meetings and presentations as well as electronic tools such as newsletters, monthly emails and webinars.

Ohio EPA's Office of Emergency Response (ER) is a specialized group of staff stationed throughout Ohio who coordinate with first responders and other Federal, State and local responders and support entities on environmental emergencies such as train wrecks, facility malfunctions, highway crashes, fish kills, oil and gas releases, natural disasters, etc., to minimize and abate the impact these releases cause to the environment.

ER is capable of responding 24-hours a day, seven days a week. Responders are fully trained in the Incident Command System. On-scene coordinators (OSCs) are available to help first responders address environmental emergencies and pollution incidents, including chemical and petroleum spills.

Statewide, Ohio EPA records more than 5,000 incident reports annually through calls to our emergency response spill hotline from citizens, companies, law enforcement, emergency responders and other agencies.

The Division of Environmental Response and Revitalization oversees investigation and cleanup of contaminated sites including federal facilities; provides assistance to companies and communities that clean up and reuse brownfield sites; and oversees the permitting, inspection, compliance and reporting of hazardous waste sites.

The Division of Environmental Services provides laboratory services to other Ohio EPA divisions, state and local agencies and private entities. The division chemists and biologists analyze water, air, sediment and fish tissue samples, inspect and certify laboratories and provide technical assistance.

The Office of Fiscal Administration provides fiscal services to the Agency including purchasing, accounts payable, accounts receivable, payroll, grants administration, budgeting, economic analysis and internal accounting control review. The office also publishes Sewer and Water Rate Surveys that show residential rates for these services throughout Ohio.

The Office of Legal Services provides general counsel to Ohio EPA's divisions and districts and evaluates, prepares and negotiates administrative enforcement actions. In addition, Agency attorneys prepare trade secret claim determinations; prepare and review contracts; assist in the development or review of legislation and rules; and address public records request issues.

The Division of Materials and Waste Management implements Ohio's solid waste, infectious waste and construction and demolition debris programs. In addition to the traditional regulatory program, the division is also committed to research and promotion of emerging concepts and technologies associated with resource conservation, materials management and sustainability. The division also oversees state and local planning for long-term solid waste management.

Ohio EPA is committed to providing each of its employees a safe and healthy work environment, free from any recognized hazards. The Health and Safety office oversees a dynamic, comprehensive program to protect the health and safety of all Ohio EPA employees while working in any of the Agency's facilities or during the performance of field activities.

The Public Interest Center responds to citizen and media inquiries regarding environmental issues and Agency actions; prepares news releases; facilitates public hearings; and implements public involvement activities for citizen organizations, community leaders and other parties interested in environmental issues. The office oversees publications, the website and video production.

The Division of Surface Water ensures compliance with the federal Clean Water Act and works to increase the number of water bodies that can be safely used for swimming and fishing. The division issues permits to regulate wastewater treatment plants, factories and storm water runoff; develops comprehensive watershed plans aimed at improving polluted streams; and samples streams, lakes and wetlands—including fish, aquatic insects and plants—to determine the health of Ohio's water bodies.

Partners

- Joint Committee on Agency Rule Review (JCARR)
- Ohio Air Quality Development Authority
- Ohio Attorney General
- Ohio Business Gateway
- Ohio Department of Health (ODH)
- Ohio Department of Agriculture (ODA)
- Ohio Development Services Agency

- Ohio Department of Natural Resources (ODNR)
- Ohio Emergency Management Agency
- Ohio Power Siting Board
- Ohio River Valley Sanitation Commission (ORSANCO)
- Ohio State Fire Marshal–Bureau of Underground Storage Tank Regulations (BUSTR)
- Ohio Water Development Authority
- Ohio Water Resources Council
- Ohio Lake Erie Commission
- Environmental Council of the States (ECOS)
- Interstate Technology and Regulatory Council
- U.S. EPA

29. Brownfield Redevelopment Guide*

PENNSYLVANIA DEPARTMENT
OF ENVIRONMENTAL PROTECTION

Pennsylvania has a rich industrial history. Communities across Pennsylvania have a story to tell. Whether it's the successful cleanup of a town's former industrial complex or the remediation of the corner gas station, these brownfields success stories illustrate the improved quality of life for people living and working in Pennsylvania.

Pennsylvania's approach to brownfield redevelopment has proven to be a national model for transforming abandoned, idle properties into safer places that contribute to greater economic opportunity and revitalize communities. Under the Land Recycling and Environmental Remediation Standards Act (Act 2) of 1995, thousands of brownfield sites in Pennsylvania have been returned to productive use, providing jobs and tax revenues, and benefiting local communities. Existing infrastructure, historic buildings and close proximity to transportation are among the many cost-effective benefits for reuse of brownfields. DEP has the experience and ability to work with local governments, communities, developers and remediators to meet the challenges of brownfield redevelopment and reuse.

Providing Assistance to Communities, Owners and Local Governments

Brownfield properties vary widely, from a single abandoned gas station located on a rural road to large operating factory complexes covering many acres in an urban setting. The amount and need for DEP assistance depend on the property ownership (privately or publicly owned) and the stage of the cleanup or development.

And, because each project is unique, it is not a one-size-fits-all approach. DEP recognizes it has a role as a partner throughout the many facets of brownfield redevelopment, beyond its role as regulator of the cleanup and site development process.

---

*Public document originally published as Pennsylvania Department of Environmental Protection, "Brownfield Redevelopment Success Stories," https://www.dep.pa.gov/Business/Land/Redevelopment/Pages/default.aspx (January 2020).

Developing Inventories and Assessing Properties

DEP strongly encourages local governments to identify and market brownfield sites within its boundaries through its statewide Brownfields Inventory. Developed in partnership with Team Pennsylvania Foundation and the Pennsylvania Department of Community and Economic Development (DCED), this valuable marketing tool is available free of charge to users as part of Pennsylvania's premier "PA Site Search" database of land and buildings with GIS features. It is used by professionals seeking properties for redevelopment opportunities, and the PA Site Search data feeds into the national database "Zoomprospector."

The Governor's Action Team, a group of experienced economic development professionals that serve as a single point of contact for companies looking to establish or expand new business operations in Pennsylvania, uses the database to respond to inquiries from national and international company officials looking for potential properties. Environmental site assessments (ESA) are typically conducted in phases and are used to determine whether a site is contaminated. A Phase I ESA is a review of property records, including past and current land uses.

The DEP files are available at DEP's six regional offices to assist consultants in performing initial property assessments that help local governments and economic development agencies prepare market analyses and zoning approvals and assist purchasers in performing due diligence. If there is a potential for contamination, the assessment proceeds to the next phase. A

Phase II ESA involves sampling to help determine the extent, types and sources of soil and/or groundwater contamination and the level of risk to humans and the environment.

Phase I and II ESAs need to meet requirements established by U.S. Environmental Protection Agency (EPA) for All Appropriate Inquiry investigations to qualify for liability protection under the federal Comprehensive Environmental Response, Compensation and Liability Act or Superfund.

Identifying Sources of Financial Assistance

Financial incentives are available for brownfield projects from public sources, such as DCED, EPA, local municipal governments and economic development agencies. Private sources of funding are available for some projects. Tax incentives are offered at federal and state levels. DEP assists local governments, property owners and developers in locating potential sources of public financing. A list of financial assistance programs.

DCED offers many state assistance and incentive programs for brownfields projects. These programs can be easily accessed through a Funding and Program Finder through a single application on the website. The Industrial Sites Reuse Program, a widely used program for local governments and Economic Development Agencies, offers grants and loans for assessment and cleanup of industrial sites.

DEP personnel participate in the review of submittals for certain state programs offered through DCED. EPA offers a number of federal brownfields grants on a periodic basis using a competitive rating process to assist communities with revitalization. DEP can provide letters of support and eligibility determinations as required by specific grant program conditions. The Brownfields Assessment Grant provides funding for property characterization, assessments, inventories and community involvement plans. EPA also provides revolving loan funds.

Other federal sources include the U.S. Department of Housing and Urban Development (HUD), U.S. Department of Agriculture (USDA), and the U.S. Department of Commerce. HUD provides block grants and competitive awards for revitalizing entitlement communities, offers federally guaranteed loans for large economic development projects, and provides grants for HUD Empowerment Zone or Enterprise communities (targeted to low-income or distressed areas). USDA provides loans and grants through the Rural Development division that can assist rural communities. U.S. Department of Commerce provides programs through its Economic Development Administration and Small Business Administration.

Engaging Communities, Planning and Outreach

DEP promotes the redevelopment of brownfields by supporting site and community planning efforts and providing information and education through outreach and training. Efforts include the following:

- DEP participates on local brownfields planning teams.
- Environmental advocate coordination is available for environmental justice communities to engage these communities before, during and after the permitting process.
- Pennsylvania's Brownfields Conference is the largest gathering of brownfields consultants, planners, redevelopment authorities, local officials, and technical and legal professionals in Pennsylvania. The conference includes dozens of educational sessions and networking opportunities with industry professionals, state regulators and regional leaders
- Videos and fact sheets about successful brownfields projects are available for viewing on DEP's YouTube channel at www.youtube.com/user/pennsylvaniadep and DCED's website. A collection of videos features interviews with public and private partners who describe the vision, planning and re-use of a brownfield site and how challenges were met and overcome. Contact the Bureau of Environmental Cleanup and Brownfields in Harrisburg to share a brownfield success story.
- Technical training and program outreach events are offered to all stakeholders. DEP can partner with professional associations like the Pennsylvania Council of Professional Geologists and Engineers' Society of Western Pennsylvania to provide quality sessions to interested individuals. Webinars, regional sessions and workshops focused on brownfield topics are being developed to assist communities.

Meeting Cleanup Challenges

Act 2 establishes a cleanup process and remediation standards that are proven to work for brownfield redevelopment. Act 2 provides:

- Uniform cleanup standards based on end use of
- the property that are protective of public health and the environment.
- Protection from environmental liability for sites attaining an Act 2 cleanup standard.
- Established report review deadlines that provide dependable timeframes for remediators, developers and financial partners.

In addition, through its extensive experience, DEP has developed many tools that are specifically designed to achieve results, including:

- One Cleanup Program provides concurrent relief of environmental liability from DEP and approval from EPA on federal corrective action obligations. The program reviews site characterization work plans, remediation work plans, data evaluation, risk assessments, fate and transport modeling, post remediation care plans and environmental covenants.
- Buyer/Seller Agreements allow for the re-use of a property while remediation activities are being completed. A Buyer/Seller Agreement provides
- details of the proposed sale, remediation plan for the property and obligations of all parties with respect to implementing the remediation plan. (See model legal agreement on the Land Recycling webpage).
- Special Industrial Area Consent Order and Agreements can be used to address immediate, direct or imminent threats on properties located in designated enterprise zones or where there is no financially viable responsible person to clean up the contamination.

Permitting Site Development Activities

Brownfield site cleanup and development can restore the environment and provide significant economic benefit to Pennsylvania. As such, brownfield sites are eligible for prioritization of permit reviews under DEP's policy for implementing its Permit Review Process and Permit Decision Guarantee.

A key component of the Permit Review Process establishes the Permit Review Hierarchy, which prioritizes review of permits as a workload management tool. The first tier for review is "applications necessary for protection of public health, safety or the environment from imminent threats or that are necessary to support restoration of the environment or that support broader environmental improvement goals." The second tier for review is "applications necessary for economic development projects that create and/or retain jobs in Pennsylvania, leverage private investment in Pennsylvania, and/or provide significant economic benefit to Pennsylvania communities."

Pre-application conferences with DEP staff are highly recommended for brownfield projects. The purpose of pre-application conferences is to discuss site development and interplay with remediation activities, which are important for high-quality, complete permit applications. During conferences, permit review priority information can be presented and evaluated by DEP staff.

Permit applicants are advised to provide the following information during pre-application conferences:

152   Part III. Practices and Innovations • B. State

- Are there any imminent threats to public health, safety or the environment at the site?
- Is the project enrolled in DEP's Act 2 program?
- Is DCED Governor's Action Team coordinating site development?
- Is the brownfield site located within an enterprise zone, as designated by DCED?
- Is the project located in an environmental justice and/ or high unemployment area?
- What economic benefits are expected, including number of jobs created and retained and added tax revenues?
- What private investment dollars are anticipated?
- Has the project been approved for state funding assistance?

The Permit Application Consultation Tool (PACT) can help applicants who are considering expanding or siting a new project. This tool can quickly and easily determine which types of environmental permits, authorizations or notifications may be required for their projects. PACT is a useful foundation for a pre-application conference with DEP to discuss and verify tool results and permit coordination. Please be advised that, because of the complexity of potential projects and the diverse nature of state and federal environmental regulations, no tool can substitute for a detailed analysis of individual project plans.

Success Stories

Philadelphia Wholesale Food Produce Market: Modern industrial land occupied by new food warehouse. Philadelphia was known at the turn of the 20th Century as the Workshop of the World due to its large and innovative manufacturing base. Philadelphia's current industrial attributes feature a transportation infrastructure including a sophisticated highway network, passenger and freight rail, an international airport and the largest freshwater port in the world. Philadelphia's location at the center of the Northeastern region; its companies, buoyed by the people that live, work and attend school there; and the continued investments by both the public and private sectors make Philadelphia an ideal choice for modern industry.

Today the city's industrial base includes traditional manufacturing, ranging from food to fashion to helicopters; advanced manufacturing such as pharmaceuticals; and transportation and logistics to support global enterprises. Underutilized properties can be transformed into modern industrial land, occupied by laboratories, flex space, warehouses and distribution centers, or purpose-built manufacturing buildings.

Hamilton Health Center: Once-vacant properties now provide medical services and jobs. In September 2012, Hamilton Health Center opened its new 117 South 17th Street facility in the city of Harrisburg. Funding for this $17 million project was provided by DEP and DCED as well as the Dauphin County Gaming Commission and the Harrisburg Redevelopment Authority. New Markets Tax Credit, bank financing and other commitments provided the majority of the funding. Hamilton Health Center is launching a capital campaign to complete the project with additional improvements to its building space.

When investigative work began in 2004 at the former Allison Hill Automotive property, the brownfield site consisted of abandoned buildings in various states of disrepair, as well as vacant land overgrown with vegetation. The site has undergone environmental remediation through the Land Recycling Program (Act 2) as a part of the development of the health center, including excavation activity, removal of soils and capping with an asphalt surface. The center is located in an environmental justice area, providing essential services to a poor and underserved community.

30. Oregon Brownfields Initiative*

OREGON DEPARTMENT OF ENVIRONMENTAL QUALITY
and OREGON BUSINESS DEVELOPMENT DEPARTMENT

A "brownfield" is generally defined in federal and state law as: real property where expansion or redevelopment is complicated by the actual, potential, or perceived presence of environmental contamination.

DEQ can help remove environmental barriers to redevelopment by providing technical assistance and other services to assist parties with investigating, cleaning up, and planning reuse of brownfields. See DEQ's brownfields fact sheet. Many federal, state, and local programs also assist with brownfields. Below are links to programs and funding sources commonly used to assist in brownfield investigation, cleanup, and redevelopment.

Identifying Brownfields in Oregon

Every Oregon city and county, whether rural or urban, has vacant, underused and potentially contaminated properties. To get lists of sites that DEQ considers brownfields (sites that have received financial or technical assistance), visit the DEQ Environmental Cleanup Site Information query page, and click on "Search complete ECSI database." Then, when the fill-in form appears, click the box at the bottom right labeled "Return only Current or Former Brownfield Sites," enter other limiting parameters as desired, and click "Submit."

Opportunities to redevelop old mill sites: DEQ partners with other Oregon state agencies on the Oregon's Collective Impact Mills Project to provide a centralized searchable inventory and map of over 500 abandoned or diminished wood-product mill sites, which are a significant subset of Oregon's brownfield sites. The inventory and map can be used to identify the status, location or footprint of abandoned or diminished wood-product mill sites in Oregon.

Business Oregon also provides a comprehensive database of Oregon brownfield sites and buildings. The Oregon Prospector GIS web tool provides easy access to information about local industrial sites and economy. You can use it to evaluate land supply and pricing data.

---

*Public documents originally published as Oregon Department of Environmental Quality, "Brownfields in Oregon," https://www.oregon.gov/deq/Hazards-and-Cleanup/env-cleanup/Pages/Brownfields.aspx (January 2020), and Oregon Business Development Department, "Financing Brownfields Redevelopment in Oregon," https://www.orinfrastructure.org/assets/docs/brownfields.pdf (2020).

Metro offers a tool to identify contaminated cleanup and leaking underground storage tank sites, as well as marginalized communities and park areas, in Clackamas, Multnomah and Washington counties. Visit METRO Interactive Site Locator.

Environmental Cleanup Site Information Database

A state law passed in 1987 required DEQ to "develop and implement a comprehensive statewide program to identify any release or threat of release [of hazardous substances] from a facility that may require remedial action." A year later, DEQ created the Environmental Cleanup Site Information (ECSI) database, to identify and track sites with known or suspected hazardous substance contamination. At that time, DEQ's Cleanup program developed broad but informal criteria for adding sites to ECSI. In 2000, the program formalized guidelines for ECSI entry.

Environmental Cleanup Site Information is an electronic database that the Oregon Department of Environmental Quality has used since 1989 to track sites with known, suspected, or cleaned up hazardous substance contamination. ECSI, which assigns unique identification numbers to individual sites, summarizes information about sites and their investigative/remedial status, as well as Cleanup Program recommendations for further action. ECSI also includes sites at which DEQ has determined that no further action is necessary.

Data in ECSI is "working information" used by DEQ's Environmental Cleanup Section. Please note that:

- Some information in ECSI may be unconfirmed, outdated, or incomplete.
- Data in ECSI is summary in nature, rather than comprehensive.
- There may be contaminated sites in Oregon that are unknown to DEQ and do not appear in ECSI. Conversely, the appearance of a site in ECSI does not necessarily mean that the site is contaminated. Information in ECSI is subject to change at any time.

Each ECSI entry contains basic data such as site name and location. For most sites, ECSI also indicates how and when the site became contaminated, qualitative risks the contamination may pose to human health or the environment, investigative and cleanup actions that have occurred, and prioritized further actions, if any, that are required. At many sites, ECSI documents contaminants found in soil, surface water, sediments, and groundwater, with associated concentrations and sampling dates. ECSI categorizes current site status as either: (1) under investigation; (2) on the Confirmed Release List or Inventory of Facilities Needing Further Action (Inventory); or (3) cleaned up to DEQ standards (No Further Action, or NFA). ECSI also lists past and present site operations, owners/operators, and site contacts. The amount of data entered for each site varies greatly and depends on the nature of site issues, how long the site has been active in DEQ's Cleanup Program, and the priority DEQ has assigned to the site.

Sites in ECSI comprise a wide variety of sizes, locations, features, contaminant profiles, and degrees of Cleanup Program information. What all sites have in common is documented, suspected, or remediated hazardous substance contamination in groundwater, surface water, soil, or sediments. Some ECSI sites have minimal information available and need an initial evaluation, while others have completed investigative and remedial actions, and have earned an NFA decision from DEQ. Sites range from urban industrial complexes to isolated rural facilities contaminated by disposals or spills. Most sites are either industrial or commercial, but the Cleanup Program sometimes adds highly contaminated residential properties to ECSI.

ECSI also includes study areas, which are groups of individual sites that may be contributing to a larger, area-wide problem. For example, when DEQ discovers regional groundwater contamination where the sources of contamination are not known, it will create a study area for this region. Then, DEQ will add sites within the region's boundaries to this study area, and these sites may be investigated to determine if they're potential sources of contamination. DEQ has also created study areas of sites that could threaten Vulnerable Areas such as drinking water sources or streams with endangered fish species.

DEQ's Cleanup program adds sites meeting any of the criteria below to the ECSI database:

- Sites with documented contamination that are eligible for the Confirmed Release List (Oregon Revised Statute 465.405).
- Sites that are the subject of a cleanup report submitted to DEQ.
- Sites at which the weight of evidence suggests the presence of contamination beyond de minimis proportions.
- Sites that DEQ Site Assessment staff intend to evaluate and are likely to refer to the Voluntary Cleanup, Site Response, or Orphan programs for follow-up.
- Sites at which DEQ oversight or review is requested through the Voluntary Cleanup Program or Independent Cleanup Pathway.
- Landfill sites permitted under DEQ's Solid Waste program, if contaminants that could threaten human health or the environment migrate beyond landfill boundaries, or site issues otherwise exceed the Solid Waste program's regulatory authority.
- Sites that DEQ's Spill program refers to Site Assessment for further action.
- Potentially contaminated sites requiring detailed or time-consuming preliminary file reviews to determine whether further Cleanup program evaluation is needed.

Brownfields and Public Health

Including strategies that address health inequities and promote the health of communities living nearby brownfields is crucial throughout the redevelopment and land use planning process. OHA supports efforts that engage the communities living nearby brownfield properties, involve local leaders, foster cross-sector collaboration, and prevent harmful exposures to contamination.

Mill Sites Inventory and Mapping Project

The OHA-Brownfield Initiative, Department of Environmental Quality, Business Oregon and the Department of Land Conservation and Development (DLCD) teamed up with interns from the urban and regional planning graduate program at Portland State University to create the first centralized inventory and map of abandoned or diminished wood-product mill sites ("sites"), a significant subset of Oregon's brownfield sites. Using the definition of mill site in ORS 197.719, the team identified shared interests in potential for reuse that addresses cross cutting needs in economic development, environmental restoration, land use, and health.

Case Studies

Cully Park. From 2011 to 2018 the Let Us Build Cully Park! coalition worked with the OHA-Brownfield Initiative and the NW Region Brownfields Program in the Department of Environmental Quality to assess and redevelop a former landfill located in the Cully neighborhood of northeast Portland.

Cully Park: Improving health through community partnerships provides an account of the community engagement and educational process for the site assessment phase of this project.

Cully Park Health Consultation report and summary available in English, Spanish, and Somali languages. The Cully Park Community Health Indicators Report, (Spanish) and summaries available in English, Spanish and Somali.

The first phase of Cully Park development includes a community garden, a playground, a tribal plant gathering garden, a basketball court, a youth soccer field, a picnic area, an off-leash dog area and walking fitness trails. Parking and pedestrian access improvement efforts are also underway.

Linnton Action Model Project. Federal, state and local government, private industry, community-serving organizations and community residents joined together to pilot the ATSDR Action Model in the Linnton neighborhood—located within industrial northwest Portland. The pilot project was an opportunity for government, industry and local residents to explore concerns about environmental conditions in the area, and to promote health through neighborhood-level changes.

The ATSDR Action Model provided the platform for re-establishing trusting relationships between neighborhood residents and the government agencies. The Linnton Health Fair event connected Linnton residents to health care service providers, free or reduced cost blood-lead level testing, and environmental, health and municipal organizations and agencies that serve the community.

The EPA funded Vision to Action effort provided a hands-on way for Linnton residents to come together and imagine a healthier community. Linnton residents created a series of drawings that depict their vision of possibilities for redevelopment including the former mill site, promoting recreation along the river, connecting the community through infrastructure improvements that promote physical activity, and creating safe spaces for community gatherings.

The Linnton Photovoice project shares perspectives of neighbors about brownfield redevelopment and health through photography. The resulting collection travels the city as an exhibit to raise awareness of how health can be promoted through brownfield redevelopment.

Financing Brownfields Redevelopment in Oregon

The purpose of Business Oregon's Brownfields Program is to assist individuals, non-profit organizations and local governments with financing to evaluate, cleanup and redevelop brownfields. The department manages two brownfields financing programs: the Oregon Brownfields Redevelopment Fund funded by proceeds from the sale of state revenue bonds; and, the Oregon Coalition Brownfields Cleanup Fund capitalized through a revolving loan grant from the U.S. Environmental Protection Agency.

Oregon Brownfields Redevelopment Fund

The Brownfields Redevelopment Fund is a direct loan and grant financing program to assist property owners to conduct environmental actions and assessment through cleanup on brownfields. Eligible Applicants Any individual, business, non-profit organization, prospective purchaser, municipality, special district, port or tribe may apply to the Brownfields Redevelopment Fund. For program purposes there are two types of applicants: (1) Municipal and (2) Non-municipal. Cities, counties, tribes, ports and special districts are municipal applicants. All other applicants are non-municipal.

The Brownfields Redevelopment Fund provides both grant and loan funding, but is primarily a loan program. Grants can be awarded, up to program limits, on a case-by-case basis depending on a financial analysis of the applicant's debt capacity and the public benefits of the proposed redevelopment project. Financial analysis of an applicant's ability to repay a loan is the primary method the department uses to manage and allocate limited grant resources. Examples of public benefits that factor into the funding decision include family wage job creation, assistance to rural or economically distressed communities, or addressing urgent health and/or safety needs of a local population directly impacted by identified environmental contamination on the property.

Case Study: SeQuential Biofuels Project, Eugene, OR, Recipient of the 2007 National UST Phoenix Award

Located along the McVay Highway in Eugene on the former Franko #15 service station property, the SeQuential Biofuels retail station was the first alternative fuel retail station in the Pacific Northwest offering biofuel blended with petroleum as well as ethanol blends for flex-fuel vehicles. The station and adjoining coffee shop/natural food market is substantially run on renewable power through its self-contained solar array and wind power.

The former Franko #15 service station was left abandoned after petroleum contamination was discovered on the site in 1991, and became the property of Lane County through tax foreclosure by 2004. In an effort to revitalize the site, Lane County entered into negotiations with ODEQ and SeQuential Biofuels. A Brownfields Cleanup Grant from the U.S. EPA in 2005 along with a matching brownfields cleanup loan from Business Oregon started the cleanup, which included soil excavation, installation of monitoring wells, and collection and treatment of groundwater. Today, the property's unique features are designed to prevent recontamination. In addition, "green" features include solar canopies at the dispensers that provide 30 to 50 percent of the site's electrical power, an ecoroof, an interior constructed from untreated wood interior and architectural design features that allow the store's interior to heat and cool naturally. SeQuential Biofuels has a loyal following of patrons, serving approximately 300 customers daily. SeQuential Biofuels is both paving the way for future alternative fuel facilities while cleaning up a site impacted from an "old-line" service station. It is a pivotal representation of what tomorrow's brownfields can encompass, and the potential to accommodate alternative energy options.

31. Brownfields in Alaska*

Alaska Department of Environmental Conservation

Brownfields are abandoned, unused, or underused properties that are hindered from desired reuse or redevelopment by real or perceived environmental contamination. A brownfield can be anything from a 200-acre industrial property, to an old lumber mill, or a small abandoned corner gas station.

Every Alaskan city and borough—both urban and rural—have vacant or underused properties whose redevelopment is complicated by potential contamination. DEC strongly supports and promotes the assessment, cleanup, and reuse of brownfields. In particular, the DEC Brownfields Program can help identify brownfields, assess potential contamination, and assist in arranging for necessary cleanup activities to help local governments and tribes achieve their community's visions for reusing those sites. The DEC Brownfields Program also provides outreach and training opportunities, identifies other available funding and resources, and provides site-specific technical assistance to tribes, Alaska native corporations, municipalities, and borough governments.

Common Types

Alaska's urban areas have many of the same brownfield concerns as large urban centers in the rest of the country: former industrial sites, petroleum and chemical storage areas, abandoned commercial businesses, old gas stations, railroad yards, and many others. However, Alaskan rural communities have brownfields that are unique to their remote locations. Some of these sites include:

- old canneries and fish processing facilities
- old fuel-storage tank farms
- abandoned, inactive dump sites
- shooting ranges
- logging camps
- old mines and mining operations
- old civilian federal facilities such as schools and hospitals
- formerly used defense sites

Very often, these brownfields may directly affect a subsistence resource or recreational area.

---

*Public document originally published as Alaska Department of Environmental Conservation, "Brownfields in Alaska," https://dec.alaska.gov/spar/csp/brownfields.htm#assess (January 2020).

Common Contaminants

Contaminants are any physical, chemical, biological, or radiological substances that have an adverse effect on air, water, or soil. The contaminants most commonly found in Alaska are among those commonly found elsewhere in the U.S. and include petroleum, polychlorinated biphenyls (PCBs), solvents, asbestos, and metals, including lead, mercury, and arsenic.

Soil, water, and air contamination occur from a variety of sources and activities. Government, public, industrial, or commercial facilities, as well as households, can generate or use chemicals that cause contamination when improperly used. However, some chemicals considered contaminants occur naturally in the environment. Many metals, for example, are commonly found in soil.

Understanding a site's background and previous activities can help instruct which contaminants may be present at the property.

Common Steps

Typical brownfields projects include the following steps from site identification through reuse and redevelopment. Depending upon the stage of the brownfields cleanup and reuse process, DEC can play a supporting role (for example, assisting in identifying potential properties) or in regulatory capacity (for example, approving work plans for site assessment and cleanup).

Site Identification. Local stakeholders, municipalities, and tribes are often in the best position for identifying which sites may be most appropriate for a specific reuse based on the unique needs, drivers, and other factors of the local community.

Environmental Assessment. The site is investigated in terms of the property's ownership history and use, previous activities, and documenting any known or suspected spills, releases, or disposal of petroleum or hazardous substances. In addition, the site is characterized and assessed based on field sampling and laboratory analyses, as appropriate, to determine what contaminants are present, at what concentrations, and whether cleanup is necessary.

Cleanup Options and Planning. Based on the results of the site assessment, a cleanup plan may be required to address any existing contamination on the property. One common approach for outlining potential cleanup options could be in an Analysis of Brownfields Cleanups Alternatives (ABCA), which is a requirement for projects that have received federal brownfields funding. If the site is being addressed pursuant to DEC's Contaminated Sites Program, a Site Cleanup Work Plan would be submitted to DEC, which would describe who will do the work, how the site will be cleaned up, the sampling and analyses that will be conducted, among other details to ensure the site is cleaned up to the appropriate levels and by employing he appropriate methods.

Cleanup. How a site is cleaned up depends on several factors, including the source and extent of contamination, the threat to human health and the environment, and the intended reuse envisioned for the property. Common cleanup activities include:

- Excavation of contaminated soil, which is transported offsite for treatment or disposal.
- Tank Removal and excavation and disposal of related petroleum-contaminated soil.
- Capping of contaminated areas with synthetic barriers or clean soil to reduce exposure pathways.
- In-situ treatment using chemicals or natural-occurring microbes to break down contaminants onsite.
- Abatement of lead and asbestos materials, which is removed and disposed offsite by licensed professionals.

Post-Cleanup and Reuse. Post-cleanup obligations depend upon the cleanup decisions made and the way the site is being reused. For example, some sites may require monitoring and ongoing engineered controls (for example, fencing) and institutional controls (for example, deed restrictions) to ensure the protection of human health and the environment.

Common Reuses

Reuse options for Alaska's brownfields vary significantly depending upon their location (urban or rural) and the needs of the community. Some common reuses of Alaskan brownfields include:

- Subsistence fishing and berry picking
- Recreation and green space
- Community centers
- Historic/cultural education centers
- Gardens
- Local housing
- Mixed use
- Commercial buildings

Benefits of Brownfield Reuse

Left abandoned and unaddressed, brownfields can serve as barriers between neighborhoods, an impediment to local investment, eyesores, and potentially have health risks associated with contaminated land or water. On the other hand, cleaning up and reusing brownfields can create several local environmental, economic, and social benefits for a community.

Environmental. Cleaning up and addressing brownfields can improve local environmental quality by remediating contaminated soil and water. Redeveloping brownfields in urban areas, also known as infill, can have additional environmental benefits such as reduced vehicle miles traveled and the associated air emissions, as well as reduced energy consumption. Reusing brownfields also reduces the need for additional greenfield development, thus conserving undeveloped land elsewhere in the community.

Economic. Brownfields reuse and redevelopment can create local jobs, provide additional tax revenue, and grow the local tax base by increasing area property values. Investing in the cleanup and reuse of brownfields often attracts new private investment in an area that would not have otherwise existed.

Social. Cleaning up and addressing contamination at brownfields can remove the risk of exposure, protecting human health and improving the safety of the local community. Reusing brownfields can also create new commercial, residential, and recreational opportunities, improving the quality of life for the local community.

DEC Brownfields Program

The Alaska Department of Environmental Conservation's (DEC) Contaminated Sites Program protects human health and the environment by managing the cleanup of contaminated soil and groundwater in Alaska. Many contaminated sites—due to their location, past historic or cultural significance, or other factors—may have unique drivers to incentive their cleanup and reuse. Recognizing these "brownfields" existed across Alaska, DEC created a program to help properties with an identified vision for reuse and strong community support get cleaned up and productively reused.

Since 2001, the DEC Brownfields Program has worked with local governments, tribes, and community stakeholders to assess, cleanup, and reuse brownfields to improve the environmental, economic, and social well-being of their communities. Recognizing the unique opportunities and challenges inherent to Alaska's brownfields given its size, remoteness, and history, the DEC Brownfields Program employs a multi-pronged approach to address and revitalize dormant properties across the state. Specifically, DEC:

- provides technical assistance and services through DEC Brownfields Assessment and Cleanups (DBAC) Program;
- provides regulatory guidance;
- assists stakeholders apply for and implement additional grants;
- facilitates community outreach and training; and
- manages its inventory of brownfield properties.

DEC Brownfield Assessment and Cleanup (DBAC) Services DEC works closely with communities across Alaska to identify, assess, and cleanup brownfields to put those properties back into productive use. By assisting Alaskan tribes, native corporations, municipalities, and non-profits in conducting environmental site assessments and cleanups at brownfield sites, DBAC services help identify and reduce the environmental uncertainties or actual conditions. Since 2004, DEC has provided nearly 200 community and tribal partners an array of reports and resources to assist their projects navigate the brownfields development process. Through DBAC services, DEC helps communities:

- determine whether an environmental problem at a site is limiting its desired reuse;
- identify the nature and extent of contamination;
- identify recommendations for addressing potential contamination and estimate costs for additional assessment, if needed;

- identify cleanup options and provide an estimate of cleanup costs, if indicated; and
- conduct cleanup activities designed to enable reuse of a site.

Regulatory Guidance

The DEC Brownfields Program can assist stakeholders better understand and meet applicable state and federal environmental regulations and policies. Relevant laws and regulations may include, among others: State Regulations:

- 18 Alaska Administrative Code (AAC) 75.300-.396. Discharge Reporting, Cleanup, and Disposal of Oil and Other Hazardous Substances; and
- Alaska Statute (AS) 46.03.822. Strict Liability for the Release of Hazardous Substances. Federal Laws, Regulations, and Policies:
- Comprehensive Environmental Response, Compensation, and Liability Act (CERCLA, or Superfund); Small Business Liability Relief and Brownfields Revitalization Act (SBLRBRA, commonly known as the Brownfields Amendments); and
- Brownfields Utilization, Investment and Local Development Act (BUILD).

In addition, DEC's Contaminated Sites Program has developed a number of guidance and policy documents on various parts of the cleanup process (characterization, cleanup level determination, risk, cleanup alternatives, etc.), which DEC's Brownfields Program can assist with finding and understanding.

Grant Application Assistance

The DEC Brownfields Program also helps educate Alaska's brownfield stakeholders about potential grant opportunities and other resources and make connections with the relevant agencies or parties offering financial or other technical support. For example, when an eligible entity applies for a competitive brownfield grant from the U.S. Environmental Protection Agency (EPA), DEC can assist with application development (scoping, review/comment, etc.), and will write a letter to EPA in support of that application. Similarly, DEC can introduce interested parties to other sources of technical assistance, such as EPA's Technical Assistance to Brownfields (TAB) providers and Targeted Brownfields Assessment (TBA) program.

Community Outreach and Training

Community outreach and training is an important component of the DEC Brownfields Program, which provides these services in a number of ways, including: developing outreach materials such as fact sheets, case studies, and issue papers; organizing annual trainings and workshops for State and Tribal Brownfield Response Programs; presenting on Alaskan brownfields topics at state and national conferences and providing these presentations on the DEC Brownfields website; and providing community-specific visioning sessions and communication planning.

State Contaminated Sites Database

To provide tribes, Village Corporations, Regional Corporations, municipal and borough governments, and other interested stakeholders with known information regarding potential contamination at a site, DEC maintains a database of contaminated sites that have been identified throughout Alaska. The DEC Brownfields Program ensures that brownfield sites that it supports or manages are included in the state database, as well as any relevant reports, as appropriate.

32. Brownfields

Transform the Past, Build for the Future[*]

NEW YORK STATE DEPARTMENT
OF ENVIRONMENTAL CONSERVATION

New York State has a long history of brownfield redevelopment. Our brownfield programs have already addressed hundreds of properties, and as you will see in this brochure, many of these sites have been put back into productive use.

Environmental contamination is often the most obvious feature of a brownfield. However, transforming these properties into productive community assets includes many factors: planning, financing, community involvement, liability issues, technology selection, regulatory requirements, and the coordination of stakeholders.

Brownfield revitalization is a crucial issue for New York State. We hope this brochure encourages you to join with other businesses, developers, local officials, environmentalists and community leaders in this important initiative. As we continue to focus energy and resources on brownfields, the future of these sites, along with the environmental and economic future of our state, continues to brighten.

Brownfield Redevelopment in New York State

Nearly every community in New York State is affected by brownfield sites. Contaminated and abandoned properties exist in big cities, small towns, sprawling suburbs and the countryside. Left untouched, brownfields pose environmental, legal and financial burdens on a community and its taxpayers. However, after cleanup, these sites can again become the powerful engines for economic vitality, jobs and community pride that they once were.

New York State's brownfield programs have evolved to include:

- Streamlined cleanup processes
- Community involvement and planning
- Increased availability of financial assistance
- Liability clarification and relief

---

[*]Public document originally published as New York State Department of Environmental Conservation, *Brownfields: Transform the Past Build for the Future*, http://www.dec.ny.gov/docs/remediation_hudson_pdf/brownfields.pdf (January 2017).

- Valuable partnerships with agencies within New York State and across the country
- Resources for all project stages, from planning to cleanup and redevelopment

Our Results Are Real

Municipalities, businesses, and nonprofit organizations across New York State have taken advantage of DEC s brownfield programs. Hundreds of abandoned and underused sites are being turned into vital and productive properties.

Our Programs Work

Environmental Restoration Program Provides municipalities with financial assistance for site investigation and remediation at eligible brownfield sites. Municipalities are reimbursed 90 percent of on-site costs and 100 percent of off-site costs. Brownfield Cleanup Program (successor to the Voluntary Cleanup Program) was developed to enhance private sector cleanup of brown fields and to reduce development pressure on greenfields. Brownfield Opportunity Areas Program provides technical and financial assistance to municipalities and community-based organizations to conduct redevelopment planning for areas containing brownfield sites.

Our Mission Is Clear

The Department's brownfield programs promote environmental restoration and preservation, public health protection, economic development, job creation and community revitalization throughout the state.

DEC has more than 20 years of experience in cleaning up contaminated properties. While maintaining strict cleanup standards, we also provide appropriate liability relief and funding for investigation and remediation of brownfields. Creativity and innovation at the state level provide for collaboration among all levels of government, businesses, and nonprofits to transform brownfields into productive, beneficial areas that improve the quality of life for all New Yorkers.

Lakeside Commerce, City of Buffalo, Erie County

This site is located on prime waterfront property just south of down-town Buffalo, in an area once renowned as the hub for steel and iron manufacturing in Western New York. Abandoned for the last 20 years, the area is gradually awakening from its industrial past through projects like this one. The site's current owner, Krog USC Associates I LLC, initiated a cleanup project through the Brownfield Cleanup Program to revitalize the vacant site. DEC issued the Certificate of Completion for this project in December 2005. The site is now home to a 275,600 square foot manufacturing facility that is already occupied by a local plastic manufacturer. Krog is committed to maintaining the site as an industrial facility. The once barren site now boasts a hopeful future and is encouraging neighboring properties to undergo a similar transformation.

Paper Mill Island Park, Village of Baldwinsville, Onondaga County

This project transformed a former paper mill from an abandoned, contaminated site into a popular water-front park and amphitheater, complete with Seneca River boating access. The Village of Baldwinsville received substantial grant funding from New York State, and also partnered with several private entities to complete the project.

The park, which opened in September 2000, now hosts concerts and events from May through September and has become a popular destination for village residents and tourists alike. "The effort was a model of how a complex project with multiple sources of public and private financing can be accomplished on a fast-track schedule." Dale Vollmer, Plumley Engineering

Water's Edge Senior Campus City of Port Jervis, Orange County

Affordable senior housing is now more readily available in the City of Port Jervis thanks to the investigation and remediation of a former chemical manufacturing site. After the old industrial facility was razed and the property was cleaned to meet residential standards, a developer constructed new senior housing which overlooks the Neversink River near the Port Jervis downtown center. This development has helped to address a shortage of affordable senior housing in the area. "This facility will assure senior residents that they can remain in their community to enjoy their retirement years." Mayor Ross Decker, City of Port Jervis.

Jamestown Development Corporation, Village of Falconer, Chautauqua County

Jamestown Development Corporation opened a new 170,000-square-foot facility in an economic development zone of the village, on a parcel of land which was previously abandoned. The new building is used by DC Rollforms and Inscape to manufacture roll-formed metal parts and office partitions. DEC received a "Key to the Village of Falconer" in appreciation of its efforts in this brownfield redevelopment.

Richmond County Bank Ballpark at St. George, Staten Island

Under New York State's Voluntary Cleanup Program, the New York City Economic Development Corporation turned a contaminated rail yard in the St. George waterfront area along the North Shore of Staten Island into the Staten Island Yankees' ballpark stadium.

The Richmond County Bank Ballpark is a 6,500-seat facility that has hosted hundreds of thousands of fans since opening in 2001. The stadium has created 200 jobs and more than $16 million in annual revenue and it represents the centerpiece of a comprehensive economic redevelopment plan for the north shore of Staten Island. "It's hard to believe that just a few years ago, this ballpark and attractive waterfront esplanade were the site of an abandoned rail yard." NYC Economic Development Corporation President Andrew M. Alper.

Greyston Bakery, City of Yonkers, Westchester County

The Greyston Bakery has operated for 20 years in the City of Yonkers, producing gourmet desserts. The bakery expanded its operations by remediating a brownfield site near the Hudson River. Following remediation, a new $9 million bakery was constructed, which more than tripled the bakery's capacity and will allow the company to expand its existing 50-person staff. The bakery actively recruits and hires employees who have had difficulties finding employment in the past and uses profits to support the Greyston Foundation's other community projects. www.greystonbakery.com/index.html and www.greyston.org "The Greyston Bakery is committed to remaining in Southwest Yonkers, which has been our home for 20 years. This long-abandoned lot has been restored to productive use, allowing for many new, good jobs in a beautiful, new state-of-the-art building." Charles G. Lief, Chairman of the Board of Directors, Greyston Bakery.

Mitchell Park, Village of Greenport, Suffolk County

Using resources from several federal, state and local programs, the Village of Greenport redeveloped a 3.2-acre waterfront parcel that was contaminated by past uses, including a marina, shipyard and oystering activities. To develop ideas for future site uses, the village held an international design competition that attracted more than 500 submissions from 26 countries. The site now contains a public park, including an amphitheater, a historic carousel, and a harbor walk. This project has helped Greenport transform itself from a former naval shipyard to an emerging tourist destination. "It's so good to see a plan for the community come together. We'll be here all the time with our kids and grandkids." Lorraine Murphy, resident of Greenport.

Partnerships

New York State Agencies

Banking Department: Primary regulator for state licensed and state chartered financial entities, including domestic banks, foreign agencies, branches and representative offices, savings institutions and trust companies and other financial institutions operating in New York including mortgage bankers and brokers, check cashers, money transmitters, and licensed lenders, among others. www.banking.state.ny.us.

Department of Agriculture & Markets: Fosters a competitive food and agriculture industry that benefits agricultural producers and consumers alike. The remediation and redevelopment of brownfields reduces the need to develop greenspace or agricultural land. www.agmkt.state.ny.us.

Department of Health: Coordinates with DEC to ensure cleanups are protective of public health and promotes infra structure improvements of public and private drinking water systems. www.health.state.ny.us.

Department of State: The Division of Coastal Resources provides funding and technical assistance to waterfront com munities to prepare and implement redevelopment strategies, including the redevelopment of abandoned buildings, for urban areas containing brownfield sites. DOS partners with DEC to administer the Brownfield Opportunity Areas Program which provides technical and financial assistance for brownfield planning and assessment in areas with a multitude of brownfield sites. www.dos.state.ny.us.

Department of Transportation: Helps to fund transportation projects that facilitate economic development by improving site access. www.dot.state.ny.us.

Department of Taxation and Finance: Collects tax revenue and provides associated services in support of government services in New York State. Responsible for administering the Brownfield Redevelopment Credit, the Remediated Brownfield Credit for Real Property Taxes and the Environmental Remediation Insurance Credit associated with the Brownfield Cleanup Program. www.tax.state.ny.us.

Empire State Development: Funding and redevelopment assistance. www.empire.state.ny.us.

Energy Research and Development Authority: Funding and technical assistance to promote the development and deployment of innovative and energy efficient technologies. www.nyserda.org.

Division of Housing and Community Renewal: Technical and financial assistance to communities to prepare sites suitable for affordable housing. www.dhcr.state.ny.us.

Environmental Facilities Corporation: Provides funding for water quality improvement projects such as water and sewer infrastructure, land acquisition for water quality protection, and water quality protection components of municipal brownfield projects. www.nysefc.org.

Governor's Office of Regulatory Reform: Oversees the regulatory process of all New York State agencies. www.gorr.state.ny.us.

Governor's Office for Small Cities: Administers the Federal Community Development Block Grant to small communities to help low- or moderate-income individuals, revitalize neighborhoods, or address threats to health and safety. www.nysmallcities.com.

Insurance Department: Responsible for supervising and regulating all insurance business in New York State. Provides guidance for insurers on the minimum standards for environmental remediation insurance and the Environmental Remediation Insurance Credit associated with the Brownfield Cleanup Program. www.ins.state.ny.us.

Office of Parks, Recreation and Historic Preservation: Funding for land acquisition, water recreation projects, projects that enhance the cultural or historical aspect of water bodies and the acquisition and development of parks. www.nysparks.state.ny.us.

Interstate Technology and Regulatory Council (ITRC): State led coalition of regulators, industry experts, citizen stakeholders, academia and federal partners who work to achieve regulatory acceptance of environmental technologies. DEC s participation on ITRC s brownfields team, keeps New York State on the cutting edge of technology and policy issues related to brownfields. www.itrcweb.org.

Other Organizations

Quality Communities Working Group: Studies community growth in New York State and develops measures to assist communities in implementing effective land development, preservation and rehabilitation strategies that pro mote economic development and environmental protection.www.qualitycommunities.org.

State University of New York (SUNY) Center for Brownfield Studies: Provides brownfield stakeholders with expertise for redeveloping brownfields. http://sunybrownfields.esf.edu/.

University of Buffalo Center for Integrated Waste Management/Brownfield Action Project (BAP): University personnel from several disciplines critical to successful remediation and redevelopment of brownfields focus on increasing research opportunities in site remediation, providing technical assistance to municipalities seeking to redevelop environmentally contaminated properties, and expanding local workforce training opportunities in environmental restoration. www.ciwm.buffalo.edu.

United States Environmental Protection Agency (EPA): EPAs Brownfields Economic Redevelopment Initiative provides New Yorkers with funding, technical assistance and resources to clean up brownfields. New York State is a member of EPA s Brownfields Interagency Work Group. www.epa.gov/region02/brownfields/index.html.

33. Louisiana Brownfields*

LOUISIANA DEPARTMENT OF ENVIRONMENTAL QUALITY

Voluntary Remediation Program Description

Parties wishing to receive a Certificate of Completion must perform an investigation and remediation following the requirements of the Voluntary Investigation and Remedial Action statutes and regulations.

Investigation of the site begins with a Voluntary Remedial Investigation Application. The application consists of the Application form, $500 application fee, and an Investigation Work Plan. The work plan shall be designed to identify the nature and extent of contamination at the identified area of immovable property.

After approval and implementation of the investigation work plan, an investigation report shall be submitted for approval. If the nature and extent of contamination has been identified, the department will issue an approval letter stating those facts.

Upon approval of the investigation report, a Voluntary Remedial Action Application may be submitted. The Voluntary Remedial Action Application consists of a Voluntary Remedial Action application form, $500 application fee, and a Voluntary Remedial Action Work Plan. See Voluntary Remedial Action Process Flowchart

Mission

The Louisiana Voluntary Remediation Program (VRP) provides a mechanism by which property owners (or potential owners) or others can clean up contaminated properties and receive a release of liability for further cleanup of historical contamination at a site. This release of liability flows to future owners of the property as well. Through the Voluntary Remediation Program, LDEQ hopes to provide administrative, technical, and legal incentives in order to encourage the redevelopment and reuse of brownfields properties.

Legal Authority

Louisiana Voluntary Investigation and Remedial Action (VIRA) statute (La. R.S. 30:2285–2290)

Louisiana Voluntary Remediation Regulations (LAC 33:VI.Chapter 9)

---

*Public document originally published as Louisiana Department of Environmental Quality, "Brownfields," https://deq.louisiana.gov/page/brownfields (2020).

Eligibility

All properties are eligible for participation in the VRP, except the following:

a. Sites listed on the National Priorities List or formally proposed to be listed,
b. Permitted hazardous waste management units (HWMU), however, if the HWMU is located within a larger site, then only that portion of the site inside the HWMU is ineligible,
c. Trust-fund-eligible underground storage tank sites, and
d. Sites that have pending, unresolved federal environmental enforcement actions (not simply cost-recovery actions) that are related to the proposed voluntary remediation.

All persons are eligible except that only non-responsible persons (as defined in LAC 33:VI.903) are eligible to perform Partial Voluntary Remedial Actions.

Investigation and Remediation

A Voluntary Remediation must begin with an investigation that is consistent with the methods and processes provided by the Louisiana Risk-Based Corrective Action Program (RECAP) and must include the determination of the nature and extent of potential threats to human health and the environment through data collection and site characterization, and the development of remedial action goals. A Voluntary Remediation must be protective of human health and the environment and comply with RECAP standards as determined by the VRP Regulations.

In the VRP, investigation and remediation are performed on an identified area of immovable property and the release of liability is granted for that specific property. Also, no Certificate of Completion can be issued for a property unless some form of remediation is performed on the property. Contamination cannot be simply risked away in order to obtain a Certificate.

Applications and Fees

Parties wishing to receive a Certificate of Completion must perform an investigation and remediation following the requirements of the Voluntary Investigation and Remedial Action statutes and regulations.

Investigation of the site begins with a Voluntary Remedial Investigation Application. The application consists of the Application form, $500 application fee, and an Investigation Work Plan. The work plan shall be designed to identify the nature and extent of contamination at the identified area of immovable property.

After approval and implementation of the investigation work plan, an investigation report shall be submitted for approval. If the nature and extent of contamination has been identified, the department will issue an approval letter stating those facts.

Upon approval of the investigation report, a Voluntary Remedial Action Application may be submitted. The Voluntary Remedial Action Application consists of a Voluntary Remedial Action application form, $500 application fee, and a Voluntary Remedial Action Work Plan.

Public Notice

After a satisfactory review, the Voluntary Remediation Application is accepted for public review and the Voluntary Remedial Action Plan must undergo a thirty-day public notice and comment period. The participant must place this public notice in the local newspaper and must also provide a direct notice of the Plan to adjacent landowners by certified mail.

Completion

Upon a satisfactory completion of a voluntary remedial action and the submission of a Voluntary Remedial Action Report that demonstrates that the remedial action goals have been met, the participant receives a Certificate of Completion, from which flows a release from liability of the participant for the cleanup costs of historical contamination at the property.

Partial Voluntary Remedial Actions

A Partial Voluntary Remedial Action is one in which not all discharges or disposals or threatened discharges or disposals are removed. Partial Voluntary Remedial Actions, however, must be protective of public health and the environment for the intended use of the property and corresponding use restrictions for the property must be recorded in the parish records.

Only non-responsible persons, as defined in LAC 33:VI.903, may apply to perform a Partial Voluntary Remedial Action or receive a Certificate of Completion for a Partial Voluntary Remedial Action. Applicants for a Partial Voluntary Remedial Action follow the same process as above, except that they must also submit a Partial Voluntary Remediation Supplemental Application Form at the time of application.

Surveillance. The OEC Surveillance Division protects the citizens of the state by conducting inspections of permitted and non-permitted facilities, by responding to environmental incidents such as unauthorized releases, spills and citizen complaints, natural disasters, and other emergency situations, by providing compliance assistance to the regulated community when appropriate, by assessing and monitoring air and water quality for compliance with standards, and by promoting case information management for vigorous and timely resolution of issues of non-compliance.

Remediation Division. The mission of the Remediation Program is to maintain and enhance the environment of the state to promote and protect the health, safety and welfare of the people of Louisiana. This program provides an efficient means to develop, implement, and enforce regulations. It also pursues efforts to prevent and to remediate contamination of the environment. This program pursues a unified approach to remediation, simplifies and clarifies the scope of the remedial process, increases protection of human health and the environment by addressing remediation consistently, allows for fast track remediation, where applicable, reduces review time and labor, increases responsiveness to the public and regulatee, and increases accountability.

The Remediation Program meets its mission my performing the following duties: site investigations/evaluation, corrective action, corrective action monitoring, field verification, communication, documentation, training and research.

Corporate Recycling Tax Credits. Taxpaying entities who purchase qualified new recycling manufacturing or process equipment, and/or qualified service contracts, may be eligible for a tax credit of 14.4 percent against Louisiana income and corporation franchise taxes. The equipment must be new machinery or apparatus used exclusively to process post-consumer waste material, and/or recovered material, or new manufacturing machinery used exclusively to produce finished products from >50 percent post-consumer waste material in the state of Louisiana. Applicants must complete an Application for Income Tax Credit for Qualified New Recycling Equipment. More information can be found in the DEQ Solid Waste regulations, LAC 33:VII.Chapter 104.

Annual Recycling Report Form for Parishes and Municipalities. The Louisiana Department of Environmental Quality (LDEQ) is required by the Louisiana Revised Statutes 30:2413.A.9, to submit an annual update report to the Legislature on the status of resource recovery and recycling programs in the parishes and municipalities throughout the state. LDEQ in turn is authorized to collect and compile data from the parishes and municipalities on resource recovery and recycling programs in those jurisdictions.

Success Stories

Louisiana Brownfields Association. Late in 2004, a group of interested parties believed that the creation of a state brownfields organization in LA. could help promote further redevelopment and revitalization of potentially contaminated property in LA. In July of 2006, the Louisiana Brownfields Association was born. Our mission is to promote a broad range of Brownfields-related objectives and initiatives, including environmental restoration, economic revitalization, natural resource preservation, conservation and recreational-based beneficial reuse, enhancement of financial and regulatory incentives, job creation and training, public health, environmental equity and justice and community outreach and education.

The Louisiana Brownfields Association, through community outreach and education, promotes a wide array of Brownfields-related goals, objectives and initiatives, including environmental restoration, economic development and revitalization, natural resources preservation, enhancement of financial and regulatory incentives, and protection of human health. The Louisiana Brownfields Association strives to accomplish this mission through a diverse membership that includes a wide variety of stakeholders, including property owners; developers; local, State, and Federal agency representatives; urban and regional planners; regulatory experts; community leaders; legal experts; financial and insurance industry representatives; environmental professionals, and other parties that may be interested in promoting Brownfield-related goals. In 2014, the Louisiana Brownfields Association achieved 501(c)6 non-profit status.

RPC's Brownfield Redevelopment Program. Supported by grants from the U.S. Environmental Protection Agency (EPA), the Regional Planning Commission's (RPC's) Brownfield Redevelopment Program provides technical guidance and environmental assessments to facilitate the redevelopment of Brownfield sites in the city of New Orleans and the surrounding parishes of Jefferson, Plaquemines, St. Bernard, St. Charles, St. John, St. Tammany and Tangipahoa in southeast Louisiana, converting these properties from community liabilities into community assets.

South Central Planning and Development Commission. SCPDC is a diverse, ever-changing commission serving many different constituencies made specially for and by local governments in the South Central Region. We perform a variety of services to meet the ever-changing needs and challenges of its member governments. These services include long-range planning, state and federal liaison, current issues, membership services and services to business and citizens.

34. Brownfields in Washington

Washington State Department of Ecology

Brownfields are abandoned or underutilized properties that may have environmental contamination. Brownfields are common in communities of all sizes—they may be old gas stations, drycleaners, industrial facilities, smelters, or former agricultural land.

Negative perceptions of brownfields, along with potential environmental liability concerns, can complicate a community's redevelopment plans. Local governments encounter brownfields as they plan to revitalize downtowns, make improvements to infrastructure, and redevelop old properties to meet community needs.

The Department of Ecology is proud to protect, preserve, and enhance Washington's environment for current and future generations. Our innovative partnerships sustain healthy land, air, and water in harmony with a strong economy.

Spills & Cleanup. We prevent and clean up toxic leaks and spills across the state. We respond to spills, inspect chemical storage and transport facilities, and clean up complex contaminated sites that threaten the health of people and the environment.

Waste & Toxics. We work to safely manage solid, hazardous, and nuclear waste and reduce toxic chemicals in the products you use. We regulate the threats found in everyday household products and help businesses promote green practices to turn waste products into valuable resources.

Water & Shorelines. We improve and protect water quality, manage and conserve water resources, and effectively manage coastal and inland shorelines to assure our state has sufficient supplies of clean water for communities and the natural environment.

Air & Climate. Everyone living in and around our state deserves clean air to breathe and a sustainable future that is responsive to challenges presented by climate change. To reach these goals, we regulate harmful emissions from vehicles, burning, and industrial activities which protects air quality and reduces greenhouse gases that are warming our planet.

Our Brownfields Program helps communities put those properties back into use so they can bring their redevelopment visions to life.

What does the Brownfields Program do? Our Brownfields Program works with local governments, non-profits, tribes, and community stakeholders across the state who are interested in cleaning up brownfields for redevelopment. We help them navigate a full range of environmental activities—from environmental assessments and cleanup, to redevelopment planning.

---

*Public document originally published as "Brownfields in Washington." https://ecology.wa.gov/Spills-Cleanup/Contamination-cleanup/Brownfields (2020).

As part of the Brownfields Program, we formed the State Brownfields Team. The team has members from Ecology, the Washington State Department of Commerce, and the U.S. Environmental Protection Agency (EPA). We work together to promote and support brownfield redevelopment opportunities throughout Washington. We work with communities to provide information, funding resources, technical assistance, and outreach.

Where can I find funding and technical assistance for my brownfield project? Our State Brownfields Team can help match your project to one or more of the wide range of federal and state funding and technical assistance opportunities. Download Brownfields Funding Opportunities in Washington State for a more comprehensive list.

We conduct outreach through participation in local, regional, and national conferences. Our team can also help you host brownfield workshops focused on a single community or brownfields redevelopment topic.

Ecology Funding and Technical Assistance. We provide funding for site assessments, environmental cleanup, and reuse planning through our remedial action grant program, including integrated planning grants (IPGs). IPGs help communities make informed decisions about acquiring and reusing a potentially contaminated property.

Ecology can also provide funding to local governments and non-profits for environmental assessments for eligible brownfields using funds from our EPA State Response Program grant.

We provide technical assistance as part of managing cleanups under the Model Toxics Control Act (MTCA). This includes providing technical assistance for projects funded by our partners.

Commerce Funding. The Commerce team manages Washington's Brownfields Revolving Loan Fund (BRLF) Program. The BRLF helps local and regional governments, non-profits, and private businesses cleanup and redevelop brownfield sites. They also provide technical assistance to people interested in redeveloping properties.

The benefits of redeveloping brownfields. When communities clean up and redevelop brownfields properties, they can:

- Stimulate a community's economy, create more jobs, and increase local tax base.
- Provide healthy sites for community priorities such as affordable housing.
- Turn their community's perceived problem into an asset and improve their image.
- Enable efficient land use and minimize the construction of new service infrastructure.
- Facilitate the resolution of environmental justice issues.
- Protect human and environmental health, and mitigate public health and safety concerns.
- Provide opportunities for habitat restoration, parks, or other public spaces.

Paying for Cleanups. Environmental cleanups can be costly but are always worth the effort. They protect and restore natural resources, remove blight, invigorate communities, and make way for new economic opportunities. We offer several types of grants and loans to help local governments revitalize contaminated sites and return them to beneficial uses. These grants also lessen the trickle-down costs of cleanup to taxpayers and ratepayers and help provide safe drinking water to people living in contaminated areas.

The Brownfields Sites List shows known brownfields cleanup sites in Washington

State. Brownfield sites are abandoned or underused properties where there may be environmental contamination. Redevelopment efforts are often hindered by the liability for the cleanup or the uncertainty of cleanup costs. Brownfield sites that are not cleaned up represent lost opportunities for economic development and for other community improvements.

Cleanups in My Community (CIMC) enables you to map and list hazardous waste cleanup locations and grant areas, and drill down to details about those cleanups and grants and other, related information.

Voluntary Cleanup Program. Under the Voluntary Cleanup Program, people who independently clean up a contaminated site may request fee-based services from Ecology, including:

- Technical assistance on how to meet cleanup requirements
- Written opinions on whether your cleanup meets those requirements

Under the state's cleanup law, you have several options for cleaning up a contaminated site and achieving regulatory closure.

The Voluntary Cleanup Program is designed for simpler sites with routine cleanups. Under the program, you can perform a cleanup independently and request technical assistance and written opinions from Ecology on the sufficiency of your cleanup. Such opinions are often required by lenders when buying or selling contaminated property. However, you cannot settle your cleanup liability under the Voluntary Cleanup Program.

35. North Dakota's Brownfields Program*

NORTH DAKOTA DEPARTMENT OF ENVIRONMENTAL QUALITY

The North Dakota Department of Environmental Quality (DEQ)'s vision is for a sustainable, high quality environment for current and future generations. Our Mission is to conserve and protect the quality of North Dakota's air, land and water resources following science and the law.

In cooperation with the general public, industry and government at all levels, the department implements protective programs and standards to help maintain and improve environmental quality. The concept of the DEQ's Brownfields Program is to take contaminated or potentially contaminated, underdeveloped, unproductive property and convert it into productive real estate. Brownfield sites are defined as abandoned, idled or underused industrial or commercial properties whose redevelopment is complicated by real or perceived environmental contamination.

To date, the Department continues to receive Brownfields State Response grants from the EPA. The grant can be used by the Department for environmental assessment and hazardous material cleanup activities at Brownfield sites. The assessment activities include environmental activities preliminary to cleanup such as site assessment, site characterization and site response, or cleanup planning and design for areas that have an actual or threatened release of a hazardous substance, pollutant, or contaminant.

Brownfield assessment and cleanup funds may only be used at sites where there is release, or substantial threat of release, of a hazardous substance, or there is a release, or substantial threat of release, of a pollutant or contaminant which may present an imminent and substantial danger to public health or welfare. In addition, funds may be used at sites where there is a reason to believe that a release has occurred or is about to occur. Examples of potential Brownfield sites in North Dakota include: An abandoned retail commercial building which has or is suspected to have asbestos in the ceiling tiles, wall insulation, or on the heating boiler in the basement or pipes coming off the boiler, and An abandoned gas station with soil contamination.

The Division of Waste Management Brownfields Program is application based, and cities, counties or local development groups may apply for assistance. Two documents have been developed to assist in the application process.

---

*Public document originally published as North Dakota Department of Environmental Quality, "Brownfields Program," https://deq.nd.gov/WM/Brownfields/ (2020).

The first is a Brownfields Introduction letter. The letter provides prospective applicants background information on Brownfields and how the Division's Brownfields Program will work.

The contents states in North Dakota we tend to think of Brownfields sites as large, abandoned industrial properties such as steel mills or large manufacturing plants located in cities like Chicago or Detroit. In reality, Brownfields' sites could be former service stations, dry cleaners, factories, warehouses, parking lots, hangars, lots where heavy equipment was stored or repaired, or bus facilities. These sites could be changed from potential liabilities into successful developments that will generate revenues and jobs for the community.

The Department has been active in the Brownfields Program since 2002 and to-date has made possible the assessment and/or cleanup of 38 properties throughout the state. The Department has received its latest State Response grant from the EPA. The grant can be used by the Department for environmental assessment and cleanup activities at Brownfields sites. These activities include environmental activities preliminary to cleanup such as site assessment, site characterization and site response, or cleanup planning and design for areas that have an actual or threatened release of a hazardous substance, pollutant, or contaminant as well as the actual remediation itself. Brownfields assessment funds may only be used at sites where there is release, or substantial threat of release, of a hazardous substance, or there is a release, or substantial threat of release of a pollutant or contaminant which may present an imminent and substantial danger to public health or welfare. In addition, funds may be used at sites where there is a reason to believe that a release has occurred or is about to occur.

Examples of sites that have been addressed by the state's Brownfields Program include:

1. In January 2009, the former Good Samaritan Nursing Home in Mott, ND was assessed and remediated for asbestos floor tiles and sheet rock with funding provided by the Brownfields Program. The building is scheduled for demolition and the lot for redevelopment.

2. In November of 2008, an abandoned auto dealership with soil contamination and leaking underground storage tanks, located in Grafton, ND, was assessed and remediated with funding provided by the Brownfields Program. The property is scheduled for commercial redevelopment

We would expect that the city, county or local economic development group has plans for the property that involves:

1. Renovating the building for reuse;
2. Removing the existing building and rebuilding a new building for occupancy; or
3. Removing the building and creating a "green way/green space." This could be as simple as planting grass and trees, and placing park benches on the site

The second is an Application Guideline for Brownfields Assistance In North Dakota. The guideline identifies the minimum requirements for submitting an application for a single potential Brownfields site. There are no limits on the number of sites that may be submitted for consideration, however, there is a limit on funds available to the Program.

Applicants submitting more than one site are asked to prioritize the applications based on local importance for redevelopment.

Sites will be prioritized should the number and potential assessment costs for all sites submitted exceed available funds. The Division envisions that factors such as level of contamination and community commitment toward cleanup and redevelopment will be considered during prioritization.

36. Tribal Brownfields and Response Programs*

U.S. Environmental Protection Agency

There are 565 federally recognized tribes within the United States. Each tribe is an independent, sovereign nation, responsible for setting standards, making environmental policy, and managing environmental programs for its people. While each tribe faces unique challenges, many share similar environmental legacies.

Environmental issues in Indian country range from developing basic administrative infrastructure to passing sweeping new laws; from controlling illegal open dumping to developing wastewater and drinking water infrastructure; from controlling and removing leaking underground storage tanks to asbestos and lead abatement and removal; and from air pollution to the cleanup and reuse of contaminated land.

Given each tribe's unique history and culture and the complexity of jurisdictional issues, the ability to address environmental issues in Indian country calls for new approaches and ways of thinking. The EPA Brownfields Program provides these approaches, and progress and results are occurring across Indian country.

Brownfields and Contaminated Land in Indian Country

Brownfields and other contaminated lands are found throughout the United States. Often legacies of an industrial past or bygone business, they dot the landscape of large and small communities. Brownfields are defined as "real property the expansion, redevelopment, or reuse of which may be complicated by the presence or potential presence of a hazardous substance, pollutant, or contaminant." They come in many forms and sizes. Brownfields can be the abandoned warehouse or corner gas station, the local mill site or abandoned mine. In Indian country they are as diverse as the communities in which they are found.

To address environmental issues in Indian country, many tribes establish their own environmental protection and natural resource management offices. To clean up and reuse contaminated lands, many create brownfields programs or "Tribal Response Programs." However, tribal communities often lack funding to sustain environmental program capacity building and continue to need outside technical assistance and expertise.

---

*Public document originally published U.S. Environmental Protection Agency, "Tribal Brownfields and Response Programs," https://www.epa.gov/sites/production/files/2015-09/documents/tribalreport11.pdf (2019) (January 2020).

Additionally, many tribes seeking to address brownfields in their communities face problems that are found in many small or rural areas in the United States. Rural locations typically do not have the technical resources that many larger communities have, nor the economic drivers associated with more dense populations that might spur cleanup and reuse. Tribes may seek to return contaminated land to a non-economic reuse (e.g., returning land to a culturally beneficial reuse), which often must be funded by the public sector or tribal government and which may not attract the interest of those with private cleanup dollars.

Despite the challenges, revitalization of contaminated lands is an environmental issue being addressed successfully across Indian country. With the assistance of grants and other resources available through EPA's Brownfields Program, tribes are making great strides in cleaning up and returning contaminated land back to productive use. By using the grants and tools available, tribes address their fundamental environmental and revitalization goals and enrich the health and welfare of their communities.

U.S. EPA Brownfields Resources for Revitalization of Contaminated Land in Indian Country

Since the inception of EPA's Brownfields Program in 1995, the program's goal has been "to empower states, tribes, communities, and other stakeholders in economic development to work together in a timely manner to prevent, assess, safely clean up, and sustainably reuse brownfields." The program provides financial and technical assistance for brownfields revitalization, including annual competitive grants for environmental assessment, revolving loan funds (RLF), cleanup, and job training, and non-competitive funding for state and tribal response programs. In 2002, the passage of the Small Business Liability Relief and Brownfields

Revitalization Act—referred to as the Brownfields Amendments—codified many of the policies EPA developed. The Brownfields Amendments authorized, among other things, two main sources of funding that may assist tribes in revitalizing contaminated land in Indian country:

1. (1)Section 128(a) State and Tribal Response Program funding
2. (2)Section 104(k) Competitive Grant Program funding

Tribal Response Program Grants

Tribal Response Program funding—referred to as "Section 128(a)" funding after the section of the Comprehensive Environmental Response, Compensation and Liability Act (CERCLA) that it falls under—can be used to create new or to enhance existing environmental response programs. Authorized at $50 million per year and shared among states, tribes and territories, the funding is awarded on an annual basis.

The funding can also be used for limited site assessments or cleanups at brownfield sites; for other activities that increase the number of response actions conducted or overseen by a state or tribal response program; to capitalize revolving loan funds for cleanup; to purchase environmental insurance; or to develop other insurance mechanisms for brownfields cleanup activities.

The primary goal of the funding is to ensure that response programs include, or are taking reasonable steps to include, the following four elements in their programs:

1. Timely survey and inventory of brownfield sites.
2. Oversight and enforcement authorities or other mechanisms and resources to ensure that a response action will protect human health and the environment.
3. Mechanisms and resources to provide meaningful opportunities for public participation.
4. Mechanisms for approval of a cleanup plan and verification and certification that cleanup is complete

Assessment, Revolving Loan Fund, and Cleanup Grants (ARC Grants)

The 104(k) competitive grants are awarded through an annual competition. Most federally recognized tribes are eligible to apply for this funding.3 ARC grants may be used to address sites contaminated by petroleum and hazardous substances, pollutants or contaminants (including hazardous substances co-mingled with petroleum). Opportunities for funding are as follows: Brownfields Assessment grants (each funded up to $200,000 over three years); Brownfields Revolving Loan Fund (RLF) Grants (each funded up to $1,000,000 over five years); and Brownfields Cleanup Grants (each funded up to $200,000 over three years).

Job Training Grants

Job Training grants—competitively awarded on an annual basis—are also available to most federally recognized tribes. To help residents located in areas affected by brownfields take advantage of jobs created by the assessment and cleanup of these properties, EPA initiated the Brownfields Job Training grants.

Among other things, the Job Training grant funds may be used for:

- Training residents in the handling and removal of hazardous substances, including training for jobs in sampling, analysis, and site remediation.
- Training in the management of facilities at which hazardous substances, pollutants, contaminants, or petroleum contamination are located.
- Training for response activities often associated with cleanups such as landscaping, demolition and ground water extraction.
- Development or refinement of existing training curriculum.
- Training participants in the techniques and methods for cleanup of leaking underground storage tanks and other sites contaminated by petroleum products, asbestos abatement, or lead abatement where these topics are a component
- of a more comprehensive hazardous waste management training course or environmental technology training course.

Passamaquoddy Tribe

The Passamaquoddy Tribe is using Section 128(a) Tribal Response Program funding to inventory contaminated properties on its lands. The tribe occupies two separate locations in Maine, Perry and Princeton; they are commonly referred to as the Pleasant Point and Indian Township Reservations, respectively. In 2005, the Passamaquoddy Tribe at Pleasant Point received assistance from the Maine Department of Environmental Protection's Brownfields Program to conduct Phase I and Phase II assessments at the Sipiyak Corner Store property, which included a vacant gas station. The investigations found contaminated soil associated with the former tanks and pump island. An immediate removal of four underground storage tanks (UST) was conducted with funding through the state's Groundwater Fund. The cleanup is complete and the property is ready for redevelopment.

The tribe is also conducting an inventory on properties on the Pleasant Point Reservation. Through its inventory efforts, the tribe identified—and is currently working to complete an assessment on—the former Gates building. This former upholstery manufacturing building has suspected soil contamination resulting from previous manufacturing activities. The tribe is targeting a privately owned junk yard on tribal land. The tribe plans to conduct an assessment on the property and create an ordinance that prevents private landowners from operating dumps on the reservation in the future. The tribe conducted Phase I and Phase II assessments at a former museum; a leaking UST was identified and contaminated soil was removed and replaced. And, Phase I and Phase II assessments were completed on a private piece of property located adjacent to the reservation. It is expected that this property will be the future home of a new tribal elementary school.

Seneca Nation

Seneca Nation is using Section 128(a) Tribal Response Program funding to actively locate and identify brownfields properties and build an inventory of properties to determine areas of concern within its reservation boundaries. Most of the property information has come from the community's historical knowledge of the tribal lands. The tribe uses public meetings and announcements in its bi-monthly newsletter to inform and educate tribal members about brownfields efforts, and to ask for assistance in identifying former uses of abandoned or underutilized properties on the reservation. The community identified several properties with past oil spills and provided valuable information regarding an historic rail yard property. The tribe's Environmental Protection Department worked extensively with the community to determine the past use and potential risk of contamination associated with the former rail yard property. The tribal environmental staff also used Section 128(a) Tribal Response Program funding to attend brownfields training sessions to broaden its knowledge regarding brownfields issues and tribal response programs. The tribe plans to prioritize the properties in its inventory and use Section 128(a) Tribal Response Program funding to assess properties and get them ready for cleanup.

Seminole

Managed under the ERMD, the Seminole Tribal Response Program assessed many properties; these assessments help pave the way for redevelopment that improves the lives of tribal members. The Seminole Tribe developed a brownfields inventory using geographic information system technology to successfully identify and characterize brownfields and help define the extent of contamination on the tribe's land. Using its inventory to prioritize sites, the Seminole Tribe assessed over 25 properties throughout its six reservations. The tribe conducted assessment and cleanup activities at the Snake Road Pond 2 on the Big Cypress Reservation. The tribe is working with the Bureau of Indian Affairs, the Florida Department of Transportation, and the Federal Highway Administration on improvements to Snake Road and one of the projects included the reconstruction of a bridge on a contaminated portion of the roadway. An environmental assessment discovered arsenic impacted soils.

ERMD working with the tribe's Transportation Department, regulatory agencies and other stakeholders, evaluated the affected area and soil excavation, removal and proper disposal was conducted in an effective and efficient manner. The tribe is also in the process of developing a comprehensive tribal development plan to ensure that once properties are assessed and cleaned up, they are put back into productive reuse. A key component in this process is community participation and input. Response program staff use the Seminole Water Commission meetings as a way to provide information to the public about brownfields properties and to gather feedback regarding community needs and priorities. In addition, the tribe developed an ordinance that provides a code of law focusing on storage tanks, permitting processes, treatment and transport of substances, and cleanup targets. This comprehensive set of guidelines allows the program to be more proactive and provide the authority to address brownfields challenges.

Keweenaw Bay Indian Community

KBIC is using Section 128(a) Tribal Response Program funding to actively locate and identify brownfields properties and build an inventory of potential brownfield sites within the L'Anse Reservation boundaries. It is developing an inventory by talking to tribal elders, using historical society resources, and talking with tribal members about former uses of abandoned or underutilized properties on the reservation. KBIC's Natural Resources Department is developing protocols and cleanup standards that will establish a process for moving properties through the assessment and cleanup phases and result in beneficial property reuse. KBIC completed the assessment and cleanup of the Sand Point property using tribal general funds, EPA Brownfield Cleanup funds, Great Lakes Basin program funds, and Section 128(a) Tribal Response Program funding.

The Sand Point property consists of shoreline property impacted by copper ore processing waste, known as stamp sands. Stamp sands contain low level concentrations of heavy metals. As part of the cleanup, a soil and vegetation cap was constructed over more than 33 acres of stamp sand area. KBIC transformed the property into a recreational area for use by tribal members and the general public. KBIC's long-term plan is to incorporate attractive greenspace and landscape architectural design and provide hiking trails, wildlife viewing, and areas for personal reflection. KBIC will focus on increasing community awareness regarding contaminant issues in the area, and developing assessment and cleanup protocols in the coming years. The tribe plans to conduct outreach to develop the vision for the cleanup and reuse of brownfields properties; it will continue to visit area schools and work with youth in the community to teach children about the importance of land stewardship.

• C. City •

37. The Factories of the Past Are Turning into the Data Centers of the Future*

GRAHAM PICKREN

We live in a data-driven world. From social media to smart cities to the internet of things, we now generate huge volumes of information about nearly every detail of life. This has revolutionized everything from business to government to the pursuit of romance.

We tend to focus our attention on what is new about the era of big data. But our digital present is in fact deeply connected to our industrial past.

In Chicago, where I teach and do research, I have been looking at the transformation of the city's industrial building stock to serve the needs of the data industry. Buildings where workers once processed checks, baked bread and printed Sears catalogs now stream Netflix and host servers engaged in financial trading.

The buildings themselves are a kind of witness to how the U.S. economy has changed. By observing these changes in the landscape, we get a better sense of how data exist in the physical realm. We are also struck with new questions about what the rise of an information-based economy means for the physical, social, and economic development of cities. The decline of industry can create conditions ripe for growth—but the benefits of that growth may not reach everyone in the city.

"Factories of the 21st century"

Data centers have been described as the factories of the 21st century. These facilities contain servers that store and process digital information. When we hear about data being stored "in the cloud," those data are really being stored in a data center.

But contrary to the ephemeral-sounding term "cloud," data centers are actually incredibly energy- and capital-intensive infrastructure. Servers use tremendous amounts of electricity and generate large amounts of heat, which in turn requires extensive investments in cooling systems in order to keep servers operating. These facilities also need to

---

*Originally published as Graham Pickren, "The factories of the past are turning into the data centers of the future," *The Conversation*, https://theconversation.com/the-factories-of-the-past-are-turning-into-the-data-centers-of-the-future-70033 (January 3, 2017). Reprinted with permission of the publisher.

be connected to fiber optic cables, which deliver information via beams of light. In most places, these cables—the "highway" part of the "information superhighway"—are buried along the rights of way provided by existing road and railroad networks. In other words, the pathways of the internet are shaped by previous rounds of development.

An economy based on information, just like one based on manufacturing, still requires a human-made environment. For the data industry, taking advantage of the places that have the power capacity, the building stock, the fiber optic connectivity and the proximity to both customers and other data centers is often central to their real estate strategy.

From Analog to Digital

As this real estate strategy plays out, what is particularly fascinating is the way in which infrastructure constructed to meet the needs of a different era is now being repurposed for the data sector.

In Chicago's South Loop sits the former R.R. Donnelley & Sons printing factory. At one time, it was one of the largest printers in the U.S., producing everything from Bibles to Sears catalogs. Now, it is the Lakeside Technology Center, one of the largest data centers in the world and the second-largest consumer of electricity in the state of Illinois.

The eight-story Gothic-style building is well-suited to the needs of a massive data center. Its vertical shafts, formerly used to haul heavy stacks of printed material between floors, are now used to run fiber optic cabling through the building. (Those cables come in from the railroad spur outside.) Heavy floors built to withstand the weight of printing presses are now used to support rack upon rack of server equipment. What was once the pinnacle of the analog world is now a central node in global financial networks.

Just a few miles south of Lakeside Technology Center is the former home of Schulze Baking Company in the South Side neighborhood of Washington Park. Once famous for its butternut bread, the five-story terra cotta bakery is currently being renovated into the Midway Technology Center, a data center. Like the South Loop printing factory, the Schulze bakery contains features useful to the data industry. The building also has heavy-load bearing floors as well as louvered windows designed to dissipate the heat from bread ovens—or, in this case, servers.

It isn't just the building itself that makes Schulze desirable, but the neighborhood as a whole. A developer working on the Schulze redevelopment project told me that, because the surrounding area had been deindustrialized, and because a large public housing project had closed down in recent decades, the nearby power substations actually had plenty of idle capacity to meet the data center's needs.

Examples of this "adaptive reuse" of industrial building stock abound. The former *Chicago Sun-Times* printing facility became a 320,000-square-foot data center earlier last year. A Motorola office building and former television factory in the suburbs has been bought by one of the large data center companies. Even the once mighty retailer Sears, which has one of the largest real estate portfolios in the country, has created a real estate division tasked with spinning off some of its stores into data center properties. Beyond Chicago, Amazon is in the process of turning an old biscuit factory in Ireland into a data center, and in New York, some of the world's most significant data center properties are housed in the former homes of Western Union and the Port Authority, two giants of 20th-century modernity.

What we see here in these stories is the seesaw of urban development. As certain industries and regions decline, some of the infrastructure retains its value. That provides an opportunity for future savvy investors to seize upon.

Data Centers and Public Policy

What broader lessons can be drawn about the way our data-rich lives will transform our physical and social landscape?

First, there is the issue of labor and employment. Data centers generate tax revenues but don't employ many people, so their relocation to places like Washington Park is unlikely to change the economic fortunes of local residents. If the data center is the "factory of the 21st century," what will that mean for the working class?

Data centers are crucial to innovations such as machine-learning, which threatens to automate many routine tasks in both high and low-skilled jobs. By one measure, as much as 47 percent of U.S. employment is at risk of being automated. Both low- and high-skilled jobs that are nonroutine—in other words, difficult to automate—are growing in the U.S. Some of these jobs will be supported by data centers, freeing up workers from repetitive tasks so that they can focus on other skills.

On the flip side, employment in the manufacturing sector—which has provided so many people with a ladder into the middle class—is in decline in terms of employment. The data center embodies that economic shift, as data management enables the displacement of workers through offshoring and automation.

So buried within the question of what these facilities will mean for working people is the larger issue of the relationship between automation and the polarization of incomes. To paraphrase Joseph Schumpeter, data centers seem likely to both create and destroy.

Second, data centers present a public policy dilemma for local and state governments. Public officials around the world are eager to grease the skids of data center development.

In many locations, generous tax incentives are often used to entice new data centers. As the Associated Press reported last year, state governments across the U.S. extended nearly US$1.5 billion in tax incentives to hundreds of data center projects nationwide during the past decade. For example, an Oregon law targeting data centers provides property tax relief on facilities, equipment, and employment for up to five years in exchange for creating one job. The costs and benefits of these kinds of subsidies have not been systematically studied.

More philosophically, as a geographer, I have been influenced by people like David Harvey and Neil Smith, who have theorized capitalist development as inherently uneven across time and space. Boom and bust, growth and decline: They are two sides of the same coin.

The implication here is that the landscapes we construct to serve the needs of today are always temporary. The smells of butternut bread defined part of everyday life in Washington Park for nearly a century. Today, data is in the ascendancy, constructing landscapes suitable to its needs. But those landscapes will also be impermanent and predicting what comes next is difficult. Whatever the future holds for cities, we can be sure that what comes next will be a reflection of what came before it.

38. Cleaning Up House*

Marcus Humberg, Martha Faust,
Cheryl Ann Bishop *and* Lyn Hikida

In the early 1940s, a small dry-cleaning business, Mt. Baker Cleaners, opened in South Seattle.

Several years later, a run-of-the-mill corner gas station set up shop across the street. For decades, it was business as usual. But as the years wore on, these small businesses were slowly creating a big environmental problem. Dry cleaning chemicals, solvents, and petroleum found their way into the soil, slowly and silently leaching down to the groundwater. By the mid-2010s, the dry cleaner had moved to a new location and the gas station closed after changing hands many times. Both lie vacant since, leaving an array of environmental problems yet to be discovered.

This is a typical story of a brownfield. While the name itself inspires images of fenced off, unused grassy acres, brownfields are often just run-down, abandoned businesses or dusty gravel lots with crumbling buildings. Brownfields can seem like a Pandora's box, just waiting to unleash their toxic—and potentially costly—secrets to the unsuspecting property buyer. Or they could be nothing more than an unused property with little to no environmental contamination on the surface, but with no one willing to pay to find out.

While there is no one definition that can describe a "typical" brownfield, the problems faced are the same: How can you clean it? How can you redevelop it? And who is going to pay for it? The next question, of course, is what brownfield cleanups have to do with affordable housing? What sane planner or project manager would want to combine the complexity of both issues? After all, how do you redevelop a brownfield property with unknown costs and uncertainty when you are already trying to navigate limited housing budgets, grant requirements, and strict timelines?

The current need for affordable housing for low-and middle-income families has reached crisis levels in many areas. Cities struggle with finding available land, while costs continue to rise. It is easy to see where housing demand has outstripped supply. And it is happening in urban, suburban, and even rural markets, driving up home prices and rents faster than incomes are rising. Formerly affordable neighborhoods are gentrifying, displacing lower income families, leaving them nowhere to go.

Here lies the conundrum—brownfields are developable land in potential, but can take a lot of time, money, and work to be economically viable again. Affordable housing

---

*Marcus Humberg, Martha Faust, Cheryl Ann Bishop, and Lyn Hikida, "Cleaning Up House," *PM* (December 2019, Vol. 101: 11) by ICMA, the International City/County Management Association; reprinted with permission.

is greatly needed, but it's becoming more difficult to build economically and administratively—especially in the current real estate markets many areas across the country are experiencing.

So, how can local governments leverage the opportunities brownfields offer while minimizing their drawbacks to build affordable housing—all without busting budgets or timelines? When faced with public policy challenges of this magnitude, it takes a lot of dedication and determination to blaze a trail through the twin minefields of brownfields and affordable housing. But success can be found where others are unwilling to venture. Enter the innovators.

Schmidt Artist Lofts in Saint Paul, Minnesota

In the eastern half of the Twin Cities of Minneapolis-Saint Paul, lies Ramsey County. It includes the bustling capital city of Saint Paul and is the only county in Minnesota that has been fully built out. Even before the recent shift in market preferences toward infill development, county planners realized that redevelopment of existing properties was the only path to create new housing, jobs, and even green space. And this redevelopment, by definition, required tackling costly environmental legacy issues head on.

In 1997, Ramsey County, along with neighboring Hennepin County—home of the other twin city of Minneapolis—approached the State Legislature to help them establish a special fund. The goal of this fund was to offset the costs of environmental and brownfield remediation and enable urban land recycling for a range of new uses, including affordable housing.

By 2004, Ramsey County launched their new Environmental Response Fund, funded by a mortgage registry and deed tax. This tax collects one dollar for every $10,000 in value for every property transaction in the county—around $25 for the average $250,000 home. Funding is split equally between the city of Saint Paul and its surrounding suburbs, providing a critical tool in reviving the urban and suburban core of the Twin Cities Metropolitan Area.

The philosophy of the Environmental Response Fund is to be the last public money into a project, helping leverage private investment into brownfield properties, and increasing the county's tax base. Many of these brownfields are located next to existing infrastructure, transit networks, and other services, making them especially desirable for redevelopment. Since its inception, the fund has helped remediate 330 acres of land, assisted the development of over 600 affordable housing units and 775 market-rate housing units, creating over 4,370 jobs.

Patching an Urban Tapestry

In the heart of the working-class West Seventh neighborhood, just southwest of downtown Saint Paul, stands the towering, castle-like Bottling House and Brew House. This former Schmidt Brewery complex has been given a new life as affordable live-work units for area artists. For over 100 years, the 18-acre site was home to a series of breweries and at one time was the largest brewery in Minnesota. Shortly after Prohibition, it was serving thirsty Minnesotans as the nation's seventh-largest brewery. But in the face of increasing competition, the facility shuttered in 2002. Following a short run as an ethanol production facility, the property was slated to be razed to make room for a Walmart, but ultimately sat vacant for over a decade. The contamination from a century of industrial use stymied any potential development. Enter local affordable housing developer, Dominium, who envisioned a new transit-oriented use for the property, drawing on its historic character and iconic architecture.

The first step in redevelopment required remediation of a myriad of environmental conditions, including soil contaminated with poly aromatic hydrocarbons (PAHs), lead, and arsenic. Removal of underground storage tanks, significant asbestos, and lead-based paint abatement, as well as installation of sub-slab vapor systems, would be required for all of the new residential uses. The total remediation costs ran upwards of $3.5 million. Ramsey County contributed $300,000 in Environmental Response Funds, other remediation grants had to be acquired, and the developer covered the remaining balance.

One of the unique steps in this project also included the historical designation of the site. Once recognized as one of "Minnesota's 10 most endangered historic places," the former brewery is now part of a new historic district listed on the National Register for Historic Places. As an adaptive reuse, the $130 million project created 247 individually unique one, two, and three-bedroom rental lofts and flats, and 13 three-bedroom townhomes on a property adjacent to the bottling house. These units are not only affordable, but attractive to artists with a $42,000 maximum income restriction for a single-person household. Onsite amenities include paint, clay, sound, and dance studios; a performance space; and a rooftop deck with views of the Mississippi River and downtown Saint Paul. The development was fully leased before opening in 2014, and remains 100 percent leased today.

Perhaps just as important as the successful adaptive reuse of the Schmidt Brewery complex is the catalytic effect the project has produced. Overnight, the restoration of the property injected new energy and historic pride into the neighborhood. In 2018, a 33,000 square-foot Keg & Case food hall opened in a former storage building in the new historic district, filled with local restaurateurs, vendors, and fittingly, a craft brewery. Keg & Case hosts a weekly neighborhood farmers market and was recently named the best new food hall in America by *USA Today*.[1]

The Schmidt Brewery redevelopment illustrates the opportunities that brownfield sites hold for potential reuse for affordable housing. Success in this case required creative vision, persistence, and public-private partnerships to overcome the significant cost challenges. Projects such as the Schmidt Artist Lofts not only provide critically needed, transit-accessible affordable housing, but also fill holes in the urban fabric, and can even spur an economic revolution through strategic redevelopment.

The Maddux in Seattle, Washington

When it comes to overheated real estate markets, Seattle and surrounding King County is still white-hot. Though prices are cooling, the median home value in King County has risen from $350,000 in 2011 to $625,000 in 2019.[2] Residents are being priced out of the market by a flood of high-paid tech workers moving to the area. This influx has pushed Seattle's lower-paid workers, who often rent their homes, to the brink—or worse, onto the streets.

One could think it odd then that only a few miles from downtown there are boarded-up businesses and vacant properties. Surely these lots would be quickly swallowed up and developed in such an insatiable, high-priced, high-demand market. But even white-hot real estate prices cannot overcome that which lies beneath.

Creating Successful Partnerships

In 1988, Washington's citizens passed Initiative 97 establishing a statewide environmental cleanup law, the Model Toxics Control Act (MTCA).[3] This act installed a tax on petroleum products, certain chemicals, and pesticides to fund cleanups across the state and prescribes the required cleanup process. The Washington State Department of Ecology (Ecology) manages the majority of MTCA funding and regulates the cleanup process for public and private properties across the state.

Until recently, MTCA cleanup funds could not be granted to private parties; they were instead routed only through local governments. When Ecology recently became involved with affordable housing-related cleanup, this limitation inspired two new variants of its main grants—Integrated Planning Grants (IPGs) and Remedial Action Grants (RAGs). These new grants support housing and community planning and cleanup activities for brownfield sites that deliver affordable housing as an end use. They can be used by local governments and tribes, as well as nonprofit and private entities.

IPGs provide $200,000–$300,000 to support planning, investigation, and public involvement related to a potential cleanup. This early funding can produce a much bigger return on investment later in the project. Whether that planning is for site assessment, or other innovative uses that benefit the public, the key is setting the stage early, which gives projects a strong foundation for later success. Affordable housing-related RAGs have no award limits and help investigation and cleanup of brownfield sites.

Inspiring Innovation in Affordable Housing[4]

In 2013, MTCA was modified to allow local governments new ways to use cleanup funds, including the creation of a Redevelopment Opportunity Zone (ROZ).[5] Within a ROZ, the local government can create a brownfields renewal authority, a municipal authority that has broad powers to help manage and fund the cleanup and redevelopment of brownfields. The ROZ also allows Ecology to connect prospective purchasers and developers with owners of brownfield properties and provide funding for parts of the project that are not directly involved with cleanup.

The city of Seattle voted in 2017 to create a ROZ encompassing two major cleanup sites—the abandoned Mt. Baker Cleaners and a run-down, former gas station and auto repair shop owned by Phillips 66. These derelict properties occupy an otherwise desirable location—a prominent corner, in real estate parlance—within walking distance of light rail, a bus station, and green space, mere minutes from downtown. It is almost everything you could want for affordable housing except, of course, for the cleanup price tag.

To kick-start the project, in 2017 Ecology offered $400,000 to help assess the contamination on the site and connect the property owner to a nonprofit developer, Mt. Baker Housing. This early funding spurred the project forward, and ultimately inspired future innovation. The environmental assessment showed the extent of the property's toxic unknowns—dry-cleaning solvents (percholorethene and trichloroethene) and petroleum contaminants (gasoline, diesel, benzene, and heavy oil) in the soil and groundwater at levels below what had been anticipated, bringing the cleanup cost estimate from as high as $31 million to around $7 million.

Using this new information, the Mt. Baker housing authority went to work, securing $56 million in private, state, and federal funding. With all the details in place, the state legislature approved $6.2 million to fund the site cleanup. In 2019, Mt. Baker Housing finalized the purchase agreements and will begin construction of the mixed-use project, including 144 affordable housing units and ground-level commercial spaces, which is essential in an area with limited retail services.

In the realms of environmental justice, cleaning up properties like Mt. Baker Cleaners in lower-income neighborhoods is a step toward a more equitable and sustainable future. Contamination and long-abandoned buildings depress property values and affect residents' social and physical wellbeing. However, brownfield properties often attract projects that can easily price out the people who stand to benefit the most—the residents who lived with the contamination and lower property values for so many years. Part of the success of the Maddux hinged on placing restrictive affordable housing covenants on the land, protecting the neighborhood from the pressures of market-rate development and gentrification.

Though providing funding through a ROZ worked for the Maddux, it was an inefficient way of providing direct funding to non-government entities. Given the success that early assessment and planning had on the Maddux, Ecology established the Healthy Housing Remediation Program, a pilot project exploring direct funding options for private, tribal, and non-profit agencies that connect the cleanup of contaminated sites to redevelopment as affordable housing.[6] This program has already produced proposals for 110-units of affordable housing in Kennewick, Washington; and a mixed-use, seven-story waterfront development in Bellingham, Washington, that includes affordable apartments and a campus with a professional communal kitchen and food truck court.

Jordan Downs in Los Angeles, California

During the height of World War II, the city of Los Angeles was going full steam for America's war effort. At the same time, it was experiencing a housing crisis due to the influx of workers recruited by the defense industry. In the Watts neighborhood of South Los Angeles, the city contracted to build Jordan Downs, a 34-acre temporary housing development with hundreds of low-rise, barracks-style buildings, next door to a steel mill built to support the war. According to the *Los Angeles Times*, Jordan Downs was dedicated in 1944 for the city's war workers including members of minority racial groups that have faced a critical housing problem.[7] In 1955, this cinder block "temporary housing" was converted into 700 units of low-income public housing. Over the decades, economic depression, racial conflicts, and disinvestment in the community contributed to its physical and social decline.

Bifurcating the Jordan Downs neighborhood today is a 21-acre industrial property that once housed the steel mill. Over time, the site was repurposed from steel manufacturing and truck repair to waste handling and storage. In 1996, environmental studies were conducted that identified significant contamination. Recognizing an opportunity to eliminate this dysfunctional property so close to their public housing, the Housing Authority of the City of Los Angeles (HACLA) acquired the site in 2008 with the intent to remediate it for future use.[8] The California Department of Toxic Substances Control with a range of affordability, along with new roads and infrastructure, community facilities, retail, parks, and open space.

Delivering Environmental Justice

In 2012, the nonprofit BRIDGE Housing, along with The Michaels Organization, was selected by HACLA to develop and lead the revitalization of Jordan Downs.[9] Ultimately, this ongoing comprehensive, long-term effort will rebuild all 700 units of distressed public housing and create an additional 650 new homes with a range of affordability, along with new roads and infrastructure, community facilities, retail, parks, and open space. While significant remediation was required, putting the old steel mill site into service as part of the Jordan Downs master redevelopment would achieve several important goals:

- Reknit the physical community, as the vacant parcel splitting Jordan Downs created turf wars and divisions between residents of the north and south sides.
- Allow the construction of the first 250 apartments and create replacement public housing units mitigating displacement of current residents.
- Enable the extension of Century Boulevard, a major thoroughfare, to reconnect Jordan Downs with the surrounding neighborhood.
- Provide land for 115,000 square feet of retail and commercial space, which is vital in a neighborhood that has had a dearth of retail services and jobs.
- Eliminate severe blight of the industrial parcel.
- Eliminate toxins immediately adjacent to Jordan High School, the public housing complex, and the community's recreation center.

The DTSC approved a remedial action plan for the former steel mill site in 2014, and remediation work began in April 2015. Based on earlier environmental studies, the conclusion was reached that only certain areas of the site had contamination requiring remediation, anticipating that the cleanup would take only six months. However, it soon became evident that heavy metals and toxic contamination were spread across the entire site. Engine oil, diesel and gasoline, paint thinners, trichloroethylene (an industrial solvent), and polychlorinated biphenyls (PCBs) had leached into the soil and groundwater. Contamination in some areas extended to a depth of over 20 feet, requiring the removal of more than 220,000 tons of impacted soil. Backfilling the space with clean soil has ensured safe occupancy for future uses. Due to the expanded scope of cleanup, the remediation costs rose to $31 million, a significant investment in a community that had been neglected for decades.

In 2016, the remediation was completed and DTSC issued a "no further action" letter for the residential parcels, allowing construction of the first residential phases, the Century Boulevard extension, and retail spaces.

As of fall 2019, BRIDGE's 115-unit Cedar Grove at Jordan Downs is now leasing. Designed to a LEED Silver certification level, the new apartments will serve existing public housing residents and other low-income families. Retail establishments are nearing completion, and the new Century Boulevard extension connects the community to the services and amenities of greater Los Angeles. The remediation and reuse of the 21-acre brownfield parcel was the critical first step in a multiphase process that is transforming Jordan Downs into a vibrant—and healthier—mixed-use community where thousands of residents will be able to thrive.

Notes

1. St. Paul's Keg and Case named Best New Food Hall, *USA Today*, January 18, 2019, accessed at https://www.10best.com/awards/travel/best-new-food-hall/.
2. Northwest Multiple Listing Service Data, 2011–2019.
3. https://ecology.wa.gov/Spills-Cleanup/Contamination-cleanup/Rules-directing-our-cleanup-work/Model-Toxics-Control-Act.
4. This section adapted in part from an article published in the Seattle *Daily Journal of Commerce*. Article is attributed to Bob Warren but was ghostwritten by Cheryl Ann Bishop. "State helps turn brownfields into affordable housing," *Daily Journal of Commerce*, September 27, 2018, https://www.djc.com/news/en/12114941.html.
5. https://fortress.wa.gov/ecy/publications/SummaryPages/1809048.html.
6. https://fortress.wa.gov/ecy/publications/SummaryPages/1809051.html.
7. Dedication of Housing Today (1944 May 28), *Los Angeles Times*, retrieved from http://newspapers.com.
8. http://uli.org/wp-content/uploads/ULI-Documents/2009JordanDownsLAReport.pdf.
9. https://bridgehousing.com/press_releases/los-angeles-celebrates-groundbreaking-of-first-residential-phase-of-jordan-downs-revitalization/.

39. The Music City Miracle*

Paula Middlebrooks

Nashville has been known as Music City and the Country Music Capital of the World for decades. A more recent designation has Nashville ranked among the top 25 most populous cities in the USA, with a population increase of more than 10 percent since 2010.[1] With rapid growth, infill is occurring at a swift pace, and infill happens on brownfields.

Increasingly, brownfields redevelopment has become an important part of economic development and community revitalization strategies across the country. Brownfields are properties which may contain real or perceived environmental contamination that hinder their redevelopment or reuse. Many brownfields are under-utilized or abandoned facilities with a history of manufacturing. Other common types of brownfields include old mills and factories, junkyards, former dry cleaners, railyards, mine-scarred lands, and abandoned gas stations.

Brownfields exist in towns of all sizes. While not all municipalities and rural areas have experienced the growth that Nashville has, the potential for brownfields redevelopment is nonetheless abundant everywhere. These idle properties can be a burden on neighbors and threaten public health, local economies, and communities. The cleanup and re-use of these properties can have significant social and community benefits, in addition to economic and environmental benefits, as illustrated by the following case studies.

Case Study: From Bridges to Climbing Walls

Located along the east bank of the Cumberland River, adjacent to downtown Nashville, the Nashville Bridge Company was originally founded as a bridge builder in the 1890s. In 1915, the company converted to shipbuilding, and by the 1960s, it was said to be the world's largest builder of inland barges. The facility closed in 1996, when it was decided a new stadium for the Tennessee Titans would be built on a portion of the property. However, the closure left the riverfront portion of the property sitting vacant.

Under the New Riverfront Park Plan, it was determined that new public parks, open space, and recreational amenities would be added along the downtown riverfront.[2] In 2008, due to the historical us of the property, environment site assessments

---

*Originally published as Paula Middlebrooks, "The Music City Miracle," *PM* (December 2019, Vol. 101: 11) by ICMA, the International City/County Management Association; reprinted with permission.

were conducted utilizing Environmental Protection Agency (EPA) Region 4 Targeted Brownfields Assessment assistance. Additional assessment and technical oversight by the Tennessee Department of Environment and Conservation, Division of Remediation (TDEC-DoR) were completed using EMPA 128(a) brownfields funds. The assessments identified several areas impacted by polycyclic aromatic hydrocarbons (PAHs), lead and arsenic that required cleanup. The TDEC-DoR and the Metro Parks and Recreation Department worked cooperatively to develop and implement plans that incorporated a combination of soils removals, engineered caps, and institutional controls to address environmental concerns and provide for a safe reuse of the property.

Today, the Cumberland Play Park is an innovative play space for children and families located on the east bank for the Cumberland River in downtown Nashville. It is a portion of an overall revitalization project on approximately three miles of land on both the east and west bank of the river. The park includes a local stone climbing wall, sand play areas, garden mazes, outdoor seating, meandering paths, and other interactive play areas.

Adaptive reuse, water harvesting for irrigation, and improved biodiversity were also included in this brownfield redevelopment project. Each year, one million gallons of stormwater are captured and reused for irrigation. Over 1.6 acres of meadow and riparian grasses were restored. There is also an outdoor amphitheater that can accommodate 1,200 people. The historic Bridge Building, originally built in 1908 for the Nashville Bridge Company, has been restored and is now home to a Metro Parks office and event space, and has earned the highest rating for sustainable buildings (LEED-Platinum) by the U.S. Green Building Council.

Case Study: From Landfill to Solar Power

A 37-acre tract of land, located approximately seven miles northeast of downtown Nashville, was formerly known as the Due West Landfill. After serving as a municipal landfill from approximately 1959 to 1973 and covered with rock excavated from the construction of Interstate 65, the land was vacant. In 1997, a portion of the property entered TDEC's Voluntary Cleanup, Oversight, and Assistance Program (VOAP). The state approved closure of the site with an engineered cover on the landfill in 2002. The property was subsequently monitored for the release of methane, iron, and manganese. Land use restrictions were also placed on the property to limit its use at the time.

But in 2016, the city of Nashville showed interest in transforming the vacant land, adjacent to a major medical center, into a property designed to showcase its environmental and community benefits. The TDEC-DoR issued a "no further action" letter for the site to address soil gas and leachate. In the spring of 2018, the Nashville Electric Service (NES) broke ground for the Music City Solar Array (MCSA), located on a portion of the former landfill, transforming 25 acres of the site into Nashville's first community solar park. In August 2018, MCSA began operating, producing renewable energy back to the power grid. The solar park gives NES customers access to sustainable, maintenance-free solar energy. The two-megawatt facility uses over 17,000 solar panels, with each panel generating an estimated 14-kilowatt hours per month of green energy for Nashville's electric grid.

Case Study: From Clay Targets to Mixed Use

A 38-acre property composed of several parcels, adjacent to downtown Nashville and Interstate 65/Interstate 40, is currently being transformed in phases into a large mixed-use development. Historical use of the property was residential in the 1800s, and gradually became commercial during the 1900s. The property was used for a variety of commercial and industrial purposes, including a car dealership with a bakery, railroad exchange yard, cold storage, bookstore, beer distributor, aluminum can collection center, restaurant, woodworking shop, clay target launcher manufacturer, coal storage, and an auto body shop, among other uses. This property is situated between an active rail line and the two interstates along Dr. Martin Luther King Blvd., adjacent to the Gulch neighborhood.

Between 2005 and 2012, environmental site assessments were conducted at the property, and environmental issues were identified. Contamination was primarily confined to the soils and consisted mainly of petroleum and automotive-related products and wastes, as well as PAHs. Some of the contaminants identified were the result of buried coal and coal wastes related to the original railroad and industrial activities in the vicinity of the site used as backfill when parcel grades were raised during the burial of the local sewers dating back to the mid–1800s. To address these issues, the property was entered into the VOAP in phases, starting in 2013.

Subsequent remedial activities at the site included the removal and proper disposal of 369 tons of contaminated soils, 20 in-ground hydraulic lifts, and one 560-gallon underground storage tank from just one of the parcels on this large site. Groundwater sampling was also done prior to construction on the property, and an oil/water separator was removed, and confirmatory sampling completed to confirm a clean closure.

A multi-disciplinary team including developers, engineers, environmental professionals, and the TDEC-DoR worked together to make this cleanup and redevelopment a success through the VOAP. Numerous brownfields voluntary agreements, land use restrictions, and soil management plans were put in place to ensure safe use of the property. The mixed-use finished project, called Capitol View, will span 38 acres and include buildings with a collective 1.1 million square feet of Class A office space, 130,000 square feet of retail and restaurant space, a 169-room hotel, grocery store, urgent-care clinic, a high-end apartment building, and a 2.5-acre park complete with free parking. The Urban Activity Park will include a dog park, playground, yoga lawn, and sand volleyball courts. The park is also a trail head for the Nashville Greenway, connecting to 190 miles of trails through Davidson County, and will be donated to Metro Nashville Government upon completion.

Addressing Brownfields

Timing is often a critical component to brownfields redevelopment. Contamination, or potential contamination, is typically identified during pre-transaction environmental due diligence screening or "all appropriate inquires." This is accomplished by performing a Phase I Environmental Site Assessment (ESA). A Phase I ESA is completed to research the current and historical uses of a property. If the findings of the Phase I ESA show additional studies are needed, a Phase II ESA may be needed to collect samples for laboratory analysis. Typically, a Phase II ESA involves sampling of groundwater, surface water, soil, and/or soil gas. Understanding the scope of environmental impacts of a property, prior to a property transaction and development of site plans, can save money and time in the property transaction and development of the site.

The TDEC works with a variety of sectors on brownfields redevelopments, including municipalities, landowners, redevelopment agencies, consulting firms, attorneys, non-profits, and other entities. State involvement early on in brownfields projects is key. The VOAP provides liability protection to purchasers of property who address environmental impacts. The VOAP has had over 500 properties enter the program across Tennessee since its inception in 2001. The state also works with EPA 104(k) brownfields grant applicants to provide support during the application process and to provide technical oversight on active grants. There has been over $5 million awarded to Tennessee recipients since 2010 for the assessment and cleanup of brownfields, and the state has overseen the technical components at no cost to the communities. Both programs serve the entire state, beyond Nashville.

Recently, Tennessee passed a state law expanding tax incentives for counties in Tennessee.[3] The 2019 law amended a previous law to expand benefits to small and mid-sized counties with greater flexibility for the size of brownfields being redeveloped. The law also expands redevelopment zones to include qualified Opportunity Zones and expands qualified costs to include investigation, remediation, or mitigation of a brownfield project. When entities work toward the shared goal of safe reuse of environmentally impacted properties, brownfields redevelopment can flourish. Proactively identifying these properties—and seeing them as an asset and part of a community's history instead of simply eyesores—is critical to growth at any pace.

Notes

1. https://www.tennessean.com/story/news/2019/05/24/nashville-population-growth-percent-us-census-2018-top-25-rank/1214610001/.
2. https://www.civicdesigncenter.org/pdfs/NashvilleRiverfrontReport.pdf.
3. http://wapp.capitol.tn.gov/apps/BillInfo/default.aspx?BillNumber=SB0355&GA=111.

40. ICMA and CCLR's Case Experiences*

Clark Henry, Tad McGalliard and Ignacio Dayrit

This article goes into colorful city case study experiences documented by the International City/County Management Association and the Center for Creative Land Recycling spanning the United States, from Roebling, New Jersey to Snow Creek, California.

Case #1: Roebling Steel Company, Roebling, New Jersey

Prior Use. Before accommodating a museum, greenspace, and a multi-modal transportation hub, the 200-acre Roebling Steel site was an industrial manufacturing facility producing steel cables, and wires. Company founder John A. Roebling began producing steel cables in the mid–1840s, and provided cables for some of the country's most iconic suspension bridges, such as the Golden Gate Bridge, in California, and the Brooklyn Bridge in New York for which he served as lead engineer.

After his death in 1869, Mr. Roebling's sons took over his business and grew it to be the most influential steel cable producer in the world. With the company's growth, the town of Roebling, New Jersey was founded to house its workforce of about 4,000 employees. By the 1950s, the manufacturing facility and business was sold, and it operated under new ownership until the early 1970s. Portions of the site were then leased to companies for various industrial uses including polymer reclamation, vinyl product storage, warehousing, shipping container restoration, equipment storage until the early 1980s when all activity on the site ceased.

Beginning in the late 1970s, the U.S. Environmental Protection Agency (EPA), began identifying significant environmental problems with the site. After several attempts to get site owners and operators to address these conditions, enforcement actions began in force in 1983 with a listing on the EPA National Priority List (NPL), commonly referred to as Superfund.

Contaminants of Concern. Contaminants of Concern (COC) on site include heavy metals (lead, chromium, cadmium), petroleum, Asbestos, Polychlorinated Biphenyls (PCB), oil/tar and associated Volatile Organic Compounds (VOC). Nearly all of these

---

*Published with permission from the International City/County Management Association (ICMA) and the authors.

COCs are found in soil, groundwater, surface water, and in the approximately 70 structures that remained on site.

Specific areas of concern on site include two sludge lagoons, slag pile, and a landfill. Offsite migration was of significant concern and impacts were identified in the Delaware River, and nearby creek and wetland.

Additional COCs on site include acids and other toxic materials stored in steel drums. During one inspection, approximately 600 barrels containing toxic material were found. Included with the drums were other material such as electrical transformers containing oil with Polychlorinated biphenyls (PCBs), abandoned storage tanks, piles of slag material, piles of old tires, chemical piles, slag heaps, and other hazardous material.

Remediation. Remediation of the Roebling Steel site has taken place over several actions starting in the early 1990s into 2013 and beyond. These efforts organize the property into different sub areas referred to as Operable Units (OU), each with its own approach and remedy.

First, removal actions were required to eliminate immediate threats to human health and the environment, including removing several hundred drums, transformers, and solid waste. Materials were taken to an appropriate facility, characterized, and disposed of, much of it in a toxic waste landfill.

In total, these actions moved, treated, disposed of, or recycled 300 lab pack containers of chemicals; 3,200 full and empty drums; 263 overpacked drums, 663 crushed drums; 120 cubic yards of crushed and emptied drums3 pounds of metallic mercury; 1 drum of cyanide; 10 compressed gas cylinders; 3,000 gallons of sulfuric acid; 2,150 gallons of phosphoric acid; and 239,000 pounds of base neutral solids; 663 crushed drums; 45,864 gallons of transformer oil and 860,709 pounds of transformer cases; 266,843 gallons of tank liquids, and 1,351 tons of sludge; 800 tons of baghouse dust; 251 tons of chemical piles and asbestos; 126 tons of burnt tires; 261 tons of recyclable tires; and 640 cubic yards of soil.[1]

In total, 67 buildings were demolished, with recyclable or reusable materials separated and managed differently. The unusable demolition material contained hazardous materials including asbestos, lead, oil and chemical lines, and contaminated soil. This material was disposed of in an offsite appropriate landfill.

Crafts Creek and the Delaware River Back Channel were dredged to remove contaminated sediment, and 3,000 linear feet of shoreline was stabilized. A stormwater drainage system was also installed to manage runoff from the village of Roebling. Approximately 240,000 cubic yards of contaminated sediments were dredged, with excavated areas backfilled with clean material and re-vegetated and adjacent wetlands restored. The dredged material was dewatered on site and placed on the portion of the property formerly used as a slag heap. The dredged material was then capped with two feet of clean soil and vegetated.

In addition to excavation and capping of contaminated soil, human and environmental health was protected through the use of Institutional Controls (IC). Deed restrictions were placed on the entire site preventing it from being used for residential uses. The integrity of capped areas is also maintained through ICs, placing restrictions on digging, or other activity in those areas that would compromise the cap.

Groundwater was also largely addressed through a combination of ICs and ongoing monitoring obligations. Monitoring wells were placed throughout the site to track the movement of groundwater and groundwater to ensure offsite migration is not taking place beyond what is currently known. Deed restrictions to prevent the installation of wells that would extract groundwater for purposes other than testing, both on site, and on properties surrounding the site.

Reuse. Today, the property is home to three community assets—a light rail commuter station, public green space, and a history museum. Each reuse involved the coordination of multiple agencies and entities including the property owner, United States Protection Agency (EPA), New Jersey Transit Authority, Florence Township Redevelopment Agency, the local historic preservation authority, and many more stakeholders.

The Roebling Steel main gate house was preserved as a historic landmark and is now the Roebling Museum, educating the public about the region and site's industrial past.

The former parking lot is now home to Roebling Station, a stop on the New Jersey Transit Authority's River Line light rail which carries approximately 9,000 passengers per weekday.

The area formerly used to dump slag waste is now the John A. Roebling Memorial Park, a 34-acre extension of the Abbott Marshlands adjacent to the Delaware River. The park is built up on the capped dredge material from Crafts Creek and the Delaware River Backwater cleanup.

Conclusion. The Roebling Steel redevelopment story is a prime example of contaminated land from the industrial revolution being transformed into a variety of assets serving an increasingly dense and populated urban environment. It also profiles the benefit of collaboration amongst multiple players working together to achieve a common purpose.

Case #2: Stanley Marketplace, Aurora, Colorado

Prior Use. What is now the Stanley Marketplace was once the home of Stanley Aviation, a pioneer in aircraft ejector seat technology and manufacturing. Operations began and grew into a 100,000 square foot manufacturing facility producing in Aurora, Colorado adjacent to the Denver region's Stapleton Airport. In the early 2000s the site became fully vacant, after nearly 50 years of operation. During the same time period, the Stapleton Airport closed, and the new Denver International Airport began operations. The former airport land was redeveloped into a large, sustainability oriented mixed-use community, and the Stanley Aviation site responded similarly.

Contaminants of Concern. While in operation, chemicals used in the manufacturing process were often released, and waste streams were managed in way that created environmental impacts requiring remediation. The main Contaminants of Concern (COC) on site were asbestos, chlorinated solvents, heavy metals, and petroleum.

Asbestos was a major concern In a portion of the property formerly used as a municipal landfill accepting construction debris. It was also found and remediated in a nearly 1-acre parking lot, and the main building's floor tiles and pipe insulation.

Chlorinated solvents were identified in soil and groundwater resulting from leaks in eroded piping under the building's foundation. Additional groundwater testing under a portion of the property used for pressure washing and hazardous waste storage found Vinyl Chloride, a chemical associated with chlorinated solvent degradation.

Groundwater and soil samples revealed petroleum and heavy metals. After evaluation, it was considered likely groundwater impacts came from an upgradient source, and not associated with Stanley Aviation.

Remediation. Remediation of the construction debris landfill included excavation and disposal at an appropriate landfill, with some remaining debris remaining in place and capped with 3 feet of clean fill. The depth of the cap was made 3 feet because depth of the planned building's sprinkler system was 1.5 feet below ground surface. If repairs needed to be made to the system, workers would still be protected by 1.5 feet of clean fill, and not be exposed to contaminants. The asbestos contaminated asphalt parking lot was also excavated and disposed of in a landfill.

To address groundwater impacted by chlorinated solvents, in-situ bioremediation sped the degradation of the contaminant. A Hydrogen Release Compound (HRC) was injected into the groundwater in-situ, significantly reducing the concentration of chlorinated solvents in the groundwater. Regulatory compliance was also achieved through an Institutional Control (IC), with restrictions on groundwater use recorded on the property's title.

Reuse. Following the repurposing of the Stapleton Airport revitalization into a mixed-use community, the Stanley Aviation site also found new life as a mixed-use facility. Developers recognized the opportunity of the site's location as well as the potential to reuse the former manufacturing facility and hangar space.

The developer worked closely with the City of Aurora to come up with a reuse scenario that added value to the broader community as well as the owners and tenants. Working toward this common goal they knew that they had to create a special place where tenants interacted with one another and created vitality amongst likeminded businesses and people. They needed to create a destination. After a $31 million construction project, the Stanley Marketplace opened in 2016 and is now a vibrant amenity with approximately 50 commercial businesses offering food, entertainment, retail, fitness, services, education, and offices. Approximately 500 people are employed in the marketplace.

The former airplane hangar space also has new life as a highly regarded event space hosting premier cultural events, festivals, and small gatherings year-round. In recognition of the site's historical significance to the City of Aurora, the developer and city worked with the local historic preservation committee to designate the building as an historic landmark. This not only honors the pioneering history of Stanley Aviation, and the modernist design of the building, but it also made $2 million of historic preservation tax credits available to help finance the project.

Another portion of the property formerly used as the parking lot is also planned as a unique multifamily residential development, Stanley Residential. This project includes over 170 rental units, and small retail space targeting millennial tenants in two five story buildings. The project reflects contemporary trends in the housing market and innovative ideas such as micro units of under 450 square feet, one-bedroom units under 1000 square feet, and two-bedroom units under 1200 square feet. In keeping with the airplane theme of the Stanley Marketplace, the building design itself calls up on design concepts of an airplane wing. Further, the residential units are being designed considering the efficient use of space in airplanes. The development is planned to have rooftop solar, and provide less than one parking space per unit, and 142 bicycle parking spaces that help reduce its environmental footprint.

Conclusion. The Stanley Marketplace demonstrates how a creative redevelopment plan inspires the willingness to move through complicated remediation and regulatory compliance. It is also a model of redeveloping large sites in incremental steps. By making the marketplace a successful amenity, they can support the market viability of the planned residential project, reducing risk for financial partners. Further, by working incrementally, they can build on relationships with the surrounding community and ensure the site's design, programming, and management meets their needs too.

Reference: Flying High Again; 2018 EPA https://www.epa.gov/sites/production/files/2018-04/documents/epa_2017_oblr_successstory_stanley_v5_release_508.pdf.

Case #3: Willow Run, Ypsilanti, Michigan

Prior Use. The Willow Run site is in one of America's automotive manufacturing communities, Ypsilanti, Michigan. As with other cities such as Detroit, Saginaw, Flint, and many others, Ypsilanti faces significant economic and environmental burden from the shift of automotive manufacturing to overseas locations. The Willow Run property is divided into two main portions—the Commercial Vehicle Operations site, and the Powertrain Plant.

Both sites had been developed by the Ford Motor Company in the early 1940s to construct B-24 bombers supporting American operations in World War II. After the war, the property was purchased by General Motor Company (GM) in the early 1950s. Between 1953 and 2010, GM used the 300+ acre Powertrain Plant facility to manufacture transmissions. The adjacent 22-acre commercial vehicle operations site was used to service and store GM corporate vehicles. At the facilities' peek of operations, over 40,000 employees worked on site. The Powertrain facility operated 39 years before needing to comply with the U.S. Resource Conservation and Recovery Act (RCRA) permits that started in 1980. GM filed for bankruptcy in 2009 and the facility ceased operations in 2010, after which extensive environmental site assessments (ESA) found significant impacts on both parcels.

Both parcels were included in a portfolio of former GM properties with known environmental conditions and put under the management of a court ordered trust, the RACER trust, in 2011. As a part of the court's actions, $40 million was set aside to address contamination on the Willow Run property.

Contaminants of Concern. Several Contaminants of Concern (COC) on the powertrain plant site, and the commercial vehicle operations site include solvents, oil, polychlorinated biphenyls (PCB), per-polyfluoroalkyl substances (PFAS), perfluorooctanoic acid (PFOA), and heavy metals. Contaminants are generally co-mingled in soil, groundwater, and stormwater runoff. On the powertrain site, approximately 40 acres of ground beneath the building's foundation is saturated with COCs after years of unregulated management and on-site disposal prior to the 1980 RCRA registration.

Impacts were also identified in groundwater samples throughout the site. Further complicating the issue is stormwater, which was captured and conveyed through a drainage system. This drainage system then carried contaminated stormwater runoff to nearby Willow Creek.

Contamination at the commercial vehicle operations site includes petroleum, paint, and PCBs left behind from vehicle maintenance operations. Paint sludge was known to be disposed of on the border of the property prior to RCRA registration in 1980.

Remediation. For both sites, remediation of contaminated soils was conducted through a combination of excavation and disposal and managed through land use restrictions (institutional controls), and caps (engineering control).

The main building of the Powertrain facility was demolished but the foundation remains in place, serving as the cap preventing exposure to contaminated soils. The cap also prevents stormwater infiltration through contaminated soils that aids contaminant migration. Remediation of contaminated soils at the commercial vehicle operation site included excavation, mixing, treatment, and disposal of soil. Once excavated, impacted soils were mixed with Persulfate, a compound that aids in chemical oxidation to bring down contamination levels of Volatile Organic Compounds (VOC). This allowed for disposal of the soil at a non-hazardous waste landfill, greatly reducing the cost of disposal. Structures on the property were retrofit with sub slab depressurization and soil vapor extraction systems to prevent contaminated soil vapor migration into the structures and off site.

The stormwater conveyance system installed in 1941 on the powertrain site was reconfigured in 2017 to separate management of stormwater and groundwater and stop its flow directly into the adjacent Willow Creek. The original stormwater management system was sealed off and replaced with a new system of shallow and surface conveyances diverting runoff into specially constructed, lined stormwater ponds. Once in the ponds, VOCs in stormwater runoff is broken down through natural attenuation.

To control contaminated groundwater, engineering controls were put in place to capture it and prevent hits horizontal migration into Willow Creek. These include a French drain system throughout the site, supplemented with bulkheads along the creek. Institutional controls further protect human and environmental health by recording restrictive covenants on the properties' titles prohibiting groundwater from being used on both sites.

Reuse. As is often the case with brownfield redevelopment, finding a suitable and feasible reuse for the Willow Run properties was complicated. The 22-acre former commercial vehicle operations facility had existing structures on site including the maintenance structure and offices, making another industrial or light industrial use appropriate. Its proximity to the Willow Run Airport proved advantageous. A nearby company, International Turbine Industries needed to expand beyond its existing facility next door and welcomed the opportunity to buy the commercial vehicle operations site.

Finding an appropriate reuse, and user, for the 300+ acre powertrain site was more complicated and required a tailored approach and solution. Property reuse was constrained due to several factors, including lack of demand for large industrial facilities in Ypsilanti, the 80 acre building slab remaining in place as part of a cap over contamination, as well as a series of easements, and utility corridors that significantly limit what can be constructed on site. In response to these dynamics, the RACER Trust worked closely with the City of Ypsilanti's economic development agency to identify unique redevelopment scenarios. Today, the site is owned by the State of Michigan, who leases it to the American Center for Mobility, the premier testing, validation, research, and certification facility for automated and connected vehicles, and other mobility technologies in the United States. The Center is available to private companies, government, research and educational organizations, and other stakeholders working to advance innovation in mobility and associated technologies.

Conclusion. The Willow Run facilities in Ypsilanti are a perfect example of the complications, and compelling outcomes, of large industrial site reuse. Having once been a center for manufacturing, employment, and economic growth, the facilities were heavily impacted by contaminants, the sites now host viable reuses serving the economy, providing jobs and protecting the environment. Their evolution from heavy manufacturing, to advanced mobility innovation, and modern aircraft maintenance uses is a poetic advancement of a cultural, and economic engines that powered Ypsilanti for generations.

Case #4: Hickory Textile Mills

Prior Use. Like many communities across the United States, Hickory, North Carolina is responding to vacant properties left behind when local manufacturing operations closed or relocated. These sites are commonly considered Brownfields or otherwise properties whose redevelopment must consider environmental remediation and regulatory compliance. Hickory is well known as a center for furniture manufacturing, hosiery, and textile mills, and by 1961 was home to more than 150 manufacturing facilities, the vast majority of which are now gone.

Now, the public and private sectors in Hickory are collaborating to reactivate these properties, bring jobs to the city and protect environmental and human health. A recent success story is the Hollar Mills project, an approximately 2-acre property that was primarily used for hosiery and textile manufacturing between 1930 and the early 2000s.

Contaminants of Concern. Like many hosiery and textile mills, operations at Hollar Hosiery used chemicals considered toxic, and are now managed under a regulatory framework. However, many sites such as the Hollar site, operated at least partially, pre-regulation, resulting in environmental impacts of toxic or hazardous waste, and pollutants referred to as Contaminants of Concern (COC) requiring assessment and remediation.

A Phase II ESA at the Hollar site revealed Tetrachloroethene (TCE), and Manganese in groundwater. Polynuclear Aromatic Hydrocarbons (PAH) from oil and grease were also found in soil, and soil vapor above regulatory standards. Additionally, the structure itself was found to have lead-based paint, and asbestos requiring remediation.

Remediation. To address each impacted media, the developer used a combination of soil removal and Engineering Controls (EC), and Institutional Controls (ICs). Each remedial action, EC, and IC were conducted subject to review and approval of the State of North Carolina. This information is recorded in a "Brownfield Agreement," a legally binding agreement between the developer and state that outlines the developer's obligations on the property, and the State's obligation to hold the developer harmless of impacts they did not cause.

The Brownfield Agreement for the Hollar site is constituted mostly of Land Use Restrictions (LUR). These restrictions limit the types of use that the property can be used for under certain conditions.

Groundwater—No groundwater or surface water cannot be used on the property at any time, for any purpose.

Soil—Areas of soil impacts on the property must be covered in a "cap," or impervious surface that prevents human contact with impacted soils, and stormwater from filtering through impacted soils.

Soil Gas—Testing of the soil gas near the structure's foundation identified up to 33 Volatile Organic Compounds regulated by the state, but levels were below the state threshold. No action was necessary to address soil gas as it did not represent a risk for vapor intrusion through the building's foundation.

Additional LUR's are subject to the Brownfield Agreement, and, in general, limit allowable land uses to residential, commercial, light manufacturing, and retail, office, and higher education.

Lead paint issues in the structure were managed through encapsulation, or by painting over it in order to prevent exposure. Limited asbestos abatement included removal following state regulatory guidelines for removal and disposal.

Reuse. The remaining Hollar Mills property retained some of its historic brick structures, making it an attractive opportunity for a developer to undertake an adaptive reuse project. By reusing the existing, and historic structures, the Hollar Mills redevelopment uses Hickory's history and identity as the foundation for revitalization. The former industrial buildings are now home to a mixed-use development offering a brewery, event space, commercial uses, and a restaurant.

Conclusion. Despite the complications of Brownfield redevelopment, underused and vacant land was reactivated to provide amenities, increased tax revenue, employment, and vitality Hickory needed. This project is a good example of how brownfield redevelopment does not necessarily require extensive, and expensive, remediation efforts in order to protect human and environmental health and activate critical spaces.

Case #5: Jacksonville Ash, Jacksonville, Florida

Prior Use. From the early 1900s until the 1960s, the City of Jacksonville, Florida disposed of its solid waste through incineration. The resulting ash was deposited as fill material in low lying areas of the city to build up the land. The City was even known to give the ash away to property owners and developers for fill material. This disposal occurred on three main sites which in total constitute approximately 1,140 acres within the City of Jacksonville. Two of the sites were the location of the city's incinerators, and the third is the site of the ash disposal.

When this city's ash disposal practice ceased in the 1960s, the land used to deposit the ash was used to accommodate Jacksonville's population growth. The result is that residential neighborhoods, schools, parks, public rights of way, and other uses were constructed on top of this fill material. In the mid–1990s, the State of Florida discovered that this fill contains levels of contaminants higher than regulations allow. After lengthy investigation and litigation, the city of Jacksonville agreed to pay for remediation estimated at approximately $100 million.

Contaminants of Concern. Contaminants of Concern (COCs) impacting the Jacksonville Ashe site include lead, arsenic, dioxin, and Polycyclic Aromatic Hydrocarbons (PAH), all regulated by federal and state agencies. The depth of the ash containing the COCs is found across the site as various depths, from less than 1' deep, to 10' deep, with most impacts are generally in the 1'–4' range. Areas of concern are not limited to those where the ash was directly deposited. Significant migration to adjacent properties is known to have occurred during disposal events, but also over time.

Extensive Environmental Site Assessments (ESA) were conducted at the request of the United States Environmental Protection Agency (EPA) specifically for a determination of whether it should be listed on the National Priorities List (NPL) and considered a Superfund site. The results showed that contaminant levels could warrant listing on the NPL, but EPA determined it qualified to be treated under a more expedient process called a Superfund Alternative Approach. This allows additional assessment, remediation, and reuse to occur under less prescriptive processes, and timelines, allowing for a more rapid reuse.

One of the main concerns over any federal designation, as opposed to a state driven process, was the stigma placed on the properties within the project area. After the extent of contamination became known, warnings that the properties were, or might be contaminated, were recorded on property titles within the study area with thousands of homes. Property owners and residents filed suit, arguing that the warning devalues their property, and is not legal. This resulted in a more extensive soil removal process, and special considerations for when restrictions remain on a property's title.

Remediation. Once the scope of contamination was understood, an ambitious remediation action commenced. The remedy included a mix of excavation and disposal, supplemented by restrictions on land uses, and capping. While the strategy is relatively straight forward, a major obstacle to performing the remediation was the fact that most of the area subject to remediation had active uses and structures that needed to remain in place.

Single family home neighborhoods, schools, parks, and commercial structures had extensive soil removal around them while they were still actively used. Where there was open space, excavation often occurred, even in the front, back, and side yards of single-family homes. In many cases, restrictions on digging in the back yard were also put in place, recorded with the property's title.

Special consideration had to be given to the time of the exaction, the impact of equipment and vehicles on the uses. Additionally, the routes taken by dump trucks and equipment through the neighborhoods were also a major consideration when planning the remediation. Many structures with basements had gravel caps placed over contaminated media to prevent human contact.

A different approach had to be taken where infrastructure such as roads, sidewalks, and utilities were constructed over contaminated fill. For most of this infrastructure, contaminated ash remains in place, and special precautions are taken during infrastructure construction and repair to ensure construction does not spread the ash or expose workers to contaminated media.

Reuse. While some of the remediated land hosted a new use after remediation was complete, most of it was used in the same manner it was sued for prior to the remediation. This includes single family home neighborhoods, multi-family developments, commercial property, and public facilities.

At the former Forest Street Incinerator site, important public amenities had to close out of contamination concerns. The Forest Street Park Community Center closed its doors, though the city plans to replace the center in a new facility on a nearby lot. The open space park portion for the property remains open with fields, and limited sport courts. Additionally, the Forest Park Head Start school had been constructed decades before investigations began and also closed its doors and was demolished.

What is now the Lonnie C Miller, Sr. Regional Park was once a site for incinerator ash disposal, and later a quail farm, as well as a junkyard. While the park actively serves the community with a variety of recreational uses, portions of the park impacted by contamination are fenced off awaiting excavation.

Conclusion. The Jacksonville Ash site demonstrates several interesting dynamics in brownfield development within the United States. It is an extreme example of how contamination, nor regulation, are limited by property lines. Additionally, it is testament to the legacy of pre-regulatory environmental practices, even from the public sector, can have long lasting and significantly negative impacts.

Case #6: Snow Creek Restoration Project, Snow Creek, California

Prior Use. Lake Tahoe, California and the surrounding area is known for its crystal-clear water, beautiful mountains, clean air, and abundant snowfall. It was these characteristics that landed the 1960 Winter Olympics, and the development surge that comes with them, in adjacent Squaw Valley. In preparation for the games, a concrete plant was constructed to support the development boom.

At the time of construction, the concrete plant was sited on approximately 6 acres of pristine pine forest, wetland meadows, and streams leading to Lake Tahoe. The concrete plant continued operating for decades after the Olympics, supplying concrete to the rapid development of the Lake Tahoe region. Unfortunately, site operations resulted in negative environmental impacts including releases of contamination from regular operations, debris, and byproducts from concrete plant, and building materials dumped throughout the property, including in the wetlands, and stream waters that feed Lake Tahoe.

In 2004, the State of California, Placer County, and the Lake Tahoe Community were tackling a significant decline in Lake Tahoe's water quality. The concrete plant was identified as a contributor to the decline. Resources were then mobilized to acquire the property, take measures to eliminate sources of contamination, and restore the land's ecological functions.

Contaminants of Concern. Contaminants of Concern (COCs) were identified sitewide, in areas where materials were stored, concrete was mixed, in and around a concrete pond washout area, a vehicle maintenance area, a fueling area and abandoned Underground Storage Tank (UST).

Concrete rubble and byproducts were found in several areas of the site, ranging in depth from six inches to nine feet. Constituents within this slag increased the PH levels of the surrounding soils and in groundwater. While not considered a recognized Contaminant of Concern, the rubble represented an obstacle to site reuse, and was the source of elevated PH levels and was addressed during the remediation process.

Around the maintenance shop area, soil and groundwater were found to be impacted by motor oil, diesel, gasoline, and benzene were detected above regulatory thresholds. Sitewide analysis also found elevated levels of diesel fuel, heavy metals (including chromium, arsenic, barium, and lead), and increased PH levels in soil and groundwater.

Another major factor addressed through site restoration was fine sediment that was migrating into Lake Tahoe. While Lake Tahoe is famed for its clear waters, its clarity had been degrading for decades due to runoff from development on the land surrounding the lake. A tributary to the lake, Snow Creek is fed by an 80 hectare watershed containing several sources of potentially contaminated runoff including roadways, parking facilities, light industrial, and commercial uses. The Snow Creek Restoration Project was an opportunity to not only address conditions on site, but to also improve runoff from an entire watershed.

Remediation. Remediation largely relied on the trusted approach of excavation and disposal, with some reliance on natural attenuation for petroleum based COCs that did not exceed regulatory thresholds. Removal of concrete rubble in soils was conducted to eliminate the source of elevated PH levels in surrounding soils and groundwater.

Remedial actions were taken to not only address concerns directly on site but to also mitigate offsite impacts resulting from stormwater runoff into nearby streams, and ultimately Lake Tahoe, making this a stormwater runoff challenge. This is a case where decisions were made that exceeded regulatory requirements for that particular property. They considered the impacts to Lake Tahoe, it is economic importance, environmental uniqueness, and their interdependency.

To address the runoff impacts, stormwater treatment facilities were designed as a series of installments that slow the flow of stormwater in stages, allowing for solids and floating debris to settle or separate from the water flow. It starts with a broad concrete chamber forebay that captures larger debris. The forebay discharges into a gravel berm that acts as a large filter to capture additional, and smaller, debris. This berm is replaced once it is clogged. After the berm, water migrates over a broad wetland area and floodplain where fine sediments settle, volatile organic compounds can naturally attenuate, and root systems and plants can sequester other materials. The floodplain is flanked on both sides by banks, between which Snow Creek's natural channel runs. The banks allow the creek to flood during high water evens but keep it in a relatively confined area.

Reuse. From the very beginning of the project, stakeholders knew that a more sustainable reuse for the former concrete plant was important to protect and improve Lake Tahoe, an asset upon which the region depends on economically and culturally.

To facilitate this, the first step was Placer County's purchase of the site in 2008. After purchasing the site, Placer County enlisted the support of the Institute for Sustainable Infrastructure (ISI) to apply their Envision Sustainability Rating System as a decision making framework. The rating system evaluates 5 areas of a project to help guide higher performance of civil infrastructure projects by the application of more sustainable choices in project planning and implementation. The categories are:

- Quality of life
- Leadership
- Resource Allocation
- Natural World
- Climate and Risk

Achieving the first Platinum rating under Envision, the project sought opportunities to reduce carbon emissions, reusing materials on site, using recycled or otherwise environmentally friendly materials, Low Impact Development (LID) stormwater infrastructure, and meaningful stakeholder engagement.

Construction and restoration efforts concluded in 2014 when the site was opened up as the Snow Creek Stream Environment Zone Restoration Project, a 3.5 acre publicly available natural area complete with restored wetlands, stream restoration, multi-use paths, interpretive and education signage.

Conclusion. Brownfield redevelopment often brings a place full cycle, and in the case of the Snow Creek Restoration Project, a pristine natural area was recovered from a degraded condition back into a critical environmental, cultural, and economic asset. These goals are not exclusive, and by integrating the Envision decision making framework into project planning and decision making from the beginning, the Snow Creek Restoration Project is a model example of sustainable brownfield redevelopment.

A Tale of Two Cities

City #1: Emeryville, California

One of the first 40 Brownfields Pilots of the EPA, no other city took charge of their fate and took risks as much as Emeryville.

The Problem: In the early 1990s, with a long industrial background, no space to grow and more that 60 percent of the city branded as untouchable, Emeryville's economy was stagnant from the perception that industries left a citywide groundwater plume, discouraging property transactions and redevelopment. The complicated California regulatory environment, where up to four regulatory agencies could potentially be involved on a site, scared away prospective purchasers and redevelopers.

The Solutions: Using an EPA grant and powers of its redevelopment agency, and partnerships with property owners, regulators, and developers, and federal partners like the EPA and U.S. Army Corps of Engineers, the city undertook an areawide approach to assessment and environmental regulation which removed the regulatory risk, streamlined and facilitated the assessment and cleanup process, while obtaining community support for economic development, affordable housing and community serving projects. The city also developed the first interactive environmental GIS that served as the model for current day state environmental databases.

The Results: Apart from receiving a Bangemann Challenge Award (now the Stockholm Challenge) from the King of Sweden in 1999 and three Phoenix Awards, Emeryville's approach facilitated the redevelopment of hundreds of brownfields acres into parks, affordable housing, commerce and job-creating enterprises, without gentrifying the community.

City #2: Milwaukee, Wisconsin

In addition to having a citywide program much like Emeryville's, Milwaukee's Menomonee Valley exemplifies reuse is not possible without nongovernmental partners.

The Problem: For thousands of years the Menomonee Valley consisted of wild rice marshes, but by the early 1800s, when Milwaukee was considered the "machine shop of the world," the valley was its engine until it became a victim of deindustrialization beginning the 1980s. What remained were hundreds of acres of inaccessible brownfield, a trash-strewn river, sparsely used railroad tracks and empty shells of companies that once employed thousands.

The Solutions: Led by the Menomonee Valley Partners and the city, led a planning and development process involving real estate, government, business, industry and community members to create a mixed-use sustainable location for recreation, entertainment and business incubation. The plan is in its second phase, maturing with the economic times.

City Conclusions. There are dozens of other cities—big and small—with notable brownfields programs, including Portland, OR, Phoenix AZ, Oklahoma OK, Missoula

MT, Council Bluffs, IA, New York, NY and many more—the key ingredients to their successes are:

1. **Planning Beyond Brownfields.** These cities obtained excellent assistance in assessing and cleaning up brownfields. But the backbone of successful programs is a well-developed neighborhood, community, reuse, sustainability or other plans.

2. **Effective Leadership.** Successful brownfield programs are not afterthoughts—and this is demonstrated by programs that retain experienced professionals and take prominent roles in the chief executive—mayor or executive director—offices.

3. **Trusted Partnerships.** Most cities cannot do it alone. They need state government help to achieve regulatory certainty. They need community guidance to develop responsive and responsible plans. They need business and industry to understand what keeps economies moving. There must be trust among all those involved in reuse.

4. **Reliable Funding and Financing, and Incentives.** EPA grants are seed funds that help start assessment, planning and cleanup activities. All the cities mentioned layered various grant programs with public financing, special taxes, infrastructure grants and loans, tax credits, and/or land use incentives to attract private funding into projects.

Note

1. Fourth five-year review report for Roebling steel superfund site; Burlington County, New Jersey: Pages 10–14; 2019.

• D. International •

41. The Reuse of U.S. Military Bases in the Philippines[*]

Severo C. Madrona, Jr.

Editor's note: Before the agreements discussed in this article were implemented, the U.S. Agency for International Development worked with the Economic Support Fund under the Ministry of Human Settlements and later, the Office of the President of the Philippines, to develop public enterprise, infrastructure and educational facilities in the areas discussed.

In 1947, owing to its past colonial relationship and strategic location, the United States established numerous military bases in the Philippines, including the crucial Clark Air Base and Subic Naval Base. Critics had called it a sign of subservience to the United States, while supporters viewed it as crucial in the U.S. defense of the Asian Region against communism (Simbulan 1983). In 1991, the Philippine Senate voted to reject the extension of the Philippine-U.S. Military Bases Agreement, accelerating the pullout of the American military forces in the U.S. Military Bases.

Philippine policymakers were not unprepared for the withdrawal of the Americans. Before 1991, the Philippine Congress has already commissioned an inter-agency study to draw up alternative plans and uses for these military bases entitled "*Kumbersyon: Comprehensive Conversion Program: Alternative Use of the Military Baselands and the Military Camps in Metro Manila,*" which envisioned the following: (a) Subic Naval Base as a Maritime Industrial Complex to include an international container port and cargo terminal as well as shipbuilding and ship repair facilities and an industrial support complex; (b) Clark Air Base, on the other hand, as an international civil aviation complex, a modern industrial estate and tourism, trade and business center for Luzon and Asia. (Legislative Executive Bases Council [LEBC] 1990:5).

To institutionalize the projected economic benefits of the military bases, then President Corazon Aquino signed Republic Act 7227 or the Bases Conversion Development Act of 1992 creating the Bases Conversion and Development Authority (BCDA) as the planning and implementing agency to manage the execution of the conversion programs proposed by the LEBC. BCDA was tasked to adapt, prepare and implement a comprehensive and detailed development program for its subsidiaries and authorities in consonance with the following directional plans (Section 2.1., E.O. No. 62, Series of 1993):

---

[*]Published with permission from the author.

- **Subic Naval Base.** To be developed as an exclusively economic and free-port zone ensuring the free flow of goods and capital following prescribed rules, to generate employment opportunities in and around the zone, and to attract and promote productive local and foreign investments. The Subic Special Economic and Freeport Zone shall be developed, operated, administered, and managed by the SBMA.
- **Clark Air Base.** To be developed as an exclusive economic zone with such incentives and privileges granted the Subic Special Economic and Freeport Zone and Export Processing Zones. The Clark Special Economic Zone Zone (CSEZ) shall form part of the growth triad connecting with Subic and Metro Manila as a buffer to in-migration to the metropolis. The CSEZ is envisioned as a new industrial townsite and a major civil aviation complex for international passenger and cargo.
- **Camp John Hay.** To be preserved, maintained, enhanced, and developed as a forest watershed and tourist destination. The natural attributes and character of the Camp shall be maintained. The facilities shall be developed with the private sector's expertise to maximize its potential for both local and foreign tourism
- **Other Baselands.** The Wallace Air Station, O'Donnel Transmitter Station, San Miguel Naval Communication Station, and Mt. Sta. Rita Station shall be developed in accordance with its best land use and the national concerns as stated in the Act and as may be determined by the President in line with national priorities
- **Other Special Economic Zones.** To create, develop, and manage other special economic zones covering the municipalities of Morong, Hermosa, Dinalupihan in Bataan and Castillejos, San Antonio, and San Marcelino in Zambales subject to economic viability studies.

Challenges for Redevelopment

At the outset, two significant challenges faced the implementers in the redevelopment of the former U.S. military bases: (a) financial—the funds to be used for the redevelopment of these former U.S. military bases and (b) environmental—the legacy of environmental damage brought about by inadequate environmental management at the former American military bases.

Financial Challenges

As to the first, the solution was direct: the conversion of several Metro Manila military camps (Philippine Army's *Fort Bonifacio* and Philippine Air Force's *Villamor Air Base*) for commercial development. The conversion would not only finance the proposed redevelopment of U.S. military bases but also abet congestion in the central business districts of the metropolitan region thereby relieving Metro Manila of further increase in congestion, pollution, traffic and other urban ills; and allay the fears on continuing military adventurism manifested by series of military coups in the 1987–1989 (Casanova 2011: 109).

BCDA has also disposed of other properties: Joint U.S. Military Advisory Group

216 Part III. Practices and Innovations • D. International

(JUSMAG) property in Quezon City for USD 6.8 million and a portion of the Fort Bonifacio land to Philippine National Oil Company (PNOC) and the Department of Energy (DOE) for USD 12 million dollars. It also commenced the Heritage Park Project as an exclusive memorial park in Fort Bonifacio. It received USD 19.6 million dollars as advance payment from the sale of Heritage Park Investment Certificates (HPICs).

Public-Private Partnerships in Redevelopment

To encourage the active participation of the private sector in transforming the military reservations and their extensions into other productive uses, BCDA has likewise engaged private corporate entities in various modalities of Public-Private Partnership—sale, joint venture agreements and lease agreements—for the conversion of military reservations, including the Fort Bonifacio Global City, Villamor Air Base' Newport City, Clark Air Base, Camp John Hay and Poro Point. Combined, the sale and profits from the sale and redevelopment, can be summarized as follows:

Facility	New Use	Mode of Disposition	Year	Net Profit (est. USD)
Fort Bonifacio	Global City	Joint Venture (JV) Agreement with Metro Pacific Consortium	1995 2004–onwards	USD 658 million
	Other Developments (McKinley Hill, Serendra, Bonifacio Capital City)	JV (with Ayala Land Inc., Megaworld Corporation Century Properties)	2004–onwards	USD 67 million
		Lease of Properties (International School Manila, British School Manila, Manila Japanese School)		USD 34 million
Villamor Air Base	Newport City	Joint Venture Agreement (JV) with Megaworld Corporation	2009	USD 282 million
John Hay	Economic Zone (EZ)	Lease Agreement (for redevelopment with Fil-Estate Consortium and IHG Group)	2007	USD 12 million
Poro Point	Free Port/EZ	Lease Agreement (for locators, hotels—Thunderbird Hotels and Resorts, Inc.)	2007	USD 10 million
Clark Air Base	Economic Zone (New Clark City)	Lease Agreement (for locators, hotels)	1993–onwards	USD 11.9 billion

Environmental Challenges

Both U.S. and Philippine environmental experts agreed on the legacy of toxic wastes in the former U.S. military bases. No less than the U.S. General Accounting Office in

1993 acknowledged that it had "identified contaminated sites and facilities that would not comply with U.S. environmental standards" at Subic and Clark (General Accounting Office 1992). GAO reported that only 25 percent of the five million gallons of sewage generated daily in the military bases were treated. There was improper disposal of hazardous wastes like lead and other heavy metals used in ship repair as these were drained directly into Subic Bay, or buried as landfill. Like in Subic, power plants have emitted untreated pollutants directly into the air in violation of the United States' clear air standards. Agreeably, the former military bases are heavily polluted.

Thus, the Philippine Government has negotiated with the U.S. Government through diplomatic means to clean up the contaminated sites. However, diplomatic efforts proved to be ineffective. Resolutions were filed before the Philippine Congress calling for Congressional investigations and inquiries about the environmental, health, and other aspects of the issue, unfortunately, the same likewise prove futile. Consistently, the U.S. Government refused to clean up these toxic wastes concealing behind the cloak of legal immunities and international agreements. Proposals were made for the Philippine Government to bring up the case before international tribunals to resolve the question of the international responsibility of the U.S. and the alleged violation of the right to a healthy environment of Filipinos (Mercado 2001). However, up to date, no such case has been brought to the international tribunals. Thus, while some brownfields financing and redevelopment tools apply, in a legal sense, these former U.S. military bases falls under Base Realignment and Closure (BRAC), which has a separate set of statutes. Similar to that of the United States, many decommissioned bases in the U.S. are still idle, many are in process, and some are successfully cleaned up and redeveloped.

Consequently, environmental watchdog group *People's Task Force on Bases Cleanup* succinctly summarized this incessant environmental challenge *"These contaminants just won't go away xxx They will keep coming up, because the sites have not been cleaned up"* (Regencia 2014).

Overcoming the Challenges

Twenty-nine (29) years after, the former military bases have achieved somewhat thriving redevelopment as shown by the following:

Clark Special Economic Zone. BCDA created the Clark Special Economic Zone (CSEZ) covering the lands consisting of the Clark military reservations, including the Clark Air Base proper and portions of the Clark reverted base lands, and excluding the areas covered by previous Presidential Proclamations, the areas turned over to the Department of Agrarian Reform (DAR), and the areas in the reverted baselands reserved for military use (Section 1, Proclamation No. 163 Series of 1993). The CSEZ is governed by the BCDA through its wholly owned subsidiary known as Clark Development Corporation (CDC) (Section 1, E.O. No. 80, Series of 1993) with an initial investment of USD 500 thousand dollars. Clark was envisioned to be an international civil aviation complex, a modern industrial estate and tourism, trade, and business center for Luzon and Asia.

Clark Special Economic Zone was designated as the site of a premier Philippine international airport which would serve as a new international gateway to the Philippines, together with its accompanying expressway and mass-transit rail access systems will attract economic and tourism activities towards Central Luzon and the North Luzon Growth Quadrangle, thereby relieving Metro Manila of further increase in migration, congestion, pollution, traffic and other urban ills (Section 1, E.O. No. 174 Series of 1994). BCDA has invested in the construction and establishment of the Clark International Airport (later known as Diosdado Macapagal International Airport). In 2005, the airport showcased full-scale operations as a hub of budget airlines servicing Asian destinations like Korea, Hong Kong, Bangkok, and Singapore (BCDA 2007 Annual Report; BCDA 2012 Annual Report). BCDA has also entered into a lease agreement with (a) Texas Instruments (T.I.) Dallas for the 87-acre area is T.I.'s first facility to put semiconductor assembly, testing, bumping, and multi-probe functions under one roof and (b) Phoenix Semiconductor Philippines Corporation, the only memory chip semiconductor firm in Southeast Asia (BCDA 2007 Annual Report; BCDA 2012 Annual Report). In 2010, FDI magazine, an affiliate of London-based The Financial Times Business Group, ranks Clark Freeport Zones as the best (No. 1) cost-effective free port in the world. It also ranks Clark, No. 7, as best economic potential under the Global Free Zones of the future for 2010 and 2011 (BCDA 2012 Annual Report).

Camp John Hay. As to John Hay Air Station covering an area of 677 hectares, it was declared for tourism, human resource development center, and multiple use forest watershed reservation purposes under the auspices of BCDA (Proclamation No. 198 Series of 1993) through the John Hay Development Corporation (JHDC), a wholly-owned subsidiary of the BCDA with an initial investment of USD 600 thousand dollars (Section 1, E.O. No. 103 Series of 1993). After that, Two Hundred Eighty-Eight and one/ tenth (288.1) hectares, more or less, of the total of Six Hundred Seventy-Seven (677) hectares of the John Hay Reservation was proclaimed as John Hay Special Economic Zone (JHSEC) (Proclamation No. 420, Series of 1994).

Poro Point. The Wallace Air Station in Poro Point, San Fernando La Union was designated as Poro Point Special Economic and Freeport Zone (PPSEFZ). It was administered by BCDA through the wholly-owned subsidiary John Hay Poro Point Development Corporation (JHPPDC) (Section 1, E.O. No. 31 Series of 1994). PPSEFZ covers the land and bay areas which include the Wallace Air Station, the San Fernando Airport, Seaport, Barangays Poro and San Vicente and portions of Barangays San Agustin, San Francisco, and Canaoay of the Municipality of San Fernando, Province of La Union, consisting of eight hundred (800) hectares (Section 1, Proclamation No. 216, Series of 1993). In 2002, JHPPDC was separated into two—the John Hay Management Corporation and Poro Point Management Corporation—as implementing corporate entities for John Hay Special Economic Zone and Poro Point Special Economic and Freeport Zone respectively (Executive Order No. 132, Series of 2002). In 2014, BCDA completed the master plan for the Poro Point Freeport and Special Economic Zone to make it an integrated sustainable hub for Northern Luzon (BCDA 2014 Annual Report).

New Clark City. BCDA has proposed a mixed-used development program which will host government center, central business district, academic institutions, research and development hub, agri-urban farms and eco-tourism infrastructure within a self-contained green community with state-of-the-art grid and cyber universities. It would promote a vast array of practices and techniques from architectural design to the construction of the buildings; the use of renewable energy; provision of a clean and affordable public transportation system; promotion of public health by producing and cultivating locally grown organic foods; and the provision of adequate access to safe potable water. It will also feature state-of-the-art information infrastructure which shall implement a communication/ internet network system designed to perform all communications functions.

The program is expected to generate more business and job opportunities attuned to the aspirations for inclusive growth (BCDA 2012 Annual Report; BCDA 2013 Annual Report; BCDA 2014 Annual Report). The NCC is a projected USD 11.9 billion dollars development project covering 9,450 hectares across Capas and Bamban in Tarlac province in Central Luzon. The NCC is dubbed as the Philippines' first "smart, green, and resilient city" technically supported by institutions like Asian Development Bank along with other government actors such as the Japan Overseas Infrastructure Investment Corporation (JOIN), Singapore's consultancy company for infrastructure and urban development Surbana Jurong, and corporations such as AECOM, Nippon Koei, and Philkoei International Inc.

Conclusion. While, the former U.S. military bases are now considered the forefront in the country's economic boom, there are legacies from past military uses which resulted in unknown environmental impacts.

References

Bases Conversion Development Authority (BCDA). *BCDA Annual Report. 2005–2018.*

Casanova, Arnel Paciano D. (2011), "Special Economic Zones and Freeports: Challenges and Opportunities in the Bases Conversion and Development Experience in the Philippines" in Connie Carter and Andrew Harding (eds.), *Special Economic Zones in Asian Market Economies.* New York: Routledge, 2011.108–123.

Commission on Audit. *BCDA Annual Audit Report.* 2006–2018.

General Accounting Office (GAO) (1992). *Report to Congressional Requesters Military Base Closures, U.S. Financial Obligations in the Philippines.*

Legislative Executive Bases Council (1990). *Kumbersyon: Comprehensive Conversion Program: Alternative Use of the Military Baselands and the Military Camps in Metro Manila.*

Mercado, Josine Ruth Remorca (2001). *The Responsibility of the U.S. Under International Law for the Legacy of Toxic Waste at the Former U.S. Bases in the Philippines.* Master of Laws Thesis, University of British Columbia.

Regencia, Ted (2014) "Toxic trail shadows US-Philippine bases deal" in https://www.aljazeera.com/indepth/features/2014/04/toxic-trail-shadows-us-philippine-military-bases-deal-20144286574888208.html.

Simbulan, Roland G. (1983). *The Basis of our Insecurity: A Study of the U.S. Military Bases in the Philippines.* Manila: Balai Fellowship.

42. Under the Hood*

KEVIN C. DESOUZA, MICHAEL HUNTER
and TAN YIGITCANLAR

Techno-centric smart and intelligent city initiatives continue to garner our attention and resources, as transforming urban areas into prosperous, livable, and sustainable settlements is a long-standing goal for local governments. Today, countless urban settlements across the globe have jumped onto the so-called "smart city bandwagon" to achieve this goal. Most smart city projects are either focused on transformation of the existing technical and physical infrastructures of a city—brownfield developments, or greenfield urban projects.[1]

Local governments around the globe are investing in partnerships with technology companies to help shape the future of cities. Companies such as Google and Microsoft have begun to show interest in the movement with the development of Toronto's Sidewalks Lab[2] and Arizona's desert city.[3] However, more commonly governments are investing in network infrastructure partnerships[4] with companies such as CISCO to develop complex networks, sensors, and data processes. For the last several months, we have been studying the range of techno-centric smart city partnerships to uncover what works and what should local governments watch out for. Here are some of the cases we have looked at.

Songdo, South Korea

Envisioned as early as 2001, Songdo[5] was born out of a political drive[6] for low-carbon sustainable growth and a push for trade-based economic growth. South Korea's economic development over the previous half century has been largely driven by manufacturing and export as the country has few natural resources. As a result, South Korea imports almost the entirety of their fuel supply to maintain their manufacturing economy.

Songdo looks to lower the economic costs of importing fuel whilst simultaneously improving the trade network of South Korea by developing a city strategically located for trade, powered by renewable energy technology. Built entirely on reclaimed land from the Yellow Sea, Songdo is situated on the tip of the Incheon Free Economic Zone.[7] However, Songdo's two-hour commute from Seoul, the nation's capital, has received criticism from the public, who believes the distance is too far for a daily commute, but not far

---

*Originally published as Kevin C. Desouza, Michael Hunter, and Tan Yigitcanlar, "Under the Hood," *PM* (December 2019, Vol. 101: 11) by ICMA, the International City/County Management Association; reprinted with permission.

enough to recognize Songdo as its own viable economic center. This is reflected by Songdo's 60 percent unoccupancy rate and 70,000 daily commuters. While this number of daily commuters alone might seem impressive, it pales in comparison to Seoul's population of 9 million and struggles to ease the bustle of the capital—as was originally advertised. Songdo's current population sits at 100,000, which while impressive for a city built from scratch, is still short of its 300,000-resident goal and for those who do live there, Songdo is considered a ghost town.[8]

Hudson Yards, New York, United States

Like Songdo, the Hudson Yards development[9] in New York City was conceptualized as early as 2001. It was originally born out of the desire to host the 2012 Olympic Games and a need for further urban space within Manhattan. To create this urban space, the Hudson Yards project looked at developing an entire district on top of a major rail center and transport hub. This extremely ambitious project has been considered the most expensive private development[10] in United States history, budgeted at roughly $25 billion USD. The development was first advertised as New York's smartest new neighborhood, with sensor technology delivering data-driven updates, allowing the developers to repeatedly improve quality of life. In a bid to become America's first "quantified community," Hudson Yards advertised sensors that would monitor air quality, noise levels, temperature, and pedestrian traffic, alongside technology typical of the smart city movement. Pneumatic waste disposal chutes would automate waste collection, micro-grid and gas fired turbines would reduce greenhouse gases, and even more sensors would monitor resource efficiency and reduce downtime.

Its highly sought-after location garnered interest from numerous multi-nationals, with investment from HSBC, Bank of China and Deutsche Bank; and current commercial renting from SAP, BCG, Warner Media, and L'Oreal. Similar to Songdo, this development's top-down approach promised technology as a means to improve quality of life within Manhattan, but has been met with its own set of criticism.[11] Hudson Yards is currently perceived as a space only available to those who can afford it, filled with up-market commercial and entertainment businesses and little public space.

As such, it's argued that the original benefits this development would have for the city are yet to be met. Hudson Yards is yet to deliver on its original purpose with data-driven analytics being pushed to the last of the head property developers focus. Main property developer "Related" initially advertised Hudson Yards as a technologically improved urban area due to its use of data analytics to improve resource efficiency. Related has since noted[12] that from the initial planning of the city, data technology has changed rapidly, and as such, increased complications regarding privacy and analytics have surfaced. Physical construction of Hudson Yards has taken a priority in its development as it provides a more tangible economic return.

Masdar City, Abu Dhabi, United Arab Emirates

Masdar City began as an incredibly ambitious project hoping to be the world' first zero-carbon city.[13] First established in 2006, Abu Dhabi looked towards developing an economic, social, and environmental sustainability blueprint of a city[14] that would help the nation's economy diversify away from its traditionally nonrenewable assets (fossil fuel and oil). Its aim was to develop large-scale renewable energy projects, become a clean-tech hub, provide homes for 50,000 people and facilities for 1,500 businesses, and develop a new institute of science and technology (MIST).

Still in development, Masdar City has faced numerous challenges due to its location and its initial sustainability projections. This project has been considered extremely ambitious due to the severe desert weather conditions; the aims for complete sustainability; the research, development, and implementation of renewable technology; and its overall greenfield nature. This project is located 17 km south east of Abu Dhabi City and is strategically placed alongside Abu Dhabi International Airport. The desert conditions noticeably affected the construction of the city, with shifting sands adding difficulty to the initial foundations and extreme temperatures affecting workers. This directly affected the budget, which in turn had a negative impact on Masdar City as an economically sustainable project. As a result, its initial "carbon free" scheme has changed to "carbon neutral," and only two of its 1,500 planned transport stations are currently active. Similar to Songdo, its "built from scratch, top-down approach" has struggled to garner interest from UAE citizens with its current population sitting close to just 3,000 people, most of which are students.

However, Masdar City has recently begun to establish numerous global partnerships and multi-national clean tech projects.[15] Thirteen years after its initial conceptualization, the research and development of renewable energy technology has become a commodity that Masdar City can now profit from. The UAE's initial economic drive to diversify assets is now realized through the hundreds of clean energy projects Masdar City technology is involved in globally.

Gujarat, India

Gujarat International Finance Tec-City (GIFT)[16] has been conceptualized amongst India's 100 Smart City Program[17] to help adapt to community and economic needs in India's future. With 70 percent of Indians living in cities by 2050 and roughly 500 million moving to urban areas, GIFT looks to develop an economic hub within the Indian Economic Zone,[18] capable of housing large amounts of multi-national companies and scaling into a business capital of the world. GIFT is also utilizing smart city technologies—such as automated waste disposal, renewable energy infrastructure, and real-time monitoring of city life—to aid in the national development of sustainability and environmental norms against the growing population crisis.

In order to do this, GIFT aims to move most of its infrastructure underground, with power, water, waste, and fire hydrant services built into wet or dry sections of a utility tunnel plan. These large service trenches aim to provide the council with access to all-important city infrastructure without a need for digging or resurfacing, allowing for a well-designed and uninterrupted urban transport plan on the surface. Its current power system demonstrates 99.9 percent reliability with roughly 5.3 minutes of outage per annum, and the efficiency of its waste disposal system is four times the national standard.

GIFT's early stages of development have been marked as its most difficult with the city struggling to garner investment or interest nationally or globally.[19] Initially, it was expected to construct over 100 skyscrapers capable of supporting one million jobs within its first decade, although it wasn't until 2014 that Prime Minister Modi introduced clear regulatory framework regarding the city's overarching goals. Furthermore, it wasn't until 2016 that the Modi government set up favorable tax motives for finance and technology firms looking to invest in GIFT and it is even argued today that foreign business is more likely to operate out of Mumbai due to its pre-existing talent pool. Similar to the other greenfield projects in this list, GIFT required a large amount of upfront investment to begin construction, as well as a more heavily weighted top-down approach to implement the necessary infrastructure of the city. Operating as a 50/50 joint venture between state government (GUDC) and private enterprise (IFSC), GIFT's construction was initially slow with only six commercial towers currently developed.

Over the past two years, GIFT has begun to demonstrate extremely high value. GIFT was recently named in the top three emerging business hubs[20] in the world (GFCI) and late last year the city announced a collaboration with Bloomberg[21] aimed at incentivizing foreign interest through best practice, transparent frameworks, and secure data/technology infrastructure. Currently, over 200 companies are operational in GIFT, including Oracle, State Bank of India, and the Indian International Exchange.

Key Learnings

Other cases we studied include Amsterdam Smart City Initiative,[22] City Verve in Manchester City,[23] Smart City 3.1 Barcelona,[24] Singapore's Jurong Lake District[25] and, Startup Smart City—Tel Aviv,[26] among others. In examining these cases, we have arrived at some key learnings.

1. **Techno-centric smart city developments seldom work**. The projects are run over budget, they under-deliver, and they never get completed on schedule. The initiatives that have struggled all share commonalities in their greenfield top-down approach to development. Masdar City and Songdo have both implemented some incredibly impressive technology, but they struggle to maintain a population capable of utilizing it. Put differently, if you build it, they are not guaranteed to come. To be successful, technology-centric development must be complemented with associated investments in social, economic, and responsible innovation policies that can result in the development of a livable and just city.

2. **Local governments must adopt the role of facilitator within the initiative**. As seen in these initiatives, the complex nature of urban transformation will incorporate numerous partners, new technologies, and environmental change for citizens; therefore, it is crucial that government provides a solid foundation to take advantage of this complexity. Complexity is not something to be shunned— local governments must embrace it and be prepared to thrive on it as emergent opportunities develop. Furthermore, we need to equip our cities with highly dynamic mechanisms to better plan their growth and manage their day-to-day operational challenges. Investing in smart governance could pay off in this regard.

3. **Ensure risks are properly shared with the private sector**. Too often, we see smart city developments where local governments own a large share of the risk, while the private sector has its commitments and risks shielded. The most expensive

initiatives on this list have included massive infrastructure upgrades which have required public/private partnerships and investment. In the extreme cases such as Hudson Yards, private ownership has deterred the initial public benefit of the project. Local governments need to get smarter when it comes to managing complex public/private partnerships and managing public finance agreements.

    4. **Be open to new innovations and think about how to gain from setbacks**. Seldom do these projects work out as planned. As such, it is important to incorporate flexibility in how one thinks about resources and being open to re-orienting focus as conditions change. Masdar City has already capitalized on the research of its wind and solar technologies through numerous global partnerships implementing the lessons learned during the construction the city. What began as a by-product of the city's development, now offers a viable stream of revenue for continued city progress. We suggest the expansion of this idea toward the digital sphere. As renewable technologies were initially the focus of smart city developments, we can now note successful smart city initiatives largely focus on the importance of data.

    5. **Smart cities should be for all citizens**. The current smart city practices, excluding the Indian cases, are at large elitist approaches to create high-quality lifestyle havens exclusive for the privileged citizens. For instance, despite the urban plan of the Masdar city dictating that 20 percent of the accommodation areas are to be assigned to low-income groups, the city is almost exclusively occupied by affluent populations. The blue-collar workers of Masdar commute long distances by private motor vehicles, contradicting one of the design principles of the city "being a car-free development."

    6. **Smart cities must consider consumption of resources**. While a massive consumption society is an integral contributor of the environmental problems we experience, the existing smart city agenda has a negligible focus on the consumption behavior change. The reason for this is that technology is seen as a lucrative commodity—constantly producing new versions and making earlier ones redundant—and its materialism is highly profitable for the technology companies that drive the corporate smart city agenda. We underline the importance of longevity of the smart city technological infrastructure—not needing constant updates and upgrades.

    7. **Renewable energy sources are imperative to long-term sustainability**. Unsustainable practice is a clear roadblock in a city's journey to become smarter. Even though some smart cities such as Amsterdam and San Francisco are widely recognized as global leaders in smart solutions for sustainable urban outcomes, emissions generated from these cities continue to rise. Naturally, smart cities are energy-hungry urban localities; hence, they must switch to renewable energy sources to not further contribute to the global climate crisis.

    8. **Smart cities are only as smart as their residents**. There is clear interest from city administrations to employ state-of-the-art digital data and technology to create efficiencies for boosting economic development, enhancing quality of life, or improving sustainability of the city. Nonetheless, what is needed is not only to make city systems smart, but to also make the city itself smart—that includes its residents. After all, it takes a smart community (a knowledgeable, conscious, forward-thinking, engaged, united, and active community) to raise a smart city.

In closing, we looked at techno-centric smart city development efforts and found no clear evidence that in its infancy the current smart city practice has the capacity to generate genuine and long-term solutions. We are at the beginning of a new era where technology and cities are converging. The knowledge on smart cities is limited, and our expectations from them are unrealistic and full of speculations. Technology is being seen by many as the silver bullet. While critical, technology alone cannot create smart cities. It takes more than just the state-of-the-art solutions to transform cities into truly smart and sustainable ones. Thus, we must ensure that the social, economic, environmental, and policy realms are accounted for with the same level of care and vigor that we pay to technology.

Notes

1. https://www.businessfirstmagazine.com.au/building-greenfield-city-centre-smart-way/25079/.
2. https://sidewalktoronto.ca/.
3. https://www.cnet.com/news/bill-gates-plans-to-build-a-smart-city-in-arizona-desert/.
4. https://www.cisco.com/c/en_au/solutions/industries/smart-connected-communities.html#~stickynav=2.
5. https://smartcityhub.com/urban-planning-and-building/songdo-model-of-the-smart-and-sustainable-city-of-the-future/.
6. https://www.theguardian.com/sustainable-business/south-korea-smart-grid-low-carbon.
7. http://www.koreatimes.co.kr/www/tech/2018/12/693_259369.html.
8. https://www.citylab.com/life/2018/06/sleepy-in-songdo-koreas-smartest-city/561374/.
9. https://www.hudsonyardsnewyork.com/.
10. https://www.businessinsider.com.au/hudson-yards-tour-of-most-expensive-development-in-us-history-2018-9?r=U.S.&IR=T.
11. https://www.theguardian.com/commentisfree/2019/mar/13/new-york-hudson-yards-ultra-capitalist.
12. https://www.metropolismag.com/cities/hudson-yards-technology-urbanism/.
13. https://www.energydigital.com/sustainability/masdar-greenest-city-world.
14. https://masdar.ae/en/masdar-city/the-city/sustainability.
15. https://masdar.ae/en/masdar-clean-energy/projects.
16. https://economictimes.indiatimes.com/markets/stocks/news/gift-international-financial-services-centre/articleshow/69642735.cms?from=mdr.
17. http://smartcities.gov.in/content/.
18. http://www.giftgujarat.in/gift-sez.
19. https://www.business-standard.com/article/economy-policy/india-s-jobs-deficit-gift-city-in-gujarat-struggling-to-create-employment-119052400221_1.html.
20. https://www.news18.com/news/business/gujarats-gift-city-named-among-top-three-emerging-business-hubs-in-world-1876885.html.
21. https://www.bloomberg.com/company/announcements/gujarat-international-finance-tec-city-gift-city-bloomberg-collaborate-advance-indias-international-financial-services-centre-ifsc-global-investors/.
22. https://smartcityhub.com/governance-economy/amsterdam-better-than-smart/.
23. https://cityverve.org.uk/.
24. http://www.urban-hub.com/cities/smart-city-3-0-ask-barcelona-about-the-next-generation-of-smart-cities/.
25. https://www.jld.sg/.
26. https://www.tel-aviv.gov.il/en/abouttheCity/Pages/SmartStartup.aspx.

43. Brownfield Sites Are Opportunities in the Heart of Towns and Cities*

Paul Nathanail

The city of Famagusta in Cyprus lies empty, as it has since the 1974 invasion that divided the island into north and south. The city its former inhabitants left behind is now a ghost town, streets overgrown with bushes, windowless buildings like concrete skulls, roofless brick homes left open to the elements.

Reviving Famagusta is a key part of the jigsaw puzzle that comprises the efforts to find a solution to Cyprus' social and ethnic tensions, a puzzle that this year's U.S.-brokered talks between Turkish and Cyprus authorities hope to solve.

While the events by which Famagusta came to be deserted, and the length of time it has remained so, are an extreme example, such abandoned brownfield land is all too common. The term brownfield, depending on your definition, refers to sites and broader areas that have been affected by their former land uses, have become derelict or underused, may have contamination issues, usually occupy space in developed urban areas and in any event require intervention to bring them back into beneficial use.

Brownfield redevelopment was among the issues Chancellor George Osborne raised at his annual Mansion House address, focusing on the urgent need to speed up the process of putting unused land to good use, specifically for housing. The Chancellor announced local authorities will be required to use Local Development Orders to pre-approve 90 percent of their brownfield sites for housing so that building can start sooner. A sum of £5m is being allocated in support of this endeavor.

The chancellor's announcement means a clear understanding of what exactly a brownfield is has returned to the heart of national politics. For example, in the U.S. brownfields are by definition contaminated. In England, the government's regeneration vehicle—the Homes and Communities Agency—uses the term as a synonym for previously developed land, although it would be more useful to restrict the term to only previously developed land that is also vacant. While the exact definition does not always matter, when funding and government policies are targeted towards sites that meet specific criteria (as in the U.S.) or allocated to government departments in order to

---

*Originally published as Paul Nathanail, "Brownfield Sites Are Opportunities in the Heart of Towns and Cities," *The Conversation*, https://theconversation.com/brownfield-sites-are-opportunities-in-the-heart-of-towns-and-cities-27955 (June 13, 2014). Reprinted with permission of the publisher.

meet targets (as was the case under the previous UK government) then definitions are vital.

Mark Twain is credited with advising "buy land—they're not making it anymore," and by and large he was right; he might have said "reuse brownfield land—they'll make plenty more of it." Some cities are shrinking (Detroit, most spectacularly), but most cities are growing, and can do so only by building up, down, or outward.

In any case citizens expect, and authorities should strive for, progress. We expect a variety of services from city land: shelter, education, entertainment, manufacturing, offices, worship, shopping, sport and culture. The structures housing these services may well outlast the service, but the land will outlast them all. We do not consume land in the way that we do food or fuel. But we do have a habit of discarding land and moving on to the next parcel to be used for the next land use.

Recycle That Land

We know reusing land is worthwhile. In the UK there's little choice, being as it is a small, densely populated island with a long history of urban settlement. While our understanding of the long-term behavior of cities as complex systems is getting better, we face the challenge of predicting the impact of different land uses, and choosing the most sustainable, or at least avoiding the obviously unsustainable. In many cases flexibility beyond the next land use is key. But for housing we are building a legacy that will last a century, perhaps more. Where we build our new homes will influence how far we travel to work, how well we interact with our neighbors, how creative we are likely to be.

Think of brownfield sites as the empty space in the eight pieces on a grid with nine spaces where the challenge is to arrange them so as to form a coherent image. In just the same way as many economists argue full employment is undesirable, so the same goes for eradicating brownfield sites. A derelict site is needed to build the new hospital while the current one continues treating patients. Only once the new facility opens its operating theater doors, can the old be demolished, in turn to become the site for a new school, perhaps, and so the land use cycle goes on turning. If an area has no immediate hard use for a site, then it can be put to interim uses: a garden, temporary car park, or an arena for outdoor performances and markets.

Meet Expectations, Not Targets

For most people the term brownfield site conjures up images of derelict factories, abandoned train stations, or closed mines. Yet by using the term to mean any previously developed land, past target-driven governments have claimed high rates of brownfield redevelopment. This nonsense extended to counting back gardens and housing estate open space as brownfields, resulting in the absurd accounting of infill development as brownfield reuse. This was eventually dropped by the coalition government, and the targets abandoned altogether. However best use of brownfield, in the colloquial sense, sites, and the challenge of wise stewardship of our cities, remains.

The question we ought to be asking is what sort of cities are we trying to create, and then considering how those empty spaces in the puzzle can help us achieve that, in addition to building high, digging deep, and even occasionally spreading out. We need to minimize our reliance on the car and encourage the design of more walkable cities—ones that the high streets imagined by Mary Portas would benefit from, and which could begin to arrest the slide into obesity and diabetes it seems we are on.

The challenge for the chancellor is to realize the Mansion has many rooms and not all can be counted. It is not only building houses on brownfield sites he should be supporting, but instead great urban places to live, work and play. He and his cabinet colleagues in the Department for Communities and Local Government should be encouraging us to create. He could keep perhaps in his pocket a child's puzzle, to remind him that space is fixed but what we do with it is not.

44. France Has a Unique Approach to Regenerating Inner Cities[*]

SEBASTIEN DARCHEN *and* GWENDAL SIMON

The regeneration of inner-city areas is a global challenge. Inner cities in France certainly have their problems, but the nation also has a good record of successful major urban regeneration projects. We have analyzed three of these initiatives to understand what factors contribute to good regeneration outcomes.

Urban regeneration can be defined as a holistic approach to revitalize under-used areas of the city. It's commonly associated, however, with the related challenges of gentrification, rising property values, and displacement of low-income groups. And these projects do not always achieve a sense of place.

French cities have much higher densities than Australian cities. For instance, Paris has 10,000 inhabitants per square kilometer, which is more than five times the population density of Sydney's 1,900/km2. Higher density and more accessibility to public transport are important for successful urban regeneration. But this is not the only explanation for its success in France.

With the post-industrial society, new approaches are emerging to solve planning challenges in France. Since the nation began decentralization in 1982, local authorities have gained more power to implement planning strategies.

At the same time, the multiplicity of urban stakeholders makes decision-making difficult. Since the 1990s, legal obligations to consult with residents have increased. Regeneration projects have to follow general planning principles but must also allow some flexibility to enable the local community to have an input.

Lyon Confluence

Lyon Confluence is the largest urban regeneration project in Europe with 150 hectares of land having been redeveloped since 2003. The project is led by public redevelopment company SPL Lyon. It is 89 percent owned by Greater Lyon, a metropolitan institution made up of 59 local authorities.

---

[*]Originally published as Sebastien Darchen and Gwendal Simon, "France Has a Unique Approach to Regenerating Inner Cities—What Can We Learn From Its Success?," *The Conversation*, https://theconversation.com/france-has-a-unique-approach-to-regenerating-inner-cities-what-can-we-learn-from-its-success-91652 (March 11, 2018). Reprinted with permission of the publisher.

SPL Lyon can set up strict planning and urban design principles. Developers are required to integrate these principles into their designs to be part of the project.

SPL sells the land to developers at a fixed rate. Developers need to win design competitions to be part of the project and not just offer the best price for the land.

Lyon Confluence has attracted foreign investors, such as Japan's NEDO, and became a model for smart positive energy buildings, which produce more energy than they consume.

Île de Nantes

The Île de Nantes regeneration project aims to transform a 337-hectare industrial area into a sustainable living and working environment. There is a strong emphasis on preserving the industrial character of the area.

Another objective is to attract creative industries firms to a creative arts district to replace the local shipbuilding industry, which closed in 1987.

A public redevelopment company known as SAMOA oversees the Île de Nantes project, which will be completed in 2037. Innovative placemaking strategies are being developed to create a sense of place connected to the area's industrial past. The project includes a lot of consultation with urban stakeholders.

Paris Rive-Gauche

The Paris Rive Gauche project is one of the most important regeneration project in the city. The 130-hectare site is in the east of Paris, on the banks of the Seine. Paris Rive Gauche means Paris Left Bank and refers to the Paris of an earlier era.

Work on the Paris Rive Gauche redevelopment began in the early 1990s and is now halfway through. The aim is to create a mixed-use neighborhood around landmarks such as the national library and Paris Diderot University.

The aim is to redevelop industrial wasteland located around the Austerlitz train station. A publicly owned local development company, SEMAPA, manages the project.

The concerted development zone, or ZAC (zone d'aménagement concertée), was launched in 1991. Works included the construction of the François Mitterrand National Library (BNF), which began in 1991 and was completed in 1995.

Despite being overseen by one leading agency, the project is based on strong public involvement and the program has been modified. Powerful local associations went to court as there was not enough public space and the density was too high. In 1997, to prevent further revisions, SEMAPA developed a meaningful public involvement process to ensure the intentions of community stakeholders are incorporated in this large-scale project; developers are obliged to integrate these intentions.

The role of the development agency is to select developers through a competitive process to achieve the best design outcomes. Paris Rive Gauche is not just another business district like La Défense, but a real urban neighborhood developed around existing urban landmarks. It combines a mix of uses (offices, housing, local retail and services, green spaces) and good access to public transport.

What Do These Projects Have in Common?

The three regeneration initiatives presented here are all led by a single development agency financed with public money. This type of governance allows for clear leadership, which is essential to complete projects with a 30-year lifespan.

Development agencies ensure through a public involvement process that these initiatives reflect local community aspirations. The creation of the ZAC as a planning instrument allows for the project's objectives to be modified as it evolves.

Development agencies have the financial capacity to sell the land below market prices and to subsidize housing for low-income households. The French planning instruments and financing mechanisms associated with public involvement in decision-making contribute to successful urban regeneration. This approach is known as "transactional urbanism," reflecting the increasing negotiations between the development agency and the community.

45. An Old German Steel Region Gets a Mindful Modern Makeover*

Christa Reicher

The world is urbanizing at a pace never before seen in human history. By 2050, 66 percent of the world is projected to live in cities.

In the developing world, this rapid explosion in urban populations has strained the absorption capacity of cities and led to shortfalls in housing, transport, plumbing and other services.

Europe's cities face a somewhat different problem. The continent urbanized and industrialized centuries ago. Today, major urban centers that grew up on manufacturing must reinvent themselves for the 21st-century economy.

Given the large scale of modern urban areas, which are more borderless metropolitan regions than self-contained cities, designing these Europolizes of the future necessarily involves numerous states, cities, towns—and, ideally, the millions of citizens that live in them. How can so many people and institutions work together to rethink their region both spatially, in terms of its physical layout, and culturally, in terms of its new identity?

The view of Europe at night clearly reveals the regionalization of cities, which have become more a network of centers than a single urban core.

Steel City No Longer

Among several useful European redevelopment experiences, that of Germany's formerly industrial Ruhr region, which began its reinvention in 2011, stands out.

With its 53 cities and municipalities, and five million residents, the region is one of Europe's five largest population centers. Once upon a time, it was one of the top-heavy industrial areas in the world, producing steel, coal, and iron.

The Ruhr is no classic metropolis. It is comprised of numerous loosely connected cities, towns and neighborhoods interwoven with a variety of open spaces, including dormant steel factories, landscapes decimated by coal mining, rivers, and brownfields.

---

*Originally published as Christa Reicher, "Redesigning the Rust Belt: An Old German Steel Region Gets a Mindful Modern Makeover," *The Conversation*, https://theconversation.com/redesigning-the-rust-belt-an-old-german-steel-region-gets-a-mindful-modern-makeover-75273 (June 23, 2017). Reprinted with permission of the publisher.

In urban planning terms, this is what is called a polycentric urban region without a dominant core city. The Ruhr is also demographically diverse, with communities at different stages of development and income levels in proximity, and infrastructure mostly dating from its industrial days.

Germany is determined to bring this post-industrial region into the modern global economy. And it wants to do so in a way that takes both climate change and citizens' radically wide-ranging needs into account: urbanism on different levels and at different speeds.

A Discursive Process

These are the challenges facing the Ruhr Regional Planning Association (Regionalverband Ruhr, or RVR) in designing a new regional plan that will soon become the shared development guidelines for all of the region's 53 municipalities, including 11 independent cities and four counties, in the coming decades.

The plan will replace parts of three existing regional plans where they overlap with the RVR's area. But rather than go to battle with residents and the dozens of local powers that be (from mayors and governors to businesses), the planning authority has decided on an innovative process based on consensus-building.

All municipalities, local universities and citizens have fed into the plan to turn this former industrial center into a modern conurbation. The project is also designed to account for the region's changing demographics, as long-term residents once employed in its factories and mills are replaced by university students, young professionals, and immigrants.

Little by little, section by section and with ever-changing working groups collaborating on each development project, the new Ruhr is coming together.

For the recently completed Phoenix Lake redevelopment in the city of Dortmund, a developer teamed up with the regional planning association and citizens to convert a polluted former mill area into Dortmund's newest urban quarter.

An abandoned factory was replaced with a 24-square-hectare artificial lake designed for swimming and water skiing, and polluted tributaries were scrubbed. New housing went up, built in an architectural style that simultaneously fits in with the modern landscape and recalls the region's past as a steel center.

Two-Scale Urbanism

The Phoenix Lake project is an example of two-scale urbanism: the successful convergence of high-quality small projects with a broad and long-term regional vision.

In employing this participatory strategy, the Ruhr region is closing the gap between disciplines: everything from urban theory and environmental studies to economics has been fed into its development plan.

It also demonstrates that communities can work on different levels at the same time, transferring knowledge from the neighborhood level up to the regional level and implementing regional infrastructure in individual cities.

Because of this discursive style, the Ruhr's final redevelopment document could deliver answers to the challenges facing many cities and regions around the world, from rapidly expanding Accra and shrinking, struggling Detroit to cities that, like Vancouver, are seeking to become "green."

Often, what we perceive as dualisms—growing developing-world metropolis versus shrinking manufacturing hub, or booming metropolis versus controlled-growth smart city—are not so different. Rather, they reveal spatial contradictions within the urban transformation processes that all cities are likely to experience at various points in their history.

City centers are booming as young professionals and older generations, who may have left the city to raise their children, are rediscovering urban life, in no small part because people prefer not to spend hours commuting from suburb to downtown and back every day.

At the same time, cities are regionalizing. The urban sphere is expanding into surrounding areas, and new multi-functional locations outside of traditional cores are arising.

With the new "aerotropolis" model of economic development, for example, we see mega airports, often located between two cities, offering not just hotels but also conference, meeting and even living spaces. Such "airport cities" are planned or completed near Amsterdam, Dubai, Paris, Hong Kong, Shanghai, Beijing, Memphis and elsewhere, according to the 2011 book Aeorotropolis.

As long as the reurbanization and regionalization trends continue apace, the world will see ever more regional conurbations that, like the Ruhr region, have numerous, interconnected "centers." This is the geography on display in the sprawling metropolitan region of São Paulo, Brazil, with its 39 municipalities and combined population of 21.5 million, and in the New York tri-state area (population 20.2 million), which encompasses large swathes of New Jersey and Connecticut.

As the Ruhr's experience has shown, it is no simple thing to respond to these different trends at all the scales present in the region, but it is possible. The local must be connected to the regional at different points—urbanism on two scales, progressing at two different speeds.

To design change in the interest of most citizens—and with visible achievements on all levels—is the core challenge in the Ruhr, and beyond.

46. Gasbrook Gasworks, Hamburg, Germany

Tad McGalliard

Prior Use

In Hamburg, Germany, a contaminated and underperforming industrial and port district found new life as a vibrant mixed-use community. Gasbrook Gasworks is 5.7-hectare (14 acres) property within the 155-hectare (383 acres) HafenCity redevelopment district, located directly on the Northern Elbe river in the heart of Hamburg. This section of Hamburg served as a major port supporting international trade, and emigration for centuries.

In the 20th century, this section of the port played a vital role in Germany's World War II efforts and was subsequently bombed extensively by allied forces. During and shortly after the war, heavy industrial use on this land grew rapidly, including the Gasbrook Gasworks coal gasification plant. By the mid–20th century, however, with the global shipping economy's shift to containerized cargo and larger ships, this land's comparatively shallow water access proved less competitive for continued growth. Other locations were invested in to accommodate these changes, and this area became increasingly disinvested.

The Gasbrook Gasworks facility produced flammable gas beginning in 1846 starting with coal gasification. Over the next several decades, the facility upgraded its process several times until operations ceased in 1976. The site sat vacant, with structures unused, and environmental conditions undefined until the 1980s when the property's environmental condition and the future of the entire area became a priority for the city of Hamburg.[1]

In the 1990s, the City of Hamburg decided the port property should go through a master planning process for an entirely new city district within city limits. In 1999 the HafenCity Master Plan articulated a dense, vibrant, multipurpose, and mixed use district organized into distinct quarters, of which Gasbrook is one. Before this could be realized, the city had to address the area's compromised environmental conditions.

Contaminants of Concern

Contaminants of Concern (COC) on the Gasbrook Gasworks site include Poly Aromatic Hydrocarbons (PAH), Cyanide, Benzopyrene, and Benzene/Toluene/

Ethylbenzene/Xylene (BTEX). Impacts were identified in the soil, surface water, and groundwater. Flooding from tidal surges and storm events had historically also impacted the property. This is not only a vulnerability for structures and infrastructure, but flooding can also spread contamination off site, and into the river.

Remediation

Remediation efforts for Gasbrook began in the 1980s with excavation and disposal of approximately 30,500 cubic meters of contaminated soil and demolition debris. The excavated areas were backfilled with sandy material and the property was left idle until 2001 when additional environmental assessment was conducted.

Additional investigation found several previously unidentified issues with the sites environmental condition. Attempts to take soil samples using standard soil sample equipment proved unsuccessful as obstacles were encountered preventing the equipment from reaching depths for soil samples. These obstacles were determined to be abandoned Underground Storage Tanks (UST), pits, and basins that remained, often collapsed, after the soil excavation in the 1980s. It was also assumed these obstacles likely contained debris, and contaminants that had not previously been characterized.

An important fact accounted for in assessment, remediation, and redevelopment was its history of being heavily bombed in World War II, meaning unexploded ordinance and other hazards were feasibly present. As such, remediation and redevelopment were supervised by a war materials disposal service to ensure workplace and public safety.

Reuse

Having made decisions in the 1990s to revitalize the area as a new mixed-use district, the City of Hamburg tapped the expertise of planners, designers, and development teams from around the world by hosting a planning competition. The winner of the competition was tasked to create the HafenCity Master Plan built around a set of key principles, each directly applicable to the Gasbrook Gasworks redevelopment.

The Master Plan articulated a vision for a mixed-use district organized into quadrants that would be developed incrementally, each offering their own character and identity. The new city would showcase the city's historic relationship with the Elbe river, and development would reflect sustainable development practices and environmentally responsible building and operations including renewable energy and stormwater management best management practices. Additionally, the plan was intended to be a living document able to adapt to conditions as they emerge through the redevelopment process. It was also created with a global audience in mind, working to set a model of replicable, and sustainable waterfront revitalization.

After decades of planning and substantial public and private investments, HafenCity is a new city within historic Hamburg. The Gasbrook district was the second completed quadrant, and now hosts approximately 2,600 commercial uses including offices, parks, schools, entertainment, commercial activity, and 278 apartments.[2]

Conclusion

HafenCity is a remarkable project that clearly demonstrates the importance of careful planning, innovative collaborative approaches, and large scale and long-term vision in redeveloping large brownfield properties into successful, vibrant places.

Notes

1. https://www.hamburg.de/contentblob/142166/1a9bb0e12ebe438de62cb992af21bae1/data/veroeff-hafencity-engl.pdf.
2. https://www.hafencity.com/en/am-sandtorpark-grasbrook-1.html.

Part IV

Private and Nonprofit Environmental Professionals

47. How Do Brownfields Companies Innovate?*

MARY HASHEM *and* STUART MINER

The field of Brownfield development as we know it today evolved from two key events that took place forty years ago. The first was the passage of the Comprehensive Response, Compensation and Liability Act (CERCLA) in 1980, better known as "Superfund." The second was the creation of early environmental risk insurance Policies.

The passage of CERCLA created a framework to allow the Federal government toaddressthe dangers of highly toxic, abandoned or uncontrolled hazardous waste sites.The liability framework created by CERCLA was, and largely remains today, joint and several, meaning any one Potentially Responsible Party (PRP) could be held jointly or individually liable for the contamination caused by one or more other PRPs that owned or operated on a site.

The fear of CERCLA liability from historical uses caused many buyers, banks and real estate investment funds to shy away from transactions involving contaminated property. In response, insurers who had been in the Environmental Impairment Liability (EIL) market, largely for asbestos abatement projects, began to craft new policies to address the kinds of environmental liabilities imposed under CERCLA.

The early pioneers of Brownfield development were thosewho could understand both the nature of environmental risk, and how to manage it effectively in real estate transactions and redevelopment. Early entrants into the Brownfield redevelopment arena included environmental consulting companies, insurance companies, real estate investment funds, and entrepreneurs with the background to grapple with the range of disciplines needed to be successful.

Our company, RE Solutions (RES) capitalizes, on our more than three decades of experience in managing environmental risk and completing brownfield redevelopments. With projects in locations ranging from New Jersey to California, we have specialized in tackling particularly complex redevelopment projects. Some of these projects were assisting other developers, some were our own, but they all demonstrate a common thread: they are successful, profitable projects completed despite a range of challenges—economic, environmental, regulatory, financial and technical. We are dedicated to overcoming challenging scenarios and supporting revitalization by utilizing our team's wealth of experience and creative problem solving to create value for our clients, our partners and the community.

---

*Published with permission of the authors.

Throughout our 30+ year careers of brownfields development, there have been progressive innovations and evolutions in how these deals are executed. The three biggest drivers for evolution have been the creation of defenses to CERCLA liability, the EPA's hugely successful brownfield grant and revolving loan programs, and changes in the environmental insurance market. Below are a few examples of our company's past and present projects in the areas of acquisition and redevelopment, remediation and development, remediation and repositioning, and consulting. These example projects show the various ways developers, sources of public and private financing, communities and responsible parties can come together to create successful revitalization on brownfield properties.

Acquisition and Redevelopment

Signal Hill, California

This property covers over eight acres and is located at 21st and Walnut Streets in the City of Signal Hill, CA, at the northern border of Long Beach. Historic refinery operations resulted in soil and groundwater contamination at the property, which had prevented its sale. The investigation and cleanup of the site is regulated by the Los Angeles Regional Water Quality Control Board (RWQCB). Refinery operations ceased in 1994, and demolition took place in 1997 and 1998. The property was put up for sale shortly after completion of the demolition and installation of an interim remedial measure.

Multiple offers were made on the property; however, none of the prospective purchasers were able to resolve the environmental issues or create a development plan that the City of Signal Hill would approve. After extensive negotiations with the industrial owner, and structuring of a comprehensive risk management program, including entering into a California Land Reuse and Revitalization Act (CLRRA) Agreement with the RWQCB, RES partnered with Xebec Realty to acquire the formerChemoil Refinery property. An additional three adjoining lots were also assembled. The acquisition closed on October 12, 2017.

The property is zoned for industrial and commercial uses. Although there is some residential development in the vicinity of the property, the immediately surrounding area is primarily commercial and light manufacturing, with some civic and institutional uses. RES believes that small industrial flex-space buildings with some office space is likely the highest and best use for the property, and this use is entitled by right. The cleanup that will be required by the RWQCB will support a light industrial or commercial reuse. A Response Plan was prepared under the CLRRA Agreement, which sets forth the requirements for completing the remaining clean up. The CLRRA Agreement will provide a covenant not to sue to the purchaser after the Response Plan is implemented and all other requirements of the Agreement are met. The development plan provides for approximately 150,000 SF of industrial buildings for sale, and is expected to break ground in early 2021.

Bayonne, New Jersey

At the Bayonne Logistics Center in Bayonne, New Jersey, RES is supporting Lincoln Equities Group (LEG) to purchase and redevelop the former Military Ocean Terminal

Bayonne (MOTBY). The former MOTBY property covers 152.9 acres and has been largely under-utilized as an automobile roll on/roll off terminal and outdoor storage yard. The entire site is reclaimed land created from material dredged from New York Harbor in the early 1900s. The dredged material that was used for construction of the "peninsula" contained a range of contaminants. After filling of the site, the United States government built several million square feet of warehouse space on the eastern half of the "peninsula" and used the western half for various military activities. The property was further contaminated during the period of its military use.

The property was closed under the Base Realignment and Closure program (BRAC) and sold to the Redevelopment Authority of the City of Bayonne, New Jersey. In the early 2000s the City of Bayonne embarked upon a plan to redevelop MOTBY for mixed-use development. However, no substantial redevelopment has occurred on the site, itself. The adjoining parcels to the south and west were raised with fill, developed with infrastructure, and a 552-unit multi-family residential building was constructed. Additionally, in 2004 Royal Caribbean opened a cruise port on the eastern corner of the peninsula, and in 2010 the Port Authority of New York and New Jersey acquired 131 acres along the southeastern quadrant of the peninsula with the intent to maintain the Peninsula at Bayonne Harbor as an industrial site.

RES' work on the project has included assisting LEG in making the offer presentation to the previous property owner, Ports America (Oaktree Capital Management) and following execution of the Purchase and Sale Agreement, managing all environmental and risk management responsibilities during due diligence. RES is currently serving as the project manager for the horizontal development of the site, including building demolition, filling of the property to create new building pads above the "post–Sandy" flood elevation, and completing other horizontal site improvements. The development plan for the property includes construction of over 1.2 million square feet of modern warehouse/distribution buildings to serve port-related shipping and logistics activities. RES has both a fee and equity interest in the project,

Denver, Colorado

Another one of our acquisition and development projects is the former Dahlia Square Shopping Center in Denver, Colorado. This 8.3-acre shopping center located in the Northeast Park Hill neighborhood of Denver was first developed in the early 1950s. From 1910–1930, the site was home to the Farrey Brick Co. When brick production ceased, former clay pits were filled with construction debris and solid waste. Once the largest African American-owned shopping center in the United States and a dynamic presence in the neighborhood, by the early 2000s Dahlia Square had fallen into a state of disrepair. With 85 percent vacancy, a parking lot marred by landfill subsidence, and an increasing rate of vandalism, a community-based redevelopment effort was initiated. However, the landfilled materials, along with other environmental concerns, were an impediment to redevelopment of the property.

Brownfield Partners (BP), a company owned by us, was selected by the Denver Urban Renewal Authority (DURA) to purchase, abate, demolish, and remediate the shopping center and provide a shovel-ready site for a mixed-use development. A public-private partnership between Parkhill Community, Inc. (a subsidiary of BP) and the City of Denver, with assistance from the U.S. Department of Housing and Urban

Development, the Colorado Housing and Finance Authority (CHFA) and EPA, deployed a financing package using grants, general funds, and loans to fund the site restoration. The cleanup and regulatory closure was achieved in just over a year. The site's redevelopment includes the Park Hill FamilyMedical Center and the Dahlia Square Senior Apartment complex, with approximately 170 affordable senior residential units.

Remediation and Repositioning

While at EnviroFinance Group, we were responsible for the acquisition and repositioning of the former National Envelope Corporation (NEC) property, located in Union, NJ. This was an approximately 15-acre industrial facility located adjacent to a New Jersey Transit rail line into Manhattan, and less than ½ mile from a new commuter rail terminal. The property became available because of the bankruptcy of NEC. Initial due diligence revealed that the property was "upside down," and that there was significant risk associated with the need to rezone the property from industrial to residential. Efforts to acquire the property in Chapter 11 bankruptcy ceased when the administrative funding was exhausted, and the case converted to Chapter 7. Faced with the likelihood of Chapter 7 abandonment of the property, representatives of the U.S. Department of Justice reached out to the RES principals to request that they continue their efforts to acquire the property.

RES principals worked with the trustee to create an acquisition structure pursuant to Section 363 of the U.S. Bankruptcy Code that was contingent upon: (1) agreement with the New Jersey Department of Environmental Protection to limit the remediation to removal of the on-site source of contamination; and (2) to close only after residential rezoning was approved by Union Township. A cooperative remedial planning and rezoning process with the NJDEP and Union Township, resulted in the regulatory negotiations and re-zoning being completed in less than 6 months. Following acquisition of the property, RES principals managed the building abatement and demolition, remediation of the site and regulatory closure. The property was sold in 2014 to a local developer for construction of both for-sale and for-rent residences.

Remediation and Horizontal Development

Situated on approximately 77 acres in Denver, Colorado, the Asarco Globe Plant was once a major employer in Globeville and the surrounding neighborhoods. The Holden Smelter began refining operations began at the property in 1886 when the Holden Smelter began producing gold and silver at the site. In 1901, the American Smelting and Refining Company (renamed Asarco Incorporated in 1975) bought the Globe Plant over the next hundred years produced a variety of specialty products and high purity metals.

Asarco declared bankruptcy in 2005, and the Globe Plant ceased all operations in November 2006. In December 2009, as part of the resolution of Asarco's bankruptcy, the property was transferred to the Asarco Multi-State Custodial Trust (Trust) along with funds to clean up the site. Brownfield Partners contracted with the Trust to manage the remediation and redevelopment of the property. The project followed the Principals of RE I Solutions to EnviroFinance Group, where they continued to direct the remediation and site development. The project benefited from the cooperative support of Adams County, the city of Denver, the Denver Urban Renewal Authority, the State of Colorado, and EPA.

Cleanup of the site was completed in early 2015, and the first property sale to Trammell Crow Commercial took place in July 2015. The property has been developed into the Crossroads Commerce Center, a modern, master-planned industrial park that provides nearly 1 million square feet of class A industrial warehouse, distribution, and support space. The project has been the recipient of numerous regional and national awards, including a Phoenix Award in 2017.

Consulting

The Carson Reclamation Authority (CRA) selected RES as the Master Horizontal Developer on an approximately 157+ acre parcel located in Carson, California. This site is the former Cal Compact Landfill site located between the Del Amo Bridge and the Avalon Boulevard exit on the 405 Freeway. There is over 2,200 linear feet of frontage on the 405 which is one of the nation's busiest freeways. The end use objectives of this landfill site are to develop a high-quality retail or mixed-use destination that establishes a regional reputation for quality and luxury.

The property is owned by the Carson Reclamation Authority (CRA), a joint powers authority set up for the City of Carson to take title to the property while also shielding the city from the potential environmental liability of owning a former landfill site. The CRA needed to bring in a Master Developer with a track record of dealing with complex environmental properties to take on the challenges of the ongoing remediation and liability of the site. RES is working closely with CRA to complete remediation of the site, install structural piles and build foundation systems and slabs for future vertical development. The CRA is negotiating development deals with the ultimate vertical developers of the site.

General Motors Corporation (GM) entered Chapter 11 bankruptcy in June 2009 in a case that was one of the largest and most complex environmental bankruptcies in U.S. history. AlixPartners L.L.P., an international corporate turnaround and financial advisory firm, was charged with leading GM (renamed Motors Liquidation Company [MLC]) through its Chapter 11 bankruptcy plan to sell assets and restructure its debt. RES Principals worked as expert consultants to MLC and AlixPartners on matters relating to real estate management, reuse and redevelopment; regulatory strategy, negotiation and settlement; and environmental risk management on legacy manufacturing plants and other properties retained in the bankruptcy. There were 89 individual legacy assets under management in the bankruptcy estate, which included over 7,000 acres of land and 48 million square feet of buildings located in 14 states.

The RES Principals' role included: supporting MLC in the on-going management of legacy properties; negotiating remediation agreements with state regulators and EPA; assisting in the estimation of total environmental liabilities; formulating environmental risk management structures using both financial and insurance instruments to manage the costs and environmental risks of the portfolio; and developing strategies to maximize the reuse/redevelopment opportunities at the properties. The consensus reached with state regulatory agencies and EPA regional and headquarters staff regarding cleanup plans and costs facilitated the resolution of over $450 million in governmental cleanup cost claims.

48. What Developers Really Want*

TODD S. DAVIS

Having gone to college in the early 1980s, I clearly missed several amazing inventions that many current university attendees couldn't have imagined living without—no smart phones, no laptops, no apps. In fact, I have been told someone invented an extraordinarily popular app called Tinder. Apparently, it works something like this: each party clicks on a profile, and if both parties like what they see, they begin to communicate, and a deal is quickly consummated. (From what I understand, the deal can involve some pretty "interesting" situations.) I am not saying I approve, yet moral issues aside, you must appreciate both the directness and simplicity of the business model! Both parties know exactly why they are there and exactly what they want from the situation. Wouldn't it be amazing for both real estate developers and communities if brownfield redevelopment projects were that straightforward?

Insight into Developers' True Desires

To approach the simplicity of the "Tinder for brownfields" business model, local government managers need to understand a brownfield developer's base needs. These are the top three requisites that developers look for when deciding to apply for a brownfield redevelopment project.

Return on Investment (ROI). ROI is the libido, the lifeblood, the driving force behind all "for-profit" developers' natural instincts. Simply stated, every investor and balance the perceived risk and return in a redevelopment project to determine whether to pursue a transaction. Due to the increased costs—and often significantly expanded timeframe and complexity—of addressing environmental issues, regulatory uncertainty, legal issues, demolition, off-site groundwater concerns, and the like, brownfield deals are among the highest-risk real estate investments. Consequently, to attract risk-adjusted investment capital, assuming typical "greenfield" investment returns demand a 12 to 18 percent ROI, brownfield deals must deliver a significantly higher ROI (and equity multiple) to attract investment capital and to be economically feasible.

Risk Reduction. To contend with the increased risk inherent in brownfield deals, any mechanism which can be employed to decrease a developer's perceived risk will help "consummate" a transaction.

---

*Originally published as Todd S. Davis, "What Developers Really Want," *PM* (December 2019, Vol. 101: 11) by ICMA, the International City/County Management Association; reprinted with permission.

Timing. Again, by definition, complex brownfield transactions often require expanded timeframes to successfully execute. Increasing timeframes will inevitably increase risk, while decreasing return, due to the time value of money. Therefore, anything developers can do to keep a on budget, materially impacts a developer's potential returns and deal underwriting.

What Can Local Governments Do to "Satisfy" a Developer's Base Needs?

Now that you clearly understand the developer's most primal desires, what can every community do to satisfy those desires and maximize the chance for a successful outcome? Surprisingly, several of the most important actions will not cost anything! All local governments, no matter what size or availability of resources, can take the following simple actions to maximize brownfield redevelopment success:

Engaged Leadership. The most successful brownfield redevelopment projects always have municipal champions. Engaging local government leaders at every level, to actively contribute to and promote a project important to the key to mitigating risk. Ask any successful developer whether they're more willing to take on the risk of an important project if the developer is confident that local government managers will actively spearhead the project, side-by-side with the developer and the answer will be a resounding "yes!"

Quick Decisions. As previously described, longer timeframes associated with brownfield projects increase risk and decrease return for all parties involved. Therefore, articulating to the developer the local government's willingness to make quick, yet pragmatic project decisions reduces project risk and potentially enhances return. Developers understand they must go through an appropriate bureaucratic process. However, knowing they have a partner willing to help, by making ethical and compliant decisions quickly throughout the development cycle, will maximize your community's opportunity for executing successful projects.

Enhanced Entitlements. Consider providing enhanced entitlements for brownfield projects. Increasing density, providing zoning waivers, variances, or added flexibility will give developers better odds of hitting their ROI goals, with little cost to the communities plagued by brownfield issues. Again, these projects truly are riskier and more costly for developers. Further, brownfield sites often pose health and development risks to communities. Arguably, these redevelopments deserve, at a minimum, increased local government assistance and accommodations.

OK, Not All the Best Things Are Free!

The foregoing discussion demonstrates that by adopting several approaches, brownfield developers will be substantially more likely to tackle a complex deal in their local community. That being said, the ability of local governments to provide or coordinate meaningful financial incentives, to offset the true increased costs and risks associated with complex brownfield deals, often tips the scales during the underwriting process. If your local government does not have its own incentives, offer to help pursue other available regional, state, or federal enhancements. Remember, brownfield projects are by definition at the high end of the real estate risk and return spectrum. To address all developers' base need for risk-adjusted returns, and simply to attract investment capital, they must make a business case to debt and equity providers. Consequently, if you want developers and their capital providers to tackle a complex redevelopment project, the ability to provide meaningful financial incentives obviously goes a long way toward success.

A New Era of Candor

Like it or not, we are all living in a new era, driven not only by technology, but also by the desire for more transparency. In that vein, it likely comes as no surprise that the search for ROI is fundamental to all development projects—particularly brownfield redevelopments. Adopting the right attitude to facilitate these higher-risk infill projects does not necessarily need to cost enormous sums of capital. Local governments must simply decide to spend both the effort and energy to make deals happen.

49. Retail Revolution and Retrofit*

DAVID S. GREENSFELDER

Understanding Today's Retail World

When retail was clustered in a downtown or town square environment, there was not a need for today's ubiquitous suburban shopping center. In contrast, by the 1950s, the automobile became commonplace, part of the trend towards suburbanization, and the utility of shopping centers became clear. Over a period of time, these malls in the increasingly decentralized suburban landscape replaced urban/downtown shopping districts.

As the advent of shopping malls began to erode the downtown shopping district's market share, discounters began to erode the traditional department store's market share. The next step in the evolution away from traditional department stores was the advent of retailers who became more efficient by specializing in a particular "department." Clustered together in what have come to be known as power centers, these "big box" and "category killer" stores were more convenient, focused narrowly on one category, but offered a wide variety of merchandise within that category, developed supply and distribution advantages extending from their narrower focus, and offered everyday low prices.

"We're not over-built, we're under-demolished." The United States has approximately 24 SF of retail per-capita, the highest in the world, compared to Canada's 16 SF, Australia's 11 SF, Europe's 4–5 SF, and China's 3 SF [GGP Investor Presentation, March 2017]. With the homogenization of department stores has come the demise of many regional malls, and with consolidation of big box chains has come the demise of many anchored strip centers. Clearly the trend towards less retail space can be expected to continue.

Downtown commercial districts historically functioned as the physical, cultural, and economic center of the community, however, exacerbating industry consolidation that has impacted shopping centers and malls, many communities throughout the nation have seen [an understandable] lack of investment in their historic downtown areas, resulting in a lack of vibrancy. Some are now rediscovering the value of their historic downtowns. With the influence of e-commerce, platforms, and influencers on the rise, urban downtowns offer opportunities for authentic placemaking that are difficult to replicate in suburban locations. With the COVID-19 pandemic, we can expect to see a shift towards a less centralized model, favoring suburbs as opposed to CBD's. How this swing of the pendulum will end is yet to be seen, however, we can expect that even in suburban environments, consumers will be looking for sense of place, variety, and authenticity.

---

*Published with permission of the author.

One size does not fit all. Each community's commercial strategy must be calibrated for a variety of local conditions, including the real estate market and consumer demographics, changes in consumption patterns, community vision, perspective and capabilities of property owners and tenants, a city's available resources, available public-private partnership (P3) resources, and other factors. Strategies should be undertaken with an eye to opening up opportunities for larger, long-term changes and transformations. In summary, we have too much retail space, today's right-sizing trend is expected, and the reuse of both urban and suburban retail space can be expected to accelerate.

With respect to retail specifically, based upon 30 years of experience performing market analysis, repositioning retail projects and districts, and developing retail real estate (including overseeing strategic store deployment programs for both independent and chain retailers), taking an approach that clearly differentiates between "Commodity" retail uses and "Specialty" retail uses is recommended. Because the factors that maximize performance of commodity retail districts and specialty districts are so different, we seek to clearly differentiate each for purposes of analysis and making strategic recommendations. [Source ULI Development Handbook].

>**Commodity Retail Goods and Services** are defined as those goods and services that are (a) consumed on a regular basis from "primary" household funds; (b) purchased without emotional connection by the consumer; and (c) purchased with primary emphasis by the consumer on selecting the combination of lowest "price" and highest "convenience." "Commodity Retailers" range from local convenience stores to drug stores, grocery stores, discounters and warehouse stores. Examples of commodity retail goods and services include food and liquor stores, banks, electronics retailers, pet superstores, locksmiths, and some services.
>
>**Specialty Retail Goods and Services,** by contrast, are defined as those goods and services that are (a) consumed on an optional basis from "discretionary" income or funds; (b) involving the expenditure of "discretionary" time; and (c) for which environment or place is an important point of reference for the consumer, as is an emotional connection with purchased item and the overall shopping experience. "Place" and "environment" are key elements to understanding specialty retail, and are always part of our evaluation process. Successful specialty shopping venues, regardless of format, deliver a unique combination of "product" (i.e., shops and restaurants) and "place" (i.e., physical and conceptual environment) that are unique and inspiring. Examples include restaurants and bars, personal services, clothing and luxury goods, tattoo parlors, etc.

The most important thing to keep in mind is that specialty and commodity retail really describes a continuum of shopping behaviors ... how we consume different sorts of goods and services. Different pieces of property will lend themselves to different shopping patterns and consumer behaviors. For example, it could be easy to consider the Apple Store or Whole Foods as either a commodity or a specialty retailer, however, the reality is that it is both, serving different sorts of consumers in different ways at different points in time. Other retailers are clearer cut. Best Buy is clearly commodity whereas a find dining establishment is clearly specialty.

The E-Commerce Revolution

The driving force behind the current sea change in retail is the rapid evolution and expansion of e-commerce. Commodity retail purchases are driven by a desire for low-cost convenience. At the outset, online retailing was most well-suited to the purchase of standardized goods and this largely applies today. This is because buyers cannot inspect the product in the same way that they would at a brick and mortar establishment. Due to shipping constraints, most buyers were still visiting brick and mortar stores for more urgent purchases, as the shipment of products purchased online could take days or weeks to arrive. With the development of robust private logistics networks, such as Amazon Prime, the online retailers have broken down many of the convenience barriers that once limited their scope to commodities, and increasingly is making headway into specialty goods.

In recent years, the influence of e-commerce has begun to extend beyond the commodity retail categories upon which it was founded. Many innovative online retailers are now looking to specialty retail products that have traditionally been purchased through brick and mortar retail stores for new expansion opportunities. Subscription services like Trunk Club, and resale platforms like Bonobos and thredUP, are providing boutique type specialty retail opportunities to online consumers. Even food and beverage products are being sold through online platforms and mobile applications like Blue Apron, Uber Eats, and BeyondMenu. Professional service providers are also entering the e-commerce market. For example, professional design services for both interior home furnishings and landscape design are now being offered through online platforms.

One factor that is driving on-line sales of specialty goods is the ability to research and order on-line, combined with an increased ease of picking-up and returning goods through other retail channels. However, many of these specialty online retailers are also coming to appreciate the value of having brick and mortar locations within key markets. As "buy online, pick-up in-store" programs expand, regional locations (for first bricks-and-mortar stores) with convenience attributes will be increasingly important for pick-ups; this is a convenience strategy to drive sales.

Reusing, Retrofit, Demo, Adapting

Commodities can be purchased across multiple retail channels, a "channel" being a place such as a bricks-and-mortar store, the internet, a catalog, where a purchase can be made. Specialty goods, including apparel, jewelry, and food and beverage, which just a few years ago were the mainstay of malls and lifestyle centers are increasingly available through channels other than traditional bricks-and-mortar stores.

The overabundance of retail space indicates that, in order to survive, retail projects will increasingly provide a wider variety of reasons to visit including quasi or non-retail uses such as medical, educational, and service uses, and these non-retail uses will drive foot traffic which will in turn drive retail sales. The implications are far reaching: Retail real estate is well located, so even retail projects that fall by the wayside have excellent locational attributes for being repurposed as other compatible uses.

A decrease in demand for bricks-and-mortar retail space is leaving cities to grapple with decreased sales and property tax revenues, and developers to grapple with projects that no longer function for their originally intended uses. Retail projects are increasingly being rethought and repurposed, sometimes as part of retail pruning strategies. Examples include malls becoming mixed-use projects, educational campuses, distribution centers, or adding residential components. The question for communities, public agencies, developers, and occupiers is, "What is the correct new use?"

One of the primary challenges facing project redevelopment is an over emphasis on ground floor retail uses as a one-size-fits-all solution. Retail should be prioritized at key locations, but the space between those key location should be allowed to evolve to a variety of uses as market conditions evolve and change over time.

Retailers and developers concentrating efforts on the projects most likely to be dominant will create the most compelling and productive retail projects that will have the biggest draw despite competing retail channels. Planners concentrating on projects that don't differentiate will pave the way for their redevelopment into productive assets for communities, occupiers, owners, and municipal tax bases.

Planning for Adaptation/Reuse/Demo/Retrofit

When adapting any project to another use, there are two primary considerations: Suitability for alternative uses in terms of location and facility, and physical redevelopment considerations and the related project-level economics.

Of all the land use categories, retail is the most sensitive to location. For example, one corner of an intersection will typically be considered to have much different utility for a retailer than another corner of that same intersection. Because retail is generally so deliberately and well located, it is often suitable for a variety of other uses. For this reason, a market analysis exploring demand for various alternative uses is typically the first step of any repositioning or redevelopment process.

A smaller retail footprint, office, residential, or a mix of these uses is most frequently considered. Large formats such as distribution, R&D, warehousing, and industrial are generally not the first choices for redevelopment of retail space because the underlying land values support higher and better uses, and also because these sorts of uses are often not desired in as high profile a location as is typically occupied even my obsolete retail space.

Once a product type, or mix of product types, has been settled upon, a feasibility and risk analysis need to be performed. The risk analysis would include understanding current zoning, and what entitlements (discretionary approvals) will be required in order to execute the desired redevelopment or repositioning, the process for obtaining required approvals, estimating community support or opposition, understanding political support or opposition, and making judgments about current and expected market conditions (rents, vacancy rates, tenant trends, development costs, etc.). This analysis should also evaluate a preliminary title report including a review of the underlying documents. Chief among these documents are anything restricting the use of the property, including (but not limited to) CC&R's, memoranda of leases, and easements. An evaluation of how much time it will take to deal with restriction should be articulated in the analysis' finding.

Only once the risk analysis points to continuing the process, a repositioning or redevelopment (as the case might be) project pro-forma needs to be developed. Pro-forma are only as good as their inputs, and more complex doesn't necessarily mean better. In fact, one of the best pieces of advice I was given earlier in my career was, "If you can't make it work on the back of a napkin, that's probably telling you something." The "something" is that there may be a fundamental economic issue with the project that should be uncovered and given serious consideration before continuing.

A project pro-forma will include hard and soft development costs in reasonable detail. It is important not to give in to wishful thinking when estimating costs ... the project is going to cost what it's going to cost, and underestimating those costs is a sure way to have serious problems later on. The pro-forma should also be transparent in how it calculates net operating income. It should show rents (by space if appropriate) less expected vacancy rates, allowances for management, expenses (operating, taxes, insurance, marketing), and reserves. It is quite possible that many pro formas will be created as part of the process of perfecting a mix of uses that is both deliverable economically and that will be accepted by the community and local government.

As part of the risk analysis and pro-forma exercise, it will be important to consider the existing condition of the property. An existing conditions report will give insight about structure, building systems, and roof condition, and what opportunities there might be to reuse some or all of them if that is desired. A geotechnical report will help a civil and structural engineer understand what sorts of foundation work will be required. Phase I and lead and asbestos reports will give insight about remediation and project execution delays that might occur. With respect to the environmental reports, it will be important to consider the following

- what the place was before it was a mall
- legal obligations and controlling documents (CC&R's, deed restrictions, easements, encumbrances, zoning, use restrictions/grandfathered uses, leases, etc.)
- Environmental: Lead/asbestos, oil tanks, liability/legally responsible parties for hazmat

Conclusion

All of this would be done before a due diligence contingency expires. In other words, these exercises tell you whether you have a viable project, or if you should get your good faith deposit back and move along to another opportunity, or approach the owner to modify the purchase terms because of things that were not previously known. Remember that terms (or time) are often as or more important than price!

50. Brownfield Redevelopment and Environmental Insurance*

Ed Morales

To some, Brownfield sites are abandoned, idled, or under-used industrial and commercial facilities with real or perceived environmental issues that may complicate their reuse. But for others, they represent a true financial opportunity.

To be a successful Brownfield project today, owners and prospective purchasers need to not only understand the financial costs involved, but evaluate the environmental risks and potential liabilities associated with such properties.

There needs to be an understanding of these risks from acquisition, to infrastructure installation, vertical construction, operations and even exit strategy. All of these phases can reveal some kind of environmental risk which in most cases can be mitigated with the use of risk transfer mechanisms such as environmental insurance.

What Is Environmental Insurance?

Environmental insurance policies provide a risk transfer mechanism to cover cleanup of contamination as required by environmental laws, third party claims for bodily injury and property damage, and associated legal expenses, resulting from pollution or contamination events, whether such events are "sudden and accidental" or "gradual" in nature. Related costs such as business interruption losses (e.g., loss of profit, loss of rental income) can also be covered.

Why Does Environmental Insurance Exist?

Environmental insurance was born out of a necessity to cover risks that other traditional commercial liability or property insurance policies would not. Up until the mid–1980s, commercial general liability policies were used to cover historic pollution releases. Since these older policies were written on an occurrence basis, insureds could tap into proceeds from historic policies so long as the insurance companies that issued them were still financially viable. Since then, commercial general liability policies were issued with an absolute pollution exclusion.

---

*Published with permission of the author.

The purpose of an environmental insurance policy is to fill the insurance coverage gaps created by pollution exclusions in commercial liability and property insurance policies. Because pollution exclusions vary a great deal in property and liability insurance policies, environmental insurance policies vary a great deal as well. Virtually any legal business activity can be insured for a fortuitous pollution loss event under an environmental insurance policy.

Life Cycle of a Brownfield Project

How can risk transfer help mitigate environmental liabilities throughout the lifecycle of a Brownfield project? Let's use this table to define the various phases of a Brownfield project and identify environmental risk. Consider the following table.

The correct insurance product(s) would be responsive to the risks to the range of development possibilities illustrated below.					
Insurance Solution Options	Acquisition Circumstances	Entitlement Process & Horizontal Development	Vertical Development	Operations	Exit Strategy Options
- Cost Containment - Liability protection - Third-party protection - Hold-harmless - Etc.	- Fee simple - Partnership - Public agency assistance - Eminent domain - Etc.	- Environmental regulatory agency requirements - Negative declaration - CEQA/NEPA - Rezoning - Map Act - Local government requirements - Special districts - Etc.	- Contractor experience and track record - Form of construction contract - Engineer and architect errors and omissions policies - Etc.	- Management contract - Owner managed - Service contractors' policies - Etc.	- Sale-lease back - Flipping - Subdivide and sell - Hold - Etc.

This table is used to ask the question whether there is an environmental insurance solution for the various phases of a Brownfield project.

This first step is **acquisition**. Typically, one would conduct environmental due diligence ahead of acquisition in order to understand what the current site conditions are prior to taking title. In addition, by using a Phase I environmental site assessment (ESA) in accordance with the latest ASTM standard, a perspective purchaser may enjoy protections from the Compensation Environmental Response, Compensation and Liability Act (CERCLA) via the All Appropriate Inquiry (AAI) rule. Since the target property is considered a Brownfield by definition, the Phase I ESA may lead to a Phase II ESA or site investigation which would entail the collection of soil and ground water samples for testing of contaminants which may have been historically used at the site. This may lead to the development of a remedial action plan to mitigate the known contamination.

The next step would be **entitlement** and **horizontal** improvements. Entitlements would be the act of getting the approvals needed to proceed with the project. This may include rezoning, use permits, utility approvals and road approvals. This also may include getting regulatory approval for cleanup objectives if required. Horizontal improvements can lead to exposures right away since it would involve the movement of soils for utilities, streets and roads. If unknown contaminants are encountered, they will have to be mitigated in accordance with environmental law.

Vertical development is the construction of buildings for commercial or mixed uses. Both this and Horizontal improvements have a contractor element. These exposures may lead to claims from unknown pollution conditions resulting from contractor activities. For instance, contaminated soils may be encountered and managed. If a contractor inadvertently spreads contaminated soil in areas where none existed before, a regulator may require it to be excavated and disposed of off-site which may lead to financial losses and project delays.

Operational risks are those associated with businesses that would occupy the new development and perhaps bring a different element of environmental risk via the use of hazardous materials or potential for mold via water intrusion that is left undiscovered.

Finally, we have an **exit strategy**. The divestiture of property to 3rd parties may not resolve the former owner from any environmental liabilities discovered by the new owner and is determined to be historic in nature.

Environmental Risk Transfer Solutions

Pollution Legal Liability (PLL) can provide meaningful insurance coverage for all of the potential exposures. PLL can provide protection from financial loss created by the following environmental risks at the insured location:

- Clean-up costs
- Third Party Claims for Clean-up
- Third Party Claims for Bodily Injury and Property Damage including Damage to Natural Resources
- Contamination created from Transportation and Non-owned Disposal sites
- Business Interruption
- Coverage for both pre-existing and new pollution conditions
- Defense Expenses

Contractors Pollution Liability (CPL) insurance can protect an insured during the horizontal and vertical construction. CPL can provide protection from financial loss created by the follow environmental risk which resulted from construction activities at the project location:

- Third Party Claims for Clean-up (from contracting activities)
- Third Party Claims for Bodily Injury and Property Damage including Damage to Natural Resources (from contracting activities)
- Contamination created from Transportation and Non-owned Disposal sites
- Defense Expenses

These two policies can help mitigate the environmental risks for the entire Brownfield project cycle. So now we can complete the table as shown below.

Insurance Solution	Acquisition	Entitlement & Horizontal	Vertical Development	Operations	Exit Strategy
PLL (unknown pre-existing)	Yes	Yes	Yes		Yes
PLL (new conditions)		Yes	Yes	Yes	Yes
CPL		Yes	Yes		

Communities engaging in Brownfield projects can benefit from new tax revenues and a new source of jobs which in turn adds to the economic vitality to the community. This does not happen with zero risk. Understanding these risks specifically environmental risk will help the success of the project. Environmental insurance can be an important tool to facilitate this success.

Case Studies

Development—St. John's District in Portland, OR

First Phase—Mixed Use Redevelopment (podium residential with street retail).
Site was a former industrial property.
Contamination generally in surficial soils, included petroleum hydrocarbons, poly-nuclear aromatic hydrocarbons and metals.
Total acreage—approximately 15 acres (First Phase is about ½ of this).
Placed a 5-year Pollution Legal Liability Policy.
Limits of $10,000,000 per pollution incident/$10,000,000 policy aggregate.
Deductible of $100,000.
Coverage for unknown pre-existing pollution conditions.
Coverage included Natural Resource Damages (key coverage component due to proximity to river).
Premium was approximately $100,000.

Development—Ventura & Los Angeles Counties, CA

Phased Redevelopment.
Over 25,000 acres.
Reuse includes residential, retail, commercial, educational, open space, agricultural and municipal.
Former and current uses include oil production.
Placed a 10-year Pollution Legal Liability policy.
Limits of $50,000,000 per pollution incident/$50,000,000 policy aggregate.
Deductible: $100,000.
Coverage for both unknown pre-existing and new pollution conditions.
Premium was greater than $1,000,000.

Industry Outlook

The environmental insurance marketplace has changed and evolved since companies like American International Group (AIG) came out with their early pollution policies back in the late 1970s and into the 1980s. As a matter of fact, AIG no longer offers stand-alone mono-line pollution policies to this day.

In addition, the remediation stop-loss policy that we did not describe in this article is still available but very restrictive in capacity, terms and conditions. There are only a small number of companies who will even consider a stop-loss product.

Other markets who have stepped up over the years have also curtailed their appetite for Brownfield risks or have existed the space all together.

There are still a handful of insurance companies that are willing to take on what I would call re-development risk. Brownfields are all about that.

In summary, although the environmental insurance marketplace has changed and may have become more restrictive to Brownfield work, there are still some key companies like Beazley and others that are not afraid of the risk. They just have to be good at underwriting it. Fundamentally, the risk has not changed. So, we should make sure to consider the companies that are willing to cover these risks part of your team.

51. Land Recycling, Brownfields and the Center for Creative Land Recycling

Ignacio Dayrit

CCLR's mission is to enable communities to develop sustainably and equitably by restoring underutilized properties to productive reuse. By restoring land that has already been used to productive use and accessing existing infrastructure, land recycling provides economic renewal to urban communities, preserves our natural areas, and reduces the carbon footprint of development. Since 2010, CCLR has assisted communities remediate and redeveloped hundreds of acres brownfields in several state, and has assisted in raising more than $60 million in grant funds.

Benefits of Land Recycling

These sites sit idle and neglected, serving as desolate eyesores within their communities. By putting these barren infill sites to use, land recycling revitalizes our communities, promotes sustainable development, and preserves precious resources. The social, economic, environmental, and other benefits of land recycling include:

Social & Economic Revitalization. Land recycling helps clean up and revitalize inner cities by returning abandoned, idle, or underused sites to productive use, bolstering community spirit, creating jobs and boosting local tax revenues. The reuse of land revitalizes communities and renews economic activity, particularly in underserved urban areas. Abandoned, idled, and vacant properties are often located in former industrial and commercial areas, typically in urban and historically disadvantaged areas. These sites can be community eyesores, negatively impacting social and economic development, and often human and environmental health. The failure to redevelop brownfields translates into potentially more exposure to toxics and the loss of economic and housing benefits that can come from appropriate redevelopment.

By putting these properties to new and productive use, land recycling encourages growth of businesses and services in such areas, helping to break up concentrations of poverty, creating jobs, and stimulating additional private investment and local tax revenue. An abandoned, well-situated, factory site can be cleaned up and redeveloped into a much-needed mixed-use development with a grocery store, senior housing, and access to public transportation. The addition of neighborhood-serving retail, affordable housing, or a clean public park in a disadvantaged community can boost local spirit and improve overall quality of life.

Sustainability. Sustainability is defined as meeting the needs of the present without compromising the ability of future generations to meet their own needs.

Land recycling is an inherently sustainable idea, based on the same common sense as recycling an aluminum can. Like other natural resources, land represents a shared investment that should be reused and recycled, rather than consumed and abandoned after use. Recycling paper saves trees, reusing land saves land.

By encouraging the recycling rather than the consumption of land, land recycling promotes smart growth and responsible, sustainable patterns of development. Studies show that for every acre of brownfield redeveloped, 4.5 acres of undeveloped land is conserved. As most brownfields and other abandoned sites are typically situated in urban areas, they tap into existing nearby infrastructure, limiting the need to build new roads, gridlines, and amenities, thereby reducing further land consumption. Each infill development prevents sprawl into open space, forests and agricultural land, preserving acres of undeveloped land.

An Alternative to Sprawl. Land recycling increases density in urban areas, by reducing urban sprawl and unplanned, low-density, automobile-dependent developments.

In sprawl development, housing, public transit, jobs, and other amenities are scattered farther apart, demanding more frequent use of cars for travel. The increase in vehicle miles traveled (VMTs) produces a range of health and environmental problems, including air pollution and increased greenhouse gas emissions, and increased incidence of traffic jams and asthma. This results in a lower quality of life for residents, ever-increasing commute times, and the health implications of smog.

By moving new jobs, economic opportunities, and community amenities farther from established populations, sprawl development can cripple once thriving cities. This trend takes a toll on the socio-economic health of urban communities as growth retreats from the urban center.

Rather than take advantage of existing infrastructure such as roads, public transit, and public works, building sprawl projects abandons these resources and demands further consumption of land and resources.

Land recycling is an intelligent alternative to sprawl development. It reuses vital infrastructure and public resources and creates compact, full-service neighborhoods that reduce vehicle use and carbon dependence. Rebuilding in urban neighborhoods generates reinvestment in vibrant economic and cultural centers, rather than drawing away much-needed resources. Compact, urban development through land recycling is essential to sustainable development and is key to managing rapid population growth across the United States and beyond. As daily commute times decrease, the general quality of life improves as residents have more time to enjoy the world around them.

Directs Development to Urban Core. Redirecting population growth and growth of businesses to areas that are already urbanized is integral to creation of sustainable communities.

Applying sustainable principles to land use and growth management requires that growth be redirected from scattered fringe areas back to our urban cores, where people, services and infrastructure already exist. Building up our urban areas positively increases population density, providing the critical mass to support local services from coffee shops to grocery stores, public transit to libraries and symphony halls. Land recycling provides opportunities for urban renewal and to build truly livable communities: efficient, compact, vibrant urban neighborhoods integrated with public transit systems, which offer a mix of uses as well as affordable housing.

Addressing Climate Change. Land recycling effectively curbs greenhouse gas emissions by encouraging smart, compact growth that reduces vehicle dependence.

Redevelopment within an urban core reduces commuting distances and therefore average vehicle miles traveled (VMTs) by creating residential, office, and other amenities within proximity. Since transportation alone accounts for a third of greenhouse gases (GHGs) emitted in the United States, land recycling is a key tool in the fight against climate change. Studies show that compact urban development, as an alternative to sprawl, could reduce VMTs by an average of 30 percent. Smart urban planning is therefore crucial to maximizing energy savings and overall reduction of greenhouse gases.

LEED certified buildings and other developments best benefit climate change when they reuse infill sites and access existing resources.

A recent focus of the green movement is the Leadership in Energy and Environmental Design (LEED) Green Building Rating System, a certification system that rewards the design, construction and operation of high-performance green buildings. LEED certification signifies incorporation of smart building design and technology to reduce energy use and minimize waste. However, even if a building is energy-efficient, the energy required to travel to and from a LEED certified site may well exceed the energy saved through energy-efficient features. A project's location and its relation to the urban center should be considered first and foremost in achieving truly sustainable design.

According to research, traditional urban development can have a greater impact than a LEED certified suburban development in mitigating waste and the release of GHGs. Studies show that a green suburban development results in 15 percent more total expended energy compared to a traditional urban development of comparable size. This stems from the fact that the suburban development's energy savings gained through green building features are overcome by a three-fold increase in transportation-related energy use. That increase bumps to four-fold when comparing the same LEED suburban development to an average urban LEED development, with an overall energy expenditure increase of 84 percent.

Green-conscious suburban development is still sprawl development, despite LEED certification for the project or building. LEED certified buildings and other developments are more energy-efficient and further benefit climate change when they recycle land and access existing resources.

Challenges

While land recycling has great economic and environmental benefits, without the right tools, skills, and knowledge, reusing land can produce certain challenges. Obstacles to redevelopment may include lack of funding and increased scrutiny. These can particularly impede projects on brownfields, which carry the stigma of contamination. Because of these concerns, the perceived ease of developing on open land, or greenfields, is alluring to many. The following factors hinder land recycling:

Market Factors. Every developer knows that in real estate only three things matter:

location, location, location. Because idled and underused infill sites are often located in distressed urban areas concerns arise about crime, safety, and access to quality education and services. These and other market factors frequently pull development to open land near traditionally desirable communities and away from urban infill sites.

Environmental Liability Risks. Although recent changes in federal law provide some liability relief to new purchasers of contaminated properties, the law is very complicated, and many state laws still have strict liability covering real property. Thus, in many cases, any current or past property owner can potentially be legally and financially liable regardless of who is responsible for contamination. This liability web continues to throw a chill on many brownfield projects even in the presence of regulatory reforms designed to encourage redevelopment. A common belief among many brownfield owners is that it is less risky and cheaper to abandon or "mothball" a facility than to conduct a site assessment that could trigger large cleanup costs and potential liability.

Uncertainty & Cost. Assessing whether a site is contaminated can be a costly process that deters land reuse. Potential purchasers are often unwilling or unable to risk an investment in a site assessment for a property that may require cleanup they cannot afford. Even if a site has been purchased, concerns over cleanup costs may further stall redevelopment. Uncertainty over time, cost or a high price for cleanup leaves many brownfield sites in development limbo.

Complicated & Confusing Regulatory Requirements. The process of redeveloping an infill site, particularly a brownfield, can be complicated and confusing. The current morass of vague, overlapping and sometimes conflicting requirements at the federal, state, and local levels often intimidates developers. Making sense of legal and regulatory requirements may be daunting and discouraging. Guidance from lawyers and consultants is often needed to guide a project through the legal and regulatory framework.

Difficulty Obtaining Project Financing. Obtaining private front-end financing for brownfield cleanup can be a difficult process. Since financing is more readily available for development on greenfields, infill and brownfield sites are often passed over.

The Lure of Greenfields. Brownfields and infill sites must compete with attractive, undeveloped suburban and rural land, also called greenfields. When considering the real or perceived risks and costs of land recycling, a greenfield development may seem more economically sensible as the immediate costs are typically less than developing on an infill or brownfield site. However, it is important to consider the long-term economic gain of land recycling and the added social and environmental rewards of sustainable development.

Remediating Brownfields

Brownfield cleanup and redevelopment follow a unique set of processes that are not always linear. There are several paths to remediating a distressed property, the following are key components of the process:

Legal & Regulatory Framework. There is a myriad of regulatory and legal considerations at the federal, state, and local levels for land recycling and brownfield redevelopment. Because state and federal statues are administered by several different regulatory agencies, it is important to understand these regulatory bodies. Establishing a strong working relationship with regulators and maintaining open communication throughout the redevelopment process is key for a successful project. It is highly beneficial to obtain appropriate legal advice and guidance early in the planning process to develop an effective strategy for enhancing cost effectiveness and minimizing project risks.

Phase I Environmental Site Assessment. Evaluating a site for potential contamination is an important first step in approaching a brownfield redevelopment project. The Phase I Environmental Site Assessment (Phase I ESA) is a widely used, industry-accepted approach used to assess environmentally challenged properties. The Phase I ESA relies heavily on-site visits, interviews with relevant parties, and historical documents and public records. The goal is to understand previous site use to help determine whether and what kind of contamination may exist. A Phase I ESA is required to qualify for federal liability defense protections and certain state protections. A Phase I ESA must be conducted by a certified environmental consultant.

Phase II Environmental Site Assessment. Conducting a Phase II ESA is useful in filling remaining data gaps when recognized environmental conditions are identified. This assessment further characterizes a site in terms of the nature and extent of contamination. Phase II ESAs rely on direct field-based sampling and analytical techniques to identify and quantify actual concentration of contaminants in soil and groundwater. They additionally provide background information necessary to develop a cleanup strategy and estimate costs. A Phase II ESA is typically conducted by a certified environmental consultant.

Cleanup Process. Following completion of environmental assessments, project managers typically work with environmental consultants to determine a remediation or cleanup strategy. Results of a Phase II ESA typically include a site conceptual model determining contaminant exposure pathways. Contaminant cleanup goals are then identified based on existing regulatory guidelines and statues. Additional analysis and a variety of additional reports may be necessary based on the regulatory agency and complexity of the cleanup. An appropriate cleanup plan is then designed, considering unique site features. Cleanup may involve soil or groundwater removal or safe encapsulation of contaminants on site. Regulatory agencies may provide guidance throughout the process. In some cases, final approval from a regulatory agency certifies the cleanup process is complete. In other cases, there may be additional requirements to ensure safety from any residual levels of contamination, which were not technically or economically feasible to remove.

Environmental Insurance. A major challenge faced when approaching a redevelopment project on environmentally impaired sites is unknown risk. Environmental insurance assists sellers, buyers, developers, and lenders in defining the costs associated with known and unknown contamination at a site. It can also serve as a powerful risk transfer technique. Understanding the project's financial and timing constraints, as well as stakeholders' risk tolerance drives the selection of various risk management and insurance solutions. Input from legal, engineering, and risk professionals should be sought early in the redevelopment process to allow maximum flexibility for your project. Environmental insurance is an effective tool bridging the risk gap on complicated brownfield redevelopment projects.

Financial Resources. Securing front-end and long-term financing for brownfield projects can be difficult. Banks are often nervous about the possibility of high cleanup costs, loan defaults, and loss of collateral. Except for larger financial institutions, most banks do not have the in-house expertise needed to properly weight environmental risks.

For these reasons, public financing at the local, state, and federal levels plays an important role in the funding of most brownfield projects. Despite the challenges with securing financial resources for environmental properties, given our strong record of providing funds.

How CCLR Helps

Our work is accomplished through training, technical assistance, partnership-building and grants and loans for communities and other interested parties attempting to turn around vacant, environmentally distressed, or infill properties.

CCLR has a strong record of helping community development corporations, affordable housing developers, and municipalities overcome the challenges to cleaning up and redeveloping infill sites including brownfields and contaminated properties. CCLR promotes the reuse of already used lands and discourages urban sprawl through creative public, private, and nonprofit partnerships.

As a provider of the U.S. EPA's Technical Assistance to Brownfields (TAB) Communities program, CCLR provides technical assistance and training to brownfields communities throughout the Western United States. As part of the TAB Program, CCLR has also created an online resource center to better serve our communities.

52. Municipal and Community Collaboration for Effective Brownfields Redevelopment*

Environmental Law Institute

Strong involvement and support from those who will be affected by the process are crucial elements of a successful brownfields redevelopment initiative. Community residents and groups who have experienced the negative health, economic, and environmental effects of contaminated and abandoned sites have an important stake in how a site is redeveloped. Thus the process should provide an opportunity for those stakeholders to weigh in on—and become invested in—the redevelopment effort, to ensure that the ultimate result advances the interests of community residents, and not only the local government and developers. This includes consideration of needed public amenities and services, as well as planning to avoid problems such as displacement of existing residents and community services.

On a practical level, support from community stakeholders can also help spur municipal agencies to act and can give projects the initial political push they sometimes need to get underway. Grassroots support can also help secure project funding from competitive public funding programs and provide greater certainty to potential developers. An effective process for collaboration among municipal officials and community members can help avoid delays and interruptions to the redevelopment process. Including a broad range of stakeholders early on can reduce the risks to private developers and encourage their involvement in a project.

New Jersey has established public notice and participation requirements related to site cleanup at brownfields and other properties (see the seventh article in this collection).[1] In addition, state brownfields funding and assistance programs may require community participation or give priority to applicants who demonstrate community involvement. The state's Brownfields Development Area program, for example, uses selection criteria that include "level and breadth of community support" and the "clarity of community vision" for the project.[2] The U.S. Environmental Protection Agency's (EPA's) Brownfields Assessment Grants program includes "Community Engagement and Partnerships" as a ranking criteria, and applicants must indicate how they will engage the

---

*Originally published as Environmental Law Institute (2010), "Municipal and Community Collaboration for Effective Brownfields Redevelopment," in *Advancing Public Health and Sustainability Through Brownfields Redevelopment in New Jersey: A Handbook for Local Officials and Communities* (ELI: Washington, D.C.). Reprinted with permission of the publisher.

community, the role of community organizations, and the partnerships that have been established.³

Strategic Considerations for Community Collaboration

▶ **Engaging in *early* and *ongoing* dialogue with the community.** As partners in the redevelopment process, community members and local officials should begin working together early in the process to develop a solid foundation for dialogue. At an early stage in redevelopment planning, municipal agencies can both *solicit* community concerns and interests and *convey* municipal goals and information about brownfields redevelopment. Early input and collaboration is particularly important because initial decisions—e.g., about which brownfield sites to focus on and about the appropriate and best uses of those sites—will affect the remainder of the redevelopment process. Similarly, community residents should be informed about and included in discussions about site cleanup, as those decisions can affect community safety and health over the long term and may involve long-term monitoring and oversight of cleanup measures.

Municipal and community collaboration throughout the brownfield redevelopment process is vital to educate the community, ensure that residents are not taken by surprise, and sustain project support. To achieve effective participation, it may not be adequate to rely on standardized mechanisms such as routine public hearings and comment periods. Municipal officials may need to be more proactive and to tailor outreach to meet the needs of those residents and stakeholders most affected—for example, by advertising meetings on local access cable channels, holding public meetings at times that accommodate work schedules, providing information in languages other than English, and engaging neighborhood groups through their meetings or listservs.⁴

▶ **Reaching out to a wide array of community members and stakeholders.** In building a framework for collaboration on brownfields projects, it is important to reach out to a broad cross-section of the community, including those who may be critical of the process. If some groups feel they have been left out of the process, time and resources will likely need to be diverted later to address their concerns. The New Jersey State Plan calls for neighborhood revitalization planning to include "participation from families, neighborhoods, schools, civic-, community- and faith-based organizations, for-profit and nonprofit groups and businesses, municipalities, utilities, school districts, counties and state agencies."⁵ In addition to working with grassroots civic and religious leaders, municipal officials can collaborate with state and local non-governmental organizations (NGOs) that work on social, environmental, and economic development issues. Those organizations can help communicate with community residents and can also bring technical expertise to a brownfields initiative.

New Jersey Organizations Working on Brownfields Issues

In addition to local organizations, there are several state-level NGOs and academic institutions in New Jersey that can provide technical assistance to municipal officials and community stakeholders on brownfields redevelopment issues.

National Center for Neighborhood and Brownfields Redevelopment

http://policy.rutgers.edu/brownfields/
Housed at the Rutgers University E.J. Bloustein School of Planning and Public Policy, this Center researches issues related to smart growth, sprawl reduction, green building, housing, and urban revitalization. It also works with community leaders to build capacity for successful neighborhood revitalization planning.

New Jersey Institute of Technology (NJIT)

http://www.njit.edu/tab/
NJIT's Technical Assistance to Brownfield (TAB) Communities program serves as a free independent resource to communities, regional entities, and nonprofits who have or are seeking to obtain EPA brownfields grants. The TAB program provides guidance throughout the cleanup process, including guidance in preparing grant applications and selecting consultants, explanation of environmental laws and regulations, advice on project management, assistance in developing financing strategies, and help in galvanizing community engagement.

Housing and Community Development Network of New Jersey

http://www.hcdnnj.org/
The Housing and Community Development Network of New Jersey is a statewide association of more than 250 affordable housing and community development corporations (CDCs), individuals, and other organizations that support the creation of housing and economic opportunities for low- and moderate-income New Jersey residents. The Network provides CDCs with targeted technical assistance and educational programs, pursues resources and improved public policies on their behalf, and conducts research on ways to enhance the impact and effectiveness of the community development sector.

New Jersey Future

http://www.njfuture.org/
New Jersey Future is a statewide research and policy group advocating an approach to development that protects open lands and natural resources, revitalizes neighborhoods, keeps housing affordable, and provides more transportation choices. The organization hosts an annual redevelopment conference, presents awards for smart growth, and produces a wide range of reports and other materials on redevelopment issues.

▶ **Creating an interagency municipal brownfields team.** Brownfields projects are long-term undertakings that involve multiple offices within the local government. An interagency municipal brownfields team coordinates administrative and technical knowledge, making it easier for community residents, private and non-profit developers, and other stakeholders to work with local agencies. An interagency team can also expedite projects by coordinating multiple local approval processes. There are a number of different models for interagency teams, but it is common to have participation from the economic development, environmental, planning, finance, and legal departments, as well as the mayor's office.[6]

In New Jersey's Passaic County, the Brownfields Assessment Program is implemented by the staff of the Department of Economic Development, in conjunction with the Departments of Health, Engineering, and Planning. The county also coordinates all activities with key county committees—the Smart Growth Committee, the Comprehensive Economic Development Strategic Committee, and the Open Space and Farmlands Preservation Committee.[7]

▶ **Establishing a stakeholder taskforce to facilitate community participation and outreach.** A community task force or workgroup consisting of diverse community stakeholders and municipal officials can be an effective mechanism for achieving the key elements for effective community outreach and participation. Such a task force also provides a forum for municipal and community leaders to work together with developers, lenders, and property owners, who will have key insight and practical information about the redevelopment potential for brownfield properties. Whether established for a specific brownfields project or for a larger municipal brownfields initiative, a community stakeholder task force can provide continuity over different stages of the redevelopment process.

The city of Paterson, New Jersey, is one of many that have taken this approach in its brownfields initiatives. Using funds from an EPA Brownfields Assessment grant, the city established the public-private Paterson Environmental Revitalization Committee (PERC) to both educate and involve the community in the brownfields process.[8]

▶ **Working with Consultants.** Brownfields projects typically involve consultants who provide site assessment, cleanup, and redevelopment services. Consultants with experience in brownfields redevelopment can also help municipalities establish their brownfields program and create an effective approach to community participation. Consultants may also be able to assist municipal agencies in navigating funding sources and preparing grant applications. The fifth article in this collection provides more information about hiring a consultant.

Key Resources for Community Collaboration

There are many listings of the principal state and federal financial assistance programs that are available to fund the various stages of a brownfield redevelopment initiative. Municipalities may be able to tap some of those resources to support early redevelopment planning and collaboration efforts. For example, EPA's *Brownfields Assessment Grant* program awards funding to governmental entities for brownfields assessments, and also for planning and community involvement activities related to brownfield sites. Municipalities may apply for a site-specific grant or a community-wide assessment grant. The total request is limited to $400,000 unless a waiver is requested due to the extent of contamination at a specific site.

Certain state programs may be available to support collaborative development of a neighborhood or redevelopment plan. One example is the *Urban Site Acquisition Program,* a revolving loan fund administered by the New Jersey Redevelopment Authority (NJRA) for the acquisition, site preparation, and redevelopment of properties that are part of a larger urban redevelopment plan in NJRA eligible communities. The NJRA's

Environmental Equity Program (E2P) also makes loans to finance the pre-development costs related to brownfields development, including planning activities.

In addition, municipalities and non-profit organizations working together to promote local employment in their brownfields initiative may wish to pursue funding through EPA's *Brownfields Job Training Grant* program. This annual EPA grant competition provides funding to recruit, train, and place unemployed and under-employed residents of brownfields-impacted communities. The focus is on teaching environmental assessment and cleanup job skills, helping residents living near brownfield sites to secure full-time employment in the environmental field.

Notes

1. N.J. Administrative Code 7:26E-1.4.
2. See NJ Dept. of Environmental Protection, 2009 Brownfields Development Area Application Guidance, available at: http://www.nj.gov/dep/srp/brownfields/bda/bda_application_guide.htm.
3. See U.S. EPA, Final FY2010 Brownfields Assessment Grant Guidelines, available at: http://www.epa.gov/brownfields/applicat.htm.
4. For more information on community participation in brownfields redevelopment, see U.S. EPA Region 4, Revitalizing Southeastern Communities: A Brownfields Toolkit, available at http://www.epa.gov/region4/brownfieldstoolkit/index.html; Nat'l. Assn. of Local Government Environmental Professionals and Northeast-Midwest Institute, Unlocking Brownfields: Keys to Community Revitalization, available at: http://www.resourcesaver.com/file/toolmanager/CustomO93C337F65023.pdf; Nat'l Center for Neighborhoods and Brownfields Redevelopment, Building Capacity: Brownfields Redevelopment for Community-Based Organizations (2008), available at: http://policy.rutgers.edu/brownfields/events/Manual_Building_Capacity.pdf. Community involvement is also addressed in the Standard Guide to the Process of Sustainable Brownfields Redevelopment, published by the American Society for Testing and Materials, available for purchase at: http://www.astm.org/Standards/E1984.htm.
5. New Jersey State Plan ("Statewide Policies") 129, available at: http://www.state.nj.us/dca/divisions/osg/plan/.
6. See generally National Association of Local Government Environmental Professionals and Northeast-Midwest Institute, Unlocking Brownfields: Keys to Community Revitalization, 115–116, available at: http://www.resourcesaver.com/file/toolmanager/CustomO93C337F65023.pdf.
7. Passaic County Brownfields Assessment Program ("Program Overview"), available at: http://www.passaiccountynj.org/Departments/window-economicdevbrownfieldinfo.htm.
8. Jessie Torrez, "Paterson's U.S. EPA Pilot Grant and PERC," in Revitalization through Brownfield Redevelopment: How Paterson Is Succeeding, and You Can Too! (Env. Law Inst., 2007), available at: http://www.eli.org/program_areas/innovation_governance_pubs.cfm.

53. Working with the Private Sector to Redevelop Brownfields*

Environmental Law Institute

Most brownfield sites ultimately are developed privately or through a public-private partnership. Municipal brownfields programs can facilitate private-sector redevelopment by taking steps to address the unique challenges and opportunities that exist in securing private financing for brownfields development.

In addition to the economic considerations inherent in all real estate development transactions, brownfields redevelopment presents economic risks that financing particularly challenging. The most significant risk is posed by the potential environmental contamination at the site. Where there is uncertainty over the extent and nature of the contamination, there is also uncertainty about liability and about the cost and timing of the cleanup. These uncertainties may deter traditional lending institutions from becoming involved in the early stages of a brownfields redevelopment project or may result in financing terms that make a project unfeasible or create significant financing gaps.[1] Potential developers may be unwilling to pursue a brownfields project in the face of the greater financial risks and uncertainties over returns on their investment.

The preceding articles in this handbook have discussed actions that municipalities can take to reduce the risks and uncertainties of brownfields redevelopment—both to advance public sector redevelopment projects and to create a stronger foundation for facilitating private redevelopment.

- *Working with community stakeholders* throughout the process to create a broad base of support for redevelopment;
- *Coordinating among local government agencies* to solidify government support and streamline municipal and state decision-making;
- *Developing a vision* for site reuse to help guide the project and ensure that community needs will be addressed; and
- *Assisting in assessment and cleanup activities* at brownfields to clarify cleanup costs or to address cleanup before financing is pursued.

There are several other steps that municipal agencies can take to spur private redevelopment of brownfield properties that are publicly or privately owned.

---

*Originally published as Environmental Law Institute (2010), "Working with the Private Sector to Redevelop Brownfields," in *Advancing Public Health and Sustainability Through Brownfields Redevelopment in New Jersey: A Handbook for Local Officials and Communities* 65. Reprinted with permission of the publisher.

Strategic Considerations for Facilitating Private Investment in Brownfields Redevelopment

▶ **Educating developers about federal and state financial assistance programs.** In many cases, private parties will be eligible for federal and state grants, loans, tax credits, and other forms of financial assistance for brownfields assessment, cleanup, and redevelopment. For properties that present significant risks and obstacles to redevelopment, combining different financing mechanisms from the public and private sectors can help build an economically sound project. Municipal agencies can spur redevelopment by providing owners and developers with timely and practical information about how to access key federal and state programs that are targeted to the private sector.

▶ **Leveraging municipal funds to facilitate private financing of brownfields redevelopment.** In some cases, a small amount of public funding can make the difference in whether a private redevelopment project goes forward. In addition to linking developers with federal and state programs, local governments in New Jersey can create financial incentives for redevelopment. Municipalities can, for example, target fees, fines, or other local revenues for redevelopment projects.

Another type of local financing tool available for brownfields projects is *tax increment financing*. As part of the New Jersey Economic Stimulus Act of 2009, the state legislature established the Economic Redevelopment and Growth (ERG) Grant Program. The program is like tax increment financing, whereby estimated incremental tax revenues derived from qualified redevelopment projects are redirected to developers to defray a portion of the project costs. The program provides incentive grants to redevelopment projects in "qualifying economic redevelopment and growth grant incentive areas" to fill in financing gaps for the projects. Developers can apply for an incentive grant up to 75 percent of the annual incremental state tax and/or local tax revenue. (See http://www.njeda.com/web/Aspx_pg/Templates/Npic_Text.aspx?Doc_Id=1186&menuid=1424&topid=718&levelid=6&midid=1175.)

Any New Jersey municipality that has designated a redevelopment area may also (either directly or through application to the NJEDA) issue tax-exempt bonds to fund the infrastructure and remediation portion of a redevelopment project. The municipality may provide a tax abatement and establish a *payments in lieu of taxes* agreement with the developer to pay the debt service on the bonds.[2]

▶ **Understanding the role of insurance in facilitating brownfields redevelopment.** Environmental insurance can help satisfy regulatory responsibilities, minimize liability for contamination, and facilitate brownfields acquisition or sales. Insurance can also help procure loans by providing lenders with the certainty that borrowers will have enough money to pay back the loans. Types of insurance for brownfields projects include: (1) *environmental remediation insurance*, to protect against releases that took place before the writing of the policy, but are discovered afterwards; (2) *stop-loss or cleanup cost-cap coverage*, to protect against cleanup costs that far exceed the estimated cleanup costs; (3) *pollution legal liability insurance*, to protect against migration of contamination to other sites or against third-party and property injury claims, and (4) *secured creditor insurance*, to insure the balance of loans when the borrower defaults and there is an environmental condition on the property.[3] Municipalities can help private developers by providing information about the types of insurance and by linking small developers or site owners with insurers.

▶ **Clarifying the liability considerations for developers who acquire brownfield sites.** Under New Jersey law, an entity that is "in any way responsible" for hazardous substances is strictly liable for all cleanup and removal costs.[4] As noted in the sixth article in this collection, local governments may be eligible for relief from liability under both state and federal law where there is an "involuntary acquisition" or other acquisition to promote redevelopment. The law also provides certain defenses to liability for private parties. For example, those who acquire property subsequent to the discharge and are not in any way responsible for the contamination may qualify for an innocent landowner exception to liability if they meet detailed requirements set out in the law, including the completion of the preliminary assessment (PA), and, if necessary, a Site Investigation (SI) at the time of purchase.[5]

The law also provides relief from liability for the payment of natural resource damages and restoration of natural resources, for an owner who acquired the real property after the hazardous substance discharge, was not in any way responsible for discharge, and has not contracted to pay the damages or to restore lost or damaged natural resources.[6] Additionally, lenders who do not participate in the management of a project will generally not be deemed a responsible party (and thus liable for cleanup) solely by virtue of their security interest in the project.[7]

Federal law also provides defenses to Superfund liability in certain circumstances. Entities that acquire property and had no knowledge of the contamination at the time of purchase may be eligible as an *innocent landowner* if they conducted all appropriate inquiries (AAI) prior to purchase and complied with other pre- and post-purchase requirements, as discussed in the fifth article in this collection. A *bona fide prospective purchaser* defense is available to persons who acquire property, even if they know or have reason to know of contamination on the property, provided they meet eight threshold criteria (including AAI) spelled out in the federal regulations, comply with ongoing obligations, and do not impede the performance of a response action or natural resource restoration. The *contiguous property owner* defense applies to those who own property that may be contaminated but is not the original source of the hazardous substance contamination, provided the landowner does not know (or have reason to know) prior to purchase, that the property is or could be contaminated.[8]

▶ **Working with community development entities.** Community Development Corporations (CDCs) play an important role in neighborhood revitalization, which may include the purchase and redevelopment of brownfield properties. Municipalities can work with CDCs to help build their capacity and to connect them with federal, state, and other brownfields resources. In addition, CDCs can seek technical support from non-governmental organizations in New Jersey. Some of the organizations described in the second article in this collection—the Housing and Community Development Network of New Jersey and the National Center for Neighborhood and Brownfields Redevelopment—help build capacity of CDCs and other community-based organizations. Another organization, the Local Support Initiatives Coalition (LISC) has an office in Newark & Jersey City that provides technical assistance to CDCs, helps guide CDC projects through city and state processes, and creates opportunities for public and private sector lenders to support the work of CDCs. (See http://www.lisc.org/content/offices/detail/609/.)

▶ **Creating a strong marketing campaign to reach developers.** Marketing is a key step for municipalities that own brownfield sites and wish to make the sites available for redevelopment in the private sector. The focus of a marketing campaign will vary depending on the characteristics of the site, the stage at which the municipality is seeking to transfer the site, and the actions that have been taken to address site conditions. In all cases, marketing efforts will benefit from a clear vision for the property, developed in concert with a broad range of community stakeholders. Local and state economic development officials can bring important experience to the marketing effort, including contacts with key business associations and groups whose members may be interested in the properties. For large projects, the municipality may consider hiring a consultant or attorney to assist in preparing detailed materials to explain the site conditions and context.[9]

There are a variety of avenues for disseminating marketing materials for brownfield sites. The New Jersey SiteMart provides a free listing of brownfields. Many municipalities have developed web pages that highlight available brownfield properties. A municipality can also create a list of tax-delinquent brownfield properties subject to municipal foreclosure and publicize the list to potential developers. The city of Milwaukee created such a list and provides the public with basic information about the process through which the properties could be foreclosed and then transferred to a private developer.[10] Marketing of brownfield sites can be done through a formal municipal procurement process via a Request for Proposals.

Key Resources for Facilitating Private Financing

The following programs provide financial assistance directly to *private* entities in the form of general project financing or grants and loans for specific aspects of brownfields redevelopment, such as site cleanup:

- *Brownfields and Contaminated Site Remediation Reimbursement Program.* Through this program, developers enter into a Redevelopment Agreement with the NJEDA and are eligible for up to 75 percent reimbursement of approved remediation costs. The developer must be a non-responsible party agreeing to undertake and complete the environmental cleanup of the site.
- *Hazardous Discharge Site Remediation Fund* (HDSRF). Innocent parties who meet the criteria spelled out in the program may be eligible for up to 50 percent of costs for PA, SI, RI, and RA activities, not to exceed $1 million. The HDSRF is jointly administered by NJDEP and NJEDA.
- *Brownfields Revolving Loan Fund.* Developers in selected municipalities may apply to NJEDA for low-interest loans for brownfields remediation activities. Funding comes from an initial $2 million grant capitalized by the U.S. EPA.
- *Economic Redevelopment and Growth (ERG) Grant Program.* The ERG program provides incentive grants to developers worth up to 75 percent of the incremental state tax and/or local tax revenue associated with the project. In addition to applying for a local government grant, developers can apply for a state grant from the NJEDA.
- *Fund for Community Economic Development.* NJEDA provides loans to stimulate real estate-based economic development projects in urban and smart growth locations. Loans up to $50,000 are available for feasibility studies and other pre-development costs. Loans up to $1.25 million are available to fill financing gaps in the development of community facilities and other projects, including associated environmental remediation costs.
- *Urban Site Acquisition Program.* This is a revolving loan fund administered by the

NJRA for the acquisition, site preparation and redevelopment of properties that are part of a larger urban redevelopment plan in NJRA-eligible communities.
- *Environmental Equity Program* (E2P). Private and nonprofit developers can apply to the NJRA for loans to help fund planning, site acquisition, remediation, and demolition activities associated with brownfields redevelopment projects in NJRA-eligible municipalities. The site must be part of a broader redevelopment plan and the scope and timeline of remediation must be known.
- *New Jersey Pre-Development Fund.* This fund supports pre-development activities in NJRA-eligible urban communities. The fund covers feasibility studies, architectural costs, environmental and engineering studies, legal and other related soft costs needed for development to proceed.
- *New Jersey Redevelopment Investment Fund.* This program provides a flexible investment fund for business and real estate ventures in NJRA-eligible urban communities. The program makes available direct loans, loan guarantees, and other forms of credit enhancements.
- *NJRA Bond Program.* NJRA issues bonds for making long-term loans at below-market interest rates to qualified businesses and non-profit organizations for redevelopment projects in NJRA-eligible urban communities. Proceeds from tax-exempt bonds may be used for land and building acquisition, new construction, or expansion, purchase of new equipment, and debt/refinancing and working capital.
- *Municipal Landfill Closure and Remediation Reimbursement Program.* NJEDA reimburses eligible developers up to 75 percent of the closure or cleanup costs associated with the remediation and redevelopment of a municipal solid waste landfill. Reimbursement moneys are derived from one-half of the sales tax revenues generated from any business located on the site.
- *New Markets Tax Credit Program.* This U.S. Department of the Treasury Program permits taxpayers to receive a tax credit for making qualified equity investments in approved Community Development Entities, who in turn use the funds to provide investments in low-income communities.

Notes

1. For more detailed information on lending institutions and the risks posed by brownfields, see the New Jersey Institute of Technology's Technical Assistance for Brownfields website, http://www.njit.edu/tab/managing/brownfield/index.php.
2. N.J.A.C. 40A:12A-66.
3. See National Association of Local Government Environmental Professionals and Northeast-Midwest Institute, Unlocking Brownfields: Keys to Community Revitalization 123–124, available at: http://www.resourcesaver.com/file/toolmanager/CustomO93C337F65023.pdf; Env. Law Inst., A Guidebook for Brownfield Property Owners 15, available at: http://www.elistore.org/reports_detail.asp?ID=459.
4. N.J.S.A. 58:10–23.11g(c)(1).
5. N.J.S.A. 58:10–23.11g (d).
6. N.J.S.A. 58:10–23.11f.22 (a).
7. N.J.S.A. 58:10–23.11g5. A holder of a security interest is considered to be actively participating in the management, while the borrower is still in possession, only if the holder exercises decision making or managerial control over the enterprise as described in state law. N.J. Stat. Ann. 58:10–23.11g4.
8. See CERCLA Sec. 107, 42 U.S.C. 9607; U.S. EPA, "Landowner Liability Protections," available at: http://www.epa.gov/oecaerth/cleanup/revitalization/landowner.html.
9. See generally, Commonwealth of Massachusetts, Smart Growth/Smart Energy Toolkit, at: http://www.mass.gov/envir/smart_growth_toolkit/pages/mod-brownfields.html.
10. See City of Milwaukee, How to Purchase a Tax Delinquent Brownfield in Milwaukee, at http://www.mkedcd.org/brownfields/bfhowpurch.html.

54. Environmental Site Assessments

Tad McGalliard

Dynamic economic, environmental, and social factors have changed the way governments, the private sector, and societies across the world are using land. Approaches to accommodate population growth, manage environmental assets, and grow the economy, are increasingly aimed at urbanization instead of sprawl, using existing infrastructure and protecting human and environmental health. These approaches give rise to the reuse of properties that had previously been used but have since become vacant or underutilized. Often called brownfields, they offer opportunities to facilitate employment, housing, public facilities, and amenities, yet they require a unique development process to do so. In general, a brownfield is a property whose environmental conditions need assessment and often remediation before it can be redeveloped.

Brownfields have access to existing infrastructure such as roads, water, wastewater, electricity, and telecommunications. They are often located in or near populated areas and markets with innate or growing demand for housing, employment, goods, services, and amenities.

Developing these sites is attractive from the perspective of all levels of government, the private sector, and communities across the world. They make more efficient use of public infrastructure investments, increase tax revenue when redeveloped, and help achieve other public objectives, such as environmental and public health protection. Unfortunately, reusing this land often entails complications due to the environmental impacts of previous uses.

Whether industrial, commercial, agricultural, or even residential, previous uses have often left contaminants behind that represent significant technical, financial, legal, and design risks and constraints that must be addressed to accommodate new development. The contamination found on and migrating from brownfield properties has also created negative public and environmental health impacts with consequences that disregard property lines, and political boundaries. Conversely, brownfield properties might simply have the perception of being contaminated and might not require significant remediation, if any.

Brownfields range in size from very large (100s of acres) to very small (fractions of an acre). They can be found in the hearts of the most densely populated cities, in small towns, and in remote locations. Uncertainty regarding a property's environmental condition represents risk across public and private sectors. Until site conditions are known, developers cannot adequately plan for costs, time, technical requirements, regulatory processes, and site management. The implications on costs and scheduling can easily turn a project "upside down," leading to the project's failure. Developers are also concerned about legal liability issues stemming from the contamination and do not want to be unduly held responsible for issues they did not create. Investors and lenders are equally concerned, and do not want a financial stake in a project that fails due to inadequately estimated environmental conditions. Not only is their investment capital at risk but they are sometimes in the position of foreclosing on the land whose environmental condition proved complicated. This risk has led to brownfield properties being unused, often for decades until market forces identify it a financially viable opportunity or public agencies take regulatory enforcement action.

In measuring that risk and reducing uncertainty, Environmental Site Assessments (ESA) are necessary to profile the property's environmental condition, followed by remediation (if any). Throughout the development process, site planning, design, and engineering must account for environmental conditions identified and measured in the ESA process. They are often conducted iteratively in tandem with ESAs and remediation as they progress.

It is most often the case that ESAs, remediation, and site planning are conducted while participating with a regulatory structure that defines standards, provides oversight, and issues determinations. Regulatory structures vary among countries, and even the states or provinces within them. Despite these complications, brownfields are being used worldwide to accommodate every type of development. For the purposes of this report, we use "brownfield" to refer to any property whose reuse is complicated by contamination, or the perception of contamination. This includes sites termed Superfund, contaminated site, or other related classifications. In the content to follow, the reader will learn more about each step of the process, emphasizing cleanup technologies. Information herein references practices and examples from the United States, Canada, and European countries.

Environmental Site Assessment (ESA)

Knowledge is power, and in the case of brownfield redevelopment, it is also the key to making informed decisions, minimizing risk, and protecting human and environmental health through redevelopment. Environmental site assessments (ESA) provide this knowledge by identifying contamination and quantifying its levels and extent of its impact.

ESAs are normally conducted by environmental professionals such as engineers, geologists, or environmental scientists. They follow a process and apply standards established by regulatory entities. In the case of the United States and Canada, these standards are established by ASTM International (ASTM) and adopted by the appropriate public regulatory agency. In the United States, this is the Environmental Protection Agency in collaboration with each state's departments of environmental protection. The Canadian system is led by the Canadian Environmental Assessment Agency in collaboration with their respective provincial counterparts. Across Europe, these standards vary from country to country, though there are efforts to create tools and coordination. In general, ESAs begin with research (Phase I), followed by sampling and testing (Phase II).

Phase I ESA

A Phase I ESA is the first step in the assessment process. It involves research into the history of the site, field reconnaissance, and interviews. No samples of soil, groundwater, or materials are taken. A Phase I identifies what the property had been previously used for. Some former sites are known to have used materials and resources considered toxic or otherwise hazardous to environmental and human health and are regulated under state and federal laws. These substances are commonly referred to as contaminants of concern (COC).

Unfortunately, it is often the case that these contaminants have been released into soil, groundwater, air, and buildings. Information obtained in Phase I ESA not only informs decisions about whether or not additional (Phase II) assessment is warranted, but also what that assessment will try to identify, and where on the property it is likely located.

Site histories are researched using a variety of approaches and resources, which vary according to the country and/or state where the brownfield is located. They oft include historical records of land uses by address, historic photographs, and other records such as phone books or local historical records. Any credible evidence that identified previous uses, the names of the businesses, permits, or other records are considered. In the United States, a resource used across the country are detailed maps from the Sandborn Fire Insurance Company dating back to the mid–1900s. These maps provided location of underground storage tanks (UST) that informed insurance company's policies. In addition, to a site's historic uses, Phase I ESAs also research regulatory databases to identified if any regulatory activities have been taken on the subject property.

Regardless of the resource through which a site's history is researched, the information obtained is supplemented by more hands-on approaches, such as site visits and interviews with people who are familiar with the site. Field reconnaissance, visual inspection, and interviews are used to identify contaminant releases that were not found in the literature. Field reconnaissance can identify indicators of contamination such as stained soils, previously undisclosed underground storage tanks (UST), or other evidence of potential contamination. Because public and private records are often incomplete, technology such as ground-penetrating radar (GPR), is used to identify potential issues underground, such as USTs, underground vaults, or large buried objects. Interviews with the property owner, previous owners, tenants, business operators, and neighbors can provide firsthand knowledge of site operations, types and locations of activity, and other information to document and consider for assessment. The goal of the research is to determine whether a recognized environmental condition (REC) is present that warrants further investigation.

Examples of RECs include, but are not limited to, a site history that identifies a previous use that used COCs and have a history of known releases; a history of regulatory enforcement; field inspections that identify soil staining or other evidence of COCs; an interview identifying the location of an undocumented UST or contamination event. The finding of a REC does not mean the property is contaminated but it does mean that a Phase II ESA should be conducted.

Phase II ESA

A Phase II ESA is the step where samples are taken of potentially contaminated media and tested for the contaminants associated with the REC. Like a Phase I ESA, this step is also conducted through involvement with a regulatory program and is performed per the standards adopted by the regulatory agency.

Media typically tested include soil, soil gas, groundwater, sediments, contents in above ground and underground storage tanks, and materials within structures. Using different approaches to collecting samples, each media is tested in qualified laboratories following testing protocol for each contaminant.

The Phase II ESA scope and approach are based on the findings of the Phase I ESA and conducted in accordance with the appropriate standards. The goal of each media tested is to first determine if the contaminant is present, and if so, at what concentrations. If the contamination is present in the samples, then additional sampling is required to determine the extent of the contamination. Phase II ESAs can be conducted iteratively, with each step based on and expanding the findings of the previous step.

Soil—To characterize the extent of contamination in soils, samples are taken to profile the horizontal and the vertical extent of contamination. In most cases, samples are taken horizontally and vertically until no contamination is found, which defines the outer boundary of that impacted area. Once the boundaries are identified, a volume of soil that is impacted can now be calculated. In addition to characterizing contaminants, soil samples are evaluated for the type of soil, variations in types of soil at different depths, and any notable characteristics like odor and color are recorded. Soil samples are collected using boring equipment, such as a direct push probe or through test pits dug with excavation equipment.

Groundwater—Groundwater is tested during discrete testing events or regularly by using groundwater monitoring wells (GMW) to collect samples. The goal again is to identify, quantify, and measure contamination if present. Samples can be taken from existing wells, but it is often necessary to install additional wells to accurately profile the depth and movement of groundwater tables. Modeling groundwater movement can be challenging, since it must account for factors such as seasonal fluctuations in groundwater volume and direction, and complex geological and hydrogeological conditions.

Soil Gas—Soil gas is the gas between soil particles below ground surface. Under normal conditions, it is comprised of naturally occurring gases such as nitrogen, oxygen, and other elements necessary for healthy soils and plants. However, some naturally occurring gases such as radon and methane, also pose risk to environmental and human health.

Whether naturally occurring or manmade, compounds in the soil often break down and release gas, commonly referred to as volatile organic compounds (VOC). Soil gas can even carry contaminants that were released in groundwater. Many VOCs are harmful to human health and environmental quality. Common harmful VOCs include benzene, toluene, xylene, polycyclic aromatic hydrocarbons (PAH), and others associated with cancer and other diseases affecting internal organs, reproductive health, and immune systems.

Through a process known as vapor intrusion (VI), soil gas enters buildings through their foundations and can become concentrated in residential, commercial, and industrial settings, exposing humans to known carcinogens. Soil gas also accumulates in underground infrastructure, such as utility corridors and vaults.

These concentrated gases are not only possibly toxic, but they can also pose a risk of explosion. Testing soil gas is conducted using specialized soil gas sampling equipment, most commonly using probes into the soil at various depths. These probes can be used during a single sampling event or can be installed on a more permanent basis allowing for regular, long-term monitoring.

Buildings—The buildings themselves can also represent risk and require testing to be reused safely. Testing for potential contamination within structures is done in locations where regulated contaminants were stored, used, and where releases are known to have occurred. Samples are also often taken of the materials used in the structure's construction. Common COCs found in buildings include lead, asbestos, and polychlorinated biphenyls (PCB). These materials were used in paint, piping, lights, flooring, ceiling tiles, insulation, and other uses that could represent exposure risk while the building is operational, during renovation, construction, and/or demolition, and debris disposal.

55. Remediation Planning, Reuse Planning and Site Design

Tad McGalliard

Once the extent of contamination has been defined, the concentration levels of each contaminant are compared to the regulatory threshold/standard for that contaminant. Under most regulatory processes, thresholds for each contaminant and goals for remediation vary, depending on what the property is going to be used for.

Most regulatory standards for remediation are referred to as "risk based," meaning the regulatory thresholds for each contaminant assume some contamination may remain in place if properly managed. There are circumstances in which regulation requires complete removal and or abatement of particular contaminants, but it is not the norm.

In general, if contaminant levels are below the threshold, no action is required. When contamination levels exceed the appropriate threshold, remediation of the contaminants is necessary to protect human and environmental health through regulatory compliance. For several reasons, remediation planning is dependent on the future use of the site, at the very least it must account for the type of land use (residential, commercial, industrial, open space, etc.). As mentioned earlier, standards for contaminant levels are based on that end use. In cases where only a general land use type is known (commercial, residential, industrial) remediation planning and remediation are often not informed enough to completely account for what is required for redevelopment. Remediation planning, reuse planning, and site design have direct influence on one another, and are often conducted concurrently.

During reuse planning, it is important to know what areas of the property are impacted and subject to remediation. This is because most brownfield redevelopment involves reuse of existing buildings and infrastructure that could be impacted by the contamination and must be remediated prior to reuse. Additionally, redevelopment often involves construction of new buildings, infrastructure, and other activity that might be on or around areas impacted by contamination. Their construction and/or restoration poses the risk of releasing the contamination during the process or creating exposure risk after construction and during active site use. Choices are often made to design, site, and orient buildings and infrastructure as to avoid those areas, which might allow for less intensive, and expensive, remediation efforts. However, it is often the case that avoiding these areas is not possible or desirable, which influences the design, engineering, permitting, construction, and maintenance plans. This is where reuse, site planning, and remediation planning merge. The buildings' design and construction can also serve a dual purpose, as a necessary component of construction that also serves to remove, mitigate, or limit the risks of contaminant exposure to humans and environmental receptors.

Reuse Planning

From a private developer's perspective, reuse planning is usually focused on the property itself. From a local government perspective, reuse planning often looks at entire districts, corridors, or portfolio of brownfields in addition to individual sites.

In the United States and Canada, local governments operate under state/provincial frameworks to manage land use policies that determine what uses are allowed to be developed and where they go. This is usually done in the form of zoning that organizes land by types of use. In general, these include residential, commercial, industrial, parks, natural/preservation, and institutional uses, each having subcategories.

In some European countries, such as Germany, zoning is also used at the local level, but encourages a greater mix of land uses within proximity to one another. While others like England maintain national land use policies that direct local municipal enforcement and management. Local governments take several approaches to plan reuse of brownfields they want to see redeveloped. In the United States, a practice referred to as Brownfield Area Wide Planning is a planning process that develops redevelopment plans for the districts or neighborhoods impacted by brownfields. Rather than ignoring them and seeing them as liabilities, they are used as catalysts for investment and development in the surrounding community.

A developer's reuse planning is more focused on the specific type of development they envision and starts with finding a site compatible with that vision. Zone changes and variances to these designations are common but they are not guaranteed and often come with controversy. To the extent possible, developers can conduct their reuse planning and account for brownfield-related constraints even before purchasing the property. They must evaluate whether they can accommodate the cost, time, and other demands of remediation and regulatory compliance; and if remediation measures do not create prohibitive site planning, construction, and operational constraints.

To make this determination, there is a variety of approaches to remediation to choose from. Some variation comes from the fact that different contaminants, and different media are addressed using approaches specific to their characteristics. Choosing which method is the best fit for a development can be difficult and should be informed by professionals who understand each approach's limitations and implications.

Institutional and Engineering Controls

An institutional control (IC) is an approach that uses policy, legal mechanisms, and administrative tools to protect human health and the environment. In the United States, they include covenants, or other legally binding agreements that limit or prohibit certain activity on a property. Conditions of the IC are often recorded with the property's title/deed. For example, an IC can prohibit the use of groundwater, and when recorded with the property's title, will prevent permits from being issued for activity that would use groundwater. Additionally, land use restrictions can limit exposure by zoning a property in a way that does not allow for more intense uses. Brownfield practitioners sometimes refer to ICs as land use controls. For example, land can be kept zoned for industrial use, and not allow residential development that requires a higher level of remediation.

Engineering controls (EC) take a more physical approach to managing exposure by using barriers, walls, fencing, and other tools to prevent contact with the contamination and prevent its migration. ECs also include mechanical systems such as ventilation and soil vapor extraction (SVE). Multiple types of ECs are common on brownfield redevelopment projects. They can also be paired with ICs to enforce the integrity of the EC.

Perhaps the most common EC is simply called a "cap." A cap controls exposure to contamination in soil by preventing people from coming in contact with the soils. Several different materials are used for caps, including soil, gravel, asphalt, and concrete. Parking lots are often used as the capped area of a property. Other EC practices include technologies such as vapor barriers and soil vapor extraction systems (SVE). For example, landfills employ multiple ECs such as caps, vapor extraction and treatment systems, fencing, lining, and leachate systems. They support ECs with ICs like restrictive zoning, legal obligations to monitor groundwater, security, and controlled site access.

As mentioned earlier, there is a nexus between remediation planning and redevelopment planning where steps taken for remediation like an EC or excavation can be accomplished as part of the construction process that must happen anyway. These needs are not always aligned, but when they are, they offer an efficiency in cost and time that can be difficult to achieve on brownfield projects.

For instance, in contaminated areas where remediation requires excavation, the excavated area might serve as subterranean parking, storage, or basements. Another common example is a building's foundation serving as a cap, which is an EC. This can be effective with existing buildings and for new construction. However, if the foundation is serving as a cap, it may also require vapor extraction that is more cost effective with new construction. In the case of the cap as EC, there are usually requirements for ICs to be used, perhaps in the form of a condition on the property's title. That ensures that in the case of demolition or additional construction, the proper steps are taken, and the property owner and/or developer can make informed decisions about expansion and redevelopment.

This kind of mutual need helps with the economic efficiency of the project by spreading the cost burden across different line items in a project's budget. In the United States, Canada, and European countries, sources of capital are often divided between remediation costs and construction costs, with sources of capital for remediation less available than for construction. By accounting for the excavation, or cap as part of construction, it reduces the burden on more limited sources of remediation capital.

56. Remediation Technologies and Remedies

Tad McGalliard

Remediation technologies and remedies vary across the type of media contaminated, and the contaminant. Most regulatory structures in the United States, Canada, and European countries operate under a risk-based system, meaning some level of contamination is left onsite. Actions taken to remediate contamination depend on the volume and concentration of the contamination and its location, availability, and the end use of the site. Media addressed in brownfield redevelopment include soil, soil vapor, water, sediment, and structures.

Engineering controls and institutional controls play a large role in bringing a brownfield to redevelopment, but they are not the only options. They are used in the context of containing contamination and limiting exposure to human or environmental receptors. Other approaches are used with them, including treating the contamination so it is no longer harmful, or removing it and disposing of it at an appropriate facility. A summary of these remedies and technologies are described in this section, organized by the media impacted.

Soil

Developers and environmental professionals have several options to remediate contaminants in the soil. Soils can be impacted by contaminants, including petroleum products, heavy metals, PCBs, chlorinated solvents, herbicides, pesticides, nitrates, perchlorates, and more. Remedies vary from excavation and disposal, to treatments that break them down into more benign compounds.

Excavation—Perhaps the most straightforward remedy is excavation. Heavy equipment is used to excavate the impacted soils, which are transported to an appropriate landfill. Even landfills have their limits and depending on the type of contamination and its concentration in the soils, disposal might be required at a specially constructed and managed toxic landfills.

Excavation is sometimes not a feasible or preferable remedy because of cost, or logistical considerations like access. Sometimes excavation is simply more expensive than the economics of the development can accommodate. Additionally, soil contamination is often found at depths beyond the reach of excavation equipment. Goals for remediation can also strive to move beyond regulatory compliance and the use of ECs and ICs. In these cases, a possible remedy is in situ or ex situ remediation.

In situ and ex situ treatment—In situ treatment is the treatment of the contaminated media while it remains in place, without excavation. Ex situ remediation sometimes called land farming, is the practice of treating the soil once excavated. Each approach serves as a potential alternative or complement to excavation and disposal, engineering controls, and institutional controls. Each approach can apply effective treatments for contaminants such as petroleum, chlorinated solvents, pesticides, herbicides, and other COCs. Some approaches also work to bind contaminants such as metals or PCBs, to limit their mobility and leachability.

Widely recognized and implemented practices for both in situ and ex situ remediation rely on chemical oxidation, and/or bioremediation. The goal of both approaches is to avoid offsite disposal costs and move toward more sustainable remediation that eliminates environmental and human health risk rather then moving it somewhere else or containing it.

- Chemical oxidation—This technology introduces oxidizing agents into the soil that cause the contaminant to oxidize, breaking them down in place. This practice ranges from simply exposing the soils to outdoor air, to the introduction of proprietary products that are either injected into the soil or mixed with the soils onsite.
- Bioremediation—This is the practice of exposing contaminants to microorganisms that degrade the contamination. This can be done aerobically by injecting oxygen into the soil which aids the growth of indigenous microorganisms that interact with the contamination (bio-stimulation). Oxygen is an electron receptor, borrowing electrons from the contaminant, speeding its degradation. Petroleum hydrocarbons and chlorinated solvents are often treated this way. Other approaches work to change the soil's PH level, making it a more hospitable environment for aerobic processes.

Soil conditions and indigenous microorganisms are not always ideally suited or available for this practice. In such cases, one alternative is to inject laboratory-grown microorganisms known to, or engineered to, speed contaminant degradation (bio-augmentation). These, too, serve as electron receptors to degrade contaminants.

Anaerobic applications include injecting electron donors (sometimes hydrogen) into the soil, which lend electrons to the contaminants, altering their chemistry. This approach is common in addressing contaminants including chlorinated solvents and the compounds they degrade into, such as vinyl chloride.

In situ treatments apply treatments by injecting the oxidizing agents and/or microorganisms directly into the impacted soils at various depths through specially constructed injection wells. In situ treatment can reach soils that are difficult to reach because they are too deep to excavate, are obstructed by buildings, or geologic formations preclude excavation.

Additionally, in cases where excavation is not feasible, engineering controls and/or institutional controls are often employed. While they work to achieve regulatory compliance, they may also limit the development potential of a property, or not achieve other goals related to environmental quality.

In ex situ remediation, excavated contaminated soils can be mixed with the upper horizons (layers) of noncontaminated soils, allowing exposure to oxygen in the atmosphere, speeding their degradation, often aided by the addition of compost or other amendments. Additionally, microorganisms can also be added to aid degradation, like in situ treatments.

Excavated soils can also be collected into bio-piles, where oxidation and/or bioremediation treatments can also be applied. Bio-piles are most often required to use systems that capture and treat the leachate (leakage) from under the pile. Depending on local regulatory practices, site constraints, and on-site operational considerations, ex situ remediation can be conducted onsite or offsite at specially permitted facilities.

Both in situ and ex situ approaches to remediation have the potential to create efficiencies in cost and time, though each site is unique and the potential for each application must reflect each site's conditions. Factors used to determine the effectiveness of each approach include local regulatory standards, microbial population and density in the soils, soil pH, moisture content, soil temperature, and soil nutrients.

Monitored Natural Attenuation—When conditions are right, contamination can remain in the soils, allowing natural processes to degrade the contamination in a practice called monitored natural attenuation (MNA). To ensure effectiveness, MNA requires extensive assessment and is subject to regular monitoring. This practice also relies on the source of contamination being removed.

Natural processes making MNA effective break out into four main categories:

Evaporation—Contaminants such as gasoline and chlorinated solvents starting as liquid will evaporate into gases, which get diluted and even further volatilized with exposure to sunlight.

Sorption—This is an effective strategy when trying to stop the migration of contaminants, as soil particles will stick to contaminants, holding them in place.

Dilution—Mostly relevant with groundwater contamination, as the contaminant mixes with water, it becomes less concentrated, making it less of a concern.

Chemical—Some contaminants react with elements found in the soil, such as iron, which catalyzes a chemical change in the contaminant, often into something less harmful.

While MNA can require smaller remediation and construction costs, it also has limitations. It is often used in concert with engineering controls and institutional controls that limit activity that can be conducted onsite, such as excavation for buildings and utilities.

The process works in the scope of years, rather than months or less, and often follows more intensive remedial actions such as excavation.

In situ thermal desorption—In situ thermal desorption (ISTD) is an in situ treatment technology that uses heat to speed the treatment of contaminants in soils and groundwater. Heating elements are placed into the soils and groundwater, normally in vertical wells.

The heating elements are capable of reaching temperatures in excess of 1000° F (538°C), heating the media around it, speeding the degradation of contamination in it. It has been applied effectively to contaminants, including volatile organic compounds (VOC), gasoline, diesel, methyl tertiary-butyl ether (MTBE), PCBs, dioxins, Furans, and more.

A vapor barrier and venting system are placed on top of the area subject to ISTD in order to capture contaminated soil gas and vapor and treating it prior to ventilation to the outside air. When used to address shallow soil contamination, the ISTD system is often laid horizontally, rather than vertically.

Electrical resistance heating—Contaminant degradation can also be enhanced with electrical resistance heating (ERH), a process that heats the soil and groundwater using alternating current (AC) electricity. A grid of wells is installed throughout the contaminated area. Each well has an electrode placed in it that is connected to a power delivery system. When electrical current passes through the electrodes, the temperature of the soil or groundwater increases. Similar to ISTD, the elevated temperature aids contaminant degradation.

Also similar to ISTD, the area above the well grid is covered with a vapor barrier and vapor extraction and treatment system. Contaminants such as VOCs, chlorinated solvents, gasoline, vinyl chloride, and others are effectively treated with ERH.

Phytoremediation—Phytoremediation technology is a broad application using plants to treat soils and/or groundwater. This technology works in six main ways:

- Phytovolatilization—Plants uptake contaminants, which are then volatilized and transpired into the atmosphere through the plant's leaves. Volatile organic compounds found in materials, including gasoline, solvents, cleaners, and adhesives, can be at least partially treated through phytovolatilization.
- Phytodegradation—Process through which contaminants are degraded or transformed within the plant's rhizosphere, roots, stems, or leaves.
- Phytoextraction—Process through which plants actually take up and store contaminants, including heavy metals and PCBs.
- Phytohydraulics—Groundwater remediation technology using plants, most likely trees, with deep roots to treat groundwater through update or volatilization.
- Rhizodegradation—Process through which the area around the plant's roots (rhizosphere) has enhanced bacterial and fungal activity, which speeds the biodegradation of contaminants.
- Phytosequestration—Process by which contaminants are immobilized/sequestered, mostly by being held in place in the rhizosphere.
- Endophyte—enhanced phytoremediation

Phytoremediation is a potential solution to many contaminants, though its effectiveness and usefulness is not uniform across all contaminants, plant species, or brownfield properties. It can require more time to accomplish its goals than other technologies and results can be unpredictable.

Mycoremediation—This is an approach using fungi/ mushrooms to remediate contaminants. Many fungi produce enzymes that can help degrade different contaminants, usually organic compounds. Some contaminants are also sometimes absorbed into the mycelium of the fungi and stored.

Mycoremediation can be applied as an in situ or ex situ approach to remediating a wide variety of contaminants, including PAHs, heavy metals, plastics, dyes, petroleum products (gasoline), PCBs, and more. While this is a promising technology, its application could be limited compared to other technologies. To be effective, mycoremediation requires that the fungi be in contact with the soils, which will often require excavation of deep contamination that could be addressed through other means.

Incineration—Contaminated soils can also be remediated though incineration, a process by which soils are excavated and burned in an incinerator. Incineration can be applied to soils, water, sludge, and gases. Incineration is known to be a time effective, yet relatively resource intensive technology. Contaminants such as hydrocarbons, PCBs, pesticides, chlorinated solvents, and more can be incinerated in mobile facilities onsite, or treated at larger offsite facilities. Incineration facilities contain multiple combustion chambers and pollution control systems ensuring the operation is not emitting the contamination it is meant to remediate.

Soil Washing—Contaminants can also be separated from the soils through soil washing, a process that mixes contaminated soils. The liquid/soil mixture is sent through a series of separation tanks where larger particles separate from the smaller particles to which contaminants bind. Larger soil particles are removed clean and can be reused onsite or elsewhere. The fine-grained sludge remaining is where most of the contamination is found, which is then disposed of or treated accordingly.

Soil washing is often used as a preliminary step to treating soils using other technologies. It is a proven method that often provides the cost-effective benefits of in situ treatment. Its main limitations are that it is relatively labor intensive and requires contaminated waste stream management (liquid/water/sludge) throughout the process. Additionally, soils are not uniform, making the washing process irregular, often requiring multiwashing formulation and cycles.

Sediment

Remediation of contaminated sediments comes with a unique set of challenges and approaches to overcome them. One of the challenging aspects of remediation sediments is their locationunder rivers, lakes, ponds, stormwater retention facilitation intracoastal waters, bays, harbors, and oceans. Access to the contaminationis complicated, requiring equipment and practices that are more costly and time consuming than aboveground soil remediation. Addition, disturbing the sediment during assessment and remediationposes significant risks of mobilizing the contamination and creation additional impacts.

Remediation technologies vary, depending on the type of contamination accessibility due to depth, water flow (conveyance), sediment stability, presence of sensitive species/habitat, and associated financial and technical constraints. Remedies often include one or more of the following technologies:

- Monitored natural recovery (MNR) and enhanced monitored natural recovery (EMNR)
- Dredging
- In situ treatment
- Engineering controls (capping, amended capping, isolation capping)
- Institutional controls (dredging restriction public health warnings, etc.)

Monitored natural recovery and enhanced monitored natural recovery—Perhaps the most passive remediation options for sediments is monitored natural recovery (MNR), which is a remedial approach that relies on naturally occurring processes in the sediment to degrade or sequester contaminants. With MNR, contaminant toxicity can be reduced through natural biological processes in the sediment through which microorganisms degrade the contaminant. This process can also aid in sequestering the contamination in place, reducing the risk of migration and exposure to human and environmental receptors. Physical processes also play a big role in MNR, as clean sediments cover up contaminated sediments, reducing risk of exposure and migration Enhanced monitored natural recovery (EMNR) is an approach that adds amendments or addition material to the sediment to accelerate or enhance the MNR. Additives/addition material is often a clean layer of sediment that helps keep the contamination in place, sometimes called a thick layer cap. Additives such as granulated carbon can also be added to the sediment to aid in binding certain contaminants, reducing their bioavailability.

Both MNR and EMNR might appear to be relatively low cost and less time intensive compared to other technologies, but that perceptions can be false. While there are no costs directly associated with dredging or other high-cost activities rigorous characterization and ongoing monitoring of sediments and surrounding conditions is necessary. These costs can sometimes exceed those of other activities underscoring careful evaluation of remedial options and risk analysis prior to selection. The most significant limitations of these technologies are that by leaving contaminationin place with no firmed barrier to keep sediment in place, there is a risk of migration due to unpredictable environmental conditions.

Dredging—Dredging involves the removal of sediment, transporting the dredged material, and relocating it to an appropriate location. Dredging is often conducted mechanically, using a "clamshell" or system of excavating equipment that physically scoops the sediment from the bottomof the body of water, most effective on more gravelly or coarse material. Dredging can also be conducted hydraulically using a pumping system to remove sediments, most effectively used for more uniform, finely grained material.

Once sediment is dredged, it must be dewatered, a process by which water drains away leaving the sediment behind. It is often necessary for the water to also be treated before returning to the waterway. Contaminated sediments can often be disposed of at municipal landfill or in cases where contaminant levels exceed their regulatory restriction disposal can occur at a toxic waste landfill. Disposal can also be done in confined disposal facilities (CDF), using a system of dikes to contain the sediment. Rarely used in environmental remediationdredging is contained aquatic disposal (CAD), where dredged material is placed back on the bottom yet in a different location of the water body. Dredging can provide some assurance that the contaminated media is managed in a setting more controlled than at the bottom of the water body. It does however come with significant risk of spreading the contaminationduring excavation, dewatering, transport, and disposal.

Capping—Similar to soil contaminated sediments are oftensequestered through capping, which is the installation of clean sediment, gravel, or manufactured materials on top of contaminated sediment. Capping can keep the contamination from migration of sometimes allowing for bioremediation processes to take place. Capping has been used in marine environments, lakes, and rivers. Each environment poses different challenges that can compromise the integrity of the cap, so careful study and modeling is needed to best predict outcomes. Most capping is considered passive, in that it is simply a physical barrier.

Active capping is a process by which the physical cap is supplemented by active materials that help bind or degrade the contaminants. Capping can be a cost-effective and relatively short-term approach to remediation contaminated sediment, but they require ongoing monitoring and replacement in the case of failure.

Groundwater

Pump & Treat—The most used technology for treating groundwater is called pump and treat (P&T). Contaminated groundwater is extracted to the surface (pump) and filtering through a treatment system (treat), and then treated water is discharged. Pump and treat systems are also known to help contain the migration of contaminated groundwater plumes by creating negative pressure underground, drawing the water in an area of influence surrounding the injection wells, preventing them from migrating to water wells, other aquifers, and other environmental receptors.

Water is pumped to the surface through extraction wells installed at the depths in the groundwater table known to be impacted by contaminants. The water is then treated in an above ground system using the appropriate technology. As with other technologies, the treatment system depends on the contaminant being treated, and may involve multiple types of treatment when groundwater has more than one type of contaminant.

Depending on the types of treatment and volume of water being treated, these systems can be relatively small units, housed in mobile trailers. Conversely, they can also be large systems housed in semi-permanent or permanent buildings.

While they are used to address many types of contamination, they are widely known to be effective at treating groundwater impacted by petroleum hydrocarbons, chlorinated solvents, and heavy metals. These treatments include:

- Granulated carbon filtration
- Electrochemical treatment
- Thermal treatment
- Chemical oxidation
- Aeration
- Others

Unlike in situ groundwater treatment, P&T systems offer the convenience of having direct access to the contaminated water, at which time several treatment options are available. They are widely recognized as reliable treatments that fit within regulatory regimes in the United States, Canada, and throughout Europe. However, unlike passive systems, P&T involves mechanical systems and energy demand that require regular maintenance and monitoring.

Regardless of the location, size, or configuration of the system, it needs electricity to pump water and power other systems. This power is not always readily available in the areas in which P&T is needed. In these cases, power must be brought in, either by connecting to the electric grid or creating an off-grid power source such as solar and/or wind. Not only does this come with costs, but it often requires permitting with the appropriate local and regulatory agencies, which takes time. Once operational, these systems require monitoring and maintenance for active remediation. These upfront and continuing costs are a major factor in determining if a more passive approach is preferable.

Air Sparging—An in situ treatment option for groundwater impacted by volatile organic compounds (VOCs). In air sparging, air is pumped through wells into groundwater. By exposing the VOCs in the groundwater to air, they volatilize. The air is then brought back to the surface through a vacuum extraction and treatment system removing the volatilized contaminants from the groundwater. The air pumped into groundwater can be amended, with additives that enhance the biodegradation process.

Air sparging is a promising technology because it removes contamination from the media (water or soil) and can be conducted in situ. Its limitations are driven by unpredictable and un-uniform subsurface conditions that can create variability in air penetration and extraction.

Permeable reactive barrier—Another technology for in situ remediation of groundwater is a permeable reactive barrier (PRB), offering a possible alternative to groundwater pump & treat systems. Acting somewhat like a filter, a PRB is a physical, yet permeable, structure placed in the subsurface. As groundwater passes through the PRB allows water to pass through it while contaminants are treated, either degrading the contaminants to less harmful compounds or to levels below regulatory thresholds. PRBs also immobilize the contaminants, thereby preventing their migration.

The PRB is filled with a "reactive media" that varies depending on the nature of contaminants being treated. Reactive media either works to chemically oxidize the contaminant or to biologically remediate the contaminants like other in situ and/or ex situ remediation approaches.

When selecting the reactive media, there are several factors to consider, including being a readily available source; having relatively consistent particle sizes so as to not block water flow; have a long life so as to avoid maintenance and replacement; and most importantly, something that will not become a source of contamination in and of itself.

Reactive media that have been used include:

- Activated carbon
- Zero-valent iron
- Limestone
- Apatite
- Zeolites
- Sand/gravel
- Ion exchange

If a PRB is the selected method, it requires confirmation testing over time to ensure the groundwater is continuing to move in the right direction (through the barrier), and that the contaminant levels are being affected by the reactive media. The benefits of PRBs are that they can reduce the time and cost of other technologies, such as pump and treat systems. Once installed, they tend to require less maintenance and are considered effective for several years with little maintenance. These benefits are not guaranteed but may be worthy of consideration in the right context.

Monitored Natural Attenuation—As with soils, monitored natural attenuation (MNA) is a strategy used to address groundwater contamination. See section on soils for more information.

Soil Vapor

Contamination in the soil and/or groundwater often volatilizes, producing harmful gases within the soil. These soil gases migrate to the atmosphere and even through foundations and into buildings where they can concentrate and pose human and environmental health risk. Mitigating these impacts is commonly addressed through soil vapor extraction (SVE). Ideally, these systems are installed as a part of new construction, but they can be incorporated into existing buildings.

The technology uses a vacuum/blower unit to draw soil gas up through extraction wells installed in the vadose zone soil layer. The gas is often treated in an above ground system, and then vented out into the atmosphere. As with groundwater pump and treat, SVE not only draws contaminated media for treatment but it also creates a pocket of negative pressure in the soil limiting the migration of the soil gas outward.

In many cases, SVE is accompanied by vapor barriers and ventilation systems underneath a building's foundation. A system of perforated piping is laid on top of the soils, with a vapor barrier laid over the piping. Common materials used for barriers include sheets of polyethylene or a latex-based spray. The piping is connected to vertical ventilation pipes allowing captured vapor to vent into the atmosphere, normally at the top of the building. The venting system can be passive, allowing natural air flow to draw vapor through the system; or active, using a ventilation fan to draw vapor through the system. Installing these systems is often done as a precaution, even when not required as part of regulatory compliance.

Common contaminants that create concerns over soil gas include petroleum hydrocarbons, chlorinated solvents, and methane. Naturally occurring gases, commonly radon, can also be addressed with vapor barriers and ventilation systems.

Structures

Brownfields are often left with the structures used during their former operations, and they, too, can have contaminants that require remediation prior to reuse or demolition. Common issues include PCBs found in fixtures such as light ballasts; asbestos used in siding, floor/ceiling tile adhesives; above-ground storage tanks (AST); and lead paint. Additionally, operations that occurred onsite are often known to have spread contamination throughout the building, saturating walls, floors, and heating/ventilation/air conditioning (HVAC) systems.

Contaminants in the soil and/or groundwater might also be creating vapor intrusion risk. All these contaminant risks, and more, must be considered when planning reuse and/or demolition. Reusing structures is often a highly attractive component of brownfield redevelopment. When rehabilitating the structures for an adaptive reuse, it is important to consider possible contaminants, including lead, asbestos, PCBs, and more. Methods of abating these issues usually fall into two categories—encapsulation or removal. In the case of lead paint, encapsulation is a relatively simple application of an additional layer of paint to seal in the lead paint. Similarly, asbestos siding and/or ceiling and floor tiles can either remain in place or be removed per the appropriate protocol established at the national, state, or provincial regulatory agencies.

Mitigating the impacts of vapor intrusion can be relatively simple, with monitoring equipment placed in strategic location in the structure. The monitors record levels of the contaminant of concern and send alerts if the concentration exceed regulatory standards. When designing the building's reuse, the HVAC system can also be used to ensure that contaminated vapor in the building is ventilated to the outside. In cases where vapor intrusion is more significant, vapor extraction wells can be installed through the foundation with extracted vapor either treated or ventilated into the atmosphere before it migrates into the structure.

Part V
The Future

57. The Importance of the Arts*

Jay H. Dick

Editor's note: Whether it's public art, placemaking, or public facilities that provide opportunities for artists and creative activities, art plays a big role in revitalizing communities. In cities like Seattle (WA), Emeryville, Oakland and San Francisco (CA), permanent and temporary art installations, art centers and creatively landscaped open spaces are integral ingredients in revitalizing and activating former brownfields.

What keeps you up at night with regard to your city or county? Crime? Opioid addiction? City livability? Economic issues? I would think that every city/ county manager would include at least one thing from this list. This is the life city/county officials lead: identifying and responding to the needs of your community—hopefully proactively and not reactively. As the topics are complex and nuanced all at the same time, this article offers an additional path to help you improve your residents' lives.

Do you use the arts and culture to help solve the issues list running through your head in the wee hours of the morning? Probably not, but that is starting to change as leaders are understanding the value that the arts and culture bring to the community.

When talking about the arts, what comes to mind? I would hazard to say that you are thinking about live theater, fine art galleries, the ballet, or opera. In other words, "high arts," perhaps art for the elite, city/ urban-centric arts, etc. But the arts are so much more than this, and they are actively working each day in your community, improving the livability and economy of your area.

Let's Dispel Some Myths

Myth: The arts are a tiny part of the economy.

According to the U.S. Department of Commerce's Bureau of Economic Analysis (BEA), in 2016, arts and culture contributed $804 billion to the economy, or 4.3 percent of the gross domestic product (GDP). For comparison to other industries, construction was $745.5 billion, transportation was $577.5 billion, and agriculture was $164 billion. In other words, the arts are larger than some of the largest industry sectors in America![1]

Myth: The arts are a big, black hole with no economic return on investment. As you can probably guess from the first myth, the arts positively impact local government budgets.

---

*Originally published as Jay H. Dick, "The Importance of the Arts," *PM* (December 2019, Vol. 101: 11) by ICMA, the International City/County Management Association; reprinted with permission.

According to Americans for the Arts' Arts & Economic Prosperity 5 study, in those regions that were studied, without using multipliers, the nonprofit arts contributed $27.5 billion to state and local government coffers. Given that nationally, all levels of government collectively invest around $5 billion in the nonprofit arts, this ends up being more than a 5-to-1 return on investment. Thus, the healthier and more vibrant a locality's nonprofit arts sector, the more the locality will collect in tax revenue (times five!).

Myth: The arts and culture sector are insular and doesn't affect other city/county issues/areas. There are at least 26 different topics that the arts authentically affect. These range from the obvious—arts in education—to the not so obvious, such as arts in healthcare to aid military veterans with their post-traumatic stress disorder treatment or to prevent suicide. The arts and culture also work to positively affect housing issues, community development, and city/county planning, to name a few.[2]

Arts and Culture in City/County Planning Community planning is more than likely a substantial part of your job. Did you know that the arts can provide creative tools to help planning and urban design professionals engage with communities affected by their projects? Using storytelling, visual arts, and technology such as social media and digital billboards, community members can play a significant role in designing safe, beautiful, and useful spaces that reflect community needs and desires.

Collaborative planning toward a common goal helps communities develop a sense of ownership among residents. There is a significant correlation between the attachment people feel to the place in which they live and GDP growth. And arts districts help retain vernacular culture, helping to arrest the homogenization that makes cities less livable.

All in all, integrating the arts into the planning of our spaces and places can make them more human, more accessible, and more innovative over time. Further, I'm sure most everyone has sat in a public meeting with irate community members upset about what a certain project might do to their community. No matter what type of project it may be—transportation, housing, or commercial—allowing the arts and culture to play a role in the process often eases opposition as the community feels more included and heard. For example, one research study reported that 20 percent of people who engaged in an arts-based community design process felt more ownership over the project and thus became supporters.[3] When people have a sense of ownership of the places they frequent, their communities become better places to live, work, and visit.

Boston, Massachusetts: The Department of Play is a nonprofit organization that creates temporary play zones in public spaces around Boston. Participants envision alternative futures, share experiences, and collaboratively create artifacts. It seeks to frame the city as a malleable, ongoing construction that any resident can experiment with and impact. The Department of Play states: "Our temporary play zones (TPZs) bring people together to imagine and create collectively.

TPZs invite passersby to engage in a creative mission in an unexpected public place located in what we term border zones—those invisible frontiers that affect residents' movement. In play, people explore their visions of the future and of other plausible worlds, while the border zones become momentarily shared places."[4]

Fergus Falls, Minnesota: These types of programs are not limited to large cities. In Fergus Falls, (population: 13,783), the local economic improvement commission, working with local arts and cultural organizations, created an original site-specific theater production on the grounds of the former Fergus Falls State Hospital based on interviews and story swaps with local residents about their connection to the building.[5]

Community Development Arts–based community development (sometimes called creative placemaking)—and the deep integration of arts and culture into communities' pursuits of healthier, more vibrant, more equitable places—has a long history in the United States that stretches back thousands of years to the first Native American tribes and laces through post-colonization history as well. Artists, arts organizations, and artistic activities in general can play a valuable role in the development and long-term health and sustainability of our communities. Research shows that communities with a vibrant cultural scene are more desirable to live in, have greater economic stability, and attract a more diverse and educated workforce.

Often when a community struggles with a social concern, arts projects can foster cooperative dialogue and bring about solutions and change. The arts drive an increased tax base, stronger social networks and community cohesion, reduced health risks, higher empathy, and more community pride. These things together make it possible for communities to progress toward their goals. As a result of using the arts for community development, communities often see an increase in tax revenue.

Phoenix, Arizona: The downtown Phoenix creativity hub yielded a 105-percent increase in tax receipts, compared to a city-wide decline of 1.04 percent.[6] Art and community development also strengthen social networks. Residents living on a block where community-based art projects took place were 1.6 times more likely to report that they felt more connected to the neighbors.

Saint Paul, Minnesota: The Irrigate Initiative was created by Springboard for the Arts along with the City of Saint Paul and Twin Cities Local Initiatives Support Corporation in response to disruptive construction of a light rail line through the urban core. Irrigate is an artist-led, creative placemaking initiative that mobilizes the skills and creativity of local artists to create innovative, meaningful, and authentic solutions to local challenges through collaborative projects. As Springboard for the Arts states: "The goal of artist projects that come from Irrigate is that by creating multiple small moments of surprise and joy and relationships, we can signal to neighborhoods that change is possible, that the people who live there can engage in and direct this change, and that their place is valuable and worth tending."[7]

Economic Development

Having a cultural organization in a community has been shown to increase the nearby residential property values by up to 20 percent.[8] Higher property values equal higher revenues as most localities' budgets are heavily based upon property taxes. Research into the role of the arts in economic development highlights five ways the arts work:

1. They create a fast-growing, dynamic business sector,
2. They help mature industries become more competitive,
3. They provide critical ingredients for innovative places,
4. They catalyze community revitalization, and
5. They deliver a better prepared workforce.[9]

Greensboro, North Carolina: Upon refurbishment of the Triad Stage, a downtown theater, nearby restaurants saw increased patronage of 20–30 percent on show nights. Its work earned it an Emerging Theater Award from the American Theater Wing, with acknowledgment of its serving as a catalyst to downtown revitalization.[10]

Phoenix, Arizona: The city's Cultural Connections program used public art to help revitalize Roosevelt Row during the 2008 financial crisis. The project titled "Ground Cover" involved an array of 300 blankets assembled on an empty lot into a floral mosaic.[11] The vast mosaic of blankets was displayed for a day, then disassembled and redistributed to the homeless. The project also resulted in increased pedestrian traffic and partnerships between city organizations and businesses.[12]

Site Remediation and Transformation Chattanooga, Tennessee: The Main Terrain Art Park serves as an example of using the arts and culture to accomplish multiple goals, including city livability, improving the health of residents, and stormwater runoff management. Indeed, the park does each of these seamlessly. The Main Terrain Art Park was a vacant 1.72-acre parcel of land just at the end of Main Street squeezed between two privately owned commercial lots. The parcel itself was narrow and long, thus, not conducive to any buildings or structures.

City planners, along with local artists and arts groups, devised a plan to fully use this space and transform it into a vibrant area. Now, the site has multiple, interactive pieces of public art that encourage residents to turn wheels, do pull-ups, walk/jog and other physical exercises. The site was also designed to help mitigate storm water issues by using the landscape to absorb and retain water run-off. The end result is a vibrant space that has attracted new residential development and is now seen as an asset to the community.

Conclusion

Hopefully, this article has offered you another view of the arts and culture as transformational to communities—something to be valued, supported, and encouraged. The arts are essential to the human experience beyond any economic value, and local government leaders should truly embrace the arts and culture given the immense opportunities they provide a community.

NOTES

1. https://www.bea.gov/news/blog/2019-03-19/arts-and-culture-economy-grows-29-percent-2016.
2. To learn more, go to www.AmericansForTheArts.org/SocialImpact.
3. Community Foundation Silicon Valley. (2001). "The Social Capital Community Benchmark Survey." https://www.americansforthearts.org/sites/default/files/socialimpact/files/3%20AFTA%20 fact_Arts%2BCivic%20Dialogue_v2.pdf.
4. http://www.deptofplay.com.
5. https://blogs.mprnews.org/state-of-the-arts/2014/09/theater-brings-fergus-falls-hospital-back-to-life/.
6. See Downtown Phoenix Partnership, "Annual Report 2012" (2013), http://www.downtownphoenix.com/downloads/17/annual-report-2012.pdf. Also, see Don Brandt and David Roderique, "It's Important to Keep Downtown Phoenix Alive," *The Arizona Republic*, November 27, 2010, http://www.azcentral.com/arizonarepublic/viewpoints/articles/2010/11/27/20101127downtown-phoenix-vision.html.
7. https://springboardforthearts.org/programs/irrigate/.
8. Markusen, A. and A. Gadwa. "Arts and Culture in Urban or Regional Planning: A Review and Research Agenda" (2010). *Journal of Planning Education and Research* 29(3) 379–391.
9. Federal Reserve Bank of San Francisco, https://www.frbsf.org/community-development/files/five-roles-for-arts-culture-and-design-in-economic-development.pdf.
10. "Art + Social Impact Explorer Fact Sheet," Americans for the Arts, https://artsandmuseums.utah.gov/wp-content/uploads/2019/10/19-AFTA-fact_ArtsEconomic-Dev_v2.pdf.
11. http://groundcoveraz.com/.
12. "Art + Social Impact Explorer Fact Sheet," Americans for the Arts, https://artsandmuseums.utah.gov/wp-content/uploads/2019/10/19-AFTA-fact_ArtsEconomic-Dev_v2.pdf.

58. How Civic Tech Can Address Urban Inequality*

STEPHEN GOLDSMITH

Editor's note: Technology is a critical element in planning for brownfields reuse. Online tools like interactive GIS data applications, including inventories, indicators and statistics inform reuse studies. Indicators such as WalkScore, EPA's EJscreen, ParkScore, Food Deserts, and H+T Index provide snapshots of livability, sustainability and environmental justice. Used properly, it can promote resilient reuse of brownfields.

For all of its best intentions, civic technology has long struggled with an inclusion problem. Data dashboards, web-based tools and mobile apps are typically built by relatively homogenous teams of developers for audiences that tend to share similar, relatively affluent demographic characteristics.

The acute growth of inequality in many of America's largest cities makes this problem even more pressing. As the urbanist Richard Florida put it in a blog post a few months ago, the "clustering of talent, business, and economic capability in large, dense, knowledge-based places ... carves deep divisions into our cities and society." According to Florida's research, growing inequality in cities is positively correlated with the urban agglomeration of high-tech jobs. Indeed, attracting and retaining the technologists needed to produce civic tech often comes hand-in-hand with the urban conditions, such as soaring rents and gentrification, that define the inequitable city.

Yet civic tech can play an important part in understanding inequality, formulating policy responses and delivering the necessary calls to action. Digital workers help address the economic divides of our cities when they create tools that better diagnose structural inequalities and amplify the voices of the underserved. And in the long run, we need to bring underrepresented groups themselves into the field of civic tech so that they can have an equal hand in designing solutions.

In Los Angeles, Mayor Eric Garcetti has worked with his staff and his Bloomberg Philanthropies-funded innovation team to begin unpacking the service imbalances that have long divided his city and many like it. Together, they are mapping residents' access to good schools, jobs, safe streets and other basic necessities critical to enabling upward mobility. Additionally, they are measuring the geographic distribution of wealth, income and economic activity to understand how the city's initiatives impact the livelihoods of residents.

---

*Originally published as Stephen Goldsmith, "How Civic Tech Can Address Urban Inequality," *Governing*, https://www.governing.com/blogs/bfc/col-civic-technology-urban-inequality.html (October 5, 2017). Reprinted with permission of the publisher.

With the understanding that analysis without action is meaningless, Garcetti and his team are using these maps to set goals and hold themselves accountable for meeting them. One such effort is addressing the problem of litter- and junk-strewn neighborhoods. The city built a Clean Streets Index, a map that depicts each city street coded on a scale of 1 to 3: clean, somewhat clean and not clean. Assessment crews manually input street-cleanliness scores into a mobile application that geocodes the presence of litter. Citizens are encouraged to help out by scheduling bulky-item pickup, reporting illegal dumping and volunteering for community cleanups.

Garcetti then declared that by 2018 there would be no city grid with a grade of 3. The Bureau of Sanitation responded by strategically deploying Clean Streets cleanup crews, and within its first year of use the app has driven down the number of unclean grids by more than 80 percent.

Once a city has identified a problem and conceived of a solution, the third—and most often overlooked—step is to make the data, visualizations and methodologies accessible to audiences from all backgrounds. In a recent Civic Analytics Network webinar, Lilian Coral, who just stepped down as Los Angles' acclaimed chief data officer, noted that by describing to city residents how the city was doing its data collection and evaluation she was able to engender trust in her team's process and commitment to improve the streets for all.

Still, cities face challenges in their efforts to enable residents in struggling neighborhoods to utilize the tools of civic tech. One approach is to work with intermediary organizations that facilitate diverse feedback and training initiatives, as is the case with Chicago's Civic User Testing Group, a foundation-supported civic organization that compensates individuals from around the city for focus-grouping civic tech products.

Another approach is to extend outreach directly. For example, with the support of the hip-hop artist will.i.am's i.am.angel Foundation and the GIS vendor Esri, Los Angeles' Roosevelt High School now teaches students how to use Esri's ArcGIS system to learn more about their communities. High-schoolers mapping brownfields and park spaces are not only learning about their city but also how to do their own research in the future. This direct form of recruitment will help ensure that the civic tech teams of tomorrow are much more diverse and inclusive than today's.

Through targeted outreach, we tap a recruitment pool that may help solve three problems in the long term: the shortage of data competence within government, the lack of diversity that encumbers civic technology, and the economic inequality that's taking place in the neighborhoods we're all eager to help. Civic tech not only has a tremendous opportunity to promote equality but also a pressing need to do so if we are to produce our best work.

59. Are Car-Free Bridges the Future?*

Alex Marshall

Editor's note: Why just bridges? Why not streets? The most vibrant places in cities and towns worldwide are those where people outnumber cars. Or where there are no cars at all. When people think of the best places to visit, people mention cities that are walkable and have good transit—not those where there's lots of parking. Automobile travel and parking are among the least sustainable uses of land. Autos stifle interpersonal interaction that generates economic activity. Single-occupancy vehicles are the worst culprit. Going car-free may not be possible. But going car-less is better for forward-looking cities.

From a distance, it's beautiful—white spears with delicate white strands holding up an arched roadway across the Willamette River. It's only when you get closer that it hits you: no cars. There are buses, trains, cyclists, and walkers, but no cars and no trucks. This is a big new bridge across a major river in a major American city, and cars were left off the invitation list. It's probably the first of its kind in a century.

The Tilikum Crossing in Portland, Ore., is in a city and state that have been at the forefront of ambitious planning efforts for decades. Since at least 1973, when the state's landmark growth boundary law was passed, Portland has made itself a denser, more urban city within a state that strongly prioritizes protecting both the environment and agriculture.

The bridge, which opened in 2015 (and whose name means "people" in the local Chinook language), fits into this agenda. Will other cities copy Portland? Will it work on its own terms? Before we can answer that, we need to understand better why Portland built it.

First, it wasn't actually Portland that built it, but TriMet, the regional transit agency formed back in 1969. When you look at Portland, what you see is a state, region and city that have been innovative in government bureaucracy and institutions, which has allowed it to be creative and forward-thinking in policy and planning. TriMet, although regional in scope, is a state agency that answers to a board appointed by the governor.

So why do a bridge without car traffic? Planners told me this allowed them to pursue several priorities more directly. "For years the political calculus was that you had to get car and truck drivers on board to get political leaders to buy into projects for trains,

---

*Originally published as Alex Marshall, "Are Car-Free Bridges the Future?," *Governing*, https://www.governing.com/columns/transportation-and-infrastructure/gov-portland-bridge-tilikum-crossing.html (December 2016). Reprinted with permission of the publisher.

bikers and so forth," says Ethan Seltzer, a professor at Portland State University's Toulan School of Urban Studies and Planning. "Tilikum says, 'Not so fast. We can do transit projects on their own merits.'"

Those merits were, first, that the transit system needed another crossing over the Willamette River. Another crossing allowed TriMet to construct more of a network of lines; before Tilikum, all the transit lines went over one old bridge to the north.

A second reason is earthquakes. Tilikum is the only bridge in the region built to modern seismic standards. If a big one hits, it may be the only one left standing.

And third, the bridge fits with and encourages the redevelopment of the east and west banks of the river, which are old industrial brownfield areas. The western side has already bloomed with tall condominiums, and the Oregon Health and Science University has many of its buildings on the west bank. The eastern redevelopment area has the Oregon Museum of Science and Industry.

These are all good reasons, but a bridge without cars has other advantages too. By building the bridge only for transit, the current roads, which are limited in capacity, will get very little new traffic. And you can move a lot more people across a bridge on trains, bikes, buses and foot than you can by putting them into individual cars. This means you can put more businesses and homes in an area, with fewer parking lots and roads.

"A bridge should be about moving people," says Veronica O. Davis, a member of the American Society of Civil Engineers' Transportation Policy Committee. "To some extent, we've been using the wrong metrics," she says, referring to her profession's previous, long-standing inclination to look first at handling cars when judging bridge or road utility and efficiency. Davis says she expects other cities to follow Portland's lead, either with new bridges or by retrofitting older ones for more transit.

That may be. But when I visited the new bridge recently, I couldn't help but notice some missed opportunities. Viewed up close, it loses much of its grace. There's too much cold, hard concrete. I know it may be sacrilegious to say, but I wonder if TriMet should have spent more money on it. The final price tag, $135 million, seems remarkably low. Could TriMet have built a lighter, airier bridge with more innovative materials and more skilled workmanship? Infrastructure should be built for the ages.

And the redevelopment at the ends of the bridge so far seems better in theory than in practice. On the western side, the lanes of the Tilikum quickly meet a tangle of highways and freeways. I saw few opportunities for creating inviting, vibrant spaces. The South Waterfront area of tall condos looked more like a part of Houston or Dallas, yet another example of the difficulty of building any new version of a walkable, urban area even in a place as progressive as Portland.

Give it time, planners told me.

Whatever happens, once again Portland and Oregon are setting a direction that others might follow. In a few decades, Portland has gone from a sleepy, faded industrial city of parking lots to a place people move to for its lifestyle of biking, transit, and artisanal breweries. It's got a booming economy and soaring real estate prices. The Tilikum fits into all of this. Time will tell if it fits in well.

60. Reuses of Brownfields

Tad McGalliard

Despite the expense, time, and complications of brownfield redevelopment, reusing our previously used land offers opportunity to accommodate our growing demand for development of all types. We can support our needs for new housing, commercial space, public facilities, industrial land, recreational uses, transportation, and conservation lands necessary to accommodate a growing population and economy. Using brownfields to do this saves land from development, improves environmental quality, limits negative environmental impacts of greenfield development, and does so efficiently by reusing existing infrastructure.

Housing

Brownfields can accommodate new housing, whether it is large multifamily developments or detached single-family home neighborhoods. It does, however, require more careful due diligence, assessment, and remediation. Regulatory standards vary depending on what country, state, or province's regulatory standards apply, but in general, housing is held to a higher regulatory standard than other uses because of the exposure risk to residents. In some cases, institutional controls may prohibit the property's use for residential uses.

In the United States, Canada, and Europe, former industrial uses were often located on waterfronts now desirable for other uses. Where access to rivers and harbors attracted manufacturing and traded sector industry in the past, population growth and increasing demand for housing in urban centers has led to using these prime locations to create housing, commercial, and civic spaces. This dynamic is not limited to larger cities. Even in smaller towns and rural areas, changing economies have left a legacy of brownfield properties that are now attractive to accommodate growth.

In Ontario, Canada, an 11-acre property housed a manufacturing facility and steel foundry from 1861 to 1988, leaving heavy metals, creosote, PAHs, PCBs, and petroleum hydrocarbons. After the property was rezoned to accommodate residential development, it underwent remediation, including a mix of excavation and disposal, bioremediation, and onsite soil reuse. Today, it is home to 598 residential units across 8 buildings, with a mix of rental and ownership units and housing for senior citizens.

Commercial

Former industrial land is often repurposed to accommodate commercial development, including retail, offices, grocery stores, restaurants, medical centers, malls, warehouses, automotive-related uses (gas stations, repair facilities, dealerships, etc.), hotels, and sports facilities. Many commercial uses, such as gasoline stations or dry cleaners, are also known to leave behind contamination. Regardless of the property's previous industrial or commercial use, environmental assessment and remediation is often conducted to accommodate new investment and growth in commercial development.

In some cases, these are completely new commercial centers, and in others, they are revitalized commercial corridors, or even single properties given new life. Similar to housing, these are not just urban projects, but are also found in rural and small towns.

What is now a LEED Silver certified, 100,000-square-foot Wilmington Convention Center (Wilmington, North Carolina), 600-car parking garage, and a 186-room hotel was once contaminated with several contaminants. Remediation was accomplished through a mix of excavation, disposal, and engineering controls.

Open Space/Green Space

Despite some misperception of incompatibility, brownfields are often redeveloped into greenspace, parks, and natural habitat. Regulatory standards can be stringent due to the potential for exposure, but the use of engineering and institutional controls, often used with other remedial measures, prove an effective means to turn a brownfield into a community and environmental asset. Properties such as former landfills are often well suited for such a reuse.

A 25-acre former landfill in the heart of Portland, Oregon's, Cully neighborhood is now home to Cully Park, a community asset providing recreation, urban agriculture, events, art, and cultural celebration. Key considerations included maintaining and enhancing the landfill's cap and soil vapor extraction/treatment system and leachate collection system so construction and operations would not compromise environmental or public health.

Renewable Energy

Brownfields are also helping the world meet its renewable energy demands. Projects around the world are using contaminated land to host renewable energy facilities. Brownfields with wide open spaces, like former landfills, are well suited for utility scale solar facilities. In addition to concerns about contamination, landfills are poorly suited to accommodate new development because of unreliable site stability. As such, solutions to make the land more productive are limited. Rather than letting this special resource go to waste, solar companies and governments are using them to generate electricity through solar.

In Hellsiek Landfill (Detmold, Germany), a structure was created serving as both a roof for the landfill, and a renewable energy generator, the 9.78 MW photovoltaic system includes 37,004 solar modules. This innovative project covered nearly 100 percent of the landfill site without spaces between solar modules, which allows the solar installation to double as a stormwater diversion system.

Transportation

As we continue to grow and reshape our cities and the transportation systems that connect them, we find brownfields standing in our path. Whether we are building new roads, highways, airports, marine terminals, and railways, or simply maintaining existing infrastructure, projects are often hindered by contamination left behind from previous uses. This is true for the infrastructure itself, but also the adjacent properties whose development is catalyzed by the infrastructure investment.

The Massachusetts Bay Transportation Authority (MBTA) reopened several stops along the Fairmount Rail Line in Boston from 2012 to 2019. The investment was made to increase transit choices for communities through which the rail line ran, but also to help catalyze transit-oriented development around the station areas. When planning began, stakeholders quickly realized that several of the properties surrounding the station areas were brownfields and required environmental assessment and remediation to accommodate development.

Industrial

While many success stories are told of the transformation of industrial land into something new, there is still strong demand for industrial land with access to infrastructure, making brownfields strong candidates. New industrial uses on old industrial land can take the form of heavy industrial, like an old steel mill operating in an older mill. Conversely, formerly heavy manufacturing facilities and land can be home to newer forms of industry, such as advanced manufacturing, research, and development facilities. For instance, a former aircraft manufacturing facility in Craiova, Romania, is now home to several types of industries including textiles, manufacturers, and more small-to-medium-size businesses.

All of the Above—District Scale Mixed-Use

A mixed-use development can also be developed on brownfield a practice which has become very popular across the United States, Canada, and Europe in recent years. This can be done on a site-by-site basis, or on a district-wide approach, developing brownfields into entirely new regional centers for commerce, living, and recreation.

In Iowa City, Iowa, an area south of downtown now known as the Riverfront Crossings District, was home to a wastewater treatment plant, industrial recycling facility, and several auto-related uses that were vacant or underutilized, limiting the districts potential. After extensive planning and public and private investments, this underutilized district is a growing mixed-use district with housing, commercial space, parks, and entertainment.

Brownfield redevelopment takes many shapes and sizes, each following its own unique trajectory from liability to asset. Despite the many challenges to their reuse, the development community, local governments, and regulatory agencies have developed a dynamic set of solutions. Put in motion, these solutions facilitate the transition of brownfields into centers for industry, housing, commerce, natural amenities, renewable energy, and public facilities.

61. Identifying Future Uses for Brownfields[*]

ENVIRONMENTAL LAW INSTITUTE

As information is gathered and sites prioritized, municipal agencies and community partners will be able to identify appropriate and best uses for redevelopment. Whether a site will be redeveloped by the municipality or by the private sector, it is important to work toward a known use from an early stage. Establishing a specific reuse or a general category of uses will help focus remediation activities. Projects that pursue cleanup before considering carefully the future use for the property may incur delays and unnecessary expenses, or may conduct remedial actions that run counter to the ultimately agreed upon use for the site.[1] Projects with an identified reuse plan and thus a clearer understanding of cleanup costs will be more attractive to private investors and to federal and state financial assistance programs. In addition, creating a vision for reuse can help to sustain community support and engagement through to the project's completion.

Against the backdrop of local real estate market conditions, reuse decisions will be influenced by environmental conditions, access to transportation/infrastructure, the need for community services, natural resource preservation, and a variety of other factors. While the evaluation of reuse options inevitably involves trade-offs between community goals, a vision for reuse that ties into established priorities can help can strengthen public and private support for brownfields projects. The New Jersey State Plan calls on communities to: "Identify sites and areas for redevelopment consistent with a community-based vision and consensus and prepare brownfields redevelopment strategies that coordinate community planning efforts with all levels of government."[2] A central consideration for local communities is thus the extent to which reuse options will serve the larger goals established in existing municipal and neighborhood plans that promote economic development and revitalization, expansion of green space, creation of affordable housing, etc.

Redevelopment to Promote Public Health. Whether a municipality plans to redevelop its own property or facilitate private redevelopment, there are good reasons to consider early on how redevelopment can improve community health. Municipal brownfields redevelopment initiatives typically focus on properties in communities that have suffered from the significant social and economic impacts of disinvestment and blight.

---

[*]Originally published as Environmental Law Institute (2010), "Identifying Future Uses for Brownfields," in *Advancing Public Health and Sustainability Through Brownfields Redevelopment in New Jersey: A Handbook for Local Officials and Communities*. (ELI: Washington, D.C.). Reprinted with permission of the publisher.

These communities also often suffer from a lack of community and public health services. On one level, any redevelopment plans for such properties will improve public health by removing unsafe and dangerous buildings, reducing exposure to contaminants, and addressing conditions that foster crime.

Beyond demolition and cleanup, however, there are many ways to advance public health when considering reuse options for specific brownfield properties. Establishing *walkable* and *transit-friendly* neighborhoods promotes physical activity and reduces air pollution from vehicles. *Parks, community gardens, and other outdoor spaces*—often lacking in distressed communities—can provide opportunities for walking, biking, and other physical activity, and can enhance civic pride and wellbeing. Moreover, green spaces can increase local property values and attract additional residents and businesses to the neighborhood. Incorporating *green building* principles for commercial and residential buildings advances public health by integrating indoor environmental and other sustainable design features. Redevelopment can also promote community health directly by providing *health-related services*, such as medical, dental, and pharmacy services, recreational facilities, and accessible grocery stores and farmers markets. Numerous brownfields projects throughout New Jersey have used these strategies to advance broad public health objectives.[3]

Practical Considerations for Identifying Reuse Options

▶ **Convening community residents and stakeholders to develop a vision for reuse.** Municipal officials should establish a process through which officials and key community stakeholders can fully and openly assess local needs, review the parameters of targeted brownfields properties, and consider the ultimate reuse goal. If the municipality has already created a brownfields working group or task force, this body can help facilitate public input and ensure ongoing outreach to residents. Including developers and business leaders in these discussions can add important insight into the constraints and opportunities for various approaches to redevelopment. A workshop or charrette can be an effective way to present information collected by the municipality and obtain community input on redevelopment options. In New Bedford, Massachusetts, for example, the city held a public charrette to enable community-wide participation in creating a vision for the redevelopment of a priority brownfield site. Over 60 people attended, including business and economic development leaders, planners, developers, nonprofit directors, neighborhood community groups, municipal agencies and other interested citizens.[4] Such a workshop can also lay the foundation for continued discussion about redevelopment strategies as the municipality obtains new information about site conditions and other factors.

Brownfields Redevelopment and Community Health Services

Brownfields are often located in areas where poverty rates are high, the population suffers from disease disparities, and the residents lack access to health care. Communities around the U.S. have succeeded in addressing public health as part of their revitalization initiatives, by establishing health clinics, community centers, specialty care clinics, and hospitals.

- The *Johnnie Ruth-Clarke Health Center Brownfields Redevelopment Project*, in St. Petersburg, Florida, received an award from EPA in 2005 in recognition for Excellence in Brownfields Redevelopment. The city Mercy Hospital, an historic African American hospital that had become a deteriorated blight within its immediate four neighborhoods. An extensive planning process established the need for health services at the site and selected the Johnnie Ruth-Clarke Health Center to occupy the site. The project obtained funds from various sources, including the EPA Brownfields Assessment Grant Program, the Allegany Franciscan Foundation, the Community Development Block Grant program, and the U.S. Department of Health and Human Services (for facility construction). The new hospital now employs over 100 people, serves several hundred patients a day, and is catalyzing other private investments. Source: *Revitalization through Brownfield Redevelopment: How Paterson Is Succeeding and You Can Too!* 83 (Env. Law Inst., 2007), available at: http://www.eli.org/program_areas/innovation_governance_pubs.cfm.
- In Clearwater, Florida, an abandoned gas station became the *Willa Carson Health Resource Center*—a free clinic for residents of the African American community of North Greenwood. The city had purchased the property with state brownfields funds and worked with the state environmental agency to complete assessment and remediation. Representatives of North Greenwood participated in redevelopment planning and recommended that the city relocate an existing non-profit clinic to this new site. The existing clinic, founded by community resident and nurse, Willa Carson, had been serving residents from a neighborhood building. Because the project addressed public health issues, Florida State Tobacco Settlement funds were appropriated for the construction of the new health care facility. The city entered into a 30-year, $1/year lease with the new clinic, whose largely volunteer medical staff provides immunizations, physicals, tests and screenings, flu shots, and counseling. Sources: Willa Carson Health Resource Center, http://www.carsonhrc.org/index.html; Florida Brownfields Assoc., http://www.floridabrownfields.org/SuccessStories/SS-WillaCarson.htm.
- The Gila River Indian Community (GRIC), an EPA Brownfields Showcase Community, facilitated the cleanup and redevelopment of a historic mission south of Phoenix into a *Diabetes Education and Research Center*. The GRIC, a federally recognized tribe, has a high poverty rate and the highest adult diabetes rate (over 50 percent) in the U.S. Using federal brownfields and other funds, the GRIC developed a comprehensive inventory of approximately 60 to 70 brownfield properties and assessed approximately 20 properties. The GRIC cleaned up several priority sites, including leaking underground storage tanks on the St. John Mission property. The property was then redeveloped into a Diabetes Education and Resource Center, which is widely used by GRIC community members. Sources: EPA, *Tribal Brownfields and Response Programs*, available at: http://www.epa.gov/brownfields/tribalreport08.pdf; *Underground Storage Tanks and Brownfields Site: Gila River Indian Community/St. John Mission*, http://www.epa.gov/oust/rags/az_gilariver.pdf.

▶ **Involving the local health department early on.** Municipal health officials can be important partners for identifying public health issues and bringing expertise to addressing those issues in the redevelopment process. Local health departments may be able to provide human health and environmental data about specific sites and communities and offer technical assistance in the decision-making process. They may be in a good position to gauge the gaps in public health services faced by different neighborhoods. Local health departments can also assist in coordinating and communicating with state and federal health agencies, such as the Agency for Toxic Substances and Disease Registry (ATSDR), which may be able to provide technical or financial resources for addressing public health in the brownfields redevelopment process.

▶ **Researching similar remediation projects.** Federal, state, and local agencies, as well as nonprofit organizations, have developed numerous publications highlighting the many successful brownfields projects that have been carried out across the county. It is likely that there have been multiple brownfield projects with the same intended *uses* as those being considered, and that those projects have been described in publications that are easily available. Alternatively, brownfields initiatives can research successful redevelopment projects that began with the same initial *property type*. There are many list of publications that describe successful brownfields projects by reuse option or type of property. EPA and New Jersey brownfields program officials also can help identify other communities that are willing to share their individual experiences directly.

▶ **Broadening the scope of redevelopment to access greater resources: brownfields development areas.** It may be possible to leverage greater state funding and technical assistance by scaling up a brownfields project. New Jersey's Brownfields Development Areas (BDA) program allows communities located within Planning Areas 1 and 2 to designate clusters of brownfield sites (a minimum of at least two sites, preferably within a contiguous area, however, depending upon the sites, they do not necessarily have to be adjacent to each other) for remediation and redevelopment. To receive BDA designation, the boundaries of the area must be consistent with the boundaries of a designated Redevelopment Area; there must be broad community support for the BDA; and the establishment of the BDA must result in a benefit to public health, public safety, and the environment.[5]

A chief benefit of the BDA designation is coordinated oversight and assistance from the state for all brownfields within the BDA, which is managed by a single Case Manager from the NJDEP Office of Brownfields Reuse. This coordination helps to streamline the environmental investigation, cleanup, and compliance process. In addition, BDAs are eligible for increased funding under the state's Hazardous Discharge Site Remediation Fund. An additional $2 million in grants per municipality per calendar year is available to perform assessment and remediation activities on contaminated property located within a designated BDA thus increasing the annual funding limit for that municipality to up to $5,000,000.[6] Interested communities must form a steering committee of local stakeholders and submit an application including the proposed BDA boundaries, sites to be addressed, a description of current activities within the area, detailed information on the demographics and economic conditions within the municipality, and a discussion regarding the planning vision of the municipality. According to the agency, it is important for applicants to have a strong and diverse steering committee for the proposed BDA and to demonstrate that their redevelopment plans are achievable.[7]

Key Resources for Redevelopment to Promote Public Health

There are numerous federal and state resources supporting brownfields redevelopment generally. Many of these programs—from EPA Brownfields Cleanup grants and HUD's CDBG funding, to New Jersey's Hazardous Discharge Site Remediation Fund (HDSRF)—can be used to advance brownfields projects focused on public health. Indeed, brownfields projects can strengthen their applications for competitive grant and financing programs by addressing identified public health needs.

There are also some federal and state brownfields resources that provide specifically for (or give priority to) projects with a public health focus. For example, up to 10 percent of a federal brownfields grant can be spent for *health monitoring*. This includes "collecting or linking baseline health and environmental measures to inform redevelopment planning options."[8] These monitoring activities may reveal a lack of health care services, open space, or recreational facilities that can be addressed through the brownfields redevelopment process.

The public health-related issue addressed most frequently by federal and state brownfields and redevelopment funding programs is *open space*—a reuse option that not only protects the environmental and natural resources, but also advances public health by providing communities with parks, recreation, and green space. In 2005, New Jersey's brownfields law was amended to specifically authorize use of the state Hazardous Discharge Site Remediation fund for recreation and conservation purposes. New Jersey's Brownfields Redevelopment Resource Kit provides a listing of state resources available by Land Use Option, including "culture/open space/recreation." Two notable state funding resources emphasizing open space are:

- *Green Acres Program.* This program, administered by NJDEP, provides low interest loans and grants to municipalities to facilitate acquisition of open space and development of outdoor recreational facilities. Green Acres encourages reclamation and restoration of former brownfields for use as public spaces, awarding one point in its scoring formula for awarding funds.
- *Environmental Infrastructure Financing Program.* New Jersey Environmental Infrastructure Trust manages this program in partnership with NJDEP, providing loans for brownfield remediation activities that improve water quality, including the acquisition of open space. Projects are eligible for loans at one-quarter or one-half of the market rate and for reduced financing costs.

In addition, the Association of New Jersey Environmental Commissions offers *Smart Growth Planning Grants* for municipalities to help develop local or regional plans, ordinances, studies or document reviews that protect natural resources and establish the land use patterns envisioned in the State Plan. Funds are awarded as one-to-one matching reimbursement grants of up to $20,000. Among the projects eligible for funding according to the 2010 program guidelines are brownfields or revitalization plans that include new open space.

Green, healthy building design and construction is another brownfields redevelopment strategy that can promote public health and is the subject of several federal, state, and non-governmental programs. The New Jersey Green Homes Office, within the Department of Community Affairs, provides a listing of financial incentives for developers of green housing. Municipal officials help connect local brownfields developers to these resources. (See http://www.state.nj.us/dca/hmfa/gho/dprograms/). Federal incentives for green building, which emphasize energy conservation, can be used to support an integrated approach to creating healthy and green buildings as part of brownfields redevelopment projects. (See http://www.dsireusa.org/incentives/index.cfm?state=us).

Notes

1. U.S. EPA Region 4, Revitalizing Southeastern Communities: A Brownfields Toolkit ("Keys to Success"), available at: http://www.epa.gov/region4/brownfieldstoolkit/index.html.
2. New Jersey State Plan (Statewide Policies) at 159, available at: http://www.state.nj.us/dca/divisions/osg/plan/.
3. For example, the cities of Trenton, Camden and Jersey City are using EPA brownfields grants for redevelopment projects that incorporate farmers markets, parks, and other community amenities to advance public health. For more information on these initiatives, see http://cfpub.epa.gov/bf_factsheets/.
4. See City of New Bedford, MA, Fairhaven Mills Site Public Charrette Final Report (2006), available at http://www.newbedford-ma.gov/Planning/Fairhaven%20Mills%20Charette%20Report.pdf.
5. N.J.S.A. 58:10B-25.1.
6. See http://www.state.nj.us/dep/srp/finance/hdsrf/factsheet.htm.
7. The program began in 2002, and as of 2009 there were 31 active BDAs statewide. For a list of BDAs, as well as more information on the BDA program and application process, see http://www.nj.gov/dep/srp/brownfields/bda.
8. U.S. EPA, Brownfields Public Health and Health Monitoring (EPA #560-F-06-210) (2006), available at: www.epa.gov/brownfields/tools/finalphandbffact.pdf.

62. As Cities Look at Options for Financing Infrastructure, They Keep an Eye Out for Low-Income Residents*

Paul W. Taylor

Faced with aging infrastructure that needs to be replaced or rebuilt, a handful of cities have been working together to identify viable financing models that would also serve the interests of their low-income residents.

Teams from Pittsburgh, St. Paul, the District of Columbia and San Francisco have completed an 18-month collaboration through the City Accelerator, an initiative of Living Cities and the Citi Foundation.

The infrastructure projects are as varied as the cities pursuing them. In the nation's capital, the D.C. team overcame public resistance to LED technologies in modernizing street lighting. The Pittsburgh team pivoted mid-project in its effort to extend the service life of the city's iconic public stairs.

St. Paul identified a latent opportunity for place making as it literally surfaced and underground water utility. And San Francisco faced the daunting challenge of preparing for the seismic reinforcement of its sea wall and began the work of confronting the prospect of a $5 Billion bill to address sea level rise.

Each of the city teams worked together for 18 months to find ways to balance competing demands of sustainable financing for major infrastructure projects and investing in the well-being of low-income residents in their respective cities.

During their final meeting together, the city teams reported out on their 18 months of work—all of which was captured in a special podcast episode.

Guests on this episode:

- Jen Mayer, Infrastructure Finance Advisor, Living Cities
- Seth Miller Gabriel, Director, Office of Public-Private Partnerships, District of Columbia
- Elizabeth Reynoso, Associate Director, Living Cities
- Kristin Saunders, Transportation Planner, Department of Mobility and Infrastructure, City of Pittsburgh, PA

---

*Originally published as Paul W. Taylor, "As Cities Look at Options for Financing Infrastructure, They Keep an Eye Out for Low-Income Residents," *Governing*, https://www.governing.com/cityaccelerator/blog/Podcast-As-Cities-Look-At-Options-For-Financing-Infrastructure.html (November 28, 2017). Reprinted with permission of the publisher.

- Wes Saunders-Pierce, Water Resource Coordinator, City of St. Paul, MN
- Kristen Scheyder, Senior Program Officer, Citi Foundation
- Brian Strong, Chief Resilience Officer, City and County of San Francisco, CA

ANNOUNCER: It's Living for the City, the voice of the City Accelerator, supported by Living Cities and the Citi Foundation and produced by *Governing*.

PAUL TAYLOR: We are talking about the City Accelerator, for the record, with Jen Mayer, the infrastructure finance advisor to Living Cities.

JEN MAYER: Hello.

PAUL TAYLOR: I am Paul Taylor, editor-at-large of *Governing* Magazine, and this is a special pop-up podcast with four cities that have been incubators of innovation, in creating a resilient and equitable model of financing public infrastructure. They are Pittsburgh, St. Paul, the District of Columbia and San Francisco. And we have a live audience here in the city by the bay, San Francisco. Jen Meyer set this up. What have these cities been up to?

JEN MAYER: Well, they've been participating…. Representatives from city government from different departments involved in infrastructure finance have been involved in an 18 month peer learning experience, looking at how they do projects, learning from other cities, and actually getting to visit projects in action.

PAUL TAYLOR: Let's meet our guests. Name, affiliation, and the briefest of descriptions of your project.

BRIAN STRONG: My name is Brian Strong, I'm the Chief Resilience Officer and the director of the Office of Resilience and Capital Planning for the city and county of San Francisco. The project that we're talking about is replacing our three-and-a-half-mile sea wall that runs from Fisherman's Wharf down to AT&T Ballpark.

PAUL TAYLOR: And the nation's capitol.

SETH MILLER GABRIEL: Hi, I'm Seth Miller Gabriel, I'm the director of the Office of Public-Private Partnerships for the District of Columbia, and our project is a conversion of our 75,000 street lights to LED lights, with a build out of free public Wi-Fi.

PAUL TAYLOR: The better of the two of the Twin Cities.

WES SAUNDERS-PIERCE: Hi Paul, I'm Wes Saunders-Pierce and I'm the Water Resource Coordinator for the city. Our project is about trying to find funding for comprehensive green infrastructure solutions at urban brownfield redevelopment sites.

PAUL TAYLOR: Finally, batting cleanup, Pittsburgh.

KRISTIN SAUNDERS: I'm Kristin Saunders. I'm with the Department of Mobility and Infrastructure, and I'm a transportation planner, and our project is looking at our 800+ public staircases that are historic right of ways and are looking at how to improve them and improve pedestrian access at the same time.

JEN MAYER: Great. Let's talk about part of the impact of being part of the accelerator, beginning with our host city of San Francisco. What did your team see, early on?

BRIAN STRONG: Thanks, Jen. I hope I can be heard here. Thanks, Jen. A lot we saw early on, and really, part of the benefit of getting here is that we had a massive infrastructure project that we recently learned was at seismic risk, that we needed to make some steps to address, and just getting our group together from San Francisco. Getting four people that work in very different offices and functions, including infrastructure, planning, finance, the Port of San Francisco. Getting us together, outside of our environment, just in and of itself, was really important. And then being able to follow up with that and share with other people. I think one of the best ways you learn is by sharing, and the opportunity to share and learn from the other jurisdictions we were with was fantastic.

JEN MAYER: And I don't know if the City Accelerator can take full credit, but I heard you got some funding shortly after getting the team together. Brian Strong: No, that's right. Part of getting people together is that you can move quickly and identify next steps, and one of those next steps was getting this project into our 10 year capital plan, and by doing that, we were able to secure $4 million in capital planning fund dollars. That's money that goes toward advanced development of projects, or pre-development of projects. And we were also able to secure $2 million from the Port of San Francisco for planning, along with $2 million from some of our other, larger departments that rely on this infrastructure.

JEN MAYER: Great.

PAUL TAYLOR: Second city toss-up, who would also like to address that?

KRISTIN SAUNDERS: The start of our project.... In decades, Pittsburgh hasn't looked at a comprehensive plan for the public staircases, so just beginning to actually scope that out and really understand what it means to look at a comprehensive plan for 800 staircases that sit in multiple neighborhoods across the whole city was really valuable in getting the right players at the table, to have that conversation.

PAUL TAYLOR: On that issue of right players, let's talk a little bit about relationships. How did you know who to build them with? How did you build those relationships, and a little bit on the results? Seth, maybe we can talk about the D.C. experience to start.

SETH MILLER GABRIEL: Sure. It's been great, just through the accelerator program, and our own program.... And incidentally, the accelerator program matched up very well to the District of Columbia with the creation of the Office of Public-Private Partnership, so I guess Jen can take credit for that too, if you want. We found it very useful, as we were trying to build the relationships for a new office, within the government of the District of Columbia, reaching out to larger, more established agencies like the Department of Transportation, Department of General Services, the Chief Financial Officer's office, of trying to explain to them what a public-private partnership is, and a lot of times, what it's not. Those conversations are always harder, to explain what a P3 is not, because generally, people have grand ideas and I have to break their heart a little, and it's not fun. We learned a lot about ourselves, and those relationships inside government, and it was great to take those fledgling relationships within the District of Columbia government and bring them to this setting, and learn and see what we were doing right, and what we were doing wrong with other governments, other cities similar to ourselves, to make sure that we're building the strong bonds that we need, internally, to make sure that our projects can be successful.

PAUL TAYLOR: Any heartbreak in St. Paul, or has all been joy?

WES SAUNDERS-PIERCE: Well, we've had some really good experiences in developing relationships, and one of the things that's really helped us a lot is relying on our innovation team to help provide a framework for us to work within, in terms of developing a project charter, and fleshing out, from the internal government side, who are the right people to bring to the table, and how do we really effect change with those people? How do we empower them? And one of the things that's been the most profound for us is, not only using tools provided to us by our innovation team to bring the right people to the table, but really getting it to a self-sustaining point, where we have relationships across departments, where people recognize the skillset, value the skillset, and can really move towards a common goal, even though at a day-to-day level, there may be competing agendas for program delivery between different departments. So it's been really fantastic to see how we've been able to weave together these different technical experts, and really get to a self-sustaining relationship as a project team.

JEN MAYER: That's great. All the City Accelerator participants came in with compelling projects and compelling stories. I'm interested in knowing how your projects evolved in the course of the accelerator. Let's hear from Pittsburgh first, because you kind of had a mid-course correction on your project.

KRISTIN SAUNDERS: We did. We had a major change in scope. We started this project thinking that we were going to look at an engineer's assessment, a conditions assessment for all of our public staircases. After bringing everyone in the room and talking to DPW, we learned how short-lived those structural assessments really are, and so we actually took on more of a planning project to understand the priorities for the steps, and really developing a prioritized list, so that we can then look at.... Maybe instead of 50 steps and the conditions assessment on a set of 50 steps, it would actually be projects that we could tackle in a reasonable amount of time, as that structural assessment lives.

JEN MAYER: And I would say, Seth's project had somewhat of a similar evolution, starting out as more of an engineering project and turning into a lot more outreach than, perhaps you planned.

SETH MILLER GABRIEL: Yes. No, you're absolutely right. I was just thinking.... When we first started, at the first convening, the idea that "oh this was changing over streetlights. What could be simpler than that? We're just going to change light bulbs. We just need to get the right engineering team." We quickly learned it was really not about streetlights. It's about the perception versus the reality of lighting within the diverse, urban area, where we have some parts of the District of Columbia that are very densely populated, some parts that are not so densely populated, and a national park in the middle of the city. How are we going to address all those different areas? And it was also very helpful for, well for me, personally. I think for the D.C. team, that coming to these convenings, we spoke to other cities that are living through the same process, and the realization of something that looks very simple and straightforward, and very similar projects to what is the reality of more.... I won't say selling the idea, but presenting the idea in a package that makes sense.

BRIAN STRONG: I mean, what could be more simple, I think, than fixing a sea wall in San Francisco?

SETH MILLER GABRIEL: Right, it's easy. You have it easy.

BRIAN STRONG: The problem, and I think we had a similar situation is that no one knows what a sea wall is. So, that's one of the things that we learned early on, from some of our data that we were collecting, is that.... Just like the term "infrastructure," it means a lot of things to a lot of different people. Well, we found out that most folks don't really know that San Francisco is supported by a sea wall, and the role that that sea wall plays in protecting jobs, and transportation, in a whole host of things. Tourism, a whole host of things that the city relies on, on a daily basis, to function and to be a place where people want to come and be.

WES SAUNDERS-PIERCE: I really think that data-driven decisions is so critical, when you're moving into uncharted territory for infrastructure delivery and.... One of the things that we did in St. Paul is we looked at new delivery of storm water management solutions. We really had to understand what the typical costs being borne by the private sector were, so we did research. We looked at five years of development projects within St. Paul, to understand what the capital costs of storm water management on those development sites was. And that is information that is really going to serve to inform our decision making in a lot of different dimensions.

PAUL TAYLOR: Anybody else on data and how it affected the project?

KRISTIN SAUNDERS: The Pittsburgh steps project.... We really use data in a couple of ways. We focused a lot of the project on public outreach, because the staircases are so well-dispersed throughout Pittsburgh, we really needed to focus on really getting out there to all the neighborhoods and making sure that we had input from several different sources, and several different means. We developed an online wiki map, so anyone could go from their home, or from the library, or from one of these community meetings and actually give us input on a particular set of steps, so that's one data set that's a little softer. You know, it is self-reported. And then we're also using the more technical data that comes from the U.S. census, transit data, GIS analysis, looking at the walksheds of the steps, to also determine their importance. So I think something that we've really learned is methods for combining those two things, in order to get to a prioritized list, combining the softer data with some of the more technical data has been really valuable for us.

JEN MAYER: Excellent. Well, a lot of the cities have encountered challenges as they're implementing their projects. What was the most challenging issue for you, as you tried to implement? I know that St. Paul was trying to change a paradigm, and kind of doing it in flight, so Wes, if you want to speak to that.

WES SAUNDERS-PIERCE: Yeah, absolutely. One of the biggest challenges for us is identifying a revenue source to pay for the long-term operation of this innovative, comprehensive green infrastructure system that we envision at these redevelopment sites. And, while trying to find the revenue in and of itself is a challenge, what really made it complex is the timing of redevelopment, compared to the initial delivery of the infrastructure. So, what I mean by that is.... What we envision is building out green infrastructure systems on redevelopment sites to serve future development, so the infrastructure will be there day one. But, the redevelopment may not come for many, many years, so where can a community find revenue to pay for O & M that will be necessary, day one, when the redevelopment that will benefit from that may not be there for several years. So really, balancing not only the revenue source identification, but trying to marry it up with the proper delivery, so we can have funds available, not only immediately, but also in the long-term for successful operation of these innovative systems.

PAUL TAYLOR: Seth, could possibly go wrong with innocuous LED lights when you put them in front of a public meeting?

MILLER GABRIEL: Thanks. Yes, correlated color temperature.... And I would invite everyone listening to this podcast, just Google that and have fun. That has really become the problem. We did not anticipate there being a public debate about the actual color of the streetlights. And frankly, that wasn't really a debate when we started, but it quickly became a global discussion about the hue of the LED light that's produced, and what is an appropriate color temperature for different settings, and what would be considered a safe color temperature. I'm the first one to admit that we probably were not as prepared as we should've been for that, but it was a good lesson for any city looking at new technology, or at least newish technology. The thing that's probably going to jeopardize your project the most will be the thing that you either least suspect or have no awareness of. So you have to plan for something you can't plan for.

PAUL TAYLOR: Did you end up landing on a number and a color at the end of the process?

SETH MILLER GABRIEL: No, we're probably going to have a spectrum of colors. It's been joked mainly by my six-year-old daughter that we should have lights that are a rainbow of colors that glitter. She has a mock-up. We did not accept a proposal from her. That would be illegal, but it would be brilliant. We are working very closely with the Department of Transportation, who will own this project, and they are going through a very rigorous process of testing different color temperature lights, to find one that is not only safe for all areas and different settings, but also effective. Because there's no point of changing over to LED lights, or any other technology change, if it's not achieving the goal that you want, and doing it in a safe way. So, they're working very hard on that. I feel that we'll probably, through this process of public debate and education, land on a much better end product, because we will have a better light for every setting, because we were kind of forced to get there.

JEN MAYER: Great. The work will not end here, we hope. This is the end of the accelerator, but what do you see the impact of this experience being, as you go forward? I know in San Francisco, you've produced the results of the finance working group on the sea wall and presented it, but how do you see this experience of the peer, cohort, going forward?

BRIAN STRONG: You know, it's a long trip. I mean, we're moving forward with some of the immediate plans to address the seismic safety of our sea wall, but to address sea level rise, it's going to be a $5+ billion project. One of the things that we really benefited from, from working with City Accelerator, was that we had access to a lot of professionals and a lot of information on different types of financings that we could use. We looked at 48 different sources of revenue, and different ways that we could do that, and the opportunity to speak with professionals was really helpful. Now we've whittled it down to about half a dozen or so, and it's going to be doing the tough work, which is collecting the data and really vetting those ideas and moving them forward.

WES SAUNDERS-PIERCE: One of the things that I think is a key impact for us, for St. Paul moving forward, is we're really learning how to take a utility, something that's traditionally been underground and buried, and we're trying to bring that to the surface, to create place-making and vitality for redevelopment, and doing that in a way that really is holistic. So, we can involve engineers, we can involve planners, we can involve our finance folks. But really, I think we're trying to transform our landscape by rethinking how we deliver what traditionally has been a very hidden utility. I think the impact is going to be on the future residents of these current, vacant, urban, brownfield properties, and will benefit in a positive way by having something that is an amenity for their new neighborhood.

PAUL TAYLOR: The City Accelerator was created by Living Cities and Citi Foundation with an explicit mandate to improve the lives of low-income residents, and how has that equity lens impacted the project, and how you've approached the problem?

BRIAN STRONG: Whenever we look at a project, we gotta look at multiple benefits, and how it cannot just prevent water from coming in to San Francisco, but also how can it help some of our lower-income residents in some of the areas of the city that are not benefiting from the economic boom that we've been experiencing. So, that's been a big part of what we're doing in looking at how we incorporate them, how we do education in those areas, how we bring in jobs for the types of work that we expect that we will be doing to improve the sea wall, how we bring the rest of the city into that discussion, and how we really engage them, so that this is not just something that benefits one specific part of the city, or one specific population.

KRISTIN SAUNDERS: Yeah, in Pittsburgh, our steps plan, I think, inherently had a low-income lens, because we are talking about walking and access to transportation and jobs by the easiest means possible, just walking. So, I think at the very onset, it does have that sort of low-income lens, but we're also trying to be really diligent about our outreach methods by using many different ways of reaching people to improve the input we get. We're going out to many, many neighborhood meetings. We're presenting the project at neighborhood meetings. We're bringing computers with us to those neighborhood meetings, so that if people don't have a computer at home, they have an opportunity to provide input at the meeting itself. We're getting volunteers to sit at senior centers and help them also put input into the wiki map, and so we're really just trying to expand the reach of our outreach.

In addition to that, we're also prioritizing steps based on low-income household rankings and access to transportation, which are both.... It's even more critically important if that set of steps that is providing a critical link to a major transportation facility from low-income residential neighborhood is out of commission, and so we really do need to prioritize those facilities that provide those links.

WES SAUNDERS-PIERCE: I think in St. Paul, we really, number one, have a very strong equity lens for how we deliver services, but also what we're trying to do is make sure that the areas that we're targeting for this higher performing infrastructure can be replicable no matter where it is in the city. We have the fortune of providing the initial innovation in areas that currently are low-income, and currently are high-diversity, so we're very happy about that. But we also know, as we move forward and have other opportunities to implement this type of rain-as-a-resource program, we want to make sure we can communicate about it, and also have support from all areas of our community, across the city. So what we're doing, to really make sure that happens is, as we look at our financing strategies, make sure we're not isolating, or disproportionately impacting those that might not be able to bear the cost, and making sure that the development community as a partner is paying their fair share, as well.

PAUL TAYLOR: And Jen, let's get super tactical on our way out here.

JEN MAYER: What is the one thing, tool, resource, site visit, way of thinking, that's had the greatest impact for you or your city? I know it's hard to choose. It's like asking what your favorite child is.

PAUL TAYLOR: But that is the question.

BRIAN STRONG: I would start with the trips that we took. I would really start with the heading out to New Orleans and experiencing and going through New Orleans and meeting with some of the people from the community and experiencing what they went through after Hurricane Katrina. I think it really sort of brings home why we're doing this work, and that it's really about the people that the infrastructure is serving. I thought that was really powerful for us to experience together, as a group, and I think really helped sort of galvanize us to move forward and push ahead.

SETH MILLER GABRIEL: Clearly the best trip we had was to Washington, D.C., so thank you all for coming. I imagine you all learned the most there. It is the prettiest of the cities. (laughs) But no, I think probably one of the things that I learned when we did go visit Denver, walking around their beautiful downtown, and how they've really improved their public transportation, but how that project that has universally been seen a net positive, has caused some other issues that they didn't anticipate. You can come up with the best possible project, but by your success, you can cause other challenges. How do you plan for those challenges that you create by being successful? That's what we've tried to work through on the streetlights. We'll see how that goes. But also, the public Wi-Fi, and the remote control monitoring, some very straightforward things that we think will bring benefits to the residents of the District of Columbia, but there's something that we're not thinking about that we're going to have to, then, have a whole other project and fix after we are done with that project.

PAUL TAYLOR: The one thing for Pittsburgh.

KRISTIN SAUNDERS: The one thing. That is hard. I think the one thing we learned is probably that data focus that I discussed earlier, and that was more through our consultant work, but we just really haven't had a comprehensive transportation planning process like this going on in the city. This coincided with us starting a new Department of Mobility and Infrastructure, so that we're really looking at transportation from planning, financing, all the way down to implementation and evaluation under one house, which is really exciting. And this step plan just happened to, or maybe catalyzed the process, and we.... This is kind of the first test for us, of doing that. I learned a lot from working closer with DPW crews. I learned that we pre-cast concrete steps in the wintertime when the crews are not working, and so maybe concrete's the best way to go. So, I think just really learning how to get everyone in one room for the first time, because we are starting this new department, has been the highest value for us.

PAUL TAYLOR: St. Paul taught the entire group that it prefers to spell out the first word in its name, but what was the one thing that St. Paul brought home?

WES SAUNDERS-PIERCE: Certainly. I talked earlier about relationships, and I think that's really a key part of what is going to have the greatest impact for us. One of the things that we were able to accomplish during the course of our accelerator tenure is we hosted a green infrastructure forum, and this was a daylong event that brought together multiple departments within the city, from leadership to management and staff. But we brought in outside experts from other parts of the country that had delivered high profile placemaking storm water infrastructure, and we had them as panelists, so we could learn from them. We had our own panel discussions as part of that forum, to help really start to address some of the myths, address some of the concerns, really start to think about the barriers for implementation. And that green infrastructure forum was really something that helped steer people towards a common goal and really understand the vision of what we were trying to accomplish. So, I think it really embeds the issues of relationships and how to really think about delivering infrastructure differently by addressing barriers. That green infrastructure forum was probably one of the things that had the most impact to our work.

PAUL TAYLOR: It has been a busy 18 months. Jen Meyer, what have we learned?

JEN MAYER: Well, I'll take the facilitator's privilege and have three favorite children. One of them is capital projects don't just live happily ever after. One of the things that in every city we've visited, the issue of how are you going to operate it, how are you going to maintain it, what happens after you build it really came up, and it's…. The capital planning processes really treat the project as the end of the game, and it really isn't. The second thing we talked about a lot was resiliency, and how to fund that when you know that protection like the sea wall, or avoiding future costs is what you're trying to deliver, and how do you finance against that? A lot of times we'd talk about our crumbling infrastructure, we look to capital as a solution, or to financing tools, or to delivery tools like P3s, and I always want to say, "It's the revenue, stupid," and how do you make revenue out of avoiding cost, and that's something that we're going to be talking about. Hopefully in the guides and the things that we look at, is a concept called nega-revenue, which I came up with as some way to name financing against avoided cost and really using those savings to deliver the infrastructure that can deliver them. The final thing that really struck us in every city that we visited, and every example that we looked at was equity. I think it's been, traditionally, a box that you check at the end of the project, and you think about, and you try to meet the quota, or the hiring goal, but you don't really build it in at the beginning. But I think we've found in a lot of examples that if you don't think about equity up front, it claps you on the back end, and sometimes quite hard. Really, looking at actual, tangible tools to deliver some of the value that these very big place-making infrastructure projects can create in communities, how to deliver some of that value back to the community before it forces the people who are living there out, just from an increase in value. And so we're looking at a lot of options, whether it's creating a community dividend like in Alaska, where the city retains some of the land and has the community that's living there get some share of the increase in development, or other options like community land trusts. Some way that makes sure that the places that you make are still there for the people that are there now.

PAUL TAYLOR: The work of the City Accelerator does not happen without the support of Citi Foundation. Kristen Scheyder, what have we learned?

KRISTEN SCHEYDER: Well first, I just want to say that we are so proud to have been able to partner with Living Cities and the four cities that participated in this cohort. We really believe that cities are in our DNA, and we want to be a partner. When we look at our estimates, we know that these cities across America need to spend about $59 trillion in infrastructure improvements over the next 15 years, and how are they going to do that? Regular resources aren't there. The U.S. government has dropped its spending on infrastructure down to 1.4 percent of the gross domestic product, so cities need to be innovative. They need to come up with new solutions. They need to look at things through a new frame, and so we were really excited to go on this journey with Living Cities and give four cities an opportunity to take 18 months and look at their priority projects in new ways. And I think one of the most dynamic things that came out of this cohort was the conversations that you all had with each other, and applying the lens of different cities' projects on your own problems, and making you look at things differently. So I think that it's just a journey that this country's just beginning. We have a long way to go, but you guys have set a really great example, and we're really excited about sharing your lessons learned with the rest of the country.

PAUL TAYLOR: Living Cities has been at the center of these discussions. It's done much of the heavy lifting and has had a catalytic and animating effect on the cities. Elizabeth Reynoso, what have we learned?

ELIZABETH REYNOSO: Investing in infrastructure means investing in people. We've been talking about, first and foremost, the outcomes and the vision, and that vision, as the heart of it, and the narrative that comes out of it is because it's for our residents. To be able to do that work means that we have to invest in all of you, all of the practitioners, all of the city departments that are represented in the infrastructure finance cohort. The beginning of our idea about, "What does it mean to have different perspectives? Be part of the conversation?" So, maybe economic development wasn't at the table in previous conversations before about the different projects that you've had, or that you didn't bring in the public works guy, the science guy like Wes Saunders, you know, peers, into a conversation until these kinds of conversations were generated. And I think that what we saw, when we wanted to get these ideas about what tools are you exploring, revenue and finance that…. Also, what you were exploring was how much expertise is within your own cities, that you are not yet tapping. And then, what expertise is in your communities that you could be pulling from. So as much as this was about infrastructure finance work, it was also about engagement. Engagement of your communities in a different way. A valuing of those residents, and their expertise and exposure, and the way that they experience your cities. And also, a valuing of your colleagues, and their work, their experience. Many of you have, I feel like, grown up within the cities that you're working in, or other cities that you've brought up. And so, I think that that is some of the heart of the City Accelerator, is that we invest in the people who are doing the work, who live and breathe in the cities and are trying to create a place for all to thrive. And your focus on low-income residents, as being the people who, if we serve them, and we solve for the issues that they are most impacted by, then we serve all our residents. So, thank you for the inspiring work that has been done, and I know that you're going to continue to inspire more of your peers around the country.

PAUL TAYLOR: That's why they call her City Nourisher on Twitter. Thank you, Elizabeth. Jen, you're putting the finishing touches on the implementation guide of the model of resilient, equitable infrastructure financing, with a special chapter on nega-funding, we just learned, right?

JEN MAYER: Absolutely.

PAUL TAYLOR: So, we'll have a link to the implementation guide, as well as some of Governing's work on public-private partnerships and all of that will be in the show notes at governing.com. That will do it from here, in San Francisco. Congratulations to Jen, the team from Living Cities, Citi Foundation. And as well, to the teams from the cities that have been doing the work themselves. Pittsburgh, St. Paul, the District of Columbia and San Francisco. Our audio engineer was Eric Koch. With Jen Meyer, I am Paul Taylor. Thanks for listening.

Appendices

A. Glossary and Acronyms of Brownfields and Economic Development Practices

Joaquin Jay Gonzalez III *and* Ignacio Dayrit

Acquisition: The process of acquiring real property (real estate) or some interest therein.

Agency: A government organization (Federal, State, or local), a non-government organization (such as a utility company), or a private person using Federal financial assistance for a program or project that acquires real property or displaces a person.

Appraisal: A valuation of property by the estimate of an authorized person for real estate or other property. A person performing an appraisal must receive authorization from the appropriate body of the state in which they reside. Real estate appraisals take into account the quality of the property, values of surrounding properties, and market conditions in the area. Valuations assist in determining the property taxes for which the owner is liable, as well as a potential sale price, if the owner wishes to sell their property.

Appropriation: Or expropriation are synonyms for the exercise of eminent domain powers. The term "condemnation" is used to describe the formal act of exercising this power to transfer title or some lesser interest in the subject property.

Artist Relocation Program: A variety of financial incentives aimed at attracting artists to live and work in their city or state, for example: exempting artists from paying sales and income taxes on their work.

"As is" sale: The transfer of a property to a buyer with no promises, assurances, or representations by the property owner about the conditions of the property.

Asset sale: The transfer of ownership of public sector assets, entities, or functions to the private or nonprofit sector.

Better Utilizing Investments to Leverage Development (BUILD): A U.S. Department of Transportation (DOT) discretionary grant program, where the DOT to invest in road, rail, transit and port projects that promise to achieve national objectives. Previously known as Transportation Investment Generating Economic Recovery, or TIGER Discretionary Grants, Congress has dedicated nearly $7.9 billion for eleven rounds of National Infrastructure Investments to fund projects that have a significant local or regional impact.

Bid Process: Public solicitation for sealed bids from private or nonprofit developers, suppliers, or contractors.

Branding Campaign: A vigorous initiative to promote the town or city as a brand to attract visitors, residents, and investors.

Brownfield: A site previously used for industrial or commercial purposes. Such land may have been contaminated with hazardous waste or pollution.

Business Climate: The environment of a given community that is relevant to the operation of a business; usually includes tax rates, attitude of government toward business, and the availability of capital.

Business Creation: A local economic development strategy that focuses on encouraging the formation of new for-profit and non-profit companies that are locally based and will remain in the community and grow in the future.

Business Improvement Districts: Or BID, is a private or a public sector (or in partnership together) initiative to improve the environment of a business district or area.

Business Incubator: An organization that helps entrepreneurs and startups plan, perform, and reach profitability.

Business Retention: Efforts by local economic developers to keep existing businesses in the community and to encourage them to expand their operations on their present sites.

Center for Creative Land Recycling (CCLR): One of the EPA's Technical Assistance to Brownfields (TAB) providers.

Certificate of Completion: A written verification from a state voluntary cleanup or brownfield program that a site has been cleaned up in a manner satisfactory to the state. In some states, a certificate provides liability protection but in most states liability relief must be obtained through another mechanism such as a covenant not to sue.

Cleanup Approval Letter: A written verification from a state voluntary cleanup or brownfield program that a site has been cleaned up in a manner satisfactory to the state.

Cluster Analysis: The examination of employment in similar industries, or clusters, for the purpose of determining strengths for possible industry attraction, expansion and retention.

Comfort Letter: A letter issued through a state voluntary cleanup program, that typically states that a site complies with the program's requirements, is clean enough for the intended use, and that no future enforcement action is expected unless conditions or uses of the site change. The letter typically does not provide legally enforceable rights such as relief from liability.

Community Branding: Multi-dimensional marketing on the positive differentiator(s) of a community, intended to help it stand out relative to the competition.

Community Development Block Grants (CDBG): Flexible funding tools that address a wide range of community and economic development needs, including decent housing, healthy living environments, and expanded economic opportunity.

Community Development Corporations (CDCs): Local non-profit organizations created to promote urban redevelopment.

Community Improvement Districts (CID) Act: Legislation authorizing local governments to impose and collect a community improvement district sales tax on retail sales.

Competition: Occurs when two or more parties independently attempt to secure the business of a customer by offering the most favorable terms usually through a bid process.

Comprehensive Environmental Response, Compensation, and Liability Act (CERCLA or Superfund): A federal statute that governs the investigation and cleanup of sites contaminated with hazardous substances. The law establishes a trust fund that can be used by the government to clean up sites on the National Priorities List.

Condemnation: Indicates proceedings for taking property by right of "eminent domain." Not to be confused with the condemning property uses for reasons of safety and health.

Contracting Out: The most popular privatization approach in the public sector involving the outsourcing of public services to business or nonprofits.

Contractor Certification: A process for assuring that contractors meet state standards and have state approval for performing specific tasks.

Contractor-Certified Cleanups: Cleanups where the state allows private contractors to make cleanup decisions on behalf of the state, including no-further-action (NFA) letters. Only a small number of states use certified contractors.

Cost-Benefit Analysis: A systematic approach to estimating the strengths and weaknesses of development alternatives.

Deed Restriction: A limitation on the use of a property that is recorded on the deed to the property. The limitations on use are legally enforceable against the owner of the property, but who may enforce the limitation depends on state law.

Developer: Also referred to as the "contractor," is a for-profit or nonprofit company which has received a redevelopment or economic development contract from a city or town.

Easement: In general, an easement is the right of one person to use all or part of the property of another person for some specific purpose. Easements can be permanent or temporary (i.e., limited to a stated period of time).

Ejectment: An action of ejectment for the possession of land usually for the removal of a contesting party. Issued for a party claiming land or other real estate, against one who is alleged to be unlawfully in possession of it. A "Writ of ejectment" is the name of a process.

Eminent Domain: The power to take private property for public use by a state, municipality, or private person or corporation authorized to exercise functions of public character, following the payment of just compensation to the owner of that property.

Enterprise Development: The assistance provided to entrepreneurship in a local community to assist entrepreneurs by connecting them to financial, human, and physical resources that can help them to start and grow their business.

Enterprise Zone: An area in which taxes and regulation could be lowered; these areas are usually set up in depressed areas, with the goal of encouraging investment and job creation.

Environmental Site Assessment (ESA): A site evaluation or investigation conducted for purposes of determining the extent, if any, of contamination on a property. An assessment can be informal or formal and can consist of several stages.

Exaction: A local government may use an exaction to require concessions from developers, such as the construction of sidewalks on land that will be developed. The exaction must further a legitimate public interest.

Fair Market Value: The price that reasonably could have resulted from negotiations between an owner as a willing to seller and a purchaser who wanted to buy it without any special considerations. The value of real property is assessed based on the highest and best uses to which the property reasonably can be put. Elements for consideration include the history and general character of the area and the adaptability of the land for future buildings.

Foreclosure: A legal action taken by a lender to take the collateral (e.g., a property) that secures the loan and to extinguish the rights of the borrower in the collateral.

General Obligation Bonds (GOB's): Bonds issued by a government entity that are backed by the full-faith-and-credit of the government agency.

Gentrification: An economic redevelopment and revitalization process in urban communities and neighborhoods, which results in increased property values but the displacement of elderly, disabled, lower-income families, mom and pop stores, neighborhood cafes, and small businesses.

Gentrifiers vs. Rustics: Pro-gentrification residents and businesses versus residents and businesses who are against (or for limited) gentrification.

Geographic Information System (GIS): Computer system for capturing, storing, checking, and displaying data related to positions on the Earth's surface.

Grants: Public money given to an entity, and the recipient of these funds does not have to pay them back.

Gravity Analysis: Attraction to shopping opportunities in a regional area depends on the size of the shopping (product assortment), distance, and customer sensitivity to travel time. Generally, bigger and closer are more attractive.

Green Infrastructure: The range of measures that use plant or soil systems, permeable pavement or other permeable surfaces or substrates, stormwater harvest and reuse, or landscaping to store, infiltrate, or evapotranspirate stormwater and reduce flows to sewer systems or to surface waters.

Greenfield Development: Development of land that has never been used (e.g., green or new), where there was no need to demolish or rebuild any existing structures. When there exist greyfield and brownfield sites with infrastructure, redevelopment of those sites may be preferable.

Greyfield: Land or property that is economically obsolescent, outdated, failing, moribund or underused.

Highest and Best Use: The property use that results in the highest present value and brings in the greatest net return over a given period or in the foreseeable future. This is a key appraisal and zoning principle employed in valuing any parcel of land or property. A property's value is related to its surrounding environment so the use has to be consistent with the neighboring land use at a given time.

Hot Spots: Specific areas where the level of contamination is very high.

Indian Community Development Block Grant Program: Provides grants to develop decent housing, suitable living environments, and economic opportunities for low- and moderate-income persons in Indian and Alaska Native communities.

Infill: Or "infill development" refers to building within unused and underutilized lands within existing development patterns, typically but not exclusively in urban areas.

Interest: An interest is a right, title, or legal share in something. People who share in the ownership of real property have an interest in the property.

International City/County Management Association (ICMA): Founded in 1914, ICMA advances professional local government through leadership, management, innovation, and ethics. Their vision is to be the leading professional association dedicated to creating and supporting thriving communities throughout the world.

Kansas State University (KSU, KState or KSU-TAB): One of the EPA's Technical Assistance to Brownfields (TAB) providers.

Leadership in Energy and Environmental Design (LEED): A sustainable environmental certification for facilities or buildings.

Leasing Arrangements: A form of public-private partnership. Under a long-term lease, the government may lease a facility or enterprise to a private-sector entity.

Lien: A charge against a property in which the property is the security for payment of a debt. A mortgage is a lien. So are taxes. Customarily, liens must be paid in full when the property is sold.

Loans: Monies given to recipients with an expectation of repayment. Public sector loans generally permit firms that have trouble obtaining loans through normal channels to secure financing either at or below market interest rates from a government entity.

Low-Income Housing Tax Credit (LIHTC): Subsidizes the acquisition, construction, and rehabilitation of affordable rental housing for low- and moderate-income tenants. The LIHTC was enacted as part of the 1986 Tax Reform Act and has been modified numerous times.

Main Street Program: Established in the early 1980s by the National Trust for Historic Preservation and now a subsidiary of that organization, is economic and community development in its best form. It is a place-based public program where a community's assets are analyzed and an economic development program built from those assets.

Market Value: The sale price that a willing and informed seller and a willing and informed buyer agree to for a particular property.

Master Plan: Or master development plan, is a comprehensive, integrated development plan of action for a certain area or zone.

Mixed Use Development: Any urban, suburban or village development, or even a single building, that blends a combination of residential, commercial, cultural, institutional, or industrial uses, where those functions are physically and functionally integrated, and that provides pedestrian connections.

National Priorities List (NPL): The Environmental Protection Agency's list of the most serious uncontrolled or abandoned hazardous waste sites.

Natural Resource Damages: Injuries caused to natural resources such as streams, wildlife, and wetlands by contamination from a site. The government can in some cases compel parties responsible for the injuries to pay damages.

Negotiation: The process used by an agency to reach an amicable agreement with a property owner for the acquisition of needed property. An offer is made for the purchase of property in person, or by mail, and the offer is discussed with the owner.

New Jersey Institute of Technology (NJIT): One of the EPA's Technical Assistance to Brownfields (TAB) providers.

New Markets Tax Credit (NMTC): A program designed to stimulate the economies of distressed urban and rural communities and create jobs in low-income communities by expanding the availability of credit, investment capital, and financial services.

NIMBY: Short for "Not In My Back Yard," is a pejorative characterization of opposition by constituents to a proposal for a new development in their area.

No-Further-Action (NFA) Letter: A written statement by a state government that it has no present intention to take legal action or require additional cleanup by a party that satisfactorily cleans up a property under a state brownfield or voluntary cleanup program.

Nonresidential Use Standard: A cleanup standard, usually expressed as a numerical ratio of parts of a specific contaminant to parts of the medium of concern (e.g., 5 parts of lead per million parts of soil) that describes the maximum concentration of the contaminant in the medium that will not present an unacceptable risk to the health of humans engaging in any activity other than residential or those other activities considered to be substantially similar to residential.

Opportunity Zone: Created under the 2017 Tax Cuts and Jobs Act to stimulate economic development and job creation, by incentivizing long-term investments in an economically-distressed community where private investments, under certain conditions, may be eligible for capital gain tax incentives.

Performance Agreement: Detailed write-up of expectations, targets, outputs for a task, program or project.

Placemaking: The development of quality public space that attracts pedestrian and other hands-on uses. The process suggests that communities can be built around well-designed places such as parks, downtowns, waterfronts, plazas, neighborhoods, streets, markets, campuses and public buildings.

Privatization: The government's use of business and corporate as well as nongovernmental organization and nonprofit practices to deliver public services.

Program or Project: Any activity or series of activities undertaken by an agency where Federal financial assistance is used in any phase of the activity.

Prospective Purchaser Agreement: An agreement between the Environmental Protection Agency (EPA) and the prospective buyer of a Superfund site that protects the prospective buyer from certain liabilities for contamination that is already on the site, usually in exchange for a payment of money and other commitments by the prospective purchaser.

Public Private Partnership (PPP or P3): Economic development partnerships between or among government, business, and nonprofits.

Public Use: Requires that the property taken be used to benefit the public rather than specific individuals. Whether a particular use is considered public is ordinarily a question to be determined legislatures with review by the courts. The courts have generally deferred to legislative intent.

Redevelopment: Any new construction or development on a geographic area or site that has pre-existing uses.

Redevelopment Agency (RDA): A government body in charge of redevelopment grants, projects, and policies.

Request for Information (RFI): A standard business process whose purpose is to collect written information about the public service capabilities of private and nonprofit contractors, vendors, or suppliers.

Request for Proposal (RFP) or Request for Qualifications (RFQ): an open solicitation to submit formal proposals or statements of qualification, often made through publicly noticed process by a public agency interested in the procurement of a product, service, or asset. The distinction of an RFP and RFQ is that RFPs typically require a cost proposal, akin to a bid, while an in an RFQ process, the winning entity is chosen through a combination of qualifications, experience and billing rates.

Revenue Bonds (RB's): Bonds where the principal and interest are repaid from the revenues generated by a capital project (e.g., toll road, museum, stadium, etc.).

Smart Growth: Considered a better way to build and maintain towns and cities. Smart growth means building urban, suburban and rural communities with housing and transportation choices near jobs, shops and schools. It is an approach that supports local economies and protects the environment.

Special Assessment: A unique charge that government agencies can assess against real estate parcels for certain economic development projects. This charge is levied in a specific geographic area known as a special assessment district.

Streetscaping: Street and sidewalk enhancements as part of urban renewal. It makes streets and sidewalks more senior, children, and disabled friendly.

Superfund: A United States federal government program designed to fund the cleanup of sites contaminated with hazardous substances and pollutants.

SWOT Analysis: An examination of Strengths, Weaknesses, Opportunities and Threats by a community or other entity. Often undertaken part of a community assessment or inventory especially where a marketing or promotional effort is being considered.

Tax Abatement: Contracts between a government entity and a holder of real estate that stipulated that some share of assessed value will not be taxed for an agreed upon time period.

Tax Increment Financing (TIF): a public financing method that is used as a subsidy for redevelopment, infrastructure, and other community-improvement projects.

Technical Assistance to Brownfields Communities (TAB): helps communities, states, tribes and others understand risks associated with contaminated or potentially contaminated properties, called brownfields, and learn how to assess, safely clean up and sustainably reuse them. EPA funds three organizations—Kansas State University (KSU), the New Jersey Institute of Technology (NJIT) and the Center for Creative Land Recycling (CCLR).

Toxic Tort Action: A legal proceeding brought to seek damages for personal injury or property damage incurred as a result of exposure to a hazardous substance.

Transportation Investment Generating Economic Recovery (TIGER): (See Better Utilizing Investments to Leverage Development [BUILD]).

Uniform Act (URA): Or the Uniform Relocation Assistance and Real Property Acquisition Policies Act is a federal law enacted in 1970 that establishes minimum standards for federally funded programs and projects that require the acquisition of real property (real estate) or displace persons from their homes, businesses, or farms.

User Fee: Or user charge, require those who use a public service or facility to pay some or all of the cost of the service.

Voluntary Cleanups: Cleanups of identified contamination that are not court or agency ordered. Most states have voluntary cleanup programs that encourage voluntary cleanups and that may provide benefits if volunteers meet specified standards.

Workforce Development: A human resource strategy focused on enhancing a region's economic stability and prosperity.

Zoning: The establishment by municipalities of districts or special areas that are restricted to certain types of commercial, residential, or mixed-use development.

References

https://www.eli.org/brownfields-program/glossary.

B. Brownfields Revitalization Act (2002)

Title: To provide certain relief for small businesses from liability under the Comprehension Environmental Response, Compensation, and Liability Act of 1980, and to amend such Act to promote the cleanup and reuse of brownfields, to provide financial assistance for brownfields revitalization, to enhance State response programs, and for other purposes.

- Small Business Liability Relief and Brownfields Revitalization Act—Small Business Liability Protection Act—Amends the Comprehensive Environmental Response, Compensation, and Liability Act of 1980 (CERCLA) to provide (with exceptions) that persons shall be liable for response costs at a National Priorities List (NPL) facility as non-owners or operators only if the total of material containing a hazardous substance that the business arranged for disposal, transport, or treatment of, or accepted for transport, was greater than specified amounts.
- Exempts a person from liability for response costs (with exceptions) at a NPL facility for municipal solid waste (MSW) as a non-owner or operator if the person is an owner, operator, or lessee of residential property from which all of the person's MSW was generated, or a certain small business or small charitable tax-exempt organization that generated all its MSW, with respect to the facility concerned.
- Makes nongovernmental entities that commence a contribution action liable to the defendant for all reasonable legal costs if the defendant is not liable based on the above-described exemptions.
- Revises conditions for de minimis settlements.
- Brownfields Revitalization and Environmental Restoration Act of 2001—Provides grants for inventorying, characterizing, assessing, remediating, and conducting planning related to brownfield sites. Defines a "brownfield site," with exceptions, as real property, the expansion, redevelopment, or reuse of which is complicated by the presence or potential presence of a hazardous substance or pollutant. Includes certain petroleum- or controlled substance-contaminated sites and mine-scarred land.
- Exempts from liability under CERCLA certain owners of real property contiguous to property on which there has been a hazardous substance release or threatened release that is not owned by such persons.
- Absolves from liability for response actions bona fide prospective purchasers to the extent liability at a facility for a release or threat thereof is based solely

on ownership or operation of a facility. Gives a lien to the United States for unrecovered response costs in any case for which the owner is not liable by reason of this section and the facility's fair market value has increased above that which existed before the action was taken.
- Deems a person, with respect to defenses to liability of an owner of after-acquired property, to have undertaken appropriate inquiry into the property's previous ownership and uses if the person demonstrates that inquiries were undertaken in accordance with specified requirements.
- Authorizes the Administrator to award grants to States or Indian tribes for response programs comprised of elements including survey and inventory of brownfield sites, public participation opportunities, oversight and enforcement authorities, and certification mechanisms.
- Restricts authority to take enforcement actions under CERCLA in cases of hazardous substance releases addressed by a State response plan. Authorizes the President to bring enforcement actions in certain instances where there is migration of contamination across State lines or onto Federal property, or there is an imminent and substantial endangerment to public health or welfare or the environment and additional response actions are likely to be necessary.
- Makes restrictions on the President's authority to take such actions applicable only at sites in States that maintain and publicize a record of sites at which response actions have been completed in the previous year and are planned to be addressed under the State response program in the upcoming year. Applies enforcement action requirements only to response actions conducted after February 15, 2001.
- Provides conditions for deferral by the President of final listing of an eligible NPL response site.

C. Brownfields Utilization, Investment and Local Development (BUILD) Act (2018)

[FRL-9979-38-OLEM]

SUMMARY: The Brownfields Utilization, Investment, and Local Development (BUILD) Act was enacted on March 23, 2018, as part of the Consolidated Appropriations Act, 2018. The BUILD Act reauthorized the Environmental Protection Agency's (EPA's) Brownfields Program, and made amendments to the Comprehensive Environmental Response, Compensation, and Liability Act (CERCLA), as amended by the 2002 Small Business Liability Relief and Brownfields Revitalization Act. These amendments affect brownfields grants, ownership and liability provisions, and State & Tribal Response Programs. The Environmental Protection Agency (EPA) is developing policy and guidance to implement the BUILD Act amendments. As part of this process, the EPA is soliciting comment on three provisions in the BUILD Act: The authority to increase the per-site cleanup grant amounts to $500,000, the new multi-purpose grant authority, and the new small community assistance grant authority.

Background

The Brownfields Utilization, Investment, and Local Development (BUILD) Act was enacted on March 23, 2018, as part of the Consolidated Appropriations Act, 2018. The BUILD Act reauthorized the EPA's Brownfields Program, and made amendments to CERCLA, as amended by the 2002 Small Business Liability Relief and Brownfields Revitalization Act. These amendments affect brownfields grants, ownership and liability provisions, and State & Tribal Response Programs. The EPA is developing policy and guidance to implement the BUILD Act. As part of that process, the EPA is soliciting comment on three provisions in the BUILD Act: The authority to increase the per site cleanup grant amounts to $500,000, the new multi-purpose grant authority, and the new small community assistance grant authority.

Cleanup Grant Policy

The BUILD Act amended CERCLA Section 104(k)(3)(A)(ii) to increase the ceiling for brownfields cleanup grant funding from $200,000 to $500,000 per site; eligible entities can request a waiver up to $650,000 per site, based on the anticipated level of contamination, size, or ownership status of the site. The applicant must own the site to expend any resources on cleanup at the site.

The Agency's primary concern is one of community access to brownfields cleanup funds. Increasing the amount of single cleanup grants will most likely decrease the total number of grants that may be awarded in any given fiscal year, therefore decreasing the number of brownfield sites cleaned-up and communities served, particularly when annual appropriations remain level or decrease.

Given these parameters, the Agency is interested in receiving comments from communities and other stakeholders on the following considerations:

1. If a community receives a $500,000 cleanup grant, how likely is it that the community could meet the 20 percent cost share statutory requirement (CERCLA 104[k][10][B][iii])? How would communities meet the 20 percent cost share requirement? Do stakeholders support a higher per grant funding amount, with cost share requirement of less than 20 percent, even if the result

2. is fewer communities will receive brownfields cleanup grants?

3. In your community's experience, how long does the average brownfield cleanup take to complete? Please provide information on the average length of time, including from the time of state review and approval of a cleanup plan to the time when the brownfield site is ready for reuse. What are the barriers your community experiences in getting a brownfield site cleaned up and ready for reuse?

Multipurpose Grant Policy

The BUILD Act established a new Multipurpose Brownfield Grant program. Under this new authority, EPA may provide a maximum of $1 million in funding per grant to an eligible entity to inventory, characterize, assess, plan for or remediate one or more brownfield sites within a target area. The statute requires that a Multipurpose Grant recipient own the brownfields property prior to expending grant resources to remediate the property. The grant funding may be made available to a grant recipient for a maximum of five years. While the EPA has authority to award multipurpose grants up to $1,000,000, the EPA is considering piloting the grants at no more than $700,000.

Given these parameters, the Agency is interested in receiving comments from communities and other stakeholders on the following considerations:

1. Do communities most need funding for brownfields inventory, planning, site assessment or site remediation activities?

2. Do communities typically have in place an "overall plan for revitalization of the one or more brownfields within the proposed area in which the multipurpose grant will be used" or would they most likely need to create this plan using multipurpose grant funds?

3. What is a reasonable number of accomplishments (e.g., brownfields site assessments and site cleanups) to expect from a grant recipient that receives a $700,000 multipurpose grant over a five-year grant period?

4. What complications and barriers will affect a grant recipient's ability to achieve these accomplishments?

128(a) Small Grant Policy

The BUILD Act added a new authority for the EPA to make grants to states and tribes to provide training, technical assistance or research assistance to support a small or disadvantaged community up to $20,000 per community. Site specific assessment and cleanup activities are not allowable expenditures under this grant authority. The EPA is developing further guidance on (1) the types of activities that are eligible expenses (including examples of such activities) and (2) the evaluation criteria that the EPA will use for evaluating and selecting proposals.

Accordingly, the EPA is soliciting comment on the following issues:

1. The EPA anticipates that state and tribes may provide the following activities to small and disadvantaged communities under this grant: Brownfields outreach

and education, technical support, economic or market analyses to support the identification of reuse options for a brownfield site, the implementation or use of the EPA's Land Revitalization tools, and preparation of a needs assessment for developing a Tribal Response Program. What other types of activities should be considered as eligible expenditures under this grant program?

2. The EPA plans to include the following evaluation criteria for proposals submitted under this grant program: Description of the target community, description/purpose of the proposed project, expected outcomes, description of key activities, what entity will be conducting the activities (e.g., state, tribe, contractor), leveraged resources being provided (as necessary), approximate timeline for completing the eligible activities, the amount of funding requested, an explanation of why existing state and tribal funding is inadequate to conduct or complete the eligible activities, and a demonstration of support from the community that will benefit from the funded activity. What other types of evaluation criteria may be useful for the EPA to use when evaluating proposals and selecting grant recipients?

Dated: June 6, 2018.

David R. Lloyd, Director, Office of Brownfields and Land Revitalization, Office of Land and Emergency Management, Environmental Protection Agency (EPA).

D. Model Brownfields Legislation for States*

ENVIRONMENTAL LAW INSTITUTE

To authorize the [Environmental/Health Agency] of [State] to take certain actions to facilitate cleanup and redevelopment of contaminated properties in [State].

BE IT ENACTED BY THE LEGISLATURE OF [STATE], That this Act may be cited as the "Brownfield Revitalization Act of 200-."

Section 1: General Provisions

Purposes and Findings

1. The purposes of this Act are to:
A. eliminate public health and environmental risks on property within [State];
B. create incentives for the voluntary cleanup and redevelopment of contaminated property;
C. develop effective and consistent environmental cleanup standards and cleanup processes for the [State];
D. ensure public involvement and public accountability in the cleanup and redevelopment of contaminated property; and
E. ensure that those responsible for contamination of property in the [State] are accountable for their actions.

2. The Legislature of the [State] finds that:
A. contamination of property in the [State] has hampered redevelopment, which in turn has limited job creation and improvement of the state's tax base;
B. a comprehensive program addressing assessment and cleanup of contaminated property is essential to protect public health, welfare and the environment consistently and fairly throughout the [State];
C. the public is entitled to understand how cleanup standards are applied to a facility through a plain language description of contamination present at a facility, the risk that it may present, and how any proposed response action will abate that risk; and
D. cleanup of contaminated land can and should be coordinated with plans for redevelopment and sustainable reuse of land whenever possible.

---

*Originally published as Environmental Law Institute (2010), "Model Brownfields Legislation," https://agh.eli.org/sites/default/files/docs/modelbrownfieldslegislation_1.pdf. Reprinted with permission from the author and publisher.

Definitions—For purposes of this Act

1. the term "act of God" means an unanticipated grave natural disaster or other natural phenomenon of an exceptional, inevitable and irresistible character, the effects of which could not have been prevented or avoided by the exercise of due care or foresight;
2. the term "applicant" means a person or persons who submit an application to participate in the voluntary program established in section 6;
3. the term "Clean Land Fund" means the Clean Land Fund established by section 8(b);
4. the term "completion report" means a report submitted to the [Environmental/Health Agency] pursuant to the procedures established in section 6(d) of this Act;
5. the term "[General Counsel/Attorney General]" means the office of [General Counsel/Attorney General] within the executive branch of the [State] government;
6. the term "due diligence" means the degree of care in evaluating property for past uses and other potential evidence of contamination prior to purchase consistent with sound commercial practices at the time of purchase considering the value of the property and the sophistication of the purchaser;
7. the term "engineering control" means any method of managing environmental and health risks at a facility by placing a barrier between contamination and the rest of a facility, thus limiting exposure pathways;
8. the term "Environmental Response Trust Fund" means the Environmental Response Trust Fund established by section 8(a) of this Act;
9. the term "facility" means (1) any building, structure, installation, equipment, pipe or pipeline (including any pipe into a sewer or publicly owned treatment works), well, pit, pond, lagoon, impoundment, ditch, landfill, storage container, truck, trailer, motor vehicle, rolling stock, aircraft, (2) any site or area where a hazardous substance has been deposited, stored, disposed of, or placed, or otherwise come to be located, or (3) any watercraft or other artificial contrivance used, or capable of being used, as a means of transportation on water. The term "facility" does not include any consumer product in consumer use;
10. the term "federal Superfund Act" means the Comprehensive Environmental Response, Compensation, and Liability Act of 1980, United States Code, title 42, section 9601 et seq., as amended;
11. the term "hazardous substance" under this Act means any substance defined as a "hazardous substance" by either (1) section 101(14) of the federal Superfund Act; or (2) substances designated by the [Environmental/Health Agency] pursuant to regulations adopted under this Act;
12. the term "Hazardous Substances Response Plan" means the Plan established pursuant to regulations under section 5(b) of this Act;
13. the term "institutional control" means a legal, institutional, or administrative mechanism designed to protect public health by reducing the potential for exposure to hazardous substances, including any measure to ensure that the use of a facility after completion of a response action under this Act continues to be compatible with the levels of any residual hazardous substances left in place at the facility.
14. the term "investigation" means a facility evaluation conducted for purposes of determining the extent, if any, of contamination on that facility;
15. the term "[Administrator]" means the [Administrator] of the [Environmental/Health Agency] of the [State]or any official or office designated by the [Administrator] for the purposes of administering this Act or any provision thereof;
16. the term "owner or operator" means "owner or operator" as that term is defined in section 101(20) of the federal Superfund Act;
17. the term "participant" means a person who submits a cleanup plan or completion report approved by the [Administrator] pursuant to the procedures for the voluntary program established in section 6 of this Act;
18. the term "person" means an individual, firm, corporation, association, partnership, consortium, joint venture, or commercial entity, the United States government and its entities,

departments, and agencies, entities of the states, territories and other offices of the United States, or the [State] including its departments, agencies and other entities;

19. the term "prospective purchaser" is a person not otherwise liable for a release who seeks to purchase property on which a release has occurred;

20. the term "release" means any spilling, leaking, pumping, pouring, emitting, emptying, discharging, injecting, escaping, leaching, dumping, or disposing into the environment (including the abandonment or discarding of barrels, containers, and other receptacles containing any hazardous substance). The term does not include:

    A. any release that results in exposure to persons solely within a workplace, with respect to a claim that such persons may assert against their employer;

    B. emissions from the engine exhaust of a motor vehicle, rolling stock, aircraft, vessel, or pipeline pumping station engine; or

    C. the normal application of fertilizer;

21. the terms "respond" or "response" mean:

    A. to clean up or remove, or the cleanup or removal of, a released hazardous substance from the environment; or

    B. to take such actions, as may be necessary:

      i. to prevent or minimize the release or threat of release of a hazardous substance;

      ii. to investigate, monitor, survey, test, assess, and evaluate the release or threat of release of a hazardous substance;

      iii. to prevent, minimize, or mitigate damage to public health, welfare or the environment that may result from a release or threat of release, including but not limited to, storage, confinement, perimeter protection, fencing, limiting access, collection of leachate and runoff, neutralization, segregation of wastes, recycling or reuse, diversion, destruction, treatment, offsite transport, incineration, dredging or excavation, repair or replacement of leaking containers, restoration of groundwater or surface water, providing alternative water supplies, temporary evacuation and housing or relocation of threatened individuals, and any other emergency assistance necessary to reduce risk to public health, welfare or the environment;

      iv. to dispose, or the disposal of, removed material; and

      v. to carry out administration, planning, oversight, enforcement, and cost recovery activities related thereto;

22. the term "responsible person" means any person liable pursuant to section 3(a);

23. the term "run with the land" means the attachment of a notice, restriction, easement, limitation or order on a property that survives the transfer or assignment of interest in all or part of that property;

24. the term "Scientific Advisory Panel" means the advisory panel that may advise the [Administrator] regarding the development of cleanup standards under section 4, the development of the Hazardous Substances Response Plan under section 5, review of cleanup plans under section 6, and perform any other functions the [Administrator] determines to be appropriate; and

25. the term "treatment" means to physically, chemically or biologically alter any substance or material for the purpose of reducing exposure or risk of harm to public health, welfare or the environment.

Section 2: General Duties and Powers

    a. The [Administrator] shall have the authority to carry out and enforce the provisions of this Act and the rules, regulations, policies and orders adopted or issued under this Act.

    b. The [Administrator] shall have authority to adopt rules and regulations for purposes of implementing this Act;

    c. The [Administrator] shall have authority to designate offices or personnel of the [State] to have specific responsibilities and perform specific functions under this Act and to delegate such responsibilities and functions.

d. The [Administrator] shall have authority to advise, consult, contract, and cooperate with the federal government, other state and interstate agencies, affected individuals or organizations, and industries to carry out the provisions of this Act.

e. The [Administrator] shall have authority to enter into cooperative agreements, cost-sharing and other agreements for which states are eligible under the federal Superfund Act and other federal statutes in order to further the purposes of this Act.

f. The [Administrator] shall have authority to delegate and assign, by contract or otherwise, duties or powers imposed on the [Administrator] by the provisions of this Act.

Section 3: Liability

a. **Liability**—Notwithstanding any other provision or rule of law, and subject only to the defenses set forth in this section, any person who:

1. owns or operates a facility;
2. at the time of disposal of any hazardous substance owned or operated any facility at which such hazardous substance was disposed of;
3. by contract, agreement, or otherwise arranged for disposal or treatment of a hazardous substance, or arranged with a transporter to transport for disposal or treatment, of hazardous substances owned or possessed by such person, by any other person or entity, at any facility owned or operated by another person and containing such hazardous substances; or
4. accepts or accepted any hazardous substance for transport to disposal, treatment or incineration facilities selected by such person, from which a release or threat of a release of a hazardous substance occurred or may occur or that contributes to a release or threat of a release of a hazardous substance, shall be jointly, severally, and strictly liable, for the following:

   A. carrying out a response action not inconsistent with the Hazardous Substances Response Plan;

   B. all costs, including interest thereon, of response incurred by the [State] or any other person pursuant to this Act and not inconsistent with the Hazardous Substances Response Plan; and

   C. the costs, including interest thereon, of any health assessment performed by the [State] or its designee that is not inconsistent with the Hazardous Substances Response Plan.

5. It is the intention of the Legislature of the [State] that this Act creates retroactive civil liability on responsible persons, as is consistent with the [State's] legal rights to abate public nuisance.

b. **Defenses to Liability**—There shall be no liability under section 3(a) for a person otherwise liable who can establish by a preponderance of the evidence that the release or threat of release of a hazardous substance and the damages resulting therefrom were caused by:

1. an act of God;
2. an act of war;
3. hazardous substances releases at a facility owned or operated by a third person, with whom the person asserting this defense has no relationship, that have migrated, flowed or moved onto the property of the person asserting the defense;
4. an act or omission of an unrelated third person, but only where the person asserting this defense also establishes by a preponderance of the evidence that he took reasonable precautions to prevent foreseeable acts or omissions by third parties;
5. an act or omission by a third person with whom the person asserting the defense has a contractual relationship and where the person establishes by a preponderance of the evidence that the acts or omissions are sufficiently outside the scope of the relationship that he could not have reasonably foreseen or prevented them;
6. acts or omissions that occurred prior to acquisition of an ownership interest in the property by the person asserting this defense, but only where the person also establishes by a preponderance of the evidence that he exercised due diligence in investigating the possible existence of releases before acquiring the property and that the releases were not discovered;

7. acts or omissions that occurred prior to acquisition of an ownership interest in the property, where the person asserting the defense is an agency or unit of the government of the [State] or a qualified economic or industrial development corporation and the person acquired an ownership interest through foreclosure for tax delinquency or condemnation to respond to blight or other threats to public health, safety and welfare; or

8. acts or omissions that occurred prior to acquisition of an ownership interest in the property by the person asserting this defense, where the person acquired the facility by inheritance or bequest

Section 4: Cleanup Standards

The [Administrator] shall promulgate or adopt by reference standards in regulations that are based on sound science for cleanups that will protect public health, welfare and the environment.

    a. **Standards**—Such standards shall include:

    1. [State]-wide numerical or performance standards describing concentrations of hazardous substances in groundwater, surface water and soils that will allow the facility to be used for any purpose.

    2. procedures that the [Administrator] shall use to establish, review and approve site-specific standards based on assessments of health and environmental risks at a facility.

    A. Such standards may rely on engineering or institutional controls protective of public health, welfare and the environment.

    B. The [Administrator] may designate through policy or regulation particularly described institutional or engineering controls that protect public health, welfare and the environment in specified circumstances, taking into account both the kind and extent of hazardous substances and the proposed land use, to be presumptive remedies. Persons proposing to utilize a presumptive remedy shall not be required to conduct a risk assessment prior to seeking approval of a proposed cleanup plan.

    b. **Scientific Advisory Panel**—The [Administrator] may seek the advice of the Scientific Advisory Panel during the development of such standards.

    c. **Interim Cleanup Standards**—Until such time that the cleanup standards required by Section 4(a) of this Act are adopted, the following standards shall apply to cleanups conducted under this Act:

    1. for hazardous substances in groundwater, maximum contaminant levels established pursuant to the federal Safe Drinking Water Act;

    2. for hazardous substances in any media, cleanup standards based on any rule or policy put into effect prior to the effective date of this Act by the [Administrator] of the [State] under the authority of any [State] environmental law; and

    3. for hazardous substances in any media for which no interim standard can be identified under subsections (1) or (2) of this section, cleanup standards established by application of the risk assessment regulations of the [State's] leaking underground storage tank program.

Section 5: Response Actions

Notification of Release

    1. All persons in charge of a facility from which there is a release of a hazardous substance after the effective date of this act, except a federally- or [State]-permitted release, in quantities equal to or greater than those determined in regulations promulgated by the [Administrator], must report such release immediately to the [Administrator]. For hazardous substances that are subject to release reporting requirements under section 103(a) of the federal Superfund Act, the reportable quantities for this section shall be the same as those specified by the United States Environmental Protection Agency unless or until superseded by regulation issued by the [Administrator].

2. The notice required under this section shall identify:
   A. the location, title, and condition of the facility;
   B. all information provided to the National Response Center or to the United States Environmental Protection Agency pertaining to such release or facility; and
   C. such other information as the [Administrator], by regulation, shall prescribe.
3. A person in charge of a facility from which a reportable release occurs who fails to notify the [Administrator] of the release as required by section 5(a) of this section, or who provides knowingly or negligently false information, may be liable for a fine of up to $25,000 per day and imprisonment not to exceed 3 years (or 5 years in the event of a second or subsequent conviction) or both.

Hazardous Substances Response Plan

1. Within one year of enactment of this Act, the [Administrator] shall, after notice and opportunity for public comment, publish in regulations a Hazardous Substances Response Plan. The [Administrator] may seek the advice of the Scientific Advisory Panel in developing the Hazardous Substances Response Plan.
2. Such Plan shall include, at a minimum, for cleanups under section 5(c):
   A. policies and procedures to require those persons responsible for a release to take or fund all response actions that may be necessary to protect public health, welfare, or the environment;
   B. policies and procedures describing site-assessment and characterization methodologies;
   C. appropriate roles and responsibilities for the [State] government, non-governmental entities, the federal government, and other persons in effectuating the Plan;
   D. policies and procedures to ensure effective public involvement in response actions;
   E. policies and procedures for evaluating the effectiveness of engineering and institutional controls at facilities with residual contamination that otherwise may threaten public health, welfare or the environment;
   F. procedures for identification, procurement, maintenance, and storage of response equipment and supplies;
   G. procedures to inventory and catalog release sites and set criteria based on protection of public health, welfare, and the environment for determining priorities among releases or threatened releases within the [State] for the purpose of taking response action, including methods for discovering and investigating facilities at which hazardous substances have been disposed of or otherwise come to be located; and
   H. procedures to address response emergencies.
3. Such Plan shall include, at a minimum, for voluntary cleanups conducted under the voluntary cleanup program established in section 6:
   A. establishment of a multi-disciplinary team comprising representatives of appropriate [State] agencies to assist developers and property owners in working through the [State's] cleanup and redevelopment processes;
   B. policies and procedures to coordinate permitting activities of several [State] agencies to create expedited permitting processes for voluntary cleanups and redevelopments; and
   C. policies and procedures to implement the voluntary cleanup program set forth in this Act including the issuance of prospective purchaser agreements.
4. The [Administrator] may revise and republish such Plan.

[State] Authority and Remedies

1. Access to Information
   A. If there may be, or may have been, a release or threat of release of a hazardous substance, the [Administrator] may request or order any person who has or may have information relevant to any of the following to furnish, upon reasonable notice, information or documents relating to:

    i. the identification, nature, and quantity of materials that have been or are generated, stored, treated, or disposed of at a facility or transported to a facility;
    ii. the nature or extent of a release or threatened release of a hazardous substance from a facility; and
    iii. the ability of a person to pay for or perform a cleanup.
  B. In addition, in response to a request or an order providing reasonable notice, a person either shall:
    i. grant the [Administrator] access at all reasonable times to any facility, establishment, place, property, or location to inspect and copy all documents or records relating to such matters; or
    ii. copy and furnish to the [Administrator] all such documents or records at the option and expense of such person.
  C. Confidentiality of Information
    i. Any records, reports, or information obtained from any person under this section shall be available to the public except upon a showing satisfactory to the [Administrator] by any person that records, reports, or information or parts thereof (other than health or safety effects data) if made public would divulge methods or processes entitled to protection as trade secrets. Such information or portions thereof shall be considered confidential except that such record, report, document or information may be disclosed by the [Administrator] when relevant in any proceeding under this chapter.
    ii. No person required to provide information under this section may claim that the information is entitled to protection unless the request for confidentiality is made in writing at the time the record, report, or information is submitted to the [Administrator].
  2. Entry, Inspection and Sampling—If there may be, or may have been, a release or threat of release of a hazardous substance, the [Administrator] is authorized to enter at reasonable times, and to issue orders as necessary to gain entry, to inspect and obtain samples from, any facility, establishment, or other place or property where:
  A. any hazardous substance may be, has been, or may have been generated, stored, treated, released, disposed of, or transported from; or
  B. entry is needed to determine the need for response, the appropriate response, or to effectuate a response action under this Act. Any such inspection and entry shall be completed with reasonable promptness.
  3. Compliance Orders—The [Administrator] may request [General Counsel/Attorney General] to commence a civil action to compel compliance with an order issued under (1) or (2) of this section. Where there may be a release or threat of a release of a hazardous substance, the court may take the following actions:
  A. in the case of interference with entry or inspection, the court may enjoin such interference or direct compliance with orders to prohibit interference with entry or inspection, unless under the circumstances of the case the order for entry or inspection is arbitrary and capricious, an abuse of discretion, or otherwise not in accordance with law; and
  B. in the case of information or document orders, the court may enjoin interference with such information or document orders, or direct compliance with the orders to provide such information or documents, unless under the circumstances of the case the order for information or documents is arbitrary and capricious, an abuse of discretion, or otherwise not in accordance with law.
  4. The [Administrator] may request [General Counsel/Attorney General] to commence a civil action for civil penalties for failure to comply with an order issued under (1) or (2) of this section. The court may assess a civil penalty not to exceed $25,000 for each day of non-compliance against any person who unreasonably fails to comply with an order issued under paragraphs (1) or (2) of this subsection.
  5. Other Authority—Nothing in this section shall preclude the [Administrator] from securing access or obtaining information in any other lawful manner.
  6. Response Action Authority—General

A. Whenever there is a release or threat of release of a hazardous substance that results or may result in an exceedance of the cleanup standards established in this Act, the [Administrator] shall have authority to issue orders directing responsible persons to take response actions to address the release or threat of release of a hazardous substances.

B. After an order becomes final:

i. the [Administrator] is authorized to request [General Counsel/Attorney General] to bring an action in a court of competent jurisdiction, to compel compliance with the order; or

ii. upon failure of a person to comply with an order, the [Administrator] may take any response actions consistent with the Hazardous Substances Response Plan that are necessary to protect public health, welfare or the environment, and the [Administrator] is authorized to request [General Counsel/Attorney General] to bring an action in a court of competent jurisdiction to recover from such person the costs of the response action taken under this paragraph.

C. Any person who without sufficient cause willfully violates, or fails or refuses to comply with, any final order of the [Administrator] issued pursuant to this section, may be liable for:

i. a civil penalty not to exceed $25,000 for each day in which such violation occurs or such failure to comply continues;

ii. an amount not to exceed three times the amount of any costs expended from the Environmental Response Trust Fund as a result of such failure to take proper action.

D. Notwithstanding any other provisions of this section, the [Administrator] may take any response action consistent with the Hazardous Substances Response Plan necessary to protect public health, welfare and the environment without having first issued an order when the [Administrator] is unable to identify a responsible person. The [Administrator] is authorized to request [General Counsel/Attorney General] to bring an action in a court of competent jurisdiction to recover the costs of the response action taken under this paragraph if the [Administrator] identifies a responsible person after initiating a response action.

7. Imminent and Substantial Endangerment Response Action Authority

A. When the [Administrator] determines there may be an imminent and substantial endangerment to the public health, welfare or environment because of a release or threat of release of a hazardous substance from a facility, he may issue such orders as may be necessary to protect public health, welfare and the environment and may request the [General Counsel/Attorney General] to commence a civil action in a court of competent jurisdiction to compel compliance with any such final order.

B. The [Administrator] may take any response actions consistent with the Hazardous Substances Response Plan that are necessary to protect public health, welfare or the environment, where an order has been issued to a responsible person and there has not been compliance with the order, or it is impracticable to issue an order to a responsible person and the [Administrator] is authorized to request [General Counsel/Attorney General] to bring an action in a court of competent jurisdiction to recover from such person the costs of the response action taken under this paragraph.

C. Any person who without sufficient cause willfully violates, or fails or refuses to comply with, any order of the [Administrator] issued pursuant to this section, may be liable for:

i. a civil penalty not to exceed $25,000 for each day in which such violation occurs or such failure to comply continues;

ii. an amount equal to three times the amount of any costs expended from the Environmental Response Trust Fund as a result of such failure to take proper action.

D. Any person who receives and complies with the terms of any order issued under this section may within 60 days after completion of the required action, petition the [Administrator] for reimbursement from the Environmental Response Trust Fund for the reasonable costs of such action, plus interest. To obtain reimbursement, the petitioner shall establish by a preponderance of the evidence that:

i. it is not liable for response costs under section 3 of this Act and that costs for which it seeks reimbursement are reasonable in light of the action required by the relevant order; or

ii. that the response action required by the order was inconsistent with the Hazardous Substances Response Plan, provided that reimbursement shall be limited to costs incurred under the order that are inconsistent with the Hazardous Substances Response Plan.

E. If the [Administrator] refuses to grant all or part of a petition made under this section, the petitioner may within 30 days of issuance of the [Administrator's] decision file an appeal in a court of competent jurisdiction.

8. The [Administrator] shall make best efforts to identify, and seek response actions from, as many responsible persons as is reasonable under the circumstances when issuing an order under (6) and (7) of this section.

9. Limitations on Response Authority—Unless the [Administrator] determines that a release or threat of a release presents an imminent and substantial endangerment to public health, welfare or the environment and no other person with authority and capability to respond will do so in a timely manner, the [Administrator] shall not provide for a response action under this section to a release or threat of release:

A. of a naturally occurring substance in its unaltered form, or altered solely through naturally occurring processes or phenomena, from a location where it is naturally found;

B. from products which are part of the structure of, and result in exposure within, residential buildings, businesses or community structures; or

C. into public or private drinking water supplies or sewage systems due to deterioration of the system through ordinary use.

10. Settlement Authority—The [Administrator], in his discretion, may enter into an agreement with any person, including a responsible person under Section 3, to perform response action if the [Administrator] determines that such action will be done properly by such person.

A. Such agreements shall be subject to public notice and comment.

B. Such agreements may include limited covenants not to sue for contamination addressed in compliance with the terms of the agreement and may provide that the person or persons shall not be liable to any other person for any response costs relating to any contamination addressed in compliance with the terms of the agreement.

C. As part of such agreements, the [Administrator] may find a person eligible to participate in the voluntary cleanup under Section 6.

11. Contribution Actions—Any person may seek contribution from any other person who is liable under section 3 of this Act during or following any civil action under the Act. Such claims shall be brought in a court of competent jurisdiction and shall be governed by [State] law. In resolving contribution claims the court may allocate response costs among liable parties using such equitable factors as the court determines are appropriate. Nothing in this section shall diminish the right of any person to bring an action for contribution in the absence of a civil action under section 5(c) of this Act. A person who has resolved its liability to the [State] in an administrative or judicially approved settlement or has been issued a certificate of completion under section 6 shall not be liable for claims for contribution regarding matters addressed in the settlement. Such settlement does not discharge any other responsible persons unless its terms provide, but it reduces the liability of the others by the amount of the settlement.

12. Citizen Suits

A. Any person may commence an action to compel the [Administrator] to perform any nondiscretionary duty under this Act. At least 60 days before commencing the action, the person shall give written notice of intent to sue by registered or certified mail or personal delivery of such notice to the [Administrator] and [General Counsel/Attorney General]. The court may award attorney's fees and other costs to a substantially prevailing party in the action.

B. Any person may commence a civil action on his own behalf against any person, including the [State], the United States, and any other governmental instrumentality or agency, to the extent permitted by the Eleventh Amendment to the Constitution, who is alleged to be in violation of any standard, regulation, requirement or order which has become effective pursuant to this Act. At least sixty days before commencing the action, the person shall give written notice of the violation in the manner prescribed in subsection (1) of this section to the [Administrator] and any alleged violator of the standard, regulation requirement or order. No action may be commenced if the [Administrator] has commenced and is diligently prosecuting an action under this Act or any other law to require compliance with the standard, regulation, requirement or order concerned.

13. Statute of Limitations

A. An action by or on behalf of the [Administrator] to recover the costs of response action under this section must be commenced within 6 years after the initiation of physical on-site response work.

B. An action to compel the [Administrator] or any other person to perform a duty brought under this section must be commenced within 2 years after the date that the duty became nondiscretionary.

C. Relationship with Other Law—It is the intention of the Legislature of the [State] that this Act is complementary of other laws in the [State] relating to the protection of the environment and public health. Nothing in this Act shall prevent the [Administrator] or other authorized official of the [State] from responding to any actual or threatened release of any hazardous substance to the environment, or any noncompliance with any law established for the protection of the environment or public health, pursuant to any other applicable law in lieu of or in addition to the provisions of this Act.

Section 6: Voluntary Cleanup

Eligibility

1. No person shall be eligible to conduct a voluntary cleanup of a facility pursuant to this section unless he first submits an application to the [Administrator] using procedures established in the Hazardous Substances Response Plan.

2. The [Administrator] may deny an application to conduct a voluntary cleanup pursuant to this section if the [Administrator] determines that:

A. the facility is listed on the National Priorities List of the federal Superfund Act or is the subject of an ongoing enforcement proceeding under a [State] or federal environmental statute or program; or

B. there are grounds to believe that the applicant lacks the intent or ability to implement a response action that will protect public health, welfare and the environment.

Voluntary Cleanup Standards

All cleanups conducted under this Act shall protect public health, welfare and the environment. This standard may be met by either meeting:

1. [State]-wide numerical standards established by the [Administrator] in accordance with the procedures and methods in section 4; or

2. site-specific standards established or approved by the [Administrator] in accordance with the procedures and methods established pursuant to section 4.

Cleanup Plans and Procedures

1. An applicant shall submit to the [Administrator] a proposed cleanup plan that demonstrates how it will achieve the applicable cleanup standards. The applicant shall provide notice of the proposed plan as provided in section 6(j). The proposed plan shall conform to any applicable requirements for voluntary cleanups set forth in the Hazardous Substances Response Plan and shall include sufficient information about the future use of the facility and

the long-term reliability of any engineering and institutional controls for the [Administrator] to determine whether the plan will meet the applicable cleanup standards. The proposed plan shall also include a brief description of the location of the facility, and a site characterization report.

    2. Review and Approval of Cleanup Plans

    A. The [Administrator] shall review the proposed cleanup plan within 90 days and may approve the plan if the plan demonstrates that the cleanup will achieve the applicable standards and all applicable requirements set forth in the Hazardous Substances Response Plan. The [Administrator] may consult the Scientific Advisory Panel concerning the adequacy of a proposed cleanup plan. The [Administrator] may request the applicant to provide additional information if necessary to make a determination as to whether the plan will achieve the applicable standards. The 90 day review period will toll upon issuance of a request for additional information and resume when the requested information is received from the participant.

    B. The [Administrator] shall consider any comments received pursuant to section 6(j) on the proposed plan in determining if the proposed plan should be approved.

    C. The [Administrator] shall determine whether the proposed plan will achieve the applicable standards and any applicable requirements of the Hazardous Substances Response Plan and shall provide a written explanation of the determination, including responses to comments, which shall be provided to the applicant and made available to the public.

    D. The applicant may submit a revised cleanup plan at any time for review pursuant to this section.

    E. If the [Administrator] does not provide a written explanation of his determination under section (2)(C) of this section within 90 days of the filing of a proposed plan, a participant, upon request, is entitled to a meeting with the [Administrator] for purposes of determining the status of the proposed plan and the [Administrator's] timetable for completing review of the proposed plan. Such meeting shall be held within 10 days after the request for a meeting has been filed.

Oversight and Review of Cleanups

    1. A participant shall grant right of access to the facility to the [Administrator] for the purpose of verifying progress in meeting the cleanup plan.

    2. Completion Reports and Certificates of Completion

    A. The participant shall submit a completion report to the [Administrator] upon completion of cleanup activities and installation of any engineering and institutional controls that are necessary to achieve the applicable standards. The completion report shall include attainment sampling results, a description of the measures taken to achieve the applicable standards, any engineering and institutional controls used to achieve the applicable standards and the measures that will be necessary to maintain those controls, a brief description of the location of the facility, a listing of any hazardous substances involved, a description of the intended future use of the facility for employment opportunities, housing, open space, recreation or other uses.

    B. The applicant shall sign a statement that the completion report is true and accurate to the best of the applicant's knowledge and belief.

    C. The applicant shall provide notice of the completion report as provided in section 6(j).

    D. The [Administrator] shall consider any comments received pursuant to section 6(j) on the completion report in determining if the completion report should be approved.

    E. The [Administrator] shall review the completion report within 90 days and if he finds that the cleanup has been completed in accordance with the approved plan, that the applicable standards have been met, and that all necessary engineering and institutional controls have been installed and implemented, the [Administrator] may approve the report and may grant the applicant a Certificate of Completion as provided in section 6(f) of this Act.

The [Administrator] shall provide a written explanation of the determination, including responses to comments, which shall be provided to the applicant and made available to the public.

F. If the [Administrator] does not provide a written explanation of his determination under section (2)(E) of this section within 90 days of the filing of a completion report, a participant, upon request, is entitled to a meeting with the [Administrator] for purposes of determining the status of the completion report and the [Administrator's] timetable for completing review of the completion report. Such hearing shall be held within 10 days after the request for a meeting is filed.

Emergency Response

The provisions of this Act shall not prevent or impede the immediate response of the [Administrator] or any responsible person to a release or threat of a release that presents an imminent and substantial endangerment to public health, welfare or the environment.

Cleanup Liability Protection

1. A Certificate of Completion granted pursuant to section 6(d) of this Act shall:
    A. state that the cleanup has been completed in accordance with the cleanup plan; that the applicable standards have been met; and that the applicable requirements of the Hazardous Substances Response Plan have been met;
    B. state that the applicant is released from further liability for cleanup of the facility under this Act and other laws of the [State] for any contamination identified in the cleanup plan;
    C. provide that the recipient shall not be liable to any other person for any response costs relating to any contamination identified in the cleanup plan; and
    D. provide that the Certificate is transferable to successors in interest.
2. Any person who holds a Certificate of Completion and is relieved of liability under this Act shall not be required to undertake additional response actions unless the [Administrator] demonstrates that:
    A. the applicant, its successors and assigns, has failed to maintain and operate engineering or institutional controls required by the approved cleanup plan;
    B. fraud was committed in demonstrating attainment of a standard at the facility that resulted in avoiding the need for further cleanup of the facility, or in obtaining approval of the cleanup plan;
    C. new information establishes the existence of hazardous substances that were not identified in the approved cleanup plan;
    D. the cleanup fails to continue to meet the applicable standards;
    E. the level of risk has increased, or is reasonably likely to increase, beyond the level determined by the [Administrator] in accordance with the Hazardous Substances Response Plan to be acceptable at a facility due to substantial changes in exposure conditions due to a change in land use. A change in use that would increase the level of risk to beyond the level determined by the [Administrator] to be acceptable shall not be permitted unless and until the person proposing the change in use undertakes such response actions as the [Administrator] determines are necessary to meet the applicable standards under this Act. The [Administrator] may also require that person to modify or implement any institutional controls that the [Administrator] determines are necessary to protect public health, welfare or the environment; or
    F. the level of risk has increased, or is reasonably likely to increase, beyond the level determined by the [Administrator] in accordance with the Hazardous Substances Response Plan to be acceptable at a facility, due to substantial changes in exposure conditions as a result of new information about a hazardous substance that revises exposure assumptions beyond an acceptable range.
3. A Certificate of Completion shall not prevent the [Administrator] from taking action to require any person to comply with institutional controls required by the cleanup plan.

4. A person shall not be considered a person responsible for a release or a threatened release of a hazardous substance simply by virtue of conducting an environmental assessment or transaction screen on a property. Nothing in this section relieves a person of any liability for failure to exercise due care in performing an environmental assessment or transaction screen.

5. Nothing in this Act shall relieve a person from liability under this Act for the release of a hazardous substance later caused by that person at that facility.

6. Except for the performance of further response action at the facility, nothing in this Act shall affect the liability or authority of any person to seek any relief available against any person who may have liability with respect to the facility. This Act shall not affect the ability or authority of any person to seek contribution from another person who may have liability with respect to the facility and did not receive liability protection under this Act.

7. If the [Administrator] changes the applicable standard or the acceptable level of risk after issuance of the Certificate of Completion and determines that additional response action is necessary, then the [Administrator] shall be responsible for any additional response action that is necessary, unless the current owner of the facility refuses to allow access to the facility as necessary to conduct the response action, in which case the [Administrator] may issue an order under section 5(c) of this Act to the owner to take whatever response action is necessary to achieve the applicable standard.

Lender Liability

No person shall be considered a responsible person under this Act by virtue of holding a security interest in a facility unless they meet the definition of an owner and operator under section 101(20) of the federal Superfund Act.

Prospective Purchaser Liability

No person otherwise liable under section 3(a) of this Act shall be liable if that person has received a prospective purchaser agreement from the [State] under the policies and procedures of the Hazardous Substances Response Plan that relieves such person of liability. A prospective purchaser agreement may be issued to a prospective purchaser of a property:

A. where the [Administrator] has reason to believe that, based on a binding legal agreement with one or more responsible persons, the facility will be cleaned up in accordance with the Hazardous Substances Response Plan, or where the [Administrator] has determined that a facility will be cleaned up with funds from the Hazardous Substances Response Fund; or

B. in such circumstances identified as appropriate in the Hazardous Substances Response Plan.

Filing of Performance Bond or Other Security

1. A participant shall file a performance bond or other security with the [Administrator] within 10 days after receiving the [Administrator's] approval of a cleanup plan and before the participant may perform any work on the facility.

2. The performance bond required shall be in an amount determined by the [Administrator] to be necessary to secure and stabilize the facility if the cleanup plan is not completed consistent with subsection (h) below.

3. The market value of other securities deposited may not be less than the amount specified in subsection (2) of this section.

4. The obligation of the performance bond filed under this section shall be void upon the issuance of a Certificate of Completion to the participant or, if the participant withdraws from the program, 16 months after the date of withdrawal.

5. The obligation of the participant under the performance bond or other security shall become due and payable upon notification by the [Administrator] that action must be taken to fulfill the withdrawal requirements in section 6(h) of this Act for stabilizing a facility.

Withdrawal from Program

1. A participant may withdraw from a voluntary cleanup at any stage before or after approval of the cleanup plan. To withdraw from the program, the participant must:
 A. file notice of intent to withdraw with the [Administrator];
 B. stabilize the facility by taking those actions necessary to ensure that work conducted at the facility has not caused greater risk to public health, welfare and the environment than existed before the cleanup commenced, and to ensure the facility will not pose an imminent and substantial threat to public health, welfare or the environment; and
 C. pay all outstanding fees associated accrued by the [Administrator] in connection with participation in the voluntary cleanup, including fees associated with facility stabilization.

2. A person that meets the requirements of subsection (1) of this section and that was not a responsible person as defined in section 3 of this Act with respect to a facility shall not become a responsible person solely as a result of participation in or withdrawal from a voluntary cleanup under this Act

Technical Assistance, Review, Investigation and Oversight

1. The [Administrator] may, upon request, assist a person in identifying Brownfields sites in the [State] and options for their redevelopment, and in determining whether real property has been the site of a release or threatened release of a hazardous substance. The [Administrator] may also assist in or supervise the development and implementation of reasonable and necessary response actions. Assistance may include review of agency records and files, and review of a requester's investigation plans and proposed cleanup plans.

2. The person requesting assistance under this subdivision shall pay the [Administrator] for the [Administrator's] costs of providing assistance to the person after the person files a formal application for participation in the program. Persons receiving assistance are not required to pay for assistance received prior to the filing of an application.

Public Involvement, Notice and Review

1. Plain language—Cleanup plans and reports submitted by participants shall contain a summary that includes a plain language description of the information in order to enhance the opportunity for public involvement in, and understanding of, the cleanup process.

2. Notice and review for proposed cleanup plan or completion reports

The following notice and review provisions apply each time a proposed cleanup plan or completion report is submitted to the [Administrator]:

 A. a participant that submits a proposed cleanup plan or completion report under this Act to the [Administrator], shall cause to be published a notice of the availability of the report or plan in the [Register] and in the local and regional paper. The notices required by this subsection shall state that a 30-day comment period will be afforded and provide the address to which comments may be sent and identify the 30 days during which comments will be accepted.

 B. the [Administrator] shall receive all comments on proposed cleanup plans and completion reports and shall provide copies to the applicant.

  i. The applicant shall review and consider all comments on the proposed cleanup plan, shall modify the proposed cleanup plan as appropriate and shall provide to the [Administrator] a summary of the actions it proposes to take in response to public comments, including why it has chosen not to act, it applicable.

  ii. The [Administrator] shall review and consider all comments on the completion report and may take action, or may request that the applicant take appropriate action, to respond to the comments.

3. Public Involvement Plans—Persons cleaning up facilities under this Act are required

to develop a public involvement plan that involves the public in the cleanup and proposed use of the facility. The plan shall propose measures to involve the public in the development and review of the cleanup plan and completion report. Depending on the facility involved, measures may include techniques such as: developing a pro-active community information and consultation program that includes door-step notice of activities related to cleanup; holding public meetings and roundtable discussions; establishing convenient location where documents related to a cleanup can be made available to the public; designating a single contact person to whom community residents can ask questions; forming a community-based group that is used to solicit suggestions and comments on the various reports required by this section; and if needed, retaining trained, independent third parties to facilitate meetings and discussion and perform mediation services.

Fees

1. The [Administrator] shall collect fees to cover the costs of implementing the provisions of this Act. The [Administrator] shall establish by regulation a fee structure for purposes of collecting these fees, and shall, to extent feasible, set a standard fee per facility. The [Administrator] may at his discretion cap the amount of costs charged to a participant.

2. Fees imposed under this section shall be deposited in the [General Fund and re-allocated] to the Clean Land Fund established in section 8 of this Act.

Relationship to Federal and [State] Programs

The [Administrator] is authorized to enter into cooperative agreements with the United States Environmental Protection Agency for receiving grants, technical assistance and liability protection under federal law to those granted liability protection under this Act.

Enforcement

1. General—The [Administrator] is authorized to use the enforcement and penalty provisions applicable to the environmental medium or activity of concern established under the laws of the [State].

2. No Defense to Illegal activities—The provisions of this Act do not create a defense against the imposition of criminal or civil fines or penalties or administrative penalties otherwise authorized by law and imposed as the result of the illegal disposal of waste or for the pollution of the land, air or waters of the [State] on the identified facility.

3. Fraud—Any person who willfully commits fraud in connection with any submission to the [Administrator] required under this section shall, upon conviction, be subject to an additional penalty for each separate offense or to imprisonment for a period of not more than one year for each separate offense, or both. Each day shall constitute a separate offense.

4. Persons who have no responsibility for contamination at a facility and participate in environmental cleanup activities under this Act shall not be responsible for paying any fines or penalties levied against any person responsible for contamination on the facility.

Financial Incentives for Voluntary Cleanup

The [Administrator] shall develop a financial incentive package for purposes of encouraging the cleanup and redevelopment of contaminated property in [State] that may include, but is not limited to, the use of revenue bonds, property tax abatements against the value of improvements, income tax credits, grants, and low-interest loans.

Section 7: Institutional Controls

[State Property Laws should be checked to verify enforceability of easements mentioned in this section]

a. **Records, Information and Education**—The [Administrator] is authorized to create, modify, maintain, and disseminate any and all records, informational systems, educational materials and other mechanisms that are necessary to protect public health, welfare, and the environment at facilities cleaned up under this Act, including providing information to the public through any means the [Administrator] determines to be appropriate.

b. **Authorization of Institutional Controls**—In order to manage threats to public health, welfare and the environment at facilities cleaned up under this Act, the following written instruments are authorized, and may be issued by the [Administrator], or other appropriate person, as part of a cleanup plan approved under section 6(c) or otherwise after reasonable notice has been provided to affected persons. All offices of [State] are authorized to take any actions necessary to implement these instruments:

1. Notice of Residual Risk, which shall describe the residual hazardous substances and their locations at a facility and any engineering or institutional controls that are in place at the facility;

2. Residual Risk Use Restriction, which may apply, as appropriate, to the use of real property, or to the use of specified resources, including surface water, groundwater, and soils. Residual Risk Use Restrictions shall restrict the use of property to uses that protect public health, welfare and the environment and are consistent with the level and location of residual hazardous substances at the facility and with any engineering and institutional controls in place at that facility; Residual Risk Use Restrictions shall be designed to allow as much flexibility in use as is consistent with protecting public health, welfare, and the environment;

3. Hazardous Substance Easement, which may authorize the [Administrator] or other person to have access to a facility for the purpose of monitoring residual hazardous substances at that facility, including monitoring the maintenance and functioning of engineering and institutional controls; a Hazardous Substance Easement may also restrict use of a facility, or specified resources, to uses that protect public health, welfare and the environment and are consistent with the concentration and location of residual hazardous substances at the facility and with any engineering or institutional controls in place at that facility. The [Administrator] or any organization or person that has the capacity to carry out the responsibilities of a holder of an easement is authorized to hold a Hazardous Substance Easement; and

4. Order that runs with the land, which the [Administrator] is authorized to issue to the owner of a facility cleaned up under this Act, or to other property that is adversely affected by residual hazardous substances that exceed applicable standards and have migrated outside the boundaries of a facility cleaned up under this Act. No Order shall be issued unless the instruments in (1)–(3) of this section are not sufficient to protect public health, welfare and the environment. An Order issued to an owner of property not the subject of a response conducted under this Act shall be designed to allow as much flexibility in use of the property or specified resources as is consistent with protecting public health, welfare and the environment, and if a responsible person has been determined to be liable for the hazardous substances that are the subject of the Order, that responsible person shall be required to pay the owner of the property subject to such Order for the fair market value of the restriction on use or for any other compensation that is required as a result of the Order.

a. **Recording Instruments**—The [County Recorder or Equivalent] is authorized to record in the registry of deeds any Notice of Residual Risk, Residual Risk Use Restriction, Hazardous Substance Easement, or Order issued under this section with the deed to the property to which it attaches in such a way as to be discoverable whenever a search is conducted for the subject property.

b. **Modification, Rescission, and Extinguishment**—Any Notice of Residual Risk, Residual Risk Use Restriction, Hazardous Substance Easement or Order issued under this section shall run with the land, shall not be declared unenforceable due to a lack of property interest in a particular parcel of land or to lack of privity of estate or contract, or to lack of a benefit to a particular parcel of land, and shall not be subject to any rule against unreasonable restraints on alienation or transfer of property. The [Administrator] is authorized to modify, rescind, or extinguish any instrument authorized by this section for good cause, consistent with the purposes of this Act. An instrument authorized under this section may be modified, rescinded, or extinguished only after the [Administrator] finds that, in the case of a modification, such modification will protect public health, welfare and the environment, or, in the case of rescission or extinguishment, such instrument is no longer necessary to protect public health, welfare or the environment. Prior to modifying, rescinding, or extinguishing any instrument authorized under this section, the [Administrator] shall provide notice to the public and an opportunity to comment on any proposal to modify, rescind, or extinguish such instrument.

    c. **Enforcement of Institutional Controls**—The [Administrator] or any other person is authorized to enforce by order or by a civil action commenced in a court of competent jurisdiction any instrument issued under this section or any other institutional control established pursuant to this Act. The [Administrator] is authorized to take any action necessary to prevent, modify or stop any use or proposed use of a facility cleaned up under this Act that is or would be incompatible with any residual hazardous substance left in place at the facility or any engineering or institutional control at the facility or that may expose users of the facility to risks that exceed the applicable standard. A cause of action in favor of the government and the people of the [State] is authorized to compel compliance with any instrument issued under this section and to require the implementation of any institutional control that is necessary to protect public health, welfare or the environment.

    d. **Operation and Maintenance of Engineering and Institutional Controls**—The participant, its successors and assigns shall be responsible for maintaining all engineering and institutional controls applicable to the facility, except those solely within the control of the [Administrator] or another person or those specifically exempted by the terms of a prospective purchaser agreement, for as long as they are necessary to achieve the applicable cleanup standards. The [Administrator] shall inspect and monitor all engineering and institutional controls to ensure that they continue to operate and function as designed so that the standards continue to be met. The owner of a facility cleaned up under this Act shall allow the [Administrator] access to the facility documents and records as necessary to inspect and monitor engineering and institutional controls at the facility.

Section 8: Environmental Response Trust Fund and Clean Land Fund

Environmental Response Trust Fund

    1. There is hereby established within the [Treasury] a revolving fund to be known as the "Environmental Response Trust Fund" ("Trust Fund").

    2. Purpose—The Trust Fund shall be used for the following purposes:

    A. to conduct facility investigations, studies and designs related to cleanups conducted under this Act;

    B. to pay [State's] governmental response costs incurred pursuant to the federal Superfund Act, including emergency response, operation and maintenance costs;

    C. to administer and enforce the [State's] Clean Land Act and Hazardous Substances Response Plan; and

    D. to reimburse persons for monies expended in conducting a response action at the order of the [Administrator] who were subsequently determined, pursuant to section 5(c)(7) not to be a responsible person under this Act.

    3. Proceeds of the Trust Fund may be invested in a prudent and reasonable manner consistent with applicable [State] government policies and procedures.

    4. The Trust Fund shall be continuing. Revenues deposited into the Trust Fund shall not revert to the [General Fund] at the end of any fiscal year or at any other time and shall be continually available to the [Administrator] for the uses and purposes set forth in this Act.

    5. The Trust Fund shall receive all funds recovered from responsible persons

conducting response actions under section 5 of this Act, and all other revenue collected by the [State] as a result of fines or penalties for violation of the statutes administered by the [Administrator], determined to be appropriate by the [Administrator].

6. The Trust Fund shall be available without fiscal-year limitation and shall be used by the [Administrator] to meet the [State's] obligations under this act described in Section 8(a)(2).

Clean Land Fund

1. There is hereby established within the [State Treasury] a revolving fund to be known as the "Clean Land Fund."

2. Purpose—The Fund shall be used to receive and disburse funds from appropriations, income from operations, fees, gifts by devise or bequest, donations, grants, investments, and revenue from any and all sources pursuant to the provisions of section 6 of this Act which establishes a Voluntary Cleanup Program.

3. Revenue deposited into the Fund is specifically designated to be expended by the [Administrator] for the administration, improvement, and maintenance of the Voluntary Cleanup Program created pursuant to section 6 of this Act.

4. Proceeds of the Fund may be invested in a prudent and reasonable manner consistent with applicable [State] government policies and procedures.

5. The Fund shall be continuing. Revenues deposited into the Fund shall not revert to the [General Fund] at the end of any fiscal year or at any other time shall be continually available to the [Administrator] for the uses and purposes set for the in section 6 of this Act.

6. The Fund shall be available without fiscal-year limitation and shall be used by the [Administrator] to maintain the [State's] Voluntary Cleanup Program in accordance with section 6 of this Act. The accounting for the Fund shall be maintained on the accrual basis, including provision for employees' accrued annual leave and depreciation of fixed assets, and financial reports shall be prepared on the basis of such accounting.

Section 9: Administrative and Judicial Review

a. A person who receives an order from or is issued a decision by a designee of the [Administrator] under this Act may seek review by the [Administrator] of such decision or order.

b. Any order or decision issued by a designee of the [Administrator] that is affirmed by the [Administrator] becomes a final order and may be appealed to a court of competent jurisdiction by the person subject to the order.

c. The court shall consider the appeal based on the record developed before the [Administrator] and shall affirm the decision unless the court finds that the [Administrator's] decision was arbitrary and capricious or not in accordance with law.

Section 10: Miscellaneous Provisions

Rights Reserved

1. This Act does not preempt other statutes of the [State] except where the terms of this Act may specifically conflict with such other statutes, in which case the specific terms of this Act will govern.

2. Remedies at law related to nuisance actions are not preempted by this Act.

3. Remedies available under this Act are intended to be additional to other current remedies at law.

4. Federal—The provisions of this Act shall not prevent the [State] from enforcing specific numerical cleanup standards or monitoring or compliance requirements specifically required by the federal government to be enforced as a condition to receive program authorization, delegation, primacy or federal funds.

5. Oil Spill Response—This Act shall not apply to the removal of a discharge under section 4201 of the Oil Pollution Act of 1990 (P.L.101–380, 104 Stat. 484).

Severability

To the extent that any provision of this statute is invalidated by a court with cognizant jurisdiction, all other provisions of this Act will remain in effect.

Rewards

The [Administrator] shall pay reward to a person who provides information leading to the successful prosecution and conviction of any person who fails to provide notice of a release in accordance with section 5(a) of this Act. The amount of the reward shall be one third of the fine collected as a result of such conviction, but not less than $100.

About the Contributors

Alaska Department of Environmental Conservation seeks to conserve, improve, and protect Alaska's natural resources and environment to enhance the health, safety, economic, and social well-being of Alaskans.

Cheryl Ann **Bishop** is the communications manager at Washington State Department of Ecology Toxics Cleanup Program in Olympia, Washington.

Brandi **Blessett** is an associate professor and director of the Master of Public Administration program at the University of Cincinnati.

Kim **Briesemeister** is the co-founder of Redevelopment Management Associates in the state of Florida.

Tom **Carroll** is a village manager in Silverton, Ohio.

Sebastien **Darchen** is a lecturer in planning at the University of Queensland.

Todd S. **Davis** is the CEO of Hemisphere Brownfield Group, a national brownfield redeveloper based in Cleveland, Ohio.

Ignacio **Dayrit** is the director of programs at the Center for Creative Land Recycling in Oakland, California.

Kevin C. **Desouza** is a professor of business, technology and strategy in the School of Management at the Queensland University of Technology Business School in Australia.

Jay H. **Dick** is the senior director of state and local government affairs at Americans for the Arts.

Lindsey **Dillon** is an assistant professor of sociology at the University of California, Santa Cruz.

James R. **Elliott** is a professor of sociology at Rice University.

Environmental Law Institute is a nonprofit organization that fosters innovative, just, and practical law and policy solutions to enable leaders across borders and sectors to make environmental, economic, and social progress.

Martha **Faust** is the redevelopment manager in Ramsey County, Minnesota.

Florida Department of Environmental Protection is the state's lead agency for environmental management and stewardship, protecting air, water and land.

Scott **Frickel** is a professor of sociology, environment and society at Brown University.

Stephen **Goldsmith** is a professor of practice at the Harvard Kennedy School and director of the Innovations in American Government Program.

Joaquin Jay **Gonzalez** III is the Mayor George Christopher Professor of Public Administration at the Edward S. Ageno School of Business of Golden Gate University in San Francisco, California.

Alan **Greenblatt** is the senior staff writer at *Governing*.

David S. **Greensfelder** is the managing principal of Greensfelder Commercial Real Estate LLC.

About the Contributors

Mary **Hashem** is a co-founder and principal of RE | Solutions, LLC (RES).

Clark **Henry** is the owner of CIII Associates.

Lyn **Hikida** is vice president of communications, BRIDGE Housing.

Marcus **Humberg** is the communications specialist in the Washington State Department of Ecology Toxics Cleanup Program in Olympia, Washington.

Michael **Hunter** is an enterprise software consultant at TechnologyOne, user-experience designer, researcher, and science and engineering faculty at the Queensland University of Technology in Australia.

Jayant **Kairam** is an independent consultant and writer on environmental policy, social justice and urban sustainability.

Roger L. **Kemp** is a distinguished adjunct professor at Golden Gate University and has worked as a city manager in the largest council-manager governments in California, New Jersey, and Connecticut.

Ron **Littlefield**, a former mayor of Chattanooga, Tennessee, is a senior fellow with the Governing Institute and its lead analyst on the City Accelerator initiative.

Louisiana Department of Environmental Quality's mission is to provide service to the people of Louisiana through comprehensive environmental protection to promote and protect health, safety and welfare.

Shefali **Luthra** is a Kaiser Health news correspondent covering consumer issues in healthcare. Her work has appeared in news outlets such as *The Washington Post*, *CNN Health* and NPR.org.

Severo C. **Madrona**, Jr., is the city legal officer of Pasay City, Philippines, and a senior lecturer at the University of the Philippines' National College of Public Administration and Governance and Ateneo de Manila University.

Alex **Marshall** is a *Governing* columnist and senior fellow at the Regional Plan Association in New York City.

Tad **McGalliard** is the director of research and development for the International City/County Management Association in Washington, D.C.

Ian **Mell** is a lecturer in environmental and landscape planning at the University of Manchester.

Paula **Middlebrooks** is the brownfields community engagement and grants program manager for the Tennessee Department of Environment and Conservation.

Stuart **Miner** is a co-founder and principal of RE | Solutions, LLC (RES).

Ed **Morales** is the Senior Environmental Broker with Willis Towers Watson.

Paul **Nathanail** is a professor of engineering geology at the University of Nottingham.

New York State Department of Environmental Conservation is New York State's environmental protection and regulatory agency.

North Dakota Department of Environmental Quality's mission is to conserve and protect the quality of North Dakota's air, land and water resources following science and the law.

Ohio Environmental Protection Agency protects the environment and public health by ensuring compliance with environmental laws and encouraging environmental stewardship.

Oregon Business Development Department, operating as Business Oregon, is the state's economic development agency.

Oregon Department of Environmental Quality is responsible for protecting and enhancing the state's natural resources and managing sanitary and toxic waste disposal.

About the Contributors

Pennsylvania Department of Environmental Protection is responsible for protecting and preserving the land, air, water, and public health through enforcement of the environmental laws.

Graham **Pickren** is an assistant professor of sustainability studies at Roosevelt University.

Christa **Reicher** is a professor of architecture and urban planning at the Technical University of Dortmund.

David J. **Robinson** is principal of the Montrose Group, an Ohio-based business consulting firm, and an adjunct professor at Ohio State University's Glenn School of Public Affairs.

Stuart **Shalat** is the director of the Division of Environmental Health and a professor at the School of Public Health at Georgia State University.

Gwendal **Simon** is an assistant professor of planning and urban planning at the Université Paris-Est Marne-la-Vallée (UPEM).

Paul W. **Taylor** is the editor of *Governing*, chief content officer for e.Republic, Inc., and a senior advisor to the Center for Digital Government.

U.S. Environmental Protection Agency is an independent agency of the United States federal government for environmental protection.

Washington State Department of Ecology protects, preserves, and enhances Washington's environment for current and future generations.

Tan **Yigitcanlar** is an associate professor of urban studies and planning at the School of Civil Engineering and Built Environment at the Queensland University of Technology in Australia.

Index

air & climate 176
Akron Airdock 17
Alaska 162–163, 326, 354
Annual Recycling Report Form for Parishes and Municipalities 174
arsenic 11, 160, 186, 192, 198, 208, 210
asbestos 10, 13, 26, 108, 115, 137, 160–161, 179–180, 182, 192, 201–204, 207, 253, 279, 291; abatement 13, 184, 208, 241
assessment grant 7, 14, 83, 85, 110, 114, 132, 136–137, 149, 268, 308
Assessment, Revolving Loan Fund, and Cleanup Grants (ARC Grants) 184

Base Closure and Realignment Commission (BRAC) 141
Bases Conversion Development Authority (BCDA) 214, 219
bioremediation 13, 204, 284, 288, 303
BRIDGE Housing 195, 355
Brownfields Law 2, 7, 57–58, 310
brownfields redevelopment 18, 41, 82, 86, 92–93, 95, 98, 128–129, 177, 197, 199–200, 265–266, 268–270, 273–274, 306, 309, 311
Brownfields Redevelopment Fund 158
Brownfields Sites List 177

California 8, 15, 33, 41, 59–63, 30, 66, 117, 194–195, 201, 210, 212, 241–242, 245, 354, 355
Canada 249, 276, 281–283, 289, 303, 305
capping 13, 16, 161, 202, 209, 287, 288
Charles Town 136–139
Chicago's South Loop 188
Clean Air Act 21, 144
Clean Land Fund 352
cleanup grant 14, 61, 88, 127, 132, 136, 158, 332
Cleanup Grant Policy 332
Cleanup Liability Protection 346
Cleanups in My Community (CIMC) 178
Clifton, New Jersey 8
Colorado 60, 111, 121, 203, 243–245
commerce funding 177
commodity retail goods and services 250
Comprehensive Environmental Response Compensation and Liability Act (CERCLA) 142
Connecticut 8, 84, 87–88, 111, 124, 127–129, 234, 355
Conover Station 116
contaminants of concern 201, 203, 205, 207–208, 210, 235, 277
corporate recycling tax credits 174

data centers 187–189
debt 24, 60, 96–97, 124, 158, 245, 248, 271, 274, 326; financing 7

Department of Environmental Quality 154–157, 171, 174, 179, 355
Department of Taxation and Finance 169
Department of Transportation 169
diversity 2, 74, 198, 300, 317
Division of Housing and Community Renewal 169
Dubuque, Iowa 84, 87, 131, 133

e-commerce 249–251
ecology funding and technical assistance 177
emergency response 145, 346, 351
Emeryville, California 212, 295
Empire State Development 169
Energy Research and Development Authority 169
engaged leadership 247
enhanced entitlements 247
environmental justice 26, 41–42, 52–53, 87–88, 107, 150, 152–153, 177, 194–195, 299
Environmental Protection Agency 1, 7, 9, 15, 17, 23, 40, 49, 50–51, 66, 77, 82, 89, 105, 108, 120, 127, 131, 136, 140, 142–143, 149, 158, 170, 174, 177, 182, 198, 201, 208, 265, 276, 327–328, 332, 334, 339–340, 349, 355–356
Environmental Response Trust Fund 352
Environmental Workforce Development and Job Training Grant (EWDJT) 14, 42, 62, 81, 85, 88, 115, 119
excavation 13, 115, 153, 158, 161, 186, 202, 204–206, 209, 211, 236, 282–286, 288, 303–304

Federal Highway Administration (FHWA) 115
Florida 186, 208, 299, 308, 354
Formerly Used Defense Sites (FUDs) 141
funding 1, 13–14, 16–17, 19, 22, 24, 27–28, 32, 40, 42–44, 56–66, 71, 73–74, 77, 82–87, 89–90, 92–101, 108–109, 111, 113, 115–118, 120, 124, 128–130, 134–139, 145, 149, 152, 154, 158–160, 166–170, 177, 180, 182–186, 213, 226, 264–265, 268–269, 271, 273, 309–310, 313, 320, 324, 332–334

Good Samaritan Nursing Home 180
governing 30, 37, 45, 76–77, 80, 301, 312–313, 320, 354–356
Governor's Office of Regulatory Reform 169
Governor's Office of Small Cities 169
greenfields 1, 9, 24, 27–28, 41, 64, 161, 166, 220, 222–223, 225, 246, 261–262, 303
Greenville, South Carolina 108–109
greyfield 32

Hazard Ranking System (HRS) 142
Hazardous Substances Response Plan 336–340, 342–351

358 Index

hazardous waste 7, 42, 51, 85, 140, 142–143, 145, 184, 203, 206–207, 217, 241, 324, 327
heavy metals 108–109, 186, 195, 201, 203, 205, 210, 217, 283, 286, 289, 303

Illinois 131, 188
in situ treatment 13, 204, 284–287, 289–290
India 110, 113, 182–183, 185–186, 222–223, 225, 308, 326, 331
Installation Restoration Program (IRP) 141
Insurance Department 169
International City/County Management Association (ICMA) 76, 72, 190, 197, 201, 213, 220, 246, 295, 326, 355
Interstate Technology and Regulatory Council (ITRC) 169
Iowa 132–134–135, 305

Job Training Grants 184
Jordan Downs 194

Keweenaw Bay Indian Community 186

lead 10, 13, 48–50, 54–55, 115, 157, 160, 198, 202, 217, 253, 279; abatement 13, 56, 161, 182, 184, 192; paint 26, 50, 55, 113, 207–208, 291; pipes 78
LEED 107, 117, 122, 129, 137–138, 195, 198, 261, 304, 326
lender liability 347
leveraging 13, 19, 28, 82, 84–87, 89, 92, 96, 99, 124, 127–128, 131–134, 136
Los Angeles, California 194
Louisiana 171–174, 355
Louisiana Brownfields Association 174
Louisiana Voluntary Investigation and Remedial Action (VIRA) 171
Louisiana Voluntary Remediation Program (VRP) 171
Louisiana Voluntary Remediation Regulations 171

Maine 185
Manila 216–217, 219, 355
Massachusetts 113, 274, 296, 305, 307
matching-share contributions 93, 95–96, 99
Meriden, Connecticut 8, 111
Military Munitions Response Program (MMRP) 141
Milwaukee, Wisconsin 26, 212, 273–274
mixed-use development (mixed-use buildings) 23, 25–27, 41, 74–75, 93, 107, 114, 116–117, 121–122, 125, 127, 129–130, 132, 135, 194, 196, 199, 203, 208, 212, 218, 230, 235–236, 243, 245, 251, 259, 305, 329
Model Brownfields Legislation 335
Multipurpose Grant 14, 58, 61–62, 85, 333
Multipurpose Grant Policy 333
Music City 197–199

Nashville 197–200
National Endowment for the Arts 118, 139
National Fish and Wildlife Foundation 110, 139
National Priorities List 1, 21, 117, 142, 172, 208, 324, 327, 330, 344
New Jersey 8, 59, 65–66, 88, 201, 203, 213, 234, 241–244, 265–274, 306–311, 327, 329, 355
New Riverfront Park 197
New York 34, 37–38, 41, 43–44, 127, 165, 170, 188, 201, 213, 219, 221, 234, 243, 355
North Dakota 179–181, 355
Notification of Release 335

Oakland, California 8, 41, 295, 354

Ohio 1, 17, 73–74, 76, 88, 143–147, 354–356
Ohio Clean 144
Ohio Environmental Protection Agency 17, 143, 355
Oregon 52, 107, 154–158, 189, 302, 304, 355
Oregon Brownfields Initiative 154–155

Partial Voluntary Remedial Actions 172
Passamaquoddy Tribe 184
permitted hazardous waste management units (HWMU) 172
petroleum 10, 16, 27, 58, 109, 131–133, 141–142, 145, 158–161, 184, 190, 193–194, 199, 201, 203, 205, 211, 257, 283–284, 286, 289, 291, 303, 330
Phase I environmental site assessment 16, 110, 132, 149, 185, 199–200, 207, 253–255, 257, 263, 276–278
Phase II environmental site assessment 16, 110, 132, 149, 185, 199–200, 207, 253–255, 257, 263, 276–278
Philippines 214–215, 218–219, 355
phytoremediation 13, 109, 286
polychlorinated biphenyl (PCB) 10, 160, 195, 201, 202, 205, 279, 283–287, 291, 303
polycyclic aromatic hydrocarbon (PAH) 10, 174, 192, 198–199, 207–208, 235, 278, 286, 303

Quality Communities Working Group 169
quick decisions 247

remediation 16–17, 24–26, 37, 46, 5861, 65, 80, 87, 111, 114, 118–119, 137, 140–141, 148, 150–151, 166–173, 180, 184, 191–192, 195–196, 200, 203–205, 207, 209–210, 236, 242, 244–245, 253, 258, 275–276, 280–291, 303–306, 308–310, 333
retrofit 81, 206, 249, 251–253, 302
return on investment (ROI) 246
reuse 1, 9, 10–13, 18, 23–24, 26–27, 40–41, 51–52, 64–65, 69, 77, 82–84, 86, 88, 91–92, 97–98, 105, 107–108, 110–112, 114, 118, 133, 135–137, 145, 148–149, 154, 157, 186, 188, 192, 196–198, 200, 203, 213–214, 219, 227, 236, 242, 245, 250, 262, 264, 270, 275–276, 279, 299, 303–310, 326, 329–330, 333–335, 337
revolving loan fund grant (RLF) 14
risk-based cleanup 12
risk reduction 246

Saint Paul, Minnesota 191, 297
San Francisco 40, 46, 80–81, 117, 218, 224, 295, 315–317, 320, 354
Schmidt Artist Lofts 191
Seattle, Washington 192
Seneca Nation 185
Small Business Liability Relief and Brownfields Revitalization Act (Brownfields Law) 7, 22, 163
Small Grant Policy 333
smart growth 15, 25, 29, 105–107, 260, 267–268, 310, 328
Snow Creek Restoration Project 210–212
South Central Planning and Development Commission 175
South Korea 220
specialty retail goods and services 250
spills and cleanup 176
State Tribal Response Program Grant (STRP) 14
State University of New York Center for Brownfield Studies 170
superfund 1, 15, 21–22, 28, 40–42, 51, 57–58, 62–63, 125, 140, 142, 149, 163, 201, 208–209, 213, 272, 276, 324, 328, 336, 338–339, 344, 347, 351
surveillance 173

technical assistance 13–14, 62, 66, 84, 84–87, 94, 99, 106, 111, 113–114, 132, 139, 144–146, 154, 159, 162–170, 177–178, 182–183, 264, 266–267, 272, 309, 324, 326–327, 329, 333, 348–349
Texas 31–32, 59, 68, 218
transit-oriented use 122, 129, 135, 192, 305
Tribal Brownfields 14, 182–183, 308
Tribal Response Program Grants 183
trusted partnerships 213
Twin Cities 117, 191, 297, 313

underground storage tank 13, 137, 147, 172, 180, 182, 184–185, 199, 236, 277–278, 308, 339
U.S. Department of Agriculture 97, 99, 109, 139, 150
U.S. Department of Housing and Urban Development 111, 113, 128, 132, 139
U.S. Department of Transportation 87, 111, 128, 132, 138

University of Buffalo Center for Integrated Waste Management/Brownfield Action Project (BAP) 170

volatile organic compound (VOC) 10
voluntary cleanup program 178

Washington 29, 31, 33, 55, 62, 92, 99, 107–108, 114, 120, 124, 134, 136, 138–139, 155, 176–177, 188–189, 192–194, 265, 306, 318, 354–356
waste and toxics 176
waste management 42, 143, 144, 146, 170, 172, 179, 184
water and shorelines 176
West Virginia 84, 87, 136–139
Wisconsin 19, 131, 212
workforce training 81, 115, 170

www.ingramcontent.com/pod-product-compliance
Lightning Source LLC
Chambersburg PA
CBHW060334010526
44117CB00017B/2831